"If you want your Children to be Intelligent, Read them Fairy Tales."

—Albert Einstein

Okeopka (Cock)
Time-Keeping Animal

ANCESTRAL LEGACY
OF
FAMILY COUNSELLING

The Wisdom of Our Parents

Chinedum Joachim Konye Nwadike
(Rose Ann), HFSN

ISBNs:

978-1-80227-428-8: eBook
978-1-80227-429-5: Paperback

Contents

DEDICATION

Mr. & Mrs. Konye Nwadike
The Parents of Rev. Sr. Chinedum Joachim Konye Nwadike

This book, Ancestral Legacy of Family Counselling, is heartily dedicated to the memory of my beloved late parents, Mr. and Mrs. Mmuoegbulem Konyezuruyahu John Nwadike and Ojukwu Monica Agim Konyezuruyahu Nwadike, whose natural wisdom and home counselling had led to my self-actualization. Dear parents, you showed all your children and me the right path to life; you never misled us. Papa na Mama, rest in peace. Your legacy will never fade away. I cherish you two. I promise to lead and guide your offspring as you did, especially those of them who will accept and emulate the good life you lived and the good footprints you left behind for us. Mama used to put across this adage to us, her children, "umu m, otu onye nwere ike duru inyinya ga na nmiri ma na ohumadu enweghi ike ime ya ka onua nmiri" (my children, one man can take a horse to the spring but twenty men cannot force it to drink). It is only when you are willing to do a thing that it is possible. It is not possible if you are not willing

ACKNOWLEDGEMENT

With God, all things are possible and with the mystery of possibility, one can always conquer impossibilities. I thank Almighty God for giving me the wisdom and discernment to nourish and cherish all the wise sayings, proverbs, idiomatic expressions, folk-tales, body sign languages, and our cultural inheritance that my mother inculcated in me since my early childhood. "Onye agwara ma yak we, ga aghota (if you listen, you will understand). I listened and understood my mother's counsel and directives.

My deep appreciation goes out to my parents for being unique role models of excellent parents. Thanks for all the love, affection, wisdom, support and kindness you lavished on me. I thank all my brothers and sisters, nephews and nieces who are following our parents' way of a good life. God bless you all. I also thank all my family members who took care of our mother during her old age; God bless and reward you seven-fold. I owe profound gratitude to my late elderly brother, Ikechi Sylvester Konye, whom I always called to inquire from his expert wisdom about some insights when I started writing this book. Dede m, I am very grateful. Ada nne'm, Odaaku Clementina late Mrs. Alisigwe, thanks so much for being a role model for me by living a good life - may your gentle soul rest in peace. Dada'm Janefrancise Mrs. Dim, thanks for carrying on the good exemplary life left behind for us by Dada'm Clementina. Dada m, Henrietta Odikanwa, is one of my sisters who took after our mother in her natural wisdom. She uses figurative words and proverbs fluently as our mother. Dada m, thanks for your contributions to this book. I am pleased. Dada m, Agwunauhu Cordelia; Mrs. Nwosu, my immediate senior, I lack words to express my heartfelt gratitude for your ardent effort and support when I was organizing this project. Thanks for devoting much of your time to this work and for jotting down my brainstorming thoughts for me. Dada m Cordelia is an expert in both speaking and in writing Igbo language. God rewards you immensely. For all the young generation of the Konye and Nwadike family, who would follow the good footprints of our parents, God bless you and if there is any of you who misses the track, please make a U-Turn, otherwise, you have yourself to blame and walk on that wrong track by yourself. Our parents had ogu and ofor for you because they did not mislead us. Mama used to say, "imara nga inosa ahu ga ebeahu chiri ogodo gi." (You know how you did the act, and you know how to undo it).

I must thank you in a special way, my mother's immediate sibling, my aunt- Lady Theresa Agu (nee Agim) for your super role-modelling in the lives of Agim descendants. Dada m, your light is still shining on us. Whenever Dada m Theresa speaks in a wise manner, one would think that my mother is speaking. Aunty, thanks enormously for your wisdom and your role modelling to our young generation. Mama used to say, "Onye nwere nmadu ka onye nwere ego-nmadu ka aku. (One who has many reasonable people is greater than one who has much money). In this vein, I am thanking those who had helped me put this work together; especially Nze Chief B.I. Onunaku, who contributed hugely with his expert wisdom for this project. God bless you and your entire families. And for all who in any form showed me a good pathway to follow, God reward you in abundance. My little nephew, Ugochukwu Konye, made immensely contributed to this project. He gave me a list of proverbs he learned from his grandmother, my mother. Wonderful! God bless you, Ugo. I acknowledge you all, men and women who advocate truth and justice; you are my role models. I am very delighted to recognize the late Mr. Onwudinjo, the former President of Orlu Town Union, for his unique role, outspokenness and truthfulness. You are a noble and fearless leader of our Orlu Town Union. May God grant you eternal repose. Amen. Thanks so much for the vital role you played during my elderly brother's murder case. You are a trustworthy leader. We need people like you to lead and guide our young generation. There are many family members and friends who guided and supported me when I was growing in our noble village,

Ndiowerre, so many thanks to you all. I owe profound gratitude to all of my primary and secondary school teachers and university tutors for shaping me to be what I am today. You motivated me a lot; you had great trust in me then by always making me a leader of works, a class leader, and other functions accorded to me which, in a way, built my self-confidence. Thanks for your trust, enlightenment, empowerment, and motivation to me. These really fortified and prepared me to attain my highest aspiration in life. You really used me to prove the adage that says, "No insignificant child was ever born." You made my "scar my star." I always believe Mrs. Hillary Rodham Clinton who stated, ***"It Takes A Village To Raise A Child."*** Yes, her book is a Gospel Truth and I believe this based on my own experiences with good people I encountered in life when I was scrambling and searching for the meaning of life both in my Motherland, Africa- Igbo-Biafra, and in the Western World, the United States of America (USA) and the United Kingdom (UK). Such people are my family members, village men and women, my indigenous priests and religious leaders, The Marist Brothers of the Schools, my teachers, friends and well-wishers, my Religious Order, the Catholic Church, my fellow students, individuals, Sisters of Immaculate Heart of Mary (IHM) PA - USA, Most Reverend James C. Timlin, D.D. Bishop of Scranton PA and Rev. Sr. M. Gabriel Kane, I.H.M. PA-USA, my noble managers - The late Mr. Aloysius Roland Clarke (AL), of Christ Kingdom Society, Washington DC, also my manager, Mr. Dan Telesca-North-Eastern Plastic Inc. Scranton, as well as my other manager - Miss Cordelia Johnson and her Colleagues of the Providence Hospital –Carroll Minor Section Washington DC-USA., Rev. Sr. Helen Scarry, R.J.M. (Former Secretary for Services for Women Religious Washington DC.-USA. All my academic institutions, especially the College of Behavioural Sciences and my Church Group -The Blessed Tansi, Igbo Catholic Mission, Washington DC, USA - these collections of groups of peoples and institutions made me whole. Subsequently, their spiritual, moral, social, cultural, academic, and financial support empowered me to become what I am now. Thanks for motivating me in all ramifications. Above all, I owe my nephew, Rev. Fr. Leonard O. Chinedozi Dim, for editing this work. Chi, I am always proud of you. Thanks so much.

Really, It Takes A Whole World To Raise A Child instead. I am fulfilled and happy. Above all, I am incredibly grateful for Patrick Walsh – PublishingPush.com and his team for doing the finishing touches to this noble book. You made it a thing of reality; I am enthused; thank you immensely. You are doing a fabulous job.

One's life cannot be complete in absence of challenges; therefore, I am deeply thankful for all who, in one way or the other, have challenged me; you encouraged me to strive harder and become what I am today - thanks greatly for empowering me towards self-actualization. If God says yes, no one can say no. "Persist Until You Succeed." (I Can Do All Things With The Help of The One Who Gives Me Strength (Philippians 4:13). "Keep running until you win" (Robert H. Schuller).

FOREWORD

I was prompted to write this book in my mother's honour on the 18th of April, 2010 in the United Kingdom where I was doing my Missionary work. I was reflecting in my room how my mother bore me, suffered for me and died for me. I was motivated to write this book entitled **Ancestral Legacy of Family Counselling.** This book will highlight the origin of counselling, its importance, and the merits of good parental care and blessings towards their children and the essentials of adequate home training and its effect. It will look at folklore, proverbs, and their importance, as well as our traditional moral guidance and its effect on the children. It will also examine closely the figurative wisdom of our ancestors, handed down to us from one generation to another, that reached me through my mother. It is highly recommended to all who would like to extract the wisdom of our ancestors to read this book. The wise sayings of my mother led me to massive success and self-actualization. I was motivated to write these wise sayings down to uphold and promote the wisdom of the **Old** which I acquired through my mom. Furthermore, I decided to record these proverbs, body sign languages, metaphoric songs and idiomatic expressions as I visualized them because the youngsters - especially my siblings - are losing hold of them. Most parents are too busy nowadays to give their children basic home training and counselling. Some even pamper them and introduce their children into a cultic membership in order to be more powerful than others. In our present era, there is no more gathering together at night for folklore, etcetera, that helps with the formation of these children. Domestic training is now handed over to television, Sky TV, Internet Explorer, cell phones, WhatsApp and to the diabolical cultic individuals to manage.

One can now see that children are moving in destructive directions all over the world. The children of this generation are indifferent towards the good traditions and culture that enhance self-confidence. They are moving at a fast rate towards the Western culture that is now a defilement our system. That's why it is good to advance and improve in a positive manner which is the wish of our ancestors. But our youths are advancing negatively. Boys dye their hair, put on earrings, tongue rings and nose rings; they also wear their trousers below their hips (sagging) like inmates dressing like mad fellows on the road in the name of fashion. Boys and girls, even some adults also dress like different kinds of animals in the bush, wearing red, yellow, green and purple hairs, etcetera. Girls dress like boys, wear trousers, expose their breasts, wear perforated trousers, smoke Indian hemp, carry guns to rob people, and take hard drugs that make them senseless as they roam about the streets. They have no sense of shame anymore. Boys and their girlfriends kiss and even have sex in public places without minding the presence of people around. They live an **"I don't care" life**. Wahoo! What is happening? One can bear me witness that if this was in the olden days when children had respect for their parents and elders, our elderly ones would have spoken out, reprimanded, and stopped them. But everybody is afraid to talk for unforeseen circumstances.

But now, who can speak? There's no respect for the elders anymore, no sense of shame, no fear of anybody, no spirit of hardworking; rather, young people choose to live a carefree life. Boys and girls want to get high to be greater than their parents and the elders. Nevertheless, are they? They end up being insane, crazy, and now our streets are full of mad young boys and girls. Before, madness came through hereditary means or through frustration, or even through accident; but presently, it is self-made through hard drugs; more so, through frustration and cultism. The question is, who is to blame? Whoever chooses the wrong pathway should walk on it alone. Children are now more powerful than their parents, as well as their elders and relatives and the world at large. Teachers in our various institutions are now powerless to control their scholars. There is no more self-control. Everybody is afraid of their unlawful behaviour. Who is losing? Who is going to replace our ancestors in their good and honourable way of living? Who will lead the next generation to a decent life? Who will pass to them our ancestral oral tradition, history, and folklore? Is everybody happy with our present situation? Our relatives abroad are afraid to come home for a visit during yearly festivals as a result of fear of diabolical people and Fulani herdsmen. Again, what is going on among the youth? What is wrong? The present youth's language now is – **"I don't care, it is my choice whether heaven falls or not." Whether successful or not.** To reinforce my position, Dorothy Veining stated:

> *"It seems we now have a world where nothing is more important than choice and it matters not what is chosen. There are no longer right or wrong choices, just my choice which is right for me."*
>
> **—Dorothy Veining,**
> **Author of http://www.musingsat85.com/myblog/**
> **Resource of the day: http://www.studentsforlife.org/.**

Dear youth, your language is incorrect. It is a language that leads to self-destructive behaviour. It is a language that has no future or progress, a language that undermines your humanness. I urge you to rethink and redress your choices. Join me to follow the good footsteps of our parents, ancestors and honourable men and women who lead to success and self-actualization. I followed and became a great and responsible individual. Why can't you follow? You never become great through taking hard drugs; never. Come out from your comfort zone and that road that leads towards self-destruction and walk towards the road of light and life which I travelled and succeeded. It is not too late to turn around. Make a **U-turn now** when it is not too late. Never be the one that Cries, "If only I had known." My mother used to tell us, in her wise sayings, "Umu'm onye agwara ma nya kwe" (One who is convinced against his opinion, is still of the same opinion). I would love you to reflect on this short biblical quotation:

> *"You were darkness once, but now you are light in the Lord; be like children of light, for the effects of the light are seen in complete goodness and right living and truth. Try to discover*

My mother used to talk to her children, saying, "wepu aka enwe na ofe tupu oburu aka mmadu" – meaning, to make hay while the sun shines. She would add "onye na amaghi anya ana ele ya si ghuru ya ghuru tunya" – meaning, one who doesn't know when things are wrong is a fool. She would end up by saying, "atura nwa omata nya mara ma aturaa nwa ofeke nya efenye ise na ohia" (a word is enough for the wise). She would then sing her famous metaphoric song that disapproved of wrongdoing - "ihuna ihe imere onwe giee, ihuna ihe imere onwe giee, ihuna ihe imere onwegi nwata nwanyi, ihuna ihe imere onwegi na okporo achara." (Have you seen how you messed up or deceived yourself before the public?) Well, my dear ones, my mum told me that a fly that has no adviser, goes to the grave with the corpse. As you make your bed, you lie on it; she told me that too. Heed the advice of the elders, respect them and honour parents and your elders so that you may have a long life and may prosper… (Deuteronomy 5:16). When I was growing up in our noble village, Ndiowerre, Orlu, we loved one another, associated with each other, and had team age-grade farm work (orumbiri). Young girls had meetings on Sundays (ibu otu umu agboghiobea). These meetings were scheduled and our parents, especially our mothers, supported us by buying food items for the meetings. Our mothers would cook a tray of rice with goat meat, prepared "ibibe" (cassava sliced food with vegetable sauce) meal, and oil-bean food for us to present and serve to our peers on that occasion. That time, we were all happier than usual. Why did this noble culture vanish? What kind of spirit is leading us now? Now, things have changed drastically. Everyone has a nonchalant attitude towards the affairs of others. Where is this kind of attitude leading us to? During that noble period, we used to fetch fire from each other's house, eat together, share vegetables and crops, move freely together, fetch water from the streams and taps together, fetch firewood from the bush and borrow things from our neighbours. We went out in the night together to pick up snails from the bush during the first rain of the year. We also used to go out together to pick "udara (African star apples) and mangos in our village square in the night-time and very early in the mornings. Both boys and girls came out in the night for moon-light play without anybody abusing each other. It was the time when we called each other sister and brother, and meant it from the bottom of our hearts (nwannem na nwanna m). It was the time when individuals were happy for the progress and achievement of others. Can we do this again in this present time? If we cannot, something is absolutely wrong somewhere. We have to think and reflect and come back to God so that he will re-bless us. Why do we allow dubious, diabolical, avaricious, and gluttonous individuals to sell hard drugs to our youths to wipe out their sense of reasoning? Don't we know these individuals who are selling these hard drugs? Do these individuals sell the drugs to their blood relatives? If not, why? "Do unto others as you would have them do unto you." According to Oprah,

> *"What you did not understand is that all of your actions, both good and bad, come back to you and must often not from the people you are acting toward"*
>
> **—Oprah Winfrey**
> **O, The Oprah Magazine**
> **The Best of Oprah's**
> **What I Know for Sure (p.6).**

Who would be the next child to take hard drugs? Mama used to tell us in the "Igbo" adage, "Umu'm, okenye ana-egwu ala n'azu ulo ya, ya gbachie nkiti, e gwuchaa ala, onye ka aga-atunye na ya"? (Old man who keeps quiet when a big hole is being dug in his back yard, whom does he expect would be thrown into it?) Therefore, this is a wise question we have to ask and answer by ourselves. Does it mean there are no more truthful and fearless individuals among our village men and women? I used to travel down the hill behind the Bishop Shanahan College (BSC)and former Bishop Shanahan Teacher's Training College, (BSTTC) Orlu alone to harvest cassava, wash tapioca in the stream, fetch firewood, and farm alone, and collect breadfruits for my mother when the land was at peace with our ancestors and nothing happened to me. Tell me, then, could I, or someone else like me, as a young man or woman do this again in this present generation? Why not? Fear of unknown circumstances is the answer. The Fulani terrorist and banditry would rape you and cut off your head. My dear people, how do you feel about this ugly situation? What do you think we can do to restore our noble traditions, culture, happiness, security, and relationships towards one another? Elderly ones no longer summon younger ones to advise them when they do wrong things.

One can infer that the reason is that most of our elderly ones do involve themselves in misleading these innocent children. Ask yourself a question if you're among those who mislead them. Younger ones and elders are called upon to rethink and redress our fading culture and our ugly situations so that things will come back to normal.

This book intends to call the attention of our elders towards our fast-fading noble culture. The noble culture in which our parents brought us up is no longer there. All hands must be on deck to revive it. If we fail to redirect our children, who do we think would do it for us? This is a big problem facing all of us. Mum used to say to us whenever something happened, umu m, otu anya beba akwa nke ozo ebebakwa (when one eye cries, the others follow suit). Let us work as a team to revive our noble culture so as to reinstate our ancestral blessings on us. When I was a teen, hardly anyone young died in the village. Just once in a while, an elderly man or woman died; even then I was thinking it was only the adults who died. Now, we are dying like poisoned chickens. Young children die before their parents which is a taboo in our noble culture. What is happening? We have to rethink. Our ancestors are no longer happy with us. Consequently, we have to make a team effort to revitalize our noble culture of oneness, one voice to help our children grow in wisdom and fear of God and respect to neighbours. Remember that nobody owns a child alone; a child is for all of us, for clan, village, town, and for the whole world at large. That is the reason why Mrs. Hillary Rodman Clinton said, "It Takes A Village To Raise A Child" (1996). Accordingly, let us join hands to help our children grow with love and unity. They are like a flowing stream. If the environmentalists fail to control it, it keeps on flowing till it overflows the banks and covers the whole surface of the land, thereby putting everybody at risk. I implore parents to strive harder without minding the pressure of the present society to raise their children according to the norms of their clans.

> *"Children are like sponges, soaking up everything they are taught, directly and indirectly, as they develop into the hugely complex being an adult is. Babies learn astonishingly fast. Things we take for granted, such as walking and talking, are immensely complicated, requiring a learning curve steeper than anything you will ever encounter again. As an adult the new things you learn will be much simpler, indeed, you may go many months without learning anything new at all."*
> **—Sarah Litvinoff**

More so, according to author Johann Christoph Arnold,

> *"Reflecting on the ways in which children so often mirror their parents – in actions, attitudes, behavioural characteristics, personal traits – my grandfather, writer Eberhard Arnold, noted that children are like barometers. They visibly record whatever influences and pressures currently affect them, whether positive or negative. Happiness and security, generosity and optimism will often show themselves in children to the same degree that they are visible in their parents. It is the same with negative emotions. When children notice anger, fear, insecurity, or intolerance in an adult – especially if they are the target – it may not be long before they are acting out the same things."*
> **—Johann Christoph Arnold**
> *Their Name Is Today*

Reclaiming Childhood in a Hostile World 2014, (pp. 78-79).

Rev. Sr. Chinedum Konye Nwadike, HFSN.

xx

ABOUT THE AUTHOR

Rose Ann Nkechinyere Konye Nwadike is a daughter of the Ndiowerri Village, Orlu, in Orlu local government Area of Imo State Igboland of Biafra in West Africa. She is the fourth among the seven surviving children of Mr. Konye Mmuegbulem John Nwadike and Mrs. Ojukwu Monica Konye Nwadike. She was born on April 18, 1958. Although she was raised in a non-Christian family, her parents allowed her to become a Catholic. As a child, she was brought up according to the Catholic traditions. Having become fully initiated into the Catholic Community, Rose Ann, as she was named in Baptism, later joined League Girls. This is an order of young Catholic girls dedicated to following in the footsteps of the Virgin Mary, Mother of Jesus. The other groups she joined as a young girl were the Confraternity of the Christian Doctrine (CCD) which empowered her to teach Catechism to both children and adults at Holy Trinity Church Orlu, presently Holy Trinity Cathedral Parish Orlu. For a long period of time, she taught Catechism to many children who were preparing for their holy communion and confirmations. It is recorded that several of those who were filled with the faith who passed through the process have become Reverend Fathers and religious Sisters. Among them was her nephew, Reverend Father Leonard Dim and Rev. Fr. Sylvester Dunu. She was also an active member of the St. Anthony of Padua Society. It was through her service with the Society that she obtained the inspiration to serve the Poor and the Needy. Today, she continues to be highly involved as a member of The Holy Family Sisters of the Needy. Although she was highly engrossed in religious movements, she did not neglect her social life as a member of her community. In her village, she became the leader of the Umuoma Ndiowerre dance group. She was so renowned for dancing that her community likened her to her mother, one of the most talented dancers of the time, becoming famous in the town. However, Rose Ann was not only known for her dancing abilities; she was also known for her wisdom and her thoughts using many proverbs learned and handed down from her parents. Among other things which she believes and enjoys are the rich and wonderful traditions and customs of her people. This earned her the love and admiration of the then traditional ruler of Orlu, the late Igwe Patrick Achulonu, the Ezeigwe of Orlu autonomous community. She is fond of the late Ezeigwe of Orlu. After the Nigeria – Biafra 1967-1970 Civil War, she started her primary school education at Practicing School 1 Orlu and completed her Primary six at Premier Primary School Amike in Orlu LGA. On the completion of primary school, she obtained her First School Leaving Certificate. She later continued her secondary education at Girls' Secondary School Ihioma Orlu LGA for the next five years. At Ihioma Girls' Secondary School, she did not forget what she learned at home; to be the best example to other students. As a reward for her good behaviour, Rose Ann was made prefect (captain) of her various classes from class one to class five. She also acquired a "Certificate of Role Model Honour," issued only to the best behaved in class. After her secondary school course, she learned how to type on old typewriters. Her typing skills, combined with hard work, enabled her to be self-employed. Soon, her typing skills opened a variety of opportunities for her to secure other jobs at Nneji and Sons Printing Press in Orlu town. As it is said, "one good turn deserves another." After one year of service at the printing press, she nursed another great desire; this time, a desire to serve not in another printing press, but in a religious community. Soon came her time to choose her religious order. She had always known that God called her to serve Him among the poor and the needy. Thus, she left the secular life for a religious life to become who she is today - Reverend Sister Chinedum – meaning

God leads me. Rev. Sr. Chinedum made her application to join the newly founded women's religious order by the name of The Holy Family Sisters of the Needy at Nekede Owerri Imo State, in South-Eastern Nigeria. Accepted by The Holy Family Sisters of the Needy, she was trained and made her first religious commitment on the 22nd of August 1990. It was in her first religious commitment that she took a new name - "Chinedum Joachim." In 1991, Sister Chinedum was sent to the United States of America for mission and studies. She achieved success in her studies and obtained an Associate Degree in Medical Secretarial Diploma with honours at Lackawanna College, Pennsylvania, USA. She also holds a Bachelor of Science in Computer Information System, Strayer University, Washington DC, USA.

Sister Chinedum returned to Nigeria and made her final religious commitment on the 2nd of September 1995. She then went back to study in the USA, earning a Master of Science Degree in Business Administration, with excellence honours, from Strayer University, Washington DC, USA. Also, at Lacrosse University, she enrolled for her Doctoral Program at the College of Behavioral Sciences and Psychology, obtaining a Doctor of Philosophy /Psychology, with honours summa cum laude. She also obtained her State of Maryland Board of Nursing Assistant Certification and The District of Columbia Nursing Assistant Certification from the University of the District of Columbia, Washington DC with a specialty in working with elderly people at Providence Hospital, Washington DC branch of Carroll Manor. She also worked at the Institute of Psychotherapy with children with challenging behavioral issues. Being religious, Sister Chinedum has mostly worked with people with various life issues. In the USA, she combined her spiritual life with brave work despite all odds. In the Catholic Archdiocese of Washington DC, she became involved with the Igbo Catholic community as their chaplain, teaching catechism and preparing children as well as adults for the reception of Holy Sacraments. She held the post of Assistant Coordinator of the Igbo Children's Catechism group. She was best remembered as the liturgical coordinator and directress of both the adult and children Igbo Lectors' Association. She was also the Spiritual Directress for the Igbo Catholic Women's Association of Blessed Tansi, Washington DC. As a result of her faithful commitment and hard work with the Igbo Catholics, Sr. Chinedum was awarded an inscribed plaque in her honour. Describing Sister Chinedum in her hard work and committed life pattern would be paying great tribute to her ever-loving parents. She learned from her parents to work before harvesting in life.

In the role of her ardent efforts, Sister Chinedum worked her way through the strict immigration lines and became a citizen of the United States of America. During her process of acquiring her Citizenship, she was called upon to provide her fingerprints and asked to take a US history test exam on the same day. However, being a person who does not take chances, she has always prepared herself for any circumstances of life. True to her unsurprising nature, she took the citizenship test and scored 100 percent. In her theology of life, she would always believe that, "with God, all things are possible and with the mystery of possibilities, one can always conquer impossibilities." Sister Chinedum is also revered as one who is obedient and one who respects authority. Being an American citizen did not deter her from moving to the United Kingdom when she was asked to be a missionary there by the Superior General of her congregation. While in Britain, Sister Chinedum took the exam for UK-Life, passed it and she secured her UK permanent residents' permit. Staying in the UK was a lot of fun for her as she worked tirelessly with the Good Counsel Network Apostolate in taking care of vulnerable single young mothers, becoming their Assistant House Manager. This led her to enrol in a Module 4 Counselling Skills Course in Cambridge Open College to enable her to help the young mothers in pregnancy crisis. Later, she left for Lancaster and embarked on the New Evangelization Ministry there in 2015 for a few months.

One of Sister's philosophies is constant self-improvement which she always followed in achieving her fundamental goals. On the 11th of February 2013, she enrolled with the Association of Christian Counseling Membership to help those in everyday crisis as part of her mission. Sister Chinedum goes to the "Abortuary center" (abortion clinics) weekly to counsel pregnant ladies who intend to go for an abortion. Through this mission, she has saved many babies from being aborted. She organized meetings and talked to all these vulnerable mothers at least once every month. She has also extended her spiritual activities to St. Pius X Catholic Church where she served as a Lector and a Spiritual Directress for the Legion of Mary of Our Lady of Good Counsel Presidium. Sister Chi, as a devoted religious woman, is always keen to help the faithful wherever they need counsel.

In her former church, St. Mary Magdalene Willesden Green, in London, she was a commissioned Eucharistic Minister for the sick. Sister Chinedum used to work at Windsor Primary School with "Play with Us Child Care Provision," East Ham Manor Way, London for seven years. She also did volunteer work at St. Joachim's Catholic Primary School, London, as an assistant teacher. Presently, Chinedum works as a Childcare Practitioner in the UK. As a dedicated leader, she was promoted to the Leadership of her Religious Community in the UK and became the first Zonal Superior of The Holy Family Sisters of the Needy (English Zone) and the first Chair of The HFSN Board of Trustees for HFSN Charity UK as well as her community local superior. She is re-elected Zonal Superior in 2022. Her belief in the mystery of possibilities leads the way to her success in life. She has always been successful in life even though she was brought up in a home where neither of her parents had a formal education. She dedicated herself to academic hard work through self-discipline. Her parents were non-Christians, yet she became the first "Reverend Sister" in her village, Ndiowerre. This is another affirmation of her philosophical belief in the "Mystery of Possibilities." There is an Ibo proverb which says, "Onye kwe chi ya kwe"- meaning, "If one agrees, one's God consents." 'With her advice, Chinedum would say; "Do not sleep; awake and work yourself *up*." She is dedicated to time management. She has used her time well and attributes her success in life to this. She has urged young people to plan their time well in order to be successful in life, because, for her, experience is always the best teacher.

Sister Chinedum is the author of 'Building Up Self-confidence - A Fundamental Way of Conquering Fear' and also 'The Pride of My Family: A Journey of Life Fulfillment.' Dada m I am proud of you. Keep up with your good works. I am pleased to contribute in writing your autobiography. Enjoy this book.

—Reverend Father Leonard O. Dim

QUEST FOR FAMILY ROOTS

Brief History of Mr. Konyezuruyahu Mmuoegbulem John Nwadike and Family

Before I proceeded home from UK to visit my mother, I called my elder brother, Ikechi Sylvester Konye (now deceased) on the phone and asked him to write down for me our family roots and about himself, as if I knew what would become of him. Thus, he wrote,

"Personal Names

Born to Konye Nwadike family of Ndiowerre, Orlu, Town.
Nwadike family head - late Mgbaja Nwadike gave me the name Ikejiofor.
Late Akarusi Agim of Umusasa Umuna, Orlu gave me the name Ofojiogu.
My father's mother gave me the name Jeremiah. All these names I cherish today as often as I think of them. When I joined the Catholic Church, at baptism I took the name Sylvester.
During the greater part of my football, running, and flute-playing days in the school, I enjoyed the names - Oganamkpa and VC10.

"Family Roots

We are born in the family of Konye Nwadike.
Konye was born in a polygamous family; his junior brother is Mr. Basil Anuele Nwadike. Their other brother was Mr. Mgbaja Nwadike with

his other brothers Mr. Raphael and Mr. Geoffrey.

Nwadike was the son of Amuba.
Amuba was a son of Okwaraojiaku.
Okwaraojiaku was a son of Okwaranosike.
Okwaranosike was a son of Okwaraofor.
Okwaraofor is our present Ndiowerre."
Narrated by the late Mr. Ikechi Sylvester Konye
A Gentle Great Teacher (Oganamkpa – VC – 10).
Dede M
Rest in Peace.

My mother used to say to us, her children, in one of her wise sayings, "umu m, emee ngwangwa emeghara odachi – meaning, if you do things promptly, you escape a mishap. Therefore, my late elderly brother's sudden death tallied with this proverb to us. Immediately after I arrived home from London in 2009 and visited him in his compound, he handed me over what he had written down for me as is shown above. If I had failed to request this from him and had postponed it, I would not have gotten this important information from him. This is an oral history I never knew about us. And many people from my village never knew that from my lineage, our village originated. I am thrilled.

About Mr. Konye John Nwadike

My father was born in the family of Mr. Nwadike and Mrs. Ogoma Nwadike in 1913. His parents named him Konyezuruyahu Mmuoegbulem. Before his last day on earth, I, the author, named him John during his baptism. He had two immediate siblings, Mr. Basil Anuele Nwadike and Mrs. Nwaibirinta Maria Nzeogu. Mmuoegbulem was uneducated, though full of wisdom and understanding, gentle, humble, peaceful, generous, and God-fearing. He was a sincere and honest man. He hated injustice and he became a victim of injustice among his neighbours. He was a man of his word; his yes was yes, and his no was no, and he never gave way or stepped down for injustices. If one took him anywhere, to justify himself, he would follow. One unique character he had was that he would not bother anybody but if being bothered, he would try to defend himself in a nonviolent manner. I am one of his children who took after him in this manner. I always believe in "live and let live" and if you don't want me to live, I would ask the question, why? but in a non-violent manner. Mama, with her usual proverb, would say to us whenever any of us was taking the upper hand or cheating others, "amutara ogbe nwa ka o-kpagbuo ibe ya? – meaning, one who is an elephant should not behave like one. Or a fat child is not born to overwhelm the tiny ones. Accordingly, she would conclude in the Igbo adage, "onye biri ibe ya birie," that is, live and let live.

My father, like my mother, used to speak the truth and he always stood by the truth even if he would suffer for it. He was creative and skilful in all aspect and hardworking, selfless and generous man. He was hardworking where domestic work was concerned. Papa Konyezuruyahu was brought up in a pagan (non-Christian) family though he believed in the Chukwu Okike Abiama (The Almighty God). He was an honest and God-fearing man.

As an honest man, he maintained a peaceful attitude, a sense of justice, truthfulness, sincerity of heart, a peaceful mindset, a love of **neighbours,** and was always generous. He always kept his hands clean. He used to say, "ihe onye metere ya soro ya." Meaning, be responsible for your action. He never planned evil against anybody. He always frowned at injustice and stood tall against it. Even when his **neighbours** were scrambling for land with him, he stood firm and believed in doing what was right. Papa never looked into people's affairs and always loved to practice, ***"Do to others as you would have them do to you."*** (Luke 6:31).

Papa always stood by love and justice. Sometimes, when he was sick, he called all his children and our mother together and made his will. Then he let us know that he owed no debt to anybody. Even though he was a man of low-income status, he was always self-content. During the Nigerian-Biafran Civil War, he was unjustly conscripted to go to war. His son was already in the Red Cross serving at the front, helping the wounded soldiers. Hence, God brought him home safely for us through the efforts of our mother, dede m Ikechi and our brother in-law, Mr. Nnanna Amara of Umuafor in Orlu town. One thing is certain, in times of difficulty, there must be a way out. Moreover, if you're a good fellow, you will never suffer and there must be someone to help you in your state of hardship.

During our traditional yearly festivals - "ngbo nwanunu, emume Nriji n'ala Igbo," all the heads of the families and all the traditional non-Christian family leaders would collect male chickens called "okeokpa" and their wives would bring hens called "nnekwu" to offer sacrifices to their highest gods "Amadioha (Chukwu Okike Abiama or the Almighty God), and "Ala"- the earth goddess. Subsequently, they did these sacrifices in their own crude way and understanding. My father, being among these traditional leaders, would bring his fowl- Okeokpa-chicken, kola-nut, wine, yellow foliage palm leaves (omunkwo) and his wife's hen -Nnekwu-chicken - to make a sacrifice to their gods and their ancestors. My mother would prepare porridge tapioca and breadfruit meal and give them to my father to offer to their gods and ancestors. These gods are Amadioha and Ala (the goddess). Hence, these gods, in my own understanding, lead to Almighty God. During this occasion, I used to stand behind my father in his shrine to listen to what he was saying to his gods and to the ancestors. This is what he used to say:

My Father's (Ancestral) Sacrificial Invocations

"Amadioha, Eze Igwe na Ala, Nna anyi Chineke ka igwe, biko nna di nma, olua oha nile, nna jike nile, bia nara onyinye anyi na enye gi ma gozie ezi na ulo anyi, gozie kwaa umu anyi, ndiogo, na di enyi nile, egbe bere ugo bere ma nke si ibe ya eberena, nku kwa ya (meaning live and let live).

My father would go on and on saying these words: biko, biko nna di nma oluaoha, odum eje mba, anyi na akpoku gi- ihia (ihia means "amen")

Na afa nna nde mbo na nde egede
Nna nde gburu e egwerieegwe
Nnampuruwa nde mpuruwa
Nde odinga nde odinga
Nde ichiamobi
Nde naelegide obi anya na nde na zobi
Anyi anurunihe nde mbonambo na ayo gi na afa
Nna Nwadike
Nna Amuba
Nna Okwaraijaku
Nna Okwaranosike
Nna Okwaraofor
Nna ndi Ndiowerre nile
Umu umunile na ndi ikwu na ibe nile ma di ogo na di enyi nile.
Anyi na ayo gi ezi- ezi, ezi ulo
Ezi nwa na-ezi nwanyi
Ezi nna na ezi nne
Ezi ikwu na ezi ibe
Ezi ndu na isi nkaonuruwa
Ezi oku na ezi enwere ezi aku na ezi uba
Obu nchari -nchari nnuri - nnuri
Obu ekpe ato ekpe ato
Anya furu iche nuriana iche
Anya furu ugo nuriana ugo
Ihe ana eme nwa di nma bu nkiri -nkiri

Anyi ewere na etokosi gi nihe nine imere na anyi, were burugodogodo na ekele gi, na ayo gi ngozi na afa nde mbo na mbo na afa onye nwe anyi ofo –o ree (Omenala Igonmuo).

After these invocations, Papa would pound hard his ofo (staff) on the ground in affirmation as the Christians say "amen", that is, ihia or iseeee.

English Translations

Please, please, Father Eternal, our leader, we invoke you, let it be done accordingly; we call on you in the name of our ancestors of times immemorial. Those were those who had earned and enjoyed illustrious estates. Those fellows who were self-realized and self-actualized, those who had earned honours because of their ripe old age and those who guarded the household with alacrity.

We beseech you to endow us with the following

Good estates and good homes
Good fathers and good mothers
Good brethren and good friends
Good health and long life
Good wives and good children
Good occupations and good savings
Good wealth and good money
Let it be all festivities and rejoicing
Let our words be delightfully interesting
Let those who meet the parrot rejoice with it
Let those who meet the eagle rejoice with it

For it is good upbringing to give credit to whom it is due.

We give you our praises for your benevolence to us by offering to you our sweet-smelling gifts for all your blessings from our ancestors through Almighty God.

Thank you for making our crops grow successfully and mature for harvest.

Successively, he went on and on thanking his "Chi" and the ancestors for successful crop production, and the protection of his families, friends and well-wishers. Dad always said, "I never planned any evil against anybody and let nobody plan any mischief against me and my families." He would add, "This year's harvest was not plenty so, let next year's one be more fruitful and plentiful." Meaning in Igbo, "nke afoo ebudi ibu, nke aka ga aka." He would then kill the cock and the hen and sprinkled their blood on the shrine along with the prepared tapioca and breadfruit meal for the ancestors to eat. My dad would give me the chickens to send to my mother to cook and I would refuse because I did not believe in their god (chi). From my father, I learned how to pray by wishing people well. Papa never wished anybody evil and that was the reason why God blessed him and he was able to raise his children well in the fear of the Almighty God; and I believed that was the reason why God chose one of his children to be the first reverend in our village, Rev. Sr. Chinedum Konye Nwadike. Since the history of Ndiowerre village in Orlu town, no one has ever become religious or a priest.

Mr. Konye was an indomitable, hardworking, respectful, kind-hearted and compassionate man. He was a big farmer, and palm-wine tapper as well as a tree sawyer. He worked tirelessly and relentlessly with his wife, Ojukwu, to bring up their children and trained them well both morally and academically.

During our primary school days, my immediate younger sister, Mrs. Livina Onyeajuwa, and I would come home from school and give him long lists for our school requirements and he would take them and ride on his bike (igwe) to our local market, as he used to call it, "ahia ugwumabiri," Orlu daily market and buy all the materials including books for us. He wouldn't allow us to be chased out of school because we hadn't paid our school fees. He always made sure we paid our school fees on time. He gave all his children every support and encouragement to be educated. I believe his wish was accomplished. His ardent empowerment and motivation fortified me to strive higher in academic pursuit and self-actualization. Papa, I am documenting this to express my appreciation to you and Mama. Your efforts were not in vain. We attained the goals of your expectation. We are proud of you as our parents. We are growing in strength and hard work as you were and wished us to be. My mother used to say to us, *Umu m, agwo aghaghi imu ihe toroogologo* - meaning, 'my children, like begets like.' I believe in this wise saying of hers because all of my brothers and sisters were and are as hardworking as our parents. When I was in the USA studying, come rain, come sun, I was out there striving till I achieved my goal as my parents used to strive. One of my mother's inspirational proverbs aided me a lot to achieve my desired goal in life. She used to say to us, "My children, a child of a poor man is never a fool, he/she is always wise; thus, a poor man's child is always frugal and not lavish." This means in Igbo adage, "Nwa, nwaogbenye anaghi awusa nkpuru ano."

Here is another testimony concerning our father's motivational encouragement to his children. When he wanted to train his first son, people were discouraging him as a result of his low-income status. But he paid no attention to them and with the help of our mother, they made a team effort and trained our elder brother, who later became a great teacher. Really, our father left a great legacy for all his children. He was a brave man and he stooped to conquer by achieving a great deal.

Konye never misled his children or allowed anybody to mislead him. He used to advise us, "My children, if anybody offers you a gift, bring it home and show your parents so that we will be able to thank the person." He always discouraged us from exhibiting gluttony as he put across this wisdom across - my children, "onu orimara butere akpiri Udele." This means, too much eating causes gluttony (akpire) like that of a vulture. Then, he would reprimand us and would never offer us that particular food in question that we craved to have in order to discipline us. He taught us to be content with what we have. Papa, like Mama, taught us forgiveness; take for example, in all the times he had land disputes with his neighbours, he never fought anybody and he still moved along with them. This is how it should be; whenever we have an issue with anybody, we should borrow a leaf from our parents' book and forgive one another and forge ahead. Remember, life is very short and short-lived. Why worry ourselves unnecessarily?

Papa preferred action over words. He was energetic about domestic work and he taught me and my siblings that which helped me to survive in the USA despite all odds. Papa, you were a truthful man, you believed in saying the truth and bearing the consequence. You disliked injustice and this made you suffer a lot in life, yet God rewarded you up by choosing your offspring as the first religious leader in our noble village even though you were a "pagan" then. My parents, through your hardworking and exemplary life, you brought up your first grandchild (Chinedozi) Onyekwu Leonard Jr. Dim as a Priest of God. Dad, I am deeply grateful; your efforts were not in vain - rest in peace.

Mama, words could never adequately express my deepest

appreciation for the gift of life and knowledge given to me. Thanks for nurturing me and initiating me into the Noble Catholic Church and more so, into precious religious life and your grandchild into the priesthood. Mama, rest in peace. I love you and Dad so much. Thanks for the wisdom you instilled in me and my siblings. You never misled us. Your good advice to your grandchild Chinedozi was not in vain; he is now a priest of God as you had wished. Mama, we all are proud of you. Your dream goals for Chinedozi and I were effective. We cherish you. I will not leave behind my ancestors who gave birth to my parents. Thank you for raising them well. May you all rest in peace. Please join hands with my parents to fight against any diabolical being who tries to sow bad seeds in our loving families.

About Mrs. Ojukwu Monica Konye Nwadike (Nee Agim)

Mrs. Ojukwu Agim Monica Konye Nwadike was born in 1914 to the family of Agim Okafor Nwaugbala of Umuokwaraibekwe, Umuokwarairobe Umusasa, Uzo-ubi. She was the third child of her parents and her mother gave birth to five children: Titus, Adaeriri, Ojukwu, Agustina, and Theresa. My mother was hardworking and followed her mother to many markets like Ore Ugwu, Orie Amaroaku, and Eke ututu to trade their wares. When she was growing, her father sent her to school and her teacher flogged her for late-coming. She went home and told her father who withdrew her from school. That was the end of her academic life which she regretted her whole life. Hence, her father gave her a thorough home education. Her father used to keep her by his side anytime he had important meetings or deliberations so that she would listen and remind him of anything he had forgotten. This opportunity granted her wonderful inspiration and wisdom. This enabled her to talk in figurative ways, with idioms, proverbs, and body sign language to approve and disapprove good or wrongdoing.

When her senior sister, Adaeriri, married our uncle, Chief Mgbaja Nwadike of Ndiowerre, Orlu, our mother, Ojukwu, constantly visited Adaeriri (Oyiridie by marriage), her sister. All this time, the eagle eyes of our uncle, Chief Mgbaja, did not miss her. He saw her as a worthy wife for his brother, Konye Nwadike, an indomitable, (determined) hardworking, respectful outgoing man. She was eventually married to our father, Konye, and they were blessed with ten children: three males and six females. Mama teamed up with our father to send us to school. Our mother showed resentment of being unable to be educated through conventional education. This made her vow that in her next coming, she must embrace formal education.

Her support for education gave the family NCE Teachers, a Philosophy/Psychology Doctoral (Ph.D.) graduate, a Master of Science Business Administration, (MSBA) and a Bachelor of Science Computer Information Systems (BSCIS). She also encouraged her grandchildren to be educated. "I would not allow you to be like me who did not go to school." Presently, we have university graduates and a priest among our nephews and nieces.

Mama was a woman of strong character, very dynamic, and ready to help solve people's problems. With her strong support for her husband, they were able to support others who sought their help. They lent people money in exchange for land for farming. Like Papa, our mother disliked injustice and cherished truth. She would always want her children to speak the truth no matter the situation. She was generous and tolerated those who came to her. From our parents, we acquired the spirit of forgiveness. We learnt a lot about tolerance, forgiveness, and forgetting ugly experiences during our childhood days that have been put aside and we were living harmoniously with one another. Though our mother was born into a "pagan" family and married into a "pagan" family, she yet inspired her daughter, Rev. Dr. Sister Chinedum Konye Nwadike, to become a Reverend Sister in the congregation of The Holy Family Sisters of the Needy. Because of this, she decided to join the Catholic faith. Despite the fact that Mama was a pagan, each time she gave birth to any of her children, she took her or him to the church for baptism. Mother was a woman of great character, a rare gem, a loving mother without comparison, a great psychologist and natural philosopher. She was a woman of wisdom and insight who spoke to her children using body language such as eying, twisting of the mouth, waving of the hand, nodding the head, etc. and usage of proverbs and idiomatic expression. She used positive or negative songs to affirm or disapprove an action. Mama was a compendium of characterful attributes such as determination, endurance, compassion, being hardworking, forgiveness, peacefulness, understanding, and prayerfulness, gentleness, and generosity. Our mother was an excellent dancer and the number one dancer in the village.

Mama Monica dancing with her village dancing group

This picture portrays her dispositional mood during a village dancing period. She used to be the first person in the line during "Ayoroyo" - Ayoroyo Dance. Ndi Igbo si, egwu amuru na nwata ukwu eji egba ya na eru ala. This implies that a dance that one learned during childhood is characterized by the fact that the dancer is able to bend gracefully in rendering it, which is not possible for a person who learnt it in old age. Mother's titled name during dancing is "Mmachin Oke Aku," and this title is also as a result of her giving birth to numerous

children and having grandchildren. In Igbo land, parents who gave birth to many children are seen as wealthy people. In Igbo, they say, nwa bu uba ugwu nna na nne ha - meaning, children accord honour and respect to their parents. "Ohu madu bu ohu."
Here are the lists of names of the children, grandchildren, and great-grandchildren she left behind.

Children of Papa and Mama Konye

1. Ikechi (God's Power) Sylvester Konye (NCE Educationist);
2. Udaaku Clementina Konye Nwadike (Mrs. Alisigwe) ((Trader);
3. Jane Frances Ngamaeme Konye Nwadike (Mrs. Dim) (Full-time housewife);
4. Henrietta Anyajiwe Konye Nwadike (Mrs. Odikanwa) (Trader);
5. Cordelia Agwunihu Konye Nwadike (Mrs. Nwosu) (NCE, Educationist);
6. Onyemaechi Konye Nwadike (died young);
7. RoseAnn Nkechinyerem Konye Nwadike (Rev. Sr. Chinedum Joachim);
8. Livina Uloaku Ngozi Konye Nwadike (Mrs. Onyeajuwa) (NCE Educationist);
9. JohnBosco Onyeachusim Konye Nwadike (Business Manager)
10. Christian Chigoziri (Trader).

Grandchildren

1. Mmachi Constance Konye (Medical Student)
2. Jacqueline Konye (Student)
3. Ikechukwu Konye Jerry (Student)
4. Izuchukwu Franklin Konye (passed on)
5. Chisom Konye
6. Chinedozi Onyeukwu Leonard Dim (Priest)
7. Nkemakolam Desmond Dim (Jos Based Businessman)
8. Onyemaucheckwu Ferdinand Dim (US Civil-Servant)
9. Ahamefule Michael Dim (Business Manager)
10. Chinoso Brendan Dim (Graduate)

11. Okwuchukukwu Remingius Dim (Graduate)
12. Onyekachi Franklin Dim (Businessman)
13. Odinachiukwu Bibiana Dim (Graduate)
14. Kelechi Camillus Odikanwa (Business Manager)
15. Kasarachi Cornelius Odikanwa (Business Manager)
16. Chinyere Juliet Omezere (Registered Nurse)
17. Chinenye Vitalis Odikanwa (Student)
18. Ifeoma Ruphina Odikanwa (Medical Graduate)
19. Ikenna Jeanarous Odikanwa (Student)
20. Oluchi Zita Odikanwa (Graduate)
21. Ijeoma Juliet Alagwu (Registered Nurse)
22. Ikechukwu Benedict Nwosu (Graduate)
23. Chinaemerem Irene Nwosu (Nursing Student)
24. Eberchukwu Joachim Nwosu (Civil servant)
25. Oluchukwu Michael Nwosu (Student)
26. Ugochukwu James Adikaibe (Mathematician – Graduate)
27. Chinedum Augustine Adikaibe (Graduate)
28. Chinye Emmanuel Adikaibe (Mathematician Graduate)
29. Chinedum Gabriel Adikaibe (English Graduate)
30. Michael Adikaibe (Graduate)
31. Ugochukwu Paschal Konye (French Graduate)
32. Chigozie Valentine Konye (Graduate Technician)
33. Chinyere Vivian Konye (Graduate Education Biology)
34. Chideraa Christopher Konye (IT Student)
35. Chikwadom Favour Konye (Student)

Our mother lived and witnessed thirty-five (35) grandchildren before she passed on.

Great-Grandchildren

1. Chidiebere David Omeozere
2. Chidarra Omeozere
3. Ugochukwu Omeozere
4. Chinenye Cynthia Alagwu
5. Glory Chidima Alagwu
6. Victor Chijioke Alagwu

7. Chidiogo Olivia Alagwu
8. Nwachukwu Robert Okoroji
9. Chinaemerem Cyril Mary Okoroji
10. Amarachukwu Stella Maris Okoroji
11. Chukwudalu Precious Dim
12. Chimeremueze Leonard Simson Dim
13. Ezinne Faith Dim
14. Emmanuel Desmond Dim
15. Caria Dim
16. Chimeremueze Ferdinand Dim
17. Chinyerem Dim

God has blessed my parents with ten children, thirty-five grandchildren and seventeen great-grandchildren just now as I am writing this legacy. More good children are coming up. Blessed be God who blessed my parents with responsible children. All my siblings are living happily in their married lives except my elder brother who died tragically as a result of his estranged marriage. It was quite unfortunate. We thank God he lived a happy life before his marriage. I am advising you, the young generation, to look well before you marry in order to live a happy and fulfilled married life like our parents. The Igbo adage says, "Agwa bu nma" (good character is beauty). Never marry a woman because she is beautiful but marry her as a result of her good behaviour.

INTRODUCTION

In ancient times, attention was paid towards cultural emancipation for the production of well-groomed group up young people, turning them into attractive gentlemen and adorable and marriageable ladies. The question is, what is the correct behaviour in all aspects of life regarding language, cultural orientation, morals, and cultural standards' application that makes you who you ought to be, your identity? I embarked on writing this book in remembrance of my late mother, Mrs. Ojukwu Monica Konye Nwadike, a daughter of Agim Okafor of Umuokwaraibekwe, Umuokwarairobie, Umusasa, Uzoubi Autonomous Community in Orlu Local Government, Imo State of Nigeria in West Africa. She was born in 1914 with great insight and wisdom. She passed at 4.45 pm on 12th November, 2009 at the age of 95. Mama was imbued with natural wisdom. She used to speak in a figurative manner which she acquired from her parents and which she also handed down to us, her children, especially the author of this book. I intend to write down all the natural wisdom she imparted to us, her children and neighbours, to help those who were not fortunate enough to be closer to her before her mysterious departure, to gain the same wisdom from her. You are not left behind; mama is still alive for you only if you believe it and make proper use of this book, which enables you to acquire the wisdom of old. Though she was uneducated according to conventual education, yet she was a great philosopher, counsellor, and a great psychologist. I will cite my proposals to prove these facts as I write along. My mother, as psychologist and counsellor, used to monitor her children, especially myself, and each time, she succeeded in reading my mind. Then she would call me and counsel me saying, "Nnem Rosa, mesa ihu gi nwa m," that is, 'cheer up, my child, and brighten your face.' My mother used to tell me this whenever she saw me look gloomy and worried. When I was growing, I used to be worried because I was always thinking what the future held in store for me. Each time I was preoccupied with thinking, she caught me and advised me. My mother, as a natural psychologist and counsellor, always read our minds and instructed us on what to do to resolve our problems.

Ancestral Legacy of Family Counselling advocates the need for parents to care, direct, counsel, lead, guide, teach, and train their children well at home without minding the advance of Western civilization. There is the different between abusing of a child and reprimanding of a child. If parents fail to raise their children well in their own homes, it would be really difficult to raise them somewhere else. Home is home.

> *"The family is the cradle of life; it is a domestic church, the first school, a miniature state, a microcosm; it is one's identity in the Igbo culture. A child is trained to be greatly endeared to the family and to grow up to hold the popular saying that "North or South, East or West, home is the best."*
>
> *—Father Greg Njoku, C.S. Sp*
> ***Counselling Is A Community Or Village Enterprise***
> ***The Sub-Clinical Therapies In Counselling Today***
> ***(An Igbo-African Perspective)***
> ***Igwebuike (Unity is Strength) Series First Edition 2001,***
> ***(p. 35.36).***

I began writing this book on my birthday, 18th of April, 2010 at 10 am. I was sitting in my room reflecting on the life of my mother, how she was struggling in the maternity ward as she was giving birth to me on a day like this. As a result, the thought of writing down her legacy came to my mind. I just remembered our mother's Tally number right away - **Tally No. 0243**. I started shedding tears. I then visualized how Chigoziri, my younger sister, and I were walking down in the Imo State University Teaching Hospital Mortuary, Orlu, to see our mother and we passed numerous corpses. I saw our mother's spot in the mortuary where she was lying lifeless, stiff and chilled, covered from head to toe. I uncovered her face and saw that it was bruised as a result of her mysterious death. I whispered something in her ears, then prayed and wept. What could I say? Mama, rest in peace; you died today for me and you will never die tomorrow. I am writing this documentary to show my respect, honour, and appreciation to you, my beloved mother. On the same day, I rang my immediate elder sister, Mrs. Cordelia Agwunihu Nwosu, and asked her to start jotting down for me all our mother's wisdom proverbs as I dictated them to her. Why on the 18th of April? It was exactly the very day our mother gave birth to me. It was the exact day she named me Nkechinyere m (God's gift). Thus, on this day, I remembered that the very person who gave birth to me was no more and I wept again. Then, I started putting together all her thoughts in writing. Though she is dead, she is still alive. Her legacy will never fade away. This legacy of our mother will pass down to the generations to come, though of course, to those who would value it.

African ancestral counselling is contained in the folklore used to develop young people from childhood to adolescence, so that they will start life, ready-made, armed with what it takes to make a successful livelihood and to live decent and honest lives. It is not like a professional therapeutic damage control process in which one who has fallen out of grace is subjected to reinstating recovery treatments.

I am not talking much about my father here because he was too quiet and he was a man of his word, hence, once he said something, he stamped it. Dad was a man of action and I learnt a lot from him too by being quiet but active. I don't believe in talking too much but in doing. My father taught me that women are meant to be seen and not heard. The children of this generation never have time to listen to their parents and elders. All of us can see the effect of this attitude on our present societies. Who is to blame? Parents don't have time for their children anymore, and elders are afraid to speak out. What is going on here? Why do we allow our children to follow a corpse into the grave like flies that have no advisers? Why do our traditional rulers allow Western Culture to ruin and influence our youngsters? My mother used to say to us, umu m ijiji na-enweghi onye ndumodu na-eso ozu ala n'ili." Meaning - 'my children, a fly that has no adviser goes to the grave with the corpse.' Her saying has manifested; in the present situation, that is the reason why our youth are missing their ways: boys are wearing gowns and earrings, while girls are wearing trousers (jeans.) men become women while women become men. (transgender). Some children abuse and brutally murder their parents for rituals. Why are children stronger than their parents or guardians nowadays? Who empowers them? Where are our local chiefs and kings? What are they doing? O God! May you give us the answer. Before, the advice of parents, elders, peer groups, teachers, friends, and well-wishers helped to call us back, but now I cannot tell what is happening. Why do young people turn deaf ears to the expert advice of our elders? If you do, who is at loss, my dear ones? Our grandparents had adorable children to remember them when they passed on; but you, the younger ones, who could represent you? Who would bear your name if you continue living in this dubious way of life of 'I don't care'? My mother would say to us, "Nwa m, were ire gi guo eze gi onu" meaning, go inside yourself and think about yourself (use your tongue to count your teeth). On the other hand, meaning research your conscience and mend your life. She would say, "Onye Chineke nyere anya abuo ya tufuo ya, obiri n'uwu ozo o ga-alo." This means that if you have been given ample opportunities and you misuse them, rarely will you get those opportunities again.

Here is an example of a guy whose parents and relatives made every effort to raise him to adorable adulthood, but he chose the wrong path that led to his destruction. He roamed about chasing women, stealing, taking hard drugs and even killing venerable men and women. His life was useless and hopeless. He became a bogus fellow and he ended up dying prematurely. Who was to blame? My mom would say in her wise saying, "Okuko lele etu esi abo okwua nwanne gi." If you are a bad fellow, you will end up like this guy. Literally, he to whom God gave two eyes and he loses them in this world, would he or she get them back in the next world? Here, I ask: which next world? The person won't even have the opportunity to enter into the next world. If you lose them in this world, you have lost everything, therefore, there is no hope for you. Opportunity comes but once. My mother would add, "nwam m, imara asu, sua n'ikwe, I ga-ama asu, sua n'ala (if you know how to pound, pound in the mortar, if not, pound on the ground or if you wish, you do the right thing, if not, you mess yourself up). Again, if a child spoils her mat, he/she lies on the floor. She always ended it with, if you have ears, hear, if you don't, that is your business. She would then conclude with "atuoro omara-omara, mana atuoro nwa ofeke, o fenye isi n'ohia" – meaning, if you advise a wise person, he understands, but if you advise a person with little mind, he will not understand. Mama would say, a snail that hibernates (seals its mouth in a dormant state) abstains from food. Mama talked to us in a rhetorical manner (azu okwu), in a figurative manner with refined proverbs and she was an expert in natural counselling. It is so even though she was uneducated and never learned her counselling skill in school. She gave out what nature imbued in her. This book will outline the proverbs mama used to direct her children, both in Igbo and English. Folk stories that she used in counselling are rich in body sign languages, lyrical songs, as well as idiomatic expressions.

CHAPTER 1

1.1. The Origin of Family Counselling and Its Importance

This book- **Ancestral Legacy of Family Counselling** - is full of childhood-accumulated wisdom from parents, especially from my mother with whom I always worked and stayed very close. Our first caretakers, teachers, counsellors, directors, theologians, psychologists, psychotherapists, leaders, etcetera, are our parents and elders as well as relatives. All parents play vital roles in the lives of their children. Each child is a typical carbon copy of either the father or the mother. Apart from this, the child could acquire his or her behaviour from a peer group. This also manifests itself in the way one behaves, talks, reasons, acts, walks, looks, eats, dresses and does things in general. They come from our family ethos, etcetera. What we are is what we learned from our parents and relatives as well as from the company we keep. One can infer that parents have a greater influence on their children's behaviour. That is the reason why our first counsellors, teachers, and leaders, etcetera, in our lives are our parents and relatives. Nevertheless, in this present era, peer groups, television, the Internet, WhatsApp and Facebook are taking an upper hand in the upbringing of children. As a result, everyone is feeling the unhealthy consequences of the effects. For this reason, basic home training is crucial and it affects the life of a child, as it did in mine. Whenever a child in the village misbehaved or did something evil, our elders would apply this wise adage, 'like begets like' meaning one always produces what resembles him/her. The root of counselling originates from our ancestors. For instance, when we were growing up, my mother used to gather us together after supper before we retired to sleep and talked to us, advised us, and checked who had performed well in our daily chores. After this, she counselled us and began to narrate some stories. After each story, she would tell us the pros and cons of each story. Then she would advise us to avoid the ones that were not worth imitating and abide by the ones that were worth emulating. She talked to us in proverbs, figurative ways, idiomatic expressions, and body languages. My mother especially paid much attention to her girls' daily activities and guarded us on how to live worthy lives as women and as good citizens. She taught us how to respect our elders, how to cook, how to do domestic chores, how to farm, and how to behave well and how to comport ourselves before men. She equally guided us on how to dance our traditional dances. Today, I, the author of this book, am a good dancer and I do dance like my mum. I am also fluent in the usage of proverbs and figurative expressions; as my mother used to say, like begets like. I took after my mother in many aspects. **Ancestral Legacy of Family Counselling** could also refer to religious or moral counselling; this reveals itself when our mothers instruct the girls to be careful about young men and when they advised us not to do things contrary to the church teachings and the ordinances of the law of the land. She did always emphasize, over and over again, the importance of the girls not mingling with men out of wedlock. She told us that if one mistakenly dates with a man and gets pregnant, she would be ostracized and would be married outside her clan because her respect is gone and no man within the clan would like to marry a prostitute. Really, our parents do explain to their children the values of life to allow them to make a rightful choice. They always catch us when we are still young. On the contrary, western parents would say, "Leave her to make her choice when she grows older." Honestly speaking, it is wrong counselling. Once children form themselves, you cannot mend them. Subsequently, catch them when they are still young. Even though Mama was unbaptized then, she always instructed us to attend Sunday masses. She even took most of her children to Church to be baptized during infancy, even as a non-

Christian. Every night, she would gather us together to pray before going to bed. Her constant prayer was: 'Our Father, Hail Mary, and Heavenly Father, we do not know anything, but it is you who knows all so direct us aright.' Likewise, our father also used to counsel the boys concerning maturity, how to handle their affairs as fully grown-up men and about things they are not supposed to do and things they should do. Our father instructed the boys on how to farm, especially on how to tend the yam foliage on the stakes and some handcrafts like building mud houses and preparing local materials for local buildings. On this fact, our mother used to tell us; "My children, either be a craft fellow or a farmer." When we were growing up, all my siblings were ardent farmers like our parents. Our uncle, Basil, used to call us "umu igirigwu" because we are many and work in teams on domestic affairs as well as farm work. In fact, I learned a lot from my parents, such as hard work, generosity, respect, forgiveness, truthfulness, sincerity, patience, kindness, gentleness, courage, etcetera. Mama, thanks enormously for being such a role model to all of us. Really, family counselling, as well as folklore, is tailored to promote social values. Any folklore that teaches the noble attributes of humanity, such as good morality and socialization, is worth embracing. I had mentioned above that media and TV have taken the upper hand in raising children. The former American President, Barack Obama, also saw the effect when he stated,

> *"Give every child a world-class education by recruiting an army of new teachers with better pay and more support, hence requiring higher standards and accountability from our classroom. This may not produce much positive result, and in telling the truth, the best education starts with parents who turn off the TV, take away the video games, and are engaged in their children's lives"*
>
> **—Barack Obama.**

Obama understood well the fundamental challenges that face parents in the upbringing of their children in this present era. Parents, it is left for you to raise your children in the proper way nature demands and not the way of confused law enforcement and the government directives. They cannot give children what they don't have. I thank God they had never influenced my parents in raising us. Our ancestors believed in giving their children adequate training that would yield them good results. It is displeasing to see a child not performing well. Most parents spend most of their time watching television, chatting on the phone, and working rather than connecting with their children. When do you have time to counsel your child (ren)? One of the Counsellors defined counselling as follows, ***"Counselling is when a Counsellor sees a client in a private and confidential setting to explore a difficulty the client is having; address what he may be experiencing or perhaps his dissatisfaction with life or his current circumstances. It is always at the request of the client and no one can properly be sent for counselling."***

Although a client herself looks for a counsellor, yet it is not the same as our native family counselling. In our native family counselling, the parents, elders, and relatives, like our mother, do observe the children very closely. In my own case, my mother would monitor my countenances and then call me privately and question me and then direct me on how to go about the situation. She knew that I was worried about being underprivileged and always wondering what to do to better myself in the future. However, as a result of her constant counselling and directives, I was able to work myself up to self-actualization. Accordingly, no child is insignificant or underprivileged; everything depends on how one chooses to live their life. If your parents could not make it a better life, make it yourself and uplift them. If you work harder, you will excel. When I found myself among an underprivileged group, I felt moody and depressed all the time and I kept on striving to better myself. As a result, this state of life helped our mother to constantly monitor my emotional moods. Once she saw a change in my mood, she would find a way to divert my attention. She always applied deviation therapy to distract me as most of the counsellors and psychologists do to distract their clients. One of the things she used to do was to call me my favourite names; that is, "Nne m Rosa, Nkechinyerem Nwa m, come and do something for me," and she would ask me then to cheer up and then send me on an errand. Each time, she would call me and talk to me. It was when I was studying psychology that I came to realize what our mother was doing then. I inferred this because most often she would tell me exactly what I had in mind. And immediately she could say to me, "Nne m, stop worrying; it shall be well with you." Actually, it is well with me and my mother lived and witnessed that aspect of my life. One can infer from this experience that the origin of "Counselling" is not far-fetched from our ancestral parents, that is to say, from our families. Even though most of our parents were and are uneducated in the academic field, yet, they have superior wisdom and natural counselling skills to direct their children. The typical example was my mother, whom I regarded as a great counsellor, psychologist, and philosopher. If one has something burning in one's mind, she could tell you what it was. She could talk to you as a philosopher and psychologist as well. No matter how one pretended, she could read your mind and tell you your worries and would then help you out of it by teaching you how to go about them. Mama could drill you with a compendium of natural wisdom. Hence, our initial counselling assessment begins from our various families. For that reason, our parents are the first Counsellors we encounter in our lives. At this juncture, I want to reinforce my stand on the Ancestral Legacy of Family Counselling skill and the role of our parents to their families and children; that it is a skill worth emulating.

When one talks about counselling, people quickly rush to think of academic or professional counselling. Nevertheless, counselling skills begin right away in our various clans with our parents, elders and relatives. Our parents are the first counsellors we encounter in our lives. Our successes, failures, or setbacks are dealt with by them. If they direct and counsel us well in our early childhood, our journey of life commences in a brilliant way, but if not, we mess up. It is our parents who breed our spiritual confidence as well as our physical dynamism. Through our parents, we acquire assertive frameworks that enable us to grow into assertive and optimistic children with the ability to carry out our daily tasks. Through our parents' formative counselling framework, they impacted self-discipline in us that helped us make everyday decisions, confronting the pros and cons of life. They make us smart, hardworking, assertive, good communicators, good students, etc. And so, counselling skills are not farfetched from our family's ethos. If the family cannot counsel its children, no one can do it either. In our context, counselling cannot take shape in a vacuum; it must be rooted and founded in psychological interaction as the system of a model of human behaviour. This model is based on three major aspects of the human person: mind, body, and spirit. In human development, the mind can be broken into (1) cognition (knowing, understanding, and thinking) (2) affection (attitude, pre-dispositions, emotions, and feelings) and (3) conation (intentions to act, reasons for doing so, and will). The body is thought of as (1) a biological or genetic process, (2) bodily activities, and (3) physical behaviour. The spirit is the force vital that connects the whole entity of the human person with the divine that insures life. In human development, the human being interacts with the immediate environment in which she finds herself, which fashions the individuals into a system or mode of behaviour resulting in the following: a cognitive system which is responsible for perception, storage, processing, and retrieval of information. There are immediate and remote influences that affect human development in the area of counselling as one grows up in life. Those responsible for the training and upbringing of children in society must take adequate note of these factors if our society is to enjoy the fruits and rewards of good family counselling, which is the essence of civil society.

The marvels and effects of Ancestral Family Counselling are good attributes exhibited by the children outside their homes. The children of such families are always good citizens, very successful and resourceful; they are always good listeners and very careful citizens as well as good ambassadors for their families and of the world at large. In a family like this, there must be peace, love and tranquility between the parents and the children. Such a family becomes a home for **the father, the mother, and the children as well as the relatives.** The same applies to our communities, institutions, and the governments of different countries, states, and nations of the world on an international level. Thus, it is incumbent on us to have at our fingertips those things that influence the development of a human being before the process of development begins with an individual. These influences stem mostly from the ecological point of view like a micro-system that results from first contacts with the family, school, religious institutions and peer groups. Our parents as good counsellors bring our emotional tranquility into order. One can see with me that our parents are originators of our success in life. I am one of the lucky ones whose parents influenced them in the proper manner. Though my parents were uneducated according to conventional education, yet they were endowed with a great deal of natural wisdom. They also made enthusiastic efforts to train all of us academically despite them being uneducated.

Parental Blessing and Its Effectiveness on Children

I am a living witness of parental blessings on their children. In 1973, my mother, my younger brother, Nna m John Bosco, my immediate younger sister, Nna m Livina, and myself Nna-m Rosa Nkechinyerem were standing in front of our old house chatting with our mother, when she started blessing the three of us as she had already done to our older siblings. She first turned to Bosco and said, "Nna m Boscoro, since you said you chose to be a trader, your business will go well for you and you will marry a good wife." Then she turned to Livina and said, "Nne m Levy, you will marry a good husband, and you will live in peace with him." Also, she turned towards me and said, "Nne m Rosa -Nkechinyerem, you will be "a Reverend Sister." I disputed it, although in pretence, because I didn't want to show that I was interested as a result of uncertainties. But she reinforced it by saying, "Nne m, I have said so," "Chineke ga edu gi." Thus, within me, I responded - Amen and Amen. It happened as she said it would. My name Chinedum originated from her wishful prayers for me "Chineke ga edu gi." I chose Chinedum (God leads me) during my first religious profession; I chose my name from "Chineke ga edu gi." Mama, as well as God, had destined my religious life. I believed so because I have met with a lot of obstacles on the way that would have prevented me from proceeding towards this noble call. But my mother's blessings and those of God sustained me throughout this journey. For instance, whenever she was making a supplication to her ancestors, she would call me to stand by her side. She would always want me to watch what she was doing.

Each time, I kept on wondering why it is always me that she would call among my siblings. Besides, whenever my father was making his yearly thanksgiving sacrifice in his shrine, I would always stand behind him listening to his incantations to his ancestors. After, he would ask me to send the hen and the cock to my mother to prepare for a meal. As usual, I would refuse to go because I did not believe in their gods. When Mama prepared the meal with the fowls, I would not eat it and each time, they would laugh at me and Mama would nickname me "Bishop Nwaedo" – meaning the holy one. She regarded the late Bishop Nwaedo of Igboland of South-Eastern Biafra land as a holy bishop.

My parents trusted me a lot, especially in terms of faith, dealing with money and relating to men. They would show me where they kept their money in case of emergency. They allowed me to associate with both male and female. They would not be afraid. If a young man was looking for me, they would allow him but if it was my other siblings, my mother especially would ask why. Both of my parents built high trust in me. I would not say that I am better than the rest of others because nature made it that way. And this helped me a lot when I was overseas. I was always conscious of their trust and what I was doing at every moment. Through my parents' support, commitments, courage, and counselling to me, I always try to represent them well even though they are no more. They were proud of me and I am proud of them too.

Now, let me tell you the result of the parental blessings. For my younger brother, Bosco, since he started his business, he has been doing well even though he met with ups and downs on the way. For my younger sister, Livina, her marriage has been superb. She and her husband love each other so dearly that nothing could come between the two of them. They are married with five God-fearing and intelligent boys, a well-educated and happy family. Economically, they are balanced. For myself, "Nne m" Rosa, I found myself in the convent and made it a successful one. I am going to celebrate my 31th First Religious Profession this year – 2022. Nonetheless, the journey is still long; I have far to travel. I am striving to reach the end. Hence, my mother's blessing is still leading me. Therefore, I absolutely believe that the spirit of my mother and the grace of God will lead me through as usual. Even though I met with numerous obstacles on the way, yet her spirit always holds me firmly. Mama, we shall never disappoint you and we ask you to always keep on interceding for all your children. At the same time, she would say, "I gave my blessings to all my children wherever they were," and it happened as she said it. The reason behind these special blessings is that Mama believed that three of us were reincarnated from her parents. Bosco, as she disclosed, was reincarnated from her father, Livy, and myself, Rosa, reincarnated from her grandmother. In fact, Mama was more fond of us although she loved others of her children too in their own unique ways. One can see here the effect of parental blessings on the children.

The same thing is applicable to a parental curse. For this reason, parents should be careful when they say any negative word to their children in anger. As a teen, I was always watching my parents and observed that they hardly cursed any of us whenever we wronged. Though our father was not a talking type, our mother could talk but she never placed a curse on us; rather, she would give out a figurative proverb to disapprove of that action and then followed it up with a song to reinforce the proverb. If any of the girls misbehaved, she would say to the person, "every woman would experience what other women had experienced." Parents, don't be afraid of training your children no matter the pressure, confrontation, and challenges of western rules and regulations that undermined the home training. Never be afraid of training your children because

> *"No one can hurt you if you are determined to do only what is right; if you do have to suffer for being good, you will count it as a blessing. There is no need to be afraid or to worry about them…"*
>
> **—1 Peter 3:13-17**
> **The Jerusalem Bible & Popular Edition**
> **Darton Longman & Todd 1974, (p. 302).**

The Western rules and regulations are trying to dismantle the ties that bind parents and their children together. Where are we heading to? Parents have no right to reprimand their children; authorities have no say over those under them. If you try to direct a child under you, the so-called social workers, law enforcement, and MPs would come over to get you. Who bears the consequence? Hence, there is a difference between reprimanding and abuse. Abuse is absolutely not allowed. Parents are called upon to work hard to restore the fading value of the family upbringing and counselling. The government system is making a lot of families and marriages dysfunctional. We now have a lot of ex-wives, ex-husbands, single mothers, and single fathers. These kinds of things are taboo in our culture and the elders should, through their rules and regulations, try to prevent these things which inhibit people from living normal lives. I will never fail to mention male and male husbandry and female and female husbandry. These are confused states of living in our time. Well, we have to judge rightly. If all men marry themselves and women do the same, what would happen about procreation? Don't tell me that miracles would happen because God did not plan it that way from the beginning. I am not judging but let us reason rightly.

Parental Curse and Its Effectiveness on Children

As the blessings of parents are effective over their children, so are the parental curses. Children should endeavour to avoid parental curses on them. A good child never receives any curse from parents, or even from the elders. Children, never let the elders curse you because their curse is very effective. Parents, avoid laying any curse on your child (ren) since your curse has a remarkable impact on them. Parents, never call any of your children good for nothing or bad names. These have a psychological impact on them. Besides, be mindful of the words you use for your children. Also, keep away from giving your children names that have negative psychological influences. As good names have good influences, so do bad names. Just as my name is Chinedum, everything I lay my hand on goes well. Even though I find myself in the midst of danger, God leads me through. Children, if your parents gave you wrong names, please change them. Those names to be avoided are as these: Ashiogo, Aghahi, Onukwuforo, Onwuka, Onwuemeanyi, Njoahia, Ufu, Udele, Usu, and Njoihe, etc. Children, avoid anything that could provoke your parents to curse you because their curse is ineffectual. One boy used to beat his mother and his mother, in turn, cursed him. This boy married and had a baby boy who, when he grew up, not only beat his father but also killed him. This was as a result of the curse from his mother. She, out of anger, cursed him that his own child would beat him to death. Always long for the blessings of your parents, not their curses.

We can see from the previous chapter that I was aware of the blessings of my parents. The same thing is applicable to parental curse. For this reason, parents should be careful whenever uttering any negative word to their children. As a teen, I was observing my parents if they would curse us when we had disobeyed them; but I could not see that. Mama would rather give out a proverb to disapprove that action and then sang a song to reinforce the proverb. If any of the girls refused to do her chores, she would say to the person, "Woman would see or experience what other women had experienced."

This book, The Ancestral Legacy of Family Counselling, is trying to re-establish and strengthen the fading family ethics which the Western culture is seemingly affecting. In one of my books, "Building Up Self-Confidence, A Fundamental Way of Conquering Fear," I laid much emphasis on fear as a huge factor undermining ones' capabilities to perform various tasks. Today, in our present time, the Western civilization and its rules and regulations are deeply exerting a negative influence on our own noble African culture and family upbringing. This creates an atmosphere of uncertainties in our modern-day parents who are now afraid to raise their children according to the norms of African culture, or any other culture they belong to. Consequently, any child could do whatever she wants without minding the presence of an adult. Children fail to pay heed to our ancestral wisdom. Our youths are called upon to re-think.

Also, it is going to examine the role of mothers on their children. As proverb has it, in any successful man, there must be a woman behind him; likewise, I add, in any productive child, there are parents behind her. I am a typical example of this. I will edify on what I know for sure. Our parents play important roles in the lives of their children. Each child is a typical picture of either the mother or the father. This magnifies itself, for instance, through the way one behaves, talks, reasons, walks, looks, eats, dresses or works, and any good qualities your child has come from either of the parents and any bad quality a child has is perceptible from both too. Any behaviour they acquire is not remote from the parents. The children learn a lot from their parents. I am telling you this based on a psychological point of view and through experiences from my own parents. That is the reason why our first teachers and leaders in our lives are our parents and relatives. Thus, Basic Home Training is crucial.

"When one talks about leadership, people quickly rush to think of political, social, or religious leaders, etc. However, leadership roles begin right away in our various families with our parents, brothers, sisters, and relatives. Our parents are the first leaders we encounter in our lives; our successes, failure, or setbacks begin with them. If they direct and lead us well in our early childhood, our journey of life begins well, but if not, we mess up. For this reason, leadership roles are not farfetched from our families. If the family cannot lead their children, no one can do it either. In our context, leadership cannot take shape in the vacuum; it must be rooted and founded in psychology interactive as the system of model of human behaviour. This model is based on three major aspects of the human person: mind, body, and spirit. In human development, the mind can be broken into (1) cognition (knowing, understanding, and thinking) (2) affection, (attitude, pre-dispositions, emotions, and feelings) (3) conation (intentions to act, reasons for doing so, and will.) the body is thought of as (1) biological or genetic process, (2) bodily activities, (3) physical behaviour. The spirit is the force vital that connects the whole entity of the human person with the divine that insures life.

In human development, the human being interacts with the immediate environment in which he/she finds himself or herself, which fashions the individuals into a system or mode of behaviour resulting in the following: cognitive system which is responsible for perception, storage, processing, and retrieval of information. There are immediate and remote influences that affect human development in the area of leadership as one grows up in life. It is necessary for those responsible for the training and upbringing of children in society to take adequate note of these factors if our society is to enjoy the fruits and rewards of good leadership which is the essence of a civil society. A good leadership in the family makes for a good family where there is peace, love, and tranquility between the parents and the children. Such a family becomes a home for the father, the mother, and the children. The same is applicable to our communities, institutions, and governments of different countries, states, and nations of the world on an international level. And so, it is incumbent on us to have at our fingertips those things that influence the development of a human being before the process of development begins with an individual person. Theses influences stem mostly from the ecological point of view like micro-system that result from first contacts with the family, school, religious institutions, and peer groups."

—Unpublished Article by Sr. Chinedum J. Nwadike's Doctoral Thesis 2002 on Leadership Role of our Parents to their Children (p. 2).

One can agree with me that our parents are originators of our success in life. I am among the lucky ones whose parents influenced them in good faith. Though my parents were unschooled in the English style, yet they acquired a great deal of natural wisdom that helped them to raise us. My parents directed us well both through natural wisdom and hard work. They made determined efforts to train all of us academically. My dad was a quiet type, dedicated to work, not the talking type but he used to speak once with effectiveness and truth. He was a truthful fellow, always opposed to any form of injustice, even for which he suffered a lot. He never allowed anybody to intimidate him once he meant to speak the truth. He was very motivational. During our primary and secondary education, he was there to support us. He provided us with all the materials we needed for school work. Papa made sure we pay our school fees in time. He always frowned upon any misbehaviour. My father used to advise us that if anybody offered us a gift on the way, we should bring it home and show it to him and our mother so that they would be able to thank the person. This is an indirect way of discipline so as not to possess anything without their knowledge.

Our mother was a strong woman, hardworking, a great dancer, the talking type, and she, like our father, frowned at injustice and never looked at anybody's face when speaking the truth. She used to talk in proverbs, sign language, songs to affirm or disapprove any good deeds or wrongdoing of her children. She always abhorred any form of injustice. She used to gather us and tell us folk stories after dinner before we went to bed to sleep. After each story, she would tell us the positive and negative effects of the story and then conclude by asking us not to follow the bad but the good way. All the time my mother was doing these, I couldn't comprehend her; I always thought she was doing foolish things. Along the line in my later life, I came to the realization of the importance of what she was doing then. These manifested in me in the United States of America when I was experiencing difficult situations. Each time I was faced with difficulties, her inspirational words began to resound in my mind, and then I would realize them myself and apply a remedy to my problems immediately. All these inspirations from our mother led me through into the USA and beyond. If my parents were exhibiting misleading behaviours then, I would have copied them. especially our mother whom I was always close to in doing the domestic work. Anytime something happens, I just retrieve them one by one including what they taught us and immediately use them effectively. One of our mother's proverbs says, "When mother goat chews grass, the baby goat watches her." This is exactly what happened here in my case; I copied from her without knowing it. I cook well like my mother, I dance well like my mother, I can speak in proverbs like my mother. I can foresee danger as she could, and I am generous like my parents. My parents were extremely generous. Some of my mother's characteristics that made me successful are, patience, endurance, forgiveness, hardworking, and determination. I must tell you, my dear ones, that I facilitated my way through determination. My father was a die-hard fellow and my mother too. Thus, I copied from them. This is more reason why parents should try to be careful with what they do and say in the presence of their children. Upon reflecting on the influence our mother had on me and on my success, I was motivated to write down all these wise proverbs I learnt from her. I know quite well that this will be of great benefit to our youngsters who are wise enough to learn and to follow the right path laid down by our parents and grandparents. On my birthday, when I began writing this book, I set out to put together all my thoughts in a notebook. Though my mother is dead, yet she is still living. This legacy of hers will pass down through the generations to come, though of course, for those who will value them. I use the word 'psychologist' here to refer to Mama because, when she was living, she could read people's minds correctly. She would say to me, "Look, this person has this in mind and I am telling the truth; just mark it." And honestly speaking, it would happen exactly the way she predicted. Most often, I arose from sleep to wonder the kind of person she was. Mama could counsel individuals in crisis and assist them with their devastating situations. This attribute of my mother led me to study Psychology. Mama, thanks a lot; your wisdom will remain with us. I will endeavour to impact your wisdom to our future generation. It is said,

"The proper study of mankind is man."

—Alexander Pope

www.branyquote.com/quote/alexander-Pope_145950

More so, proverbs from the Ancient Egyptian Temples stated:

"If you are searching for a Netter (Egyptian god), observe Nature. Man, know thyself and thou shalt know the gods. The body is the house of God, that is the reason why it is said, "Man know thyself."

—John Gage Allee
Famous Quotes and Webster's Encyclopedia of Dictionary 1983 (P. 894).

The above statements tell us that to teach a child well, we must use the child's natural things, events, and reasoning to introduce to the child how things are made and how they work to prevent the child from being afraid of learning. The human body is a model of everything God has made and must be used in teaching numbers, letters, words, signs, functions, things, events, and activities. Natural models and demonstrations are most impressive on the mind and lead from the known to the unknown very reasonably.

1.2. Who are We? The Africans: The Africans in Africa and in the World

Human lineage ancestors (hominid) were separated from other human-like cousins, like the chimpanzees and the gorillas, about 7 million years ago according to comparative biomolecular data resulting from gene analysis. We are genetically 98.99 per cent similar to chimpanzees. About 4 million years ago, bipedalism (walking upright on two limbs) appeared as a result of food - and child-carrying, watching for predators, tool use, evolving intelligence, single birth, lengthy gestation, prolonged postnatal maturation, and care of the young ones. About 3 million years ago, "Lucy," a humankind female ancestor of modern man was bipedal, 3 feet in stature, and of 480 cubic centimetres' brain size. Around 1 million years ago, fire was discovered. According to the dating of anatomically modern man, skulls from archaeological research in four sites in Africa (1) Omo, Ethiopia, (2) Laetoli, Tanzania, (3) Klasies River Mouth, South Africa, and (4) Border Cave, South Africa, showed that modern man appeared in South Africa at least 130,000 to 110,000 years ago. But according to a molecular biology report, Rebecca Cann and her colleagues, in an article entitled "Mitochondrial DNA (DNA-deoxyribonucleic acid) and Human Evolution," appearing in Nature in January 1987, in their work on mitochondrial DNA (mt DNA), were able to trace human evolution. "Echoes of the Old Darkland" by Charles S. Finch III, M.D. (p. 4-51).

Mitochondria are self-reproducing units contained in all cells of higher organisms from fungi to mammals, found in many copies per cell (around 10,000 per cell), responsible for energy production of the cell, inherited from the mother alone. The mtDNA mutation rate is said to be fairly constant over long periods of time, about 2 to 4 per cent per million years and, therefore, is used to determine how long the first common mother lived. From purified placentas of 145 persons and samples of two cell lines representing the Bushmen (Khoisan) of Southern Africa and Black Americans, Cann was able to obtain purified mtDNA from five different geographical locations: Sub-Saharan Africa, Asia, Europe, North America, and the Middle East, Australia (aborigines)/New Guinea. The results showed the most variable mtDNA signifying that the oldest mtDNA in the whole world came from the Bushmen of Southern Africa. She postulates that the female common ancestor of all surviving mtDNAs, hence of all surviving human beings, lived between 140,000 to 290,000 years ago in Eastern or Southern Africa. In an interview, she gave a mean date of 200,000 for our first female common human ancestor whom she nicknamed "Eve" and the sample of mtDNA that registered the oldest age came from a Bushman or San individual from the Kalahari Desert in Southern Africa. Then, after the appearance of the first human beings, they moved up to Ethiopia and lived there until about 100,000 years ago when the first expansion took place between 100,000 and 75,000years ago, the second expansion around 60,000 to 30,000 years ago and the last expansion around 25,000 to 13,000 years ago to Asia, Europe, Australia, and North America. About 80 per cent of them, the Africans, stayed in Africa and gave rise to the African civilization in Egypt.

The Africans of Sub-Sahara lived in the Elephantine area in Egypt (today, Aswan, in Egypt, then Ibu or Abu where the names Ibo and Yoruba came from) and departed from Egypt to Meroitic Napata (Sudan and Ethiopia) in 664-625 BC when the Egyptian Libyan army officer, Psammetichus betrayed the Egyptian army into the hands of the invading Persian army for favours to rule Egypt. The Sub-Saharan Africans left Napata in 500 BC to West Africa through Central Africa to the Senegal area and established three empires during the era called the Golden Age of West Africa, namely: Ghana Empire (300-600 AD by Berber invaders, 600-1240 AD by ruling class clan, Suisse of Soninke), capital Kumbi; Mali Empire (1240-1359 AD) capital Niani, and other cities: Walata, Gao, Timbuktu, Jenne; Songhai Empire (1475-1591 AD, then till the 17ᵗʰ Century) capital Gao. From there, they spread to Nigeria, Ghana, Congo, Tanzania and Southern Africa. The sub-Sahara Africans are connected through reference to the Ancient Egyptian language and culture. For example:

> Egypt: fa-a Khu = to kindle fire on the altars,
> Ibo: fu- oku = to kindle fire by blowing it with your mouth, fire
> Egypt: Serekh =Throne,
> Hausa: Sarik = Emir = ruler
> Egypt: Horus = Heru = God of Egypt
> Yoruba: Orisha = name of God, and
> Ibo: Chukwu/Orusa = name of God.

Sources: "Introduction to African civilizations" by John G. Jackson (pp. 198-231), "The African Origin of Civilization" by Cheikh Anta Diop (pp. 124-155), and "The Africans by Ali A. Mazrui (pp. 41-79).

Ibidem- "Introduction to African Civilizations" (p. 150).

English	Egyptian
Abode (habitation)	Abut (abode)
Attack	Atakh
Autumn (season)	Atum (the red autumnal (sun)
Canoe	Khenna (a boat)
Count (a title)	Kannt (a title)
Cow	Kaui (cow)
Foot	Fut (a measure)
Hag (witch)	Hek (magic)
Kick	Khekh (to repulse)
Mamma (mother)	Mama (to bear)
Married	Mer't (attached)
Mayor	Mer (he who rules)
Ray (of sunlight)	Ra (the Sun)
Suit (to satisfy)	Suta (to please)
Write	Ruit (to engrave)

Youth   uth (youth)

It is said that Osiris left the heavenly realm of god and became an earthly Egyptian King and conferred on the Egyptians the blessings of civilization, teaching them the cultivation of barley and wheat to raise grains.

The African Identity

Africa is a rich continent in the centre of the earth's landmass and with a totally tropical climate, stretching between 32 degrees north from the Tropic of Cancer to 32 degrees south and the Tropic of Capricorn. Its soils are still the most unused arable land in the whole world and the most endowed with natural resources of mineral complex with heavy concentrations of gold, platinum, diamonds, chromium, and other hard minerals. It is bathed in the tropical sunlight of direct vertical sun rays for a full 12 hours, thus, making for luxuriant plant growth with full nutrient development and abundant animal life. This physical tropical location of Africa with an abundance of life-sustaining materials made it possible for the first man and first woman to be grown in Africa, the Garden of Eden, and for the first human civilization to flourish for over 3000 years. Everything that moves or that is scientific is African in its nucleus. Among the relatively obvious examples is the choice of Greenwich in Britain as the "mean time" meridian for setting the alarm clocks of the human race; even when we say "Universal Standard Time" we are actually saying Greenwich Mean Time.

Why did we call it the Greenwich Meridian instead of the Gao Meridian in Africa? (Gao is the capital of Songhay Empire in Africa 1350-1600 AD). Africa deserves to be honoured because Africa was the originator of time-scheduling, dating, recording, mapping, and Africa, with its full 12 hours of daylight, was responsible for measuring the duration of 12-hour daylight, 12-hour nighttime, 24-hour day, 30-day month, and 365 days a year. This is the African identity personality.

Time Scheduling was an African identity attribute and should have been projected to be remembered, because it was impossible to obtain an accurate time reckoning in Europe where the sun is seen at an angle and the duration of day and night are unequal. Among all the continents of the World, Africa, so far, has been the least affected by major earthquakes and earth disturbances. Africa's shores have also been among the least susceptible to typhoons, hurricanes, blizzards, tornadoes, and other weather-related elemental devastations, though disease and drought rather than earthquakes and hurricanes have been nature's cruelties against Africa.

Who are the Africans?

The Africans have Three Cultural/Zonal Personalities Namely:

1) North Africans - These have Arab-oriented cultures in which Muslim religion and Arabic language dominate. Even though clothing and diet join Africans together, the North Africans behave much like Arabs.
2) Southern Africans - These are influenced by European culture and so their African cultural identity is mixed with that of the Europeans.
3) Between these two zones, you have the other Africans, South of Saharans, the West Africans, and Black Africa. These Africans are the true Africans in languages, religion, clothing (agbada, buba, Sokoto, garment, loincloth), diet (root crops and tubers) mode of life and strength of character.

So, there are three cultural influences in Africa:

1. Indigenous African Pantheism,
2. Imported monotheism,
3. Western secularism modified by Western Christianity.

1. Indigenous African Pantheism (Pantheism - Belief in Almighty God and His Deities)

Indigenous African Pantheism is the purist of Black African beliefs. They believe that God is responsible for what nature does and they give spiritual values to all natural events. For example, there is a family that can make rain fall and that can stop it from falling. That is the gift of spiritual power (compare biblical gift of tongue) which we Africans call "ihanmili na ijinmiri." Africans believe that God has the knowledge and permits natural occurrences, hence, their frequent consultation with diviners and frequent sacrifices to invoke good things to occur and bad things not to occur. They accept a universal life force that permeates nature and that is indistinguishable from God.

Africans co-existed with one another so that their beliefs are congenial to all (all the same). They identify themselves with objects or animals as symbols of solidarity, perpetuating a sense of continuity between nature and man. Africans believe that a tree, an animal and a river could all have a soul and so, Africans respect all living creatures such that some African communities cannot kill a boa constrictor (eke) or tortoise (Nnambe) because of a bond of brotherhood between the animals and themselves - their totems.

2. Imported Monotheism

Monotheism asserts that a monopoly of divine power is invested in a single deity and tends to set apart the creator on one side and the creatures on the other; God, on one side, and nature, on the other. In the monotheism of Judeo-Christian and Islamic traditions, it is believed that God existed before He created anything. Thus, monotheistic culture believes in one creator, man and a host of angels both saved and fallen. In this case, there is a sharp division between not only God and nature, but also between man and the rest of creation. Monotheism maintains that only man has a soul, all other creatures are deemed to be in the service of man and for the pleasure of man without restraint. That is ecological animal racism. Islamic monotheism at its depth dislikes anything that promotes idolatry. In order to discourage a return to idolatry, they forbade the making of art forms involving the figures of animals and human beings as the animals are no longer sacred, but the camel is humanized and is the totem of Islam. Although Islam has abolished sacred animals, it still recognizes the profane ones like the pig and the dog. Anyone in contact with the pig or dog is in "najs" (unclean state) and with najs on his hands, he is not allowed to enter a mosque or pray with others in the street; Muslims have taboos on alcoholic drinks and women.

3.   Western Secularism Modified by Western Christianity

Indigenous African religion recognizes profane animals (egugo, esu millipede and centipede (gbaranwoke gbaranwanyi) and sacred animals (sheep, lamb) (aturu Chukwu), boa-constrictor (eke) while Islam limits itself only to profane animals. Western cultures neither recognize sacred nor profane creatures but Christianity makes it accept "the lamb of God who takes away the sins of the world" as a sacred animal. It also commercializes the status of animals. Some animals are placed on an endangered list for fear that if they are not preserved, they will be extinct. Some animals are also placed in conservation game preserves to protect them from being killed or poached, and can be sold as pets or sold to zoos as souvenirs (refer ngorongoro, Serengeti animals' reserves). In short, African identity personality has been affected both in North and the South but remains intact in West Africa. Our languages, religion, diet and clothing identify us from the rest of the world.

Who are the Igbos?

According to Uzoma Onyemachi, University of Michigan, Ann Arbor (1986), the Igbos occupying the Eastern side of the Niger River Delta of Nigeria are proud, dynamic, progressive, enterprising and ambitious people and according to research by archeologists, historians, linguists and agronomists, the Igbos place their greatest emphasis on education as a means of ascending the ladder of power and prominence. Igbos originally came from Egypt through Sudan (Meroe) down to the region

Northeast of Senegal River and Northwest of the River Niger, and participated in the Empire of Ghana from 700 to 1200 AD. When the empire was sacked by Moslems from the North (Morocco), the Igbos moved down to the Niger-Benue Confluence (Lokoja) in Nigeria and thence to the present location in Eastern Nigeria.

The Characteristics of the Igbos

The characteristics of Igbos can best be demonstrated by describing the noteworthy acts of three outstanding Igbo personalities. These are men of great esteem who have stemmed from extremely humble beginnings and made it to the top with arduous creative energies. One of them is King Jaja of Opobo, an Igbo slave, named Jubo- Jubo gha; Africans called him JoJo, Europeans called him Jaja; born at Amaigbo Nkwerre Orlu, Imo State. He began life as a slave in Bonny, graduated to be a canoe-paddler, a successful trader and ultimately head of Anna Pepple House and finally became the unsurpassed King Jaja of Opobo. The Sage (perceptive) of Jaja, so charmingly written up by de Cardi (1899), Dike (1956), Jonesed (1961) etc., illustrates that the Igbo at his best, is courageous, obstinate, proud, and faithful to his friends and benefactors. The 1960s are the finest of the West Africans and of all Africans as a whole. According to Kenneth Onwuka Dike (1956) "Trade and Politics in the Niger Delta" 1830-1885 - (p. 183), he said,

"As the history of Bonny from 1867 to 1873 was in all essentials the history of Jaja, his rapid rise from obscurity to prominence is worthy of note." He led the opposition groups against the Europeans' penetration of Eastern Nigeria hinterland from 1879 until 1887 (the year of his deportation to West Indies) and the part he played in Eastern Nigeria history was more important than that of any African in the period. The Igbos today regarded him as the greatest produced by their tribe in the last century. Jaja was born at Umuduruoha village in Amaigbo Nkwerre, Orlu District, Owerri Province, and Imo State in the heart of Igboland in 1821. He was sold as a slave boy at 12 years of age to Chief Iganipu Huma Allison of Bonny

who, finding him insubordinate and headstrong, made a gift of him to Madu, a chief of Anna Pepple House. His rise from slavery to freedom, his exploits as a domestic slave of Madu and his service under British Supercargo (a ship that carries cargo), form an interesting chapter in his exceptional career. His energies were concentrated in extending his trade but by 1861, he had risen to the rank of the first line of Chiefs at Bonny and was soon to gain the leadership of his House.

—Kenneth Onwuka Dike

Another example (about the mid-20th century) is the late Sir Odumegwu Ojukwu. Sir Odumegwu Ojukwu, born in Nnewi, Anambra State, started life as a petty trader and then rose to be a produce inspector, then a multinational businessman, a dealer in transportation vehicles (a transport motor magnate), a banking financier, a financial tycoon and finally a Knight of the British Empire. The last of the three Igbos is the late Middleweight Boxing Champion of the world, Dick Tiger Ihetu, from Nkwerre-Orlu, Imo State. He started off as a used bottle-picker and then as a petty trader at Eke Oha, Aba township in 1951-1952. Within this time, he joined the boxing club and fought his way to become a world Middleweight Boxing Champion in 1960. Tiger became a businessman, a school proprietor and finally, a Member of the British Empire (M.B.E.). The reason why I cited these famous Igbo prominent men is that my mother used to cite them as an example of men worthy to be emulated. She would say, "My children, you have to start from somewhere before you become a well-known fellow."

The Currency used by the Igbos from Ancient Times up to 1945

Name: Ego Ayoro-Cowries

Count Denomination:
Otumbu – 1 Cowrie

Mbunato – 3 Cowries

Isiego – 5 Cowries

Ukwuego – 10 Cowries

Ukwunato – 30 Cowries

Ohu ukwu – 200 cowries

Ngwugwuego – 600 Cowries

Ugbugbaego – 1 Bowl of Cowries

Otumbaliego – 1000 Cowries

Cowries: Old Igbo Currency

Conclusion

Africa, the continent of clement sunshine, rich in vegetation, foodstuffs, animals and complex minerals, is unique in that her people are blessed with their own diet of fu-fu made from yams, cassava, taro banana, plantain and maize in addition to soups of egusi, okra, agbono, Ukpo, vegetables (inene, oha, okasi, olugbo, anara, ugu, ahihira) and meats (goat, chicken, cow, guinea fowl, fish, crab, etc.). Nigeria, being the most populous of all African countries and centre from which Africa expanded, has over 200 languages. Her people are recognized by the way they dress, eat, speak, and dance. Our food is unique and our music is also unique. West Africans represent Africa by being totally cultural original and untampered with by foreigners. The Igbo man is their model character personality.

(source oral interview)

CHAPTER 2

Igbo Folklore And Effect On Counselling

2.1. Folklore: The Body of Orally Preserved Traditions, Beliefs, Tales, Proverbs, Riddles, etcetera, Used in African Counselling

This chapter contains enormous parts of the proverbs in Igbo language as my mother imparted them to me. I will also highlight their meanings and their interpretations both in Igbo and in English. When I was writing these proverbs down, one of my friends said to me, "But these proverbs are general "Igbo" wise sayings." Then, I answered, "Yes, but I learnt them directly from my own mother; no one else taught them to me except my mum. Each time Mama talked, I listened to her. Sometimes, I could not comprehend the reason why she was talking in such a manner. Nonetheless, later in my life, I found out she was not talking rubbish; instead, sensibly." In ancient times, attention was paid towards cultural emancipation to encourage the well-groomed growing-up of young people into attractive gentlemen and adorable and marriageable ladies. The question is: what is the correct behaviour in all aspects of life regarding language, cultural orientation, morals, and cultural standards applicable as to what you are and what you ought to be –your identity? Yes, my mother groomed my siblings and I as well. If she failed to reprimand us or disapprove of us when we were uncooperative, we would have been irresponsible men and women. My relationship with Mama proved to me that mothers have the upper hands in the behaviour, upbringing, and downfall of their children. Mums, whether any of your children is a princess, prince, king, reverend, medical doctor, doctor of education, a drop-out from school, a thief, and a drug addict, etcetera, you are responsible. I say this because mothers are always very close to their children. Appropriately, I am proud to have the kind of mama who rendered to us proper discipline that aided us to become well-mannered and progressive citizens. She guided us well with the help of our father. What I am today, she takes 95% of it. Psychologically, whatever parents are, make a great imprint on their children especially on the mom's side. If you are a mother who does not live a good life, one of your kids will follow suit. My mother used to say: like begets like or a snake never fails to breed a long issue like itself. And so, there is a great deal of psychological impact from what children learn from their parents. Mother's wise sayings in Igbo dialect and their interpretations in English are listed here below. If mother was irresponsible, automatically, I would have been too because I mimicked her a lot. As Mama used to express in the proverbs, nne ewu na ata nkwara, nwa ya na eleya, meaning (when the mother goat chews her cud, the baby goat watches). On the other hand, whatever our elders do, the young ones learn. I never knew that all the things Mum used to convey in proverbs involuntarily registered in my memory. Blessed be God who gave me a good mother; I am blessed. Mama used to say; "Seventy times seventy times, she would reincarnate and remarry in Konye Nwadike's family". So, I am saying too that 70 times, I will reincarnate and have parents like mine again if this would have been possible. My parents were academically uneducated, nevertheless, they were instilled with natural wisdom and were self-content with what nature could endow in them. My parents gave me a comprehensive formal natural wisdom and a healthy moral upbringing. I am pleased and contented with what I have. I am honoured to be one of their daughters. Mother, when any of us was showing a sign of laziness during the farming period, would say: "nwa m aka aja na ebute onu mmanu- mmanu," meaning, 'suffer before pleasure for sweat comes before sweet; soiled hands give rise to oiled mouth or a child of labour with age of ease.' Below are the lists of proverbs Mama used to apply for approval or disapproval of any behaviour. These maxims assisted me towards success and self-actualization. The book of Ecclesiastic states,

"My son, from your earliest youth choose instruction, and till your hair is white you will keep finding wisdom. Cultivate her like the ploughman and the sower, and wait for her fine harvest, for in tilling her you will toil a little while, but very soon you will be eating her crops."
—Ecclesiasticus 6:18-19)
The Jerusalem Bible & Popular Edition
Darton, Longman & Todd 1974, (pp. 907-908).

Ancestral Cultural Relationship with Animals and Totems

According to folktales of our ancestors, long ago when the creation of living beings was completed, animals were said to speak like human beings and walk like humans. The snake had legs then but owing to its treachery by disclosing the tree of life which was hidden in the sea, to the dragon that ate it up, death came to be. However, the gods cursed the snake and made it lose its legs and go on its belly. As a matter of fact, animals are more spiritual and experienced than humans because biologists, archaeologists, scientists, and biochemists have found out, with modern accurate equipment and intelligent and empirical calculations, that birds appeared on the Planet Earth, some 150 million years ago; mammals (mammals - animals that deliver their young alive and suckle them), came to be 65 million years ago, humankind, 4 million years ago and modern man about 250,000 to 290,000 years ago. As a result, animals are older, more adapted, and more knowledgeable than human beings. That is the reason why our ancestors developed metaphors, proverbs, idioms, and the practice of faith with them as models of comparison. We use some animals as totems (emblems) for some clans like the tortoise, crocodile, and eagles; some as symbols of sacredness like the Sheep and the Boas; some as symbols of wisdom like the tortoise and the elephants; some as symbols of strength and agility like the lion, elephants and birds; some as diviners like the parrot, owl and the night jay (ajoanunu). The young people are counselled and groomed with respect to these ideas by giving them these jewels of wisdom and proper behaviour so that they can be self-sufficient and mellow in doing good works as befits a civilized modern society. There are many animals but we will discuss a number of them that are important in this book, especially the ones our elders use in figurative speeches and in idioms to groom the young ones.

Abum ududere (Ududeremagu) (Wolf Spider) anaghim emebisi ulo ntara ahuhu rua

Wolf Spider and His Web's Adage

Wolf Spider   *Web*

The above title means 'I am like the spider that never destroys the house that he built with great effort'. Then, in this sense, 'my yes is yes and no is no.' The spiders are the best animal architects. They spin and weave their silken, sticky cobweb with sticky liquid protein silk, squeezed from glands in the abdomen, which hardens on contact with air and which has a combination of strength and stretch as strong as bulletproof vests. The spider, after weaving its cobweb, will make a single thread of silk with a huge blob of sticky silk at the end and sneak away undercover to avoid being exposed to predators. Its house seems to be abandoned as an eyewitness observes in the saying above. When an unsuspecting butterfly flies into the cobweb, the spider throws the sticky blob onto the butterfly to entrap it, and then the spider pounces on the prey for a meal. We may liken the spider's action to what the European traders did in the Niger Delta Region during the pioneering era of colonialism and what the African trading middlemen also did in response. British traders' attempts to penetrate the hinterland for trade in cotton, palm oil, groundnuts, coffee, and ivory were hostilely resisted by the Niger Delta Valley middlemen who felt that the European traders were attempting to capture the palm oil trade on which they depended.

The British traders erected factories (trading stations) at Aboh, Onitsha, Lokoja, Akassa, Idah, Ndoni, Abragada, Osomari, and Egga and the hostile Niger Delta tribes, instigated by the African middlemen, attacked the stations with cannons and muskets and set fire to the stations. On this account, the European traders retaliated with warships and machine guns, destroying the native fortified points. But during the seven months of the dry season when the warships could not go up the Niger River, the native hostilities resumed. In 1879, H.M.S. Pioneer (H.M.S. = His Majesty's Ship) removed £50,000 worth of British trade goods from Onitsha station and then subjected the town to naval bombardment for three days. The following day, after destroying the section of the town on the banks of the Niger River, the British forces marched to the inner city, about three miles distance, and burnt down houses, levelling down all standing walls. Consul Easton, who led the military expedition, said*, "Our proceedings at Onitsha will have a most salutary effect up and down the Niger."*

Yamaha on the Benue River, another important inland trading station, was destroyed in the same year for attacking British traders. Idah and Aboh were bombarded and at the latter, several hundreds were killed and the streets were littered with corpses. You see, each contending party was full of strong reasons and animosity and exerted a lot of effort to uphold the status quo of their businesses. No one will allow the fruit of his labour to languish. They zealously guarded their interests like the spider watching its cobweb house. But all the same, after the thunder comes the rain. After the pacification encounter, each side recognized the legitimate right of the indigenous businessmen and the corresponding right of the foreign traders whom the native traders need to buy their products in exchange for manufactured goods. **Sources: Trade Winds on the Niger by Geoffrey L. Baker (pp.34- 36). Trade and Politics in the Niger Delta by Kenneth Onwuka Dike (pp. 171-181, 204-209).**

Ashia (Weaver Bird)

The Weaver Bird is an expert in weaving its nest with sliced palm leaves. Its feathers are golden yellow below and light golden on the wings. Its songs are noisy because weaver birds build their nests in colonies. They use their sound to scare predators, saying, *"Agha azu anaghi eri anunu na akwu maka na akwu ahia adighi egbu akpu. Gidi- gidi bu ugwu eze. "*They build their nests with the entrance facing downwards to prevent anyone from taking them unawares. This is the meaning of the sayings which are always being used in sacrifices. Through birds like Ashia, one would see the wonderful creation of God and the gift of talents to different animals such as the Weaver Bird, which is the most expert in nest-making. That is the reason why whenever my mother was talking to individuals, she talked about the uniqueness of the person. And she advised the person to accept her uniqueness and the talent as God has bestowed on her. This is exactly what counsellors tell their clients during sessions when the person feels an inferiority complex. Nature has made it that way, that everybody must be unique and have something that others would admire.

Lion and Ram (agu na ebule)
https://www.bing.com/images/search?q

With a bushy tail, ebule was very boisterous,) jostling and jumping around exhibiting its bushy tail and its horns as powerful weapons before the lion (the king of all animals). (The lion was terrified and went back but mbekwu (tortoise) went on shouting in humiliation to the ram, saying, "There is nothing in the ram's tail, nothing in the ram's tail." The lion took courage from that, came out and attacked the ram and cut off its tail, killed it and made a meal of the ram. The saying goes like this: *"ewe kwana onye ka gi mgba."* Don't accept wrestling from an opponent whose strength yours cannot match. That is, don't seek that for which you have no talent, for if you do, you are going to end up with the jaws of a formidable animal clasping around your neck. Also, never be a betrayer like the tortoise.

The lion is the king of all animals. He is full of power, strength, and confidence. He moves about quietly, deliberately with confidence in his absolute power. He is proud and self-content. Below, you will see how he is tricked and overtaken.

Agu (Lion)
https://www.bing.com/images/search?q=Lion

Agu, Aturu, na Nwaebuleako (Lion, Sheep, and Sheep's Lamb child)

Lion

Sheep & Lamb

https://uk.images.search.yahoo.com/imageses_yiy
https://www.bing.com/mages/search?q--sheep&form

Sometimes, you have to take a plunge whether or not you are prepared for what is coming on. Something like going out to fish; you don't know whether you will catch fish or not but past experience is always at the back of your mind. Let us study what happened when lion, the king of the animals, planned to eat a sheep's young ones. The lion begged a sheep to allow one of her young ones to babysit her young one. The sheep agreed but told the lion to wait for her in the night. Then the sheep summoned all her young ones to locate who was judicious enough to manoeuvre the lion so as to escape if the lion intended to kill and eat her up. She located Nwaebuleako who said that he was so alert that before you thought to kill him, he was already aware. The mother sheep sent him to the lion. The lion planned to kill Nwaebuleako in the night by causing him to sleep on the left-hand side which was the lion's powerful hand. Nwaebuleako devised his own strategy by putting the lion's baby on the left-hand side. In the middle of the night, the lion woke up and suddenly and quickly grabbed the one sleeping on the left-hand side, killed it and started to eat it. Immediately, the lion discovered that it was her baby that she had killed. She became angry and started searching for Nwaebuleako. By that time, Nwaebuleako had already slipped away and had run home. Nwaebuleako played the smart card here. It is good to be smart when you are in a danger zone. If not, you cannot sort yourself out and escape from the trap. The lesson here is that dealing with a lion is scary and fearful but the sheep, honest and harmless, decided anyway to take a plunge. He, however, depended on his past experience to deal with the lion, a formidable and fierce animal. Again, look before you leap. Also never think you cannot do it; yes, you can. Never look down on anybody because no one is insignificant. So, if you are the kind of person people have poor opinions of and look down on, show them you are able; that you can do what others do to succeed and your ardent effort to succeed depends on your ability and willingness to perform. I call it "surprise-surprise." Thus, surprise them; do not be afraid. Show them that a short man can perform wonders as David did to Goliath, according to the biblical narrative. However, I am not asking you to do as David did, but rather, show them that you are able by striving successfully in your career. Also, let them know that a slow-running stream always runs deeper than the fast-running stream. The 'Igbo' wisdom saying puts it this way: 'odi mkpukpu na eme ire' (small but mighty).

Agu na Mpampa na Eke (The Lion, the Black Soldier Ant and the Python)

Lion

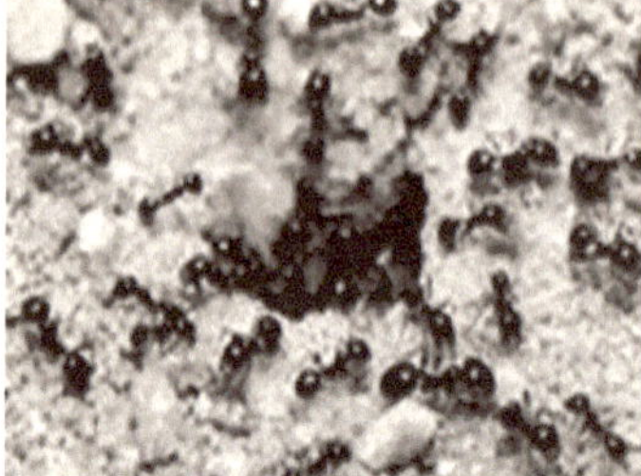

Black Soldier Ant-Mpampa

Python

Black Soldier Ant-Mpampa

https://www.com/images/search?
https://www.bing.com/images/search?

Agu, the lion, is the king of all beasts except the black soldier ant, mpampa, and eke - the python. Agu wanted to tease eke, who was asleep, by biting the tail of eke. Eke awoke, uncoiled and flung its whole length around agu and entwined itself around agu until he collapsed. Then it threw agu away for agu was too big to be swallowed. Agu managed to recover from exhaustion and ran away. Not long after, agu was resting in its den when mpampa the black soldier ant, invaded and filled agu's den. Agu was in trouble and struggled to escape but they had already got into its body, eyes, mouth, and nose. It was a raw deal for agu to handle, to escape, and clean itself up. From that day

36

on, agu, while on the hunt, sings for the appeasement of mpampa and eke: Soma (soba) Ijere (Mpampa), soma (soba) Eke, soma Ijere soma Eke. These two animals are so formidable that agu doffs his hat to them saying, 'I fear and respect ijere and eke.' We also say: *Anu esiri esi ona adi Agu nma ma oweta nke ya orie ya na ndu?* Meaning if cooked meat is good to agu (lion), why does he eat raw meat? Agu is greedy and selfish and will quickly eat raw meat to prevent anyone from sharing the meat with him. l *na akpa ike l pughi ikpachu ike agu odumodu.* If you are powerful, you cannot surpass the lion. Kings and titled men wear lion's teeth.

Mkpamkpa na Isikiri Ogbo Akwu

Everyone has something that stops him from getting on with an action. When mkpamkpa (soldier ant colony) invades a compound, the way to drive them away is to set isikiri ogbo akwu (dry fibrous woody core of palm fruit bunch) on fire and set them at different points of the area invaded by the ants. The smouldering material gives off smoke and odour which drives the ants away. Everyone has a pet aversion. (Dibe jiozo, ozo na egbu ya). In this life, there is something or somebody more powerful than the other. Therefore, we don't have it all. One can see that the lion fears the soldier ant, the python also fears the

soldier ant, the soldier ant fears the smoke and odour from isikiri ogbo akwu- dry fibrous woody core of palm fruit bunch, and the python fears a bird that preys on him. As a result, everybody has something they are afraid of. No one can claim to be more powerful than all; there is something out there more powerful than you are.

Agu: Order – Carnivora (Carnivores- Meat-Eating Cat Family)

Tiger

https://www.bing.com/images/search?q

The big cat family contains seven species viz: lion (Panthera leo), tiger (Panthera tigris), leopard (Panthera pardus), jaguar (Panthera onca), snow leopard (Panthera uncia), clouded leopard (neofelis nebulosa), and cheetah (Acinonyx jubatus).

Leopard

https://www.bing.com/images/search?q

The general distinction between the big cats (Genus Panthera) and small cats (Genus Felis) is that the big cats roar but cannot purr whereas the small cats purr but cannot roar. They vary in density of hair, colouring and patterning of the coat in relation to habitat. The basic colour is a shade of brown, grey, tawny or golden-brown, patterned with dark circles, stripes, rosettes or spots. Many species have a dark tear stripe running from the eye, past the nose to the mouth. In daylight, the cats see as much as man, but under poor light, their sight is up to six times more acute than that of man. Their eyes adapt quickly to sudden darkness. The threat to their survival comes from man who trades in their spotted skins and teeth. We are going to concern ourselves with the lion (Panthera Leo), the leopard (Panthera Pardus) and the cheetah (acinonyx jubatus).

Odum negbu Agu

Male lion

Female lion

The Lion - Agu (Genus Panthera Leo - Carnivore)

Distribution: South Sahara to South Africa, Northwest India (remnant population in Gir Forest Sanctuary).

Habitat: Varied from rich grassland of East Africa to Sands of Kalahari Desert.

Size: Males: Head/body length is 8.5 to 10.5 feet (260 to 320 centimetres); shoulder height 4 feet (1.2 metres); weight 330 to 530 pounds (150 to 240 kilograms).

Females: Head/body length 8 to 9 feet (2.4 to 2.7 metres); shoulder height 3.6 feet (1.1) metres; tail length 2 to 3.3 feet (60 to 100 centimetres); weight 270 to 400 pounds (122 to 182 kilograms).

Coat: Light tawny (golden-brown), white on abdomen and inner side of legs; back of the ears black; mane of males - hairy, tawny through reddish-brown to black. Females are tawny, no mane; Maturity: 36 to 46 months wild, 24-25 months in captivity. Litter sizes vary from 1 to 5 young with average 2 or 3.

Gestation: 100 to 119 days.

Longevity: About 15 years to 24 years in captivity.

Subspecies: Angolan Lion- Zimbabwe, Angola, Katanga; Asiatic Lion- Gir Forest, Northwest India; Masai Lion (East Africa); Transvaal Lion (Transvaal South Africa); Barbary Lion (North Africa); Cape Lion (Cape to Natal South Africa). Owing to its strength and predatory nature, the lion has been thought for centuries to be the "King of Beasts." The myth of the supernatural powers bestowed on the lion survives today. By eating or wearing parts of a lion, it is believed one can revive lost powers, cure illness and have immunity from death. The powerful image of a lion lures hunters from all parts of the world to Africa to demonstrate their ability and courage by shooting the lion, the action of which bestows a social prestige of the title "Ogbuagu" to the hunter in Igboland, and Africa at large.

Mode of Life: The lion is carnivorous (eats meat only); jaws and teeth adapted to choking an animal and eating it. Vision and hearing are of greater importance than sense of smell in locating prey. Females make kills of animals on which males survive but the male's chief role in the pride is to defend the territory and the females from other menacing males. The bulk of a lion's diet comprises rodents, gazelles, zebra, wildebeests, antelopes, and impala. When several lions stalk, that is, when they hunt, they encircle their prey, cutting off potential escape routes. Lions can reach a speed of 36 miles per hour but some of the prey can attain a speed of 50 mph. So, lions must use stealth to approach to within 100 feet of their prey before giving chase. Territorial boundaries are maintained by roaring, urine marking, and patrolling.

Adult females require about 11 pounds of meat per day per individual and adult males 15.4 pounds of meat per day per animal. The size of a pride of lions may be between 7 to 20 animals and the maximum size of territory will range over an area of between 8 and 155 square miles. **The male lion is the laziest animal**. It sleeps for ten to fifteen hours a day. From close studies made in the Serengeti National Park, Kenya, it was found out that an adult male spends 20 out of the 24 hours resting.

In courtship, which may last for several days, the courting couple may initiate copulation by rubbing heads or sniffing the other's groin. Copulation lasts for 21 seconds during which the male releases a low growl and licks or bites the female's neck, who threatens with a snarl. A pair may copulate up to 50 times in 24 hours. Several copulations are meant to initiate ovulation. In lion society, the lioness suckles the cubs of female relatives alongside her own. The lioness has grown to be tolerant toward her pride companions' offspring because they are related, but the males are intolerant of cubs not fathered by them.

The Cheetah - Agu (Genus Acinonyx Jubatus)

Family: Felidae

https://www.bing.com/images/search?q

It is a sole member of its genus. In Igboland of South Eastern Nigeria, kings use the agu as a pet or decorate their thrones with their golden spotted skin and wear the eze agu (lion's teeth) as a part of royal regalia. "Ogbuagu" is one who has bravely killed a lion, a cheetah or a leopard. He celebrates this title "Ogbuage" every year with a new yam feast celebration. What is said of a lion (odum na egbuagu) with respect to its emblematic representation of royalty and power of a monarch is also said of the cheetah. Kings appear in royal celebrations with a cheetah by their side.

Distribution: Africa, South Asia, and the Middle East.

Habitat: Most habitats are in African Savanna.

Size: Head/body length: 44 to 53 inches (112 to 135 centimetres); tail length 26 to 33 inches (66 to 84 centimetres); weight: 86 to 143 pounds (39 to 65 kilograms). Males are slightly larger than females.

Coat: Tawny with small round black spots. Face marked by conspicuous black tear stripes running from the corner of the eyes down the sides of the nose. This feature distinguishes it from the leopard.

Gestation: 91 to 95 days.

Maturity: Sexual maturity occurs at 20 to 23 months old.

Litter Size: 1 to 8, average 3 -5.

Longevity: Up to 12 years (17 years in captivity).

Subspecies: African cheetah and Asiatic cheetah and King Cheetah in South Africa (acinonyx rex) with spots along spine joined together in stripes with small blotches on the body. The cheetah is the fastest animal on land, sprinting up to 60 miles per hour (mph) (96 kilometres per hour). The cheetah hunts its prey by day, stalking in the grass from a few seconds to several hours until the prey is within 100 feet before chasing. About half of chases are successful and an average chase is 550 feet (170 metres) and lasts for 20 seconds. This high speed enables it to outstrip or outrun any other animal on earth. Against this fast speed, the cheetah has no endurance and can be exhausted after a run and has to give up and rest for some time to get its breath back.

Mode of Life: Its body build is slender and long. It does not roar but makes a cry like mew hiss. It purrs like a cat to show pleasure. It is distinguished from other cats not only by its distinctive markings but also by its loose and rangy build, small head, high-set eyes, and small flattened ears. Its usual prey consists of gazelles, impala, wildebeest, calves, and other hoofed animals of up to 88 pounds (40 kilograms). Courting females and males are already known to each other because their ranges overlap. Females in heat squirt urine on bushes, tree trunks, and rocks to attract males, which, when they discover the scent, hurriedly follow the trail, calling with yelps. The receptive female responds to the yelps by the approaching male. Mating occurs immediately with copulation lasting less than one minute. They stay together for a day or two, mating several times. There is no regular breeding season and cubs can be born in all months. Males do not help to raise the cubs, which are weaned after three months of age. Adult females are solitary except when they are raising cubs. Males are more outgoing than females and they live in a hierarchy allowing only the dominant male to mate while his companions wait nearby. Male group size is 2 to 4 members. The male's tendency to live in small groups as well as to hunt and eat together is intended to have an increased success rate in establishing and defending a territory.

Leopard (Genus Panthera Pardus) Agu Okwu, Agu Akuko

Family - Felidae

All the three Agu are regarded equally as emblems of royalty and nobility. Their skins and teeth are symbols that are worn by kings and noblemen in Igboland of Eastern Nigeria. Even bile (elu-aguis) is used as medicine.

Distribution: Africa, South of the Sahara, South Asia, North Africa, Arabia, and the Far East.

Habitat: Most areas with reasonable amounts of grass cover, a supply of prey animals and freedom from excessive persecution; from tropical rainforest to arid Savanna; from cold mountains to Urban Suburbs.

Size: Head/body length: 40 to 75 inches (100 to 190 centimetres); tail length: 28 to 37 inches (70 to 95 centimetres).

Height: 18 to 32 inches (45 to 80 centimetres).

Weight: 66 to 155 pounds (30 to 70 kilograms). Males are about 50 per cent larger than females.

Coat: Black spots on a fawn (yellowish-brown) to pale brown background. The spots are small on the head, larger on the belly and limbs and arranged in rosette patterns on the black flanks and upper limbs.

Gestation: 90 to 105 days.

Maturity: Sexual maturity: 2 ½ years.

Litter size: 1 to 6 young, average is 3. Males leave home at 2 to 3 years but females remain in mother's territory.

Longevity: Up to 12 years (20 years in captivity).

Subspecies: 7-

Amur Leopard in Amur Ussuri Region, North China, and Korea.
Anatolian Leopard in Asia Minor, Turkey.
Barbary Leopard in Morocco, Algeria, Tunisia.
North African Leopard in Africa.
Sinai Leopard in Sinai, Egypt
South Arabian Leopard in Saud Arabia.
Zanzibar Leopard in Zanzibar.

Mode: The leopard is slender and delicate but sturdy and dull compared with the cheetah. The leopard is an animal of great beauty and incarnation of grace and ferocity. The leopard is the most widespread member of the big cat family and this is due to its highly adaptable hunting and feeding behaviour. It feeds on anything it can find from rats to zebra, hedgehogs, porcupine, gazelles, and impalas. The leopards catch their prey by a combination of opportunism (surprise), stealth stalk to within a close range before making a short fast rush. Adept in tree climbing, leopards often drag their prey up trees, out of reach of scavengers and thieves (lions and cheetahs). Both the lion and the cheetah always steal kills from the leopards and leopards always avoid them. Over most ranges, the leopards have no particular breeding season. Females are sexually receptive at 3-to-7-week intervals during which mating is frequent. She cares for her young and, after they are 18 to 20 months old. she mates again. The leopard is almost entirely solitary. Females occupy territories of 4 to 12 square miles (10 to 30 square kilometres) which they mark by spraying urine onto logs, branches and tree trunks. Their main vocalization is a rough rasping sound - oom, oom, oom. It is used to both proclaim the territory holder's presence and to make contact between separated individuals and small. They young ones are kept at height they are the hiding. When in heat, a female rasps to attract the male. Their furs are highly prized as a decoration for affluent women. Their numbers are declining because man kills leopards for sport. There are still over 100,000 left.

Crocodile (Aguiyi)
https://en.wikipedia.org/wiki/crocodile

Aguiyi (Crocodile) na eme ona eri anu ona ebe akwa (when the crocodile is eating an animal, it sheds tears). It is pretending to be crying and sympathetic but it is actually enjoying the flesh. My mother did say to us in this case, ire na onu, ihe na obi - meaning, pretending to sympathize with the person whereas actually you are mocking the person. In other words, meremere na ihu ngwompiti na azu. So, when you shed crocodile tears, you are pretending. For this reason, when someone is crying scornfully or sneeringly, we call her "Aguiyi" (a pretender). In ancient Egypt, the Aguiyi (crocodile) was sacred to the god Sobek - the god of protection. Today, the crocodile is a sacred animal to the god Ochine - of owu cultural festival. It is worshipped during the owu okolosa festival in May every year. Young males have to be initiated in the shrine of the god, Ochine, after they have paid some money, eight yams, 2 gallons of palm wine, a big dish of yam fufu, a big pot of fish soup, 8 kola nuts, and 8 peppers. Owu festival dance is done in the celebration of the worship of the god Ochine, who protects and blesses with wealth and children according to ancestral belief. In the Rivers State, the crocodile is worshipped as sacred to the god of the sea at Calabari (Abonnema).

Agunkwo Na Egbe (the Hawk and the Kite)

Hawk　　　　　　　　　　*Kite*

Agunkwo (Hawk) has a long tail and short beak.

The hawk and the kite are the birds of prey, competing against each other, with the kite having the upper hand. The hawk and the kite are relatives in that they both have long tails decorated with black and white stripes but the body is white with black spots. When the kite (egbe) is around, the hawk (agunkwo) withdraws from the scene. So, when egbe migrates, (laa mba), agunkwo dominates the environment. The hawk is very subtle in deceiving chickens. It comes down amongst the chickens pretending to be one of them. That is its way of making chickens feel too care-free before it goes into action by grabbing the mother chicken and flying away. The saying is this: Egbe laa mba osi, Agunkwo elegide obodo anya – meaning, when the kite migrates, the hawk guides the environment. When agunkwo has enjoyed its meal of a chicken, it comes out flying in the sky, singing, pioo -pioo piooi; I thank God I have feasted on a chicken.

Moral Lesson: Beware of deceivers, most often, even your blood relatives; they pretend to be friends but they are not; rather, they are enemies.

Agwo na Awo (Orira jere ije nma) (the Cobra and Toad)

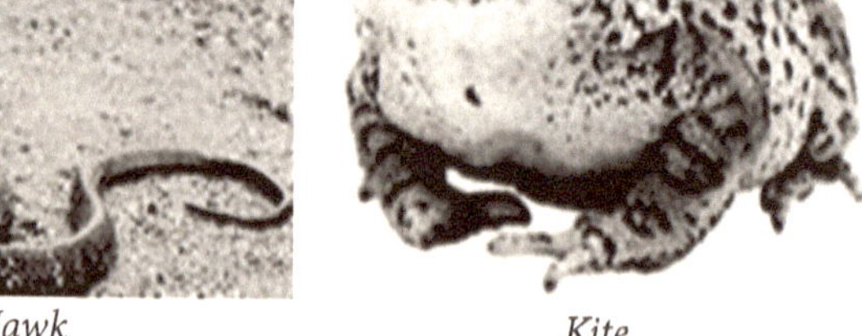

Hawk   Kite

https://www.bing.com/images/search?q

Agwonka Orira went to the chicken house and stole eggs. And so, awo told the owner of the chicken house about the incident. The owner of the chickens organized a watch to catch and kill the snake and also orira, the snake, on the run, decided to hunt down awo, the toad. Consequently, awo (toad) is always running because agwo is on its trail. A warning goes that any time you see awo running during the day, you have to be careful because agwo (snake) is chasing it. Egwu ekwe nwata gbue orira; egwu ekwe orira nyara anwu. Ibu awo no na new-nwe oso, onwere ihe na achu gi? Onye adighi ihe omere aka anaghi akpara ya. Meaning, are you running from something? Ndi Igbo si, awo anaghi agba oso ehihie na nkiti. A toad never runs in the daytime without a cause.

Sparrow (Ayoro)

The sparrow only appears during farming season. It is a harbinger of the start of farming season. She informs people of the forthcoming farming season. She calls people by their names, especially the lazy ones.

The Blue Jay (Ajoanunu)

https://www.bing.com/search?q=the+blue+jay+birds&qs

The blue night jay is known to have a tuft of feathers on top of the head and long blue tail feathers. It is a native doctor who sees the souls of those who are going to die. When it sings in the afternoon with a penetrating sound of cho-cho cho-cho-cho- chooo near someone's house, there is bound to be someone in the neighbourhood who is going to die. The community must seek the help of an oracle to ascertain the state of things. People call it **"ajoanunu" (bad bird)** because it is a revealer of ill omens. Its cry is "onye si ka onwu ka onwu ka onwu." If one wants to die, let him or her die. Whenever anybody misbehaves, our parents incite this bird as a proverb to redirect the person.

The Crow (Apia) and the Kite (Egbe)

Egbe (Kite)   Apia (Crow)

https://www.bing.com/images/search?

The crow flatters other birds by singing to them in order to steal their food. Then, there was a bush fire in which some unaware small animals (rats, snails) were unfortunately burnt to death. While the fire was yet smouldering, the crow was afraid to dare but the kite, being artfully undaunted in dealing with fire, ventured to go into the fire to get the dead animals. The crow flew around singing to the kite. Egbe nwa ori na nma, tunjele, tunjule, bia gbaram egede, tunjele, tunjele. Egbe (kite) was so pleased that mistakenly, egbe started to dance and sang in unison with apia (crow). While egbe was singing, the dead animal in her mouth fell out. Then the crow swooped down and made away with the dead animal. The kite has been deprived of its hard-earned food by a deceitfully flattering friend. When you have your treasure in your grasp, beware; do not allow any distraction to bemuse you. Also, avoid those who flatter you because they will make you loss your integrity.

The bird, apia, is a friend of children; the children make fun of him whenever he is flying around. The children would come out and sing, Apia onu gologo, okuko huu gi otie kwoo (Apia with the long bill (beak), whenever chicken sees apia, she sighs because the chicken is always afraid of him with his long beak, seeing him as a predator and enemy).

Atani -Tarsier - Small Monkey

Atani is an animal about the size of a mouse that lives in a nest of loose leaves and eats bananas, jumps from tree to tree, singing chim-chim chi chiriri in the night. It has prominent squirting eyes. It has two stories to tell: (1) its pop-eyed bulging eyes, (2) its nest of loose leaves.

1. Atani said once that its senior brother monkey, the baboon, was sick of a devastating fever and he, atani, had to make fire on a wet ground to warm the monkey up. The fire did not stay ablaze for long because of the wetness of the hearth (fireplace) and so,

atani had to kindle the fire by blowing the fire with breath from its mouth. The fire as such was smoky and the smoke caused atani's eyes to bulge out and also cause the monkey's eyes to sink into their sockets. And so, the saying is: I cho imara ihe mere anya enwe (monkey) ji di omimi, je lere anya Atani fururu y oku mgbe odara oria.

2. Atani has many predators (snakes, birds of prey) and sleeps during the day and forages during the night. Its enemies use its house to locate it. And so, to escape from them, atani decided not to have a permanent house but a temporary nest of loose leaves that is easily made, capable of giving it shelter and a chance of being able to escape the strike of a predator. Thus, if your house is a makeshift, it is said to be ulo atani because atani said he spent material and energy to build a durable house which in due course becomes an entrapment for him, therefore, he had to make it anywhere, anyhow. Osi ihe akwu emekaria la ya. In other hand, never leave a trace of you where your enemies will get hold of you. Always be careful in all your endeavours.

Lizard and Chameleon (Ogwumagala)

Lizard

Chameleon

https://www.bing.com/images/search?q

Ogwumagala (chameleon) is a lizard–like animal that has two features for catching prey. It has a camouflaging technique where it flushes the colour pigment cells of its body when it is excited, flashing its colour from reddish-orange to green-blue, back and forth, to blend with the green environment and enthrall its confused victim. It has a sticky tongue that is as long as the length of its body and that can suck in any prey instantly. You are called a chameleon if you are as changeable as weather and change your point of view very often to confuse matters and take advantage of your adversary. We say: **ibu Ogwumagala**. Ogwumagala has clasping feet and a tail such that it does not release its hold on anything easily. This feature gives it the name: Ikiri ojide ahaghi. From now, the story goes that one day, Nwanaza (wren bird) went hunting grubs (caterpillars) to feed its hatchings and unknowingly, it perched on ogwumagala's leg which blended with green leaves. A struggle ensued when the chameleon got it by its legs. Wren decided to carry chameleon home to its nest. Wren arrived at its nest but could not land because chameleon held onto the legs tightly. Instead of feeding its young ones, both wren and chameleon rolled out of the nest and fell to the ground. Then, chameleon feasted on wren. The wren's chicks said the food their mother brought home had taken their mother away. The saying goes: ihe nwanza buru kpute na akwu eburule ya pua. That is, what the wren took home has taken her away instead. You are counselled to beware before what you look down upon overpowers you.

Ram (Ebule)

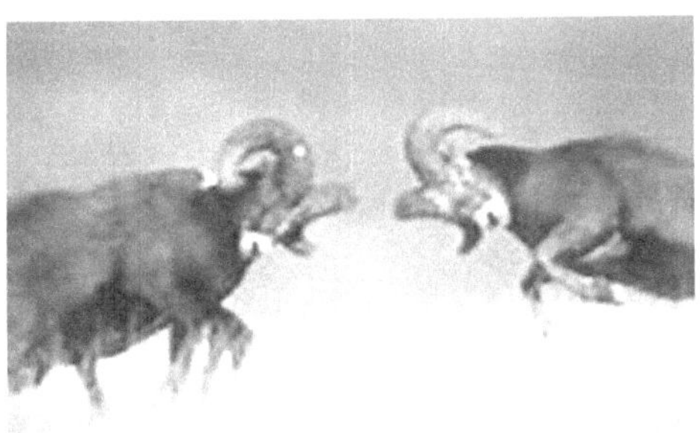

https://www.bing.com/images/search?q

Ebule (ram), in Ancient Egypt, was sacred to the god Khnum (ibo kamanu), responsible for fashioning the unborn baby in the mother's womb. Today, it is sacred to the god Agwunsi (god of war), because it is always butting with another ram. When you are called ebule Agwunsi – it means you are always fighting. Ike agwu agadi ike keta orie.

Death is King of All

One can see through the stories that all the powerful animals that could overpower others had other animals or creatures that are greater than they are. This is also applicable to human beings who claim to be more powerful than other humans and living creatures, not realising that something fiercer may lie ahead. The moral lesson from the powerful creatures shows that no one is more powerful except one thing: that is, God Almighty, who possesses all power and life. He created death that is more powerful than all the living creatures. No one can beat death and that is the reason why he goes to every living being to take them away at any time and at any stage. This is the reason why it is written thus: There is an amazing democracy about death. "It is not an aristocracy for some of the people, but a democracy for all of the people." "Kings die and beggars die; rich men die and poor men die; old people die and young people die; death comes to the innocent and it comes to the guilty. Therefore, death is the irreducible common denominator of all men and living organisms." Mahatma Gandhi said, "Death is the appointed end of all life." Yes, I concurred with him because nobody can claim to be more powerful than death is; it is God who can and to death he gives ultimate power over all living things. No one can compete with death and no one can stop it. Scientists had made several attempts to stop it but only succeeded in delaying it. Death is unbeatable, it has ultimate power, and all living things fear and obey it.

Eagle (Ugo)

https://uk.images.search.yahoo.com/search/images;

Ugo bu Ezenu, ugo nwa ori na nma (eagle, king of birds with sharp eyes). The eagle is a member of the hawk family - birds of prey. Eagles are superb fliers, soaring great heights of 20,000 feet and have excellent eyesight, strongly hooked bills and powerful talons of four toes with sharp claws for snatching their prey. The eagle's eyes function as a telescope (optical or light instrument that makes a distant object appear near). The eagle's sight is dependent on many sensory cells which no other living things have. They build their nests with sticks and decorate them with aromatic leaves to deter insect pests. Their nestlings that hatch in aromatic herbal nests cope fairly well with the stress of bad weather and return to the old nest the following year. They lay one or two eggs so as to be able to feed them adequately. They're found on mountain tops and iroko trees. They feed on rodents, squirrels, monkeys, tortoises, waterfowl and fish. The eagle is a symbol of the imperial power of many empires- falcon of the ancient Egyptian empire, Nigerian Eagle, American eagle with olive branches in one foot and a quiver of arrows in the other. The eagle is the king of birds, the status of which ancient and present people recognize by decorating their hats with eagle's feathers. In Igboland of south-eastern West Africa, where I was born, kings and nze titled men wear eagle's feathers on their crowns and hats. We Igbos call the eagle "Ugo bu Ezenu, Ugo nwa ori na nma." We sing of our dignitaries: Ugo bere na oji ka anya na ele. Onye eje nnele anaghi eru ntu- meaning much is expected of one in a high office. (Isaiah 40:31) "They shall mount up with wings as eagles." Ugo is a very intelligent bird. She trains her children to maturity, that is the reason why she lays few eggs. The modern families learnt from ugo and that is the reason why they give birth to three children and train them properly.

Eagle and Cat

When we say that someone has eagle's eyes, that person sees beyond. Eagle and cat have special eyes that see beyond. They see their prey very quickly. Cat sees well in the dark.

Eagle   Cat

Boa (Eke)

https://www.bing.com/images/search?q

In Ancient Egypt, it was sacred to the earth god, Aker. Today, Aker or Eke (snake) is regarded as sacred to the god of the land, Ali. It is called eke Obana, Eke Njaba, eke Ali, eke Urasi, eke Enyinja by different communities in Igboland. It is non-venomous. One who dares to kill it will be considered defiled and he or she must offer a cleansing sacrifice. Its songs are: nwaeke na ehiwu ala; utughutu na eme eke; nwa Iduohaeke.

Caterpillar (Egu)

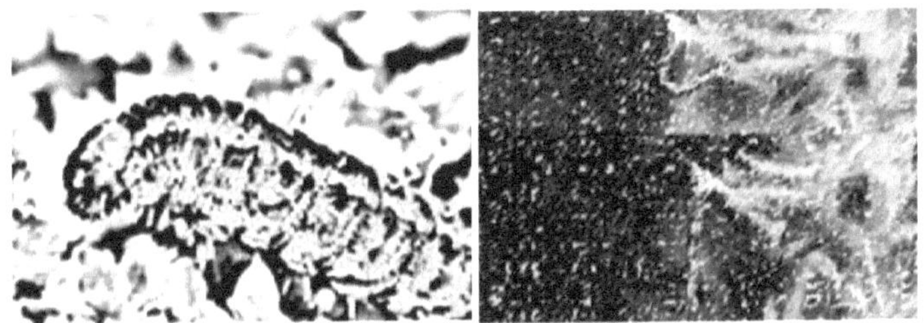

Egu *Ola or Egu Anwusi (Caterpillar - the larva of a Butterfly)*

Egu (caterpillar) is voracious in eating leaves for two reasons: (1) it must eat a lot and quickly so as to gain adequate weight and (2) it must do this in time for maturity before transforming into the pupa stage. For these two reasons, it exhibits two attitudes: (1) it defecates a lot as it eats a lot. (2) When fully fed and fully grown, it is no longer able to hold onto the twig of a tree. It falls down under its heavy weight in preparation to transform into a pupa. From these, two sayings arise:

1. Ibu egu anwusi, eri anyu (you eat and defecate)
2. Ibu egu aka siri ike na nwata ma oburu okenya, odaa. (strong when little and weak as an adult).

Egu must eat much and void the bowel in order to eat more like the Romans, to store fat enough for pupal transformation. If one eats too much and defecates much as such, we call him "Egu Anwusi eri anyu." If you are capable when young but incapable when grown-up, we call you "Egu anwusi aka sirike na nwata mana aka anwua ya na okenya."

Another version of egu eri anyu nsi: Nsi egu bu onwu ya – meaning, too much defecation of egu leads to its death.

Caterpillars of Butterflies and Moths (Egus and Ububuru)

Class: Insecta. Caterpillars are the larvae of butterflies and moths. There are various species, some of which are poisonous and some are not. The poisonous caterpillars are called ububuru and non-poisonous ones are called egu. Poisonous ones have hairs but the egus don't have hairs. The caterpillars of the swallowtail butterfly, royal moths, tiger moths, tent moths, noctuid moths, hairstreaks, white and sulphur moths and milkweed butterflies are poisonous – ububurus - whereas the caterpillars of giant silk moths and butterflies, skippers, ladies and red admirals are not poisonous. The ububurus sting with formic acid.

Body: Wormlike, segmented with three pairs of jointed legs and several pairs of fleshy legs. The vegetation they eat contains a substance that makes them toxic to birds and other predators. To contain their continuous increase in size, they periodically moult or shed exoskeleton. Following its last moult, a caterpillar stops eating, falls to the ground, finds a sheltered spot, secretes silk to enclose itself in a cocoon and becomes a chrysalis. Their colouration is varied: black and white stripes, green, reddish, and spotted. They stay in the cocoons until they mature into butterflies and moths.

When you are called egu, it means that you were active and useful when you were young but when you are adolescent, you become less active and useless. If you are called ububuru, it means you always hurt anyone who comes in contact with you. You are untouchable.

Eruru and Utunku (Grub)

Larva or Caterpillar (Eruru)
https://www.bing.com/search?q=Larva+or+Caterpillar

Eruru: The grub (larva or caterpillar) of the palm tree beetle (akirinkwu or akiringwo).

Size: 2 ½ inches long by l inch diameter.

Utunku: The grub (larva or caterpillar) of brassy metallic wood beetle (akiri osisi).

Species: Bupresidae

Size: 2 inches by ¾ inch diameter.

Eruru has a red head, fatty segment, yellow to brown meaty tissue abdomen, a small tail and no legs, working its way into the heart of a young palm tree.

Eruru Habitat: In the young palm tree shoot, found in palm tree plantation in Nigeria.

Mode of Life: Eruru is edible together with its subsequent beetle into which it develops as it grows in the young palm tree shoot. They say "Anu buru na azu bu azu." It has a luscious fatty tissue body which is highly portentous. It is a nice treat when it has been fried. Scientists have analysed the nutritional value of insects' tissues and have found out that the tissues are portentous and safe such that they are superior to that of red meat tissues of mammals because insect's protein is interlaced with polysaccharides (chitin and glycogen). Insects like eruru, utunku, beetles, crickets (ntekwuru, not mkpukpo); yam beetles (ebeji), palm tree beetles (akirinkwu or akiringwo), wood borer beetles (akiri osisi) are all edible because they eat good plants.

People go looking for young palm trees with withered leaves. That is the sign that eruru is growing inside the palm tree. Eruru can also infest a fallen old palm tree stem at the growing tip. They make themselves fat on the cambium (heart of a tree) of a young plant and then go into dormancy during which they become a pupa. Pupae develop into young adult beetles.

Utunku: Likewise, utunku has a red head and a white fatty fleshy body. It is a little bit stronger than eruru. It bores its way into the cambium of a young plant and eats it until the plant dies or it changes into an adult beetle. It is destructive to plants. Like eruru, it passes through four developmental stages of egg, larva, pupa and adult beetle. My mother told me that people name their daughters Nwaeruru or Nwauturu when the child is plump, fair in complexion, gorgeous, and good-looking. And she disclosed that if one is called Nwautunku by a senior, it means that the person is really skinny, surly and always destructive, constantly unwilling to obey orders.

Rainbow (Egwurugwu)

https://www.bing.com/images/search?q=rainbow&qs

Another symbolic event our mother taught us about is the appearance of a rainbow. The appearance of a rainbow while it is raining means the rains will soon stop, but if it is not raining and it appears, this means a bad omen, that a big man is about to die somewhere else and everybody would be afraid and wondering who could he be and where could it be and when could it happen? It also projects the seven significant beautiful colours that one of our famous Igbo writers, Rev. Father Emeka George Ekwuru, narrated in his Igbo Cosmology and Ontogeny and Hermeneutics of Igbo Sculpture: Studies in African Ethnoaesthetics as the origin of "Rainbow." According to him:

"The Rainbow (Egwurugwu)" originates from the Python. According to the folk story, he says that the rainbow is a python. One python grew so long that it could scarcely move out from its den. One day, it managed to visit a certain village and stole the child of a medicine man. The python took the child to its lair after traversing land and sea. When it reached its home, it coiled round the child, determined not to kill it but to train it to become a python. When the medicine man found that his child was missing, he called Di-ntu, a person who could find missing things. After the medicine man had consulted a diviner, who told him of his child's whereabouts, Di-ntu took up his apparatus to show him the way. He had been instructed to take in his canoe carpenters who could repair the canoe if python

destroyed it. Besides, he had to take hunters who could shoot the snake if it proved hostile. Having got everything ready, Di-ntu set out on his journey. About a mile to the python's lair, Di-ntu was terrified by the dazzling reflection of the python. When he started to panic, the medicine man began to conjure it and the python was overtaken by deep sleep until they reached it. Then the medicine man started to run his hand on the python. He had a stem of plantain tree. As the python coiled out, they directed it to coil round the tree until it unwound from the child and coiled round the plantain stem. Then, the people set out to trace their way back. Before they could go a quarter of their journey, the python, awoke from its stupor and sensing that it had been deceived, left the log and pursued the people. It pursued them in the sea; it stretched itself out and struck the canoe, damaging a section of it. The carpenters repaired the canoe; the conjurer did a bit of his work to deflect it. But it still went after them. As they ran, it pursued them until the hunters picked up courage and did their work. They shot at the python and wounded it. It went down beneath the sea. Later it appeared on the shore. And putting its tail there it went up making an arch in the sky, with its head on the other shore of the sea. Thus, we have the rainbow."

—Emeka George Ekwuru
Igbo Cosmology
The Ontogeny and Hermeneutics of Igbo Sculpture
Studies in Africa Ethnoaesthetics 2009, (p. 124).

Elephant (Enyi)

https://www.bing.com/search?q=Elephant

The elephant (Enyi) is the biggest mammal in Africa and in the world hence, Africans liken the biggest thing to elephants. For example, names of people - Ezenyi (king as an elephant), Akubuenyi (wealth as big as an elephant), Nnabuenyi (my father as big as an elephant, Enyinnunu (bird as big as an elephant - ostrich).

Proverbs

Enyi na aso ogaranya aso. Ebe enyi na alu ogu, obu ahihia na nwu. Ibu enyi ngwongwo, nwangwogo osimiri, nwa iheukwu na anyi aru. Meaning: you are as big as an elephant, as big as an ocean, a man of grand, magnificent nobility. Kings and titled men have the elephant's tusks (oduenyi) as emblems of greatness and nobility.

The Elephant and the Seven Blind Men

Outline
- What are elephants?

- The anecdote of seven blind men and the elephant's body parts.
- The purport of the story.
- Other ensuring facts from the viewpoints of people, proverbs, and the elephant as a symbol of greatness and wealth in Igboland.

What are Elephants?

The African elephant is the largest land animal in the world standing more than 11 feet (3 metres) tall and weighing 14500 pounds (6577 kilograms). The Asian elephant is slightly smaller. An elephant's most distinguishing feature is its long trunk with a snout. This trunk is used for breathing, smell, touch, sound production, collecting water and putting it into its mouth, spraying water or mud onto its body to deter blood-sucking vermin and for picking up trunks of trees. Another outstanding feature of the elephant is a pair of ivory incisor teeth that curve and protrude outward, forming tusks. The female African elephants have small tusks and the Asian elephants have no tusks. Other body parts of an elephant are: a large body with thick skin, two big ears, two small eyes, four thick legs with broad sledgehammer-like feet and a small tail. The elephants are herbivores (vegetarian), eating a lot of vegetation. They live either on grassland or in the forest. They bear 3 young ones in 10 years, one at a time, and their gestation period (period of carrying young one in the womb) is 640 days (compared to humans 280 days). The elephant's life span is 35 years.

The Tale of Seven Blind Men and the Elephant's Body Parts

One day, seven blind men went to find out what the elephant was. When they got to the spot where the elephant was, they went forward to feel the elephant's body parts with their hands.

1. One reached to the tail and described the elephant as like a small snake.
2. One got to the thick-skinned body and said that the elephant was like a big log of a tree with a bark.

3. Another one felt the trunk (proboscis) and said that the elephant was like a long flexible hose.
4. The fourth one felt the big ears and said that the elephant was like a big flapping fan.
5. The fifth one got to the ivory teeth and said that the elephant was like a long ivory shaft curved toward the end.
6. The sixth man got to the thick legs and said that the elephant was like a thick club of wood.
7. The seventh man touched the feet and likened the elephant to the head of a sledgehammer.

The Purport of the Blind Men's Story

This story portrays what usually happens in life among people. When a topic for discussion is on the floor, folks from their standpoints, the way they see the matter, express differently their opinions about the subject matter, just as the blind men had described the elephant according to what part of the body they reached. We are all human beings but all the same, we are different from one another in that one man's meat is another's poison.

For example, three people went to a restaurant to dine. One ordered a beef steak and oven-baked French fries; the second ordered chicken wings and mashed potato and the third, a lady, ordered a plate of chopped broccoli and onion soup. The three ate the food expressed in three different forms according to their likes. The same attitude of expression shows up in the way we choose clothing and other things. Some people love others for particular reasons. The same person may be liked by different people for different reasons; some like the eyes; some, the teeth; some, the legs, and others, the way she speaks. You see; different folk, different strokes. The knowledge of a subject may be dependent on one's ability to treat the subject matter. Shallow minds express things vaguely but mellow or well-matured minds detail out specifics that define clear outlines of things. Your expression depends on what you are and what your circumstances are.

Here is a story of a man and his four sons. In Igboland of Southeastern Nigeria, a certain man had four sons. In the morning, as was the normal cultural behaviour, they greeted their father, "iyee nnua," a second son, Awo man, greeted their father, "a- nna a nma," a third son Uli man, greeted their father, "nna-a nmua-a;" the fourth son, Oguta man, greeted their father, "didim do-o." After this, a quarrel arose among the four sons regarding who had greeted their father in the most acceptable expression. Their father beckoned to them, entreating them to be of a good cheer and peaceful because he himself received all the greetings with a good heart and appreciation. This can be referred to the behaviour of all religious sects which in a "holier than thou" attitude, claim they worship God in a much better way than others.

Other Ensuing Facts from the Viewpoints of People, Proverbs and the Elephant as a Symbol of Greatness and Wealth in Igboland of Southeastern Nigeria

Igboland culture is "ozuruigbo," that is, it is renowned worldwide. In the Christian bible, it is said, Psalm 18:2, "My God is my Rock. I shall take refuge in him, my Shield and my Horn of salvation." Psalm 92:10, "But you will exalt my Horn like that of a wild bull." In Igboland, we regard the elephant and its tusks as symbols of greatness by taking names or giving names relating to the elephant - "enyi" and carrying the elephant's tusks in a decorative fashion. We have names such as:
Nnabuenyi: My father is as great as the elephant.

Akubuenyi: My wealth is as great as the elephant.

Enyibuaku: The elephant is a source of great wealth.

O bu enyi na nwangwongwo osimiri: He is as great as the elephant and as vast as the ocean

Asigi buo ka enyi ma akpakwana agwa ka enyi: Grow huge as the elephant but do not act heavily on people and things like the elephant.

Iburu ibu ka enyi mana akpa nri ka nwanza: You are as huge as the elephant but eat very little food like a small muskrat.

Enyi na acho nti, nti ehuchie na ya anya: The elephant desires big ears to fit its big body, so when the ears grow on it, the ears become so large that they cover its eyes. This means you should not be too desirous when asking for something for you will lose the savour of it, if it is overwhelmingly devastating in the outcome.

Ebe enyi luru ogu obu ahihia na anwu: When two elephants fight, they go scot-free, only the grass on the battlefield dies.

Enyi na aso ogaranya aso: Elephants respect old people: All great things bow down to elders.

Obu Eze na Nze na ebu odu enyi (otoroka) na Ezeagu: It is honourable for Eze (King) and Nze (titled men) to carry elephant's tusks and wear ezeagu (lion's teeth). When a man is enthroned as a king, he is also decorated with an elephant tusk as a symbol of his greatness. He has to blow his "O du" after he has finished his sacrificial incantations to God Almighty whom he now serves. He has to blow his horn at any shrine and has to blow his horn when passing by the house of a titled man or another king as a sign of respect for a great man. The Nze (titled man) does exactly what the king does as behoves great men. They also wear eagle's feathers on their crowns as a symbol of kingliness.

Finally, to round up the discussion on the greatness of an elephant known in parts to make simple that which is great, it is worthy to quote the Holy Scriptures, referring to different personalities, different talents, and different performances thus:

> *"There is a variety of gifts but always the same Spirit; there are all sorts of service to be done, but always to the same Lord; working in all of them. The particular way in which the Spirit is given to each person is for a good purpose. One may have the gift of preaching with wisdom given him by the Spirit; another may have the gift of preaching instruction given him by the same Spirit; and another the gift of faith given by the same Spirit; another again the gift of healing, through this one*

Spirit; one, the power of miracles; another, prophecy; another the gift of recognizing spirits; another the gift of tongues and another the ability to interpret them. All these are the work of one and the same Spirit, who distributes different gifts to different people just as he chooses.
—1 Corinthians 12:4-11
The Jerusalem Bible & Popular Edition
Darton, Longman & Todd 1974, (p. 224).

Eroala (Nightjar)

Eroala (Nightjar) has feathers like the hawk. Eroala went to farm with its wife but it left for home early. When it was night, the wife did not return home and so it went about crying: *chi, chi, chi, chi, chi, chi, ri riie, chinyerem nwanyi chinararam ya, chinyerem nwanyi chinararam ya, chininyerem nwanyi chinararam ya*. It has a divining mind and can see a woman who is going to die. When it sang in the night in ancient times, people consulted a soothsayer to find out who was going to die.

Goose

The goose is either a white bird with black wing tips or a bird with a dark body and a white head and neck. There was a story about a farmer who had a goose that laid golden eggs. Wanting to get rich in an instant, the farmer decided to kill the bird and cut open the bowel to extricate more eggs. It boiled down to his surprise that there was no egg in the bowel when the bird was cut open. He lost the bird and its eggs. This gave rise to a saying: *ofo ka ofojue akpa na ebu akpo ikpo. Onwu gidi- gidi nwuga aka na ogwu. Ota cham - cham na tabiri ire.* Mama told us that having the ambition to get it all in one batch in a short time without paying due attention to what it takes to procure something always results in tremendous disappointment, loss and disaster. Never count your chickens in the eggs but allow them to hatch.

Parrot (Iche Nwaogbama Okoko)

https://www.bing.com/images
search?view=detailV2&ccid=1zLwCchm&id=

Iche Nwaogbama (parrot) is man's friend. Always, when it sees you, it observes you and begins to talk about you. It sees the future and can prophesy. It is a symbol of wisdom and happiness; hence, people decorate their hats with its feathers. We say: *nchari- nchari nnuri -nnuri ekpe ato ekpe ato, anya furu iche nuria -* that is being joyfully attractive and being happily receptive. When you see iche, you should be hospitable. When the parrot calls someone okoko, it shows that person is a bad fellow. When the owner hears him calling okoko, she becomes altered. The parrot calls okoko is a diviner.

Black Ants (Ichekiriche Na Igbogiri)

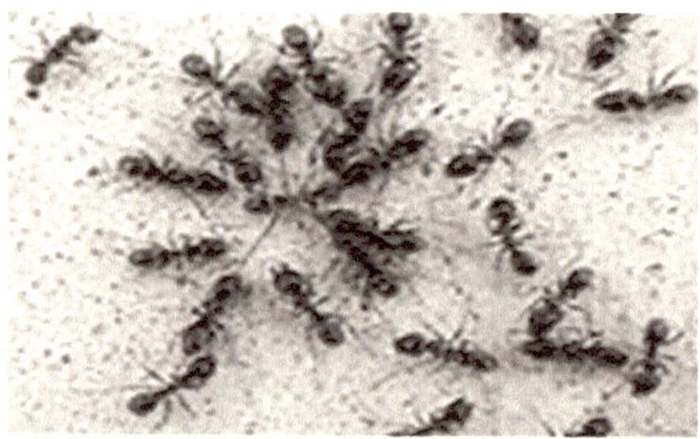

https://www.bing.com/search?

When palm fruits are harvested, the palm fronds are cut into two portions - one portion, containing leaves called ogugu, is used in making rafter frameworks on which the roof coverings of houses are placed; the other portion, with thorns close to the palm fruit bunch called igbogiri, is left to dry and then stored to be used as firewood or for making ngu (ash) for soap making. When igbogiri is put aside, it takes a while before black ants occupy it. When they do, they help igbogiri to age to a soft texture necessary for making ngu. So, the saying: *Obughi mbosi igbogiri dara na ala ka ichekiriche na abanye ya na ime.* This means that it takes time for a project to processed, progress and then reach maturity for profitability.

Swallow (Ileke)

The bluebird of the swallow family, with tail feathers of blue glossy sheen valued as an ornament on a hat. When one picks up the tail feather of ileke, one is as delighted as if you had found treasure. When you are elevated momentarily, without any visible presence of the cause, people will ask you: itutara odu ileke. (A swallow's tail feather is regarded as a symbol of good luck by the Igbos).

Crane (Igoloma)

The crane (Igoloma) is a passionate (amorous) bird with white plumage. They go about in pairs, male and female always kissing and twisting their necks together. They are majestic in behaviour, signifying a kingly attitude. Thus, kings and titled men wear their feathers on their hats: *isi turu ugo, oturu Igolobibi.* That shows that a man has attained the highest position. Igoloma is a friend of children because he makes children have fun with him whenever he flies around with his partner. Children always come out and ask him in Igbo dialect: *Igoloma, olee eshi nnegi na nna gi nwuru? I ga agwam daikwa na urashi.* Then he responds: akahu, akahu, akahu. This means: Igoloma, when did your parents die? If you don't tell me, fall into the sea. And in response, he says, last year, last year. Children are fond of the crane.

Owl (Ikwikwi egbukerempi)

https://www.bing.com/images/search?q=owl&form=

The horned or screech owl is known for its midnight muffled hoots: hoo, hoo, hoo, hoooo-hoo. It is a diviner. The owl, as a diviner, when it sees the soul of one who is going to die, will cry: ooh, ooh, ozu, ijikwa okpu gi, ooh, ooh, ooh, ohoo. The living, when they hear this owl's cry, will heat up pieces of the broken earthen pot and launch them at the owl. They will fly away but the most important thing is that she has delivered her message. Consequently, whenever Ikwikwi hoots near your house in the night, it signifies a forewarning, portraying a forthcoming foreboding omen that is around the corner. You must consult a soothsayer to find out what is to happen and what to do to avert the ominous event as disclosed by our ancestors. The owl is a nocturnal animal because it does not see well during the day. In ancient times, animals were said to have communed together to plan for the future. They put up a magnificent plan for the education of their young ones. Okwa was excited and cried out: "ejeje college, ejeje college, tutu turia ya, tutu turia ya. Immediately, obu questioned okwa saying: Ijeje College, uuh, uuh, uuh, igukwara ABCD, igukwara ABCD. Ikwikwi in unison, concurred with obu saying: hoo, hoo, hoo, hoooo-hoo, obu kwuru true, obu kwuru true. Nwanza, in supporting all said, yes, yes, yes kev, kev, kev, cha- cha -cha, ded, ded, yes, yes, yes.

Akwu Osukwu na Mbe - Soft Palm Fruit and the Tortoise

Tortise

Soft palm fruit

https://www.bing.com/images/search?=palm+tree&form

Osukwu palm fruit with soft mericarp that you can crush with teeth is the best palm fruit.

One time, Mbe planted akwu osukwu (akwu osukwu is a tasty masticable palm fruit from the palm tree). It did not take long before the tree began producing ripe fruits. When Mbe cut down a bunch of ripe fruits, he was busy eating the palm fruits alone. Neighbours called on him to say, hello but he declined to respond. Neighbours reminded him that it was time for farming. Mbe said he would not farm that year for he was satisfied with himself. But when the palm fruits got depleted and the palm tree stopped producing palm fruits, Mbe became hungry and desperate. He feverishly began to ask neighbours for help. Neighbours replied with this song: Nde oru ji neje, nda werere-werere nda, nde oru ede neje, nda werere-werere nda, nnambe na osukwu, nda werere -werere nda. Nna gi nye gi ji iju, nne gi enye gi ede iju, ta nnambe atabisimmbeleke, ta nnambe atabisim mbeleke. Nwata chue nmiri, nua nmiri. Here is a man who made a temporary provision for his life and felt that was enough for all times. He has to know when it was late that, that was a mistake.

Advice: Never spend too much time celebrating your success. Let it pay you its dividend in its due time while you get on with doing your routine duty and do not forget to share your fortune with others, in order to be covered on a rainy day. This piece of advice reminds me of my mother when she was very strong; she used to plant a lot of vegetables and her fellow women would come and call her nwunyedim (my mate), please, I need vegetables for my dinner tonight and she would allow the person to collect as much as the person needed. So, this is sharing with one another. In Igboland, sharing is one of the remarkable features of our parents. They are always caring, welcoming and compassionate.

Akwu Ojukwu Mgbaru Ogwu (Palmae)

https://www.bing.com/images/search?q=Palmae.%20&qs=n&form

Family: Palmae.

Species: Elaeis guineensis.

Ojukwu is a type of oil palm tree. Akwu - oil palm tree is a monocot and its fruit is drupe. The oil palm tree is of four types:

- Akwu Ojukwu
- Akwu okpokoro
- Akwu mgbara abubo
- Akwu osukwu.

But the technical classification of oil palm fruits recognizes three types according to the quantity of extractable oil from the fruits:

Dura: Shell 2 to 8 millimetres thick (Akwu Okpokoro) endocarp comprising 20 to 25 per cent of weight of fruit, medium mesocarp (fleshy pulp) content of 35 to 55 per cent mass.

Tenera: Shell thin, 0.5 to 4 millimetres (endocarp) (shell-endocarp-nchara ake), medium to high mesocarp content of 60 to 95 per cent, (regular Akwu and Ojukwu).

Pisifera: Shell-less - Akwu mgbaraabubo and Akwu Osukwu.

Distribution: The oil palm trees are cultivated in the equatorial regions of Africa, Southeast Asia and South America. Of all oil-bearing plants, the oil palm tree gives the highest yield of oil. In the humid regions of West Africa, yields amount to about 4.5 tons of oil per hectare per annum. In 1985, global production data for palm oil indicated that in excess of 7.6 million tons were produced, the major contributing countries being Malaysia, the Philippines and Nigeria.

Uses of Palm Oil

The palm fruit is a drupe (one kernel in a hard shell, though sometimes we have two kernels- ake mkpiri), the outer pulpy layer of which produces palm oil. Within the pulp (mesocarp) lies a hard-shelled nut containing palm kernel which gives two useful products – palm kernel oil and the residue, the palm kernel cake. Palm oil is an important part of the diet in West Africa. In addition to supplying cooking fat, it is rich in beta-carotene, a precursor of vitamin A. Palm oil, as well as palm kernel oil, is used in the manufacture of soaps. In industrialized countries, the main uses of palm oil and palm kernel oil are in the manufacture of shortening, margarine, cooking oil, salad oil, grease, soaps, candles, lubricants, cosmetics, and detergents. Palm kernel cake, the cake that remains after the extraction of oil, is used for livestock feed. The fibre that remains after the extraction of oil from the pulp is used in the making of native soap (ngu for nchaigbo). Palm wine, which is rich in vitamin B complex, is produced by tapping the immature palm fruit bunch before it sets up fruits. The ash obtained from burning the refuse which remains after stripping the fruits from the bunches is rich in potash and is used as one of the ingredients in the making of native soap. Apart from the fatty acids, the major constituents of palm oil are the fat-soluble carotenoids - chiefly carotene which gives palm oil its characteristic red colouration. The carotene content can be as high as 1000 ppm (ppm – parts per million), surpassing that of any oil. The carotenoids are responsible for the high level of vitamin A in palm oil. When in the full bearing of fruits in the mature stage, the palm tree may produce up to 12 bunches of fruits per year, the average weight of a bunch being 13 to 18 kilograms.

The traditional methods of extracting palm oil have a bad effect of producing palm oil that contains high free fatty acid (oga ukputu) up to 7 to 12 per cent. Good palm oil should contain 3 per cent free fatty acid (FFA). Free fatty acid makes oil sour (nmanuigbauka).

Local use of Akwu Ojukwu

On Emime Arusi festival (masquerade festival) when all the gods reincarnate as masquerades, some of them come along with the power of the charms, the "Odukwu," the forerunner soldiers of nmanwu (masquerades) will carry a basket of Akwu Ojukwu, okpoto root, and ogbakiki stolon and efe fruit mixed aja ala and spread them in the field of play so that those who come to watch the show will not be affected. Thus, we call the palm tree "Ojukwu mgbaru ogwu."

It has been found out that Akwu Ojukwu, because of its high free fatty acid, affects those who use it very much as cooking oil. High FFA **causes yellow** fever (akom oji) by blocking blood arteries and preventing blood circulation causing bluish skin colouration - **yellow fever**. When you are called Ojukwu, it means you are a neutralizer or an annihilator of any evil. The person is also a beautiful fellow. Also, it means that you are beautiful and charming and endowed with a strong personality. They are brilliant individuals. I believe nature destined these characteristics for them. I am interested in researching this palm fruit because my mother's name was" Ojukwu." Her mates used to call her Ojukwu-ocha and she felt proud and fulfilled when they called her so. The name Ojukwu is very significant. It is a unique name; it is a selective name to give a child and that is the reason why those who were lucky to get this are proud. Some were named Ojukwu-tulugo, Ojukwu-ocha, and Ojukwu-mma, Ojukwu Ugo, etc.

Finally, Akwu Ojukwu is medicinal. When my mother was alive and bearing children, anytime she had a stomach problem, she went and collected Akwu Ojukwu and a leaf called "njamja" and "Okwurumaosho seed" and prepared them with yam and ate it. After taking these with Akwu Ojukwu soap, her stomach problem would be cured instantly. Njamja and Okwurumaosho are natural herbs with fragrant smells.

Egwu Nmanwu na Emime Arusi Masquerade Dance Song

Obu uzo ogu*: Ime elu me ala Ojukwu mgbaru ogwu*

Odukwu: *Iye ghe eghe,*
Ojukwu mgbaru ogwu,
Ojukwu mgbaru ogwu
Ojukwu mgbaru ogwu
Iye ghe-ghe Ojukwu mgbaru ogwu

Obu uzo Ogu*: Nde - nde- nde nmiri, Ojukwu mgbaru ogwu*

Odukwu:	*Iye ghe eghe,*
	Ojukwu mgbaru ogwu,
	Ojukwu mgbaru ogwu
	Ojukwu mgbaru ogwu
	Iye ghe eghe Ojukwu mgbaru ogwu.

The African Palm Civet (Ediabali)

Family: Viverridae - Thirty-five species some of which are:

- African Palm Civet (the true Civets).
- Indian Civet.
- Malay Civet.
- Spotted linsang Civet, and
- African linsang Civet.

Distribution: Rainforest to woodlands, Savanna and mountains of Africa and Asia.

Size: African Palm Civet head/body

Length: 33 inches (84 centimetres);

Tail Length: 17 inches (42 centimetres);

Weight: 29 pounds (13 kilograms).

Coat: Various body textures: Some dark spots, bands, stripes, and banded tail.

Gestation: 80 to 90 days.

Maturity: African Palm Civets are sexually matured at 1 to 2 years of age and may produce 2 litters a year, a litter being of 1 to 3 young ones.

Longevity: 20 years (15 years in captivity).

Mode of Life: In the humid night air of the West African rainforest, a loud plaintive cry is repeated like the hooting of an owl, a series of cries penetrating the dark. It is the cry of the African Palm Civet (Why Palm Civet? Because it eats lots of palm fruits which show up in the faeces - poo). The civets are solitary but one to three females live within the home range of a dominant male and he visits them for several days as he makes his rounds. The vocal African Palm Civet (omnivorous) spends most of the time in the rainforest, feeding on fruits of trees (including palm fruits), vines, scrubs, creepers (ahihia woo woo), rodents, birds (guinea fowls), insects (scorpions) and snails and always defecates at dung heaps near its route of movement. Adult males occupy home ranges of 250 acres (100 hectares) and regularly scent-mark trees and brushes on the border of their territory. **They are known for their scent**. The name "civet" comes from the Arabic word "zabad" meaning unctuous fluid and its odour comes from the perineal glands of the deep muscular pouch on the underside associated with the genitalia, which accumulates several grams of civet oil a week. The scent of Genet Civet species has a subtle pleasant odour but that of true civets is powerfully objectionable and obnoxious. Civetone, the component of the scent that is of pleasant musky odour, has a widespread appeal to most people but the other components of the scent secretion, such as scatole, impart a fetid odour that is disagreeable.

This odour makes "Ediabali" smelly.

The scent-marking is important to the civets:

- It helps them mark the borders of their territory to warn invaders of the presence of a dominant male.
- The close association of perineal glands and the genitalia suggests that the secretion has sex functions.

The Civetone may "exalt" volatile compounds from the reproductive tract of females on heat and may carry information indicative of sex, age, and individual identity. Civet oil, once refined, is cherished within the perfume industry because its odour has the ability to exalt other aromatic compounds with a long-lasting pleasant scent. The civet oil also has medicinal uses such as reduction of perspiration, as an aphrodisiac and as a cure for skin disorders. Because of this oil, the civets are listed as potentially endangered species all over the world but because of this situation, the development of synthetic chemical substitutes has been instituted.

In the rainy season, males and females keep track of one another's whereabouts by scent-marking and calling for mating. The African Palm Civet has been elaborated upon here but the same can be said of Asian relatives for they all share many features of their natural history.

Mbele or Agbugba (Gourd or Calabash Bottle Gourds)

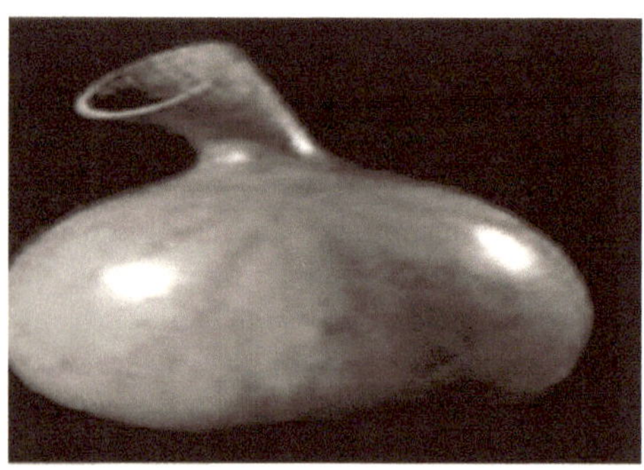

Mbele (Gourd) around 5000 years old have been found in Egyptian tombs. They have been used as utensils and containers for a long time. The gourd has various shapes - globular, flat, bottle-shaped, club-like, and coiled. It was used as bottles for palm wine, as a musical horn (opi), as a palm wine cup like a fufu plate agbugba, and as a charm emblem with the song: lyi adieri oba, meaning, oba never sinks in the sea, it always floats. When mbele is used as a palm wine bottle, there is a proverb: Nke onye na akwu nke nwa epkem mana nke mbele di ochichi onye na anu ya. That is to say: when you put palm wine in a glass bottle, its colour and content are seen but if you put the palm wine in a palm wine tapper's gourd bottle, no one sees what is inside. Simply put, if you practice your act in an open place, everyone sees it but if you practice it in a hidden place, no one knows about it.

Gazelle (Mgbada)

Mgbada is a swift graceful antelope. It usually hides in thick bush but eats grass in the open places. It has the habit of dropping its excrement wherever it goes and so hunters use the droppings to locate where it is hiding. Its skin is very tough and it is used in making drums. The sayings about Mgbada goes like this: Mgbada kere ike na ndu, kere ike na onwu. Mgbada me na okwu, me na ikporo nga ona ezenmiri agwuna. That is, mgbada is strongly swift when alive and also tough when dead, when its skin is used. And again, mgbada, because it always leaves behind its dung wherever it goes, it has no hiding place any more. When a man is so overbearing that his deeds have affected everyone, he is no longer safe with anyone.

Nduru (Dove) The Common Ground Dove or the Rock Dove)

Dove (Nduru)

Nduru - the dove is peaceful and it easily adapts to the ledges of human buildings. When it appears in a town, it means peace and tranquility. Remember, Jesus told his disciples to be docile as a dove and sharp as a serpent. The dove is a cunning bird and very wise. It is only a dove that could trick a snake; she picks up the snake by the tail and flies away, leaving the snake dangling till it dies. We release doves into the air during festivities to show pomp and pageantry. During "igbuchiahu" (initiation into the native doctor society), the nduru charm song is sung: Hapunu nwa nduru ka oturighariba ihaka ka oturighariba. Hapanu nwa nduru ka oturuighariba ihaka ka oturighariba. This means don't molest the peaceful dove while it is peaceably going about its business. This addresses the people and the Spirits.

Wren (Nwanza)

Nwanza is a bird with grey and brown feathers above, lighter below with barring on the wings and tail, and the tail often held erect. It likes "uboil nwanza" (Christmas tree flower). Nwanza is fond of asserting its righteousness in all its behaviour such that it can never err or fall off when it is swinging from branch to branch of trees or palm trees singing: yes, yes, yes, cha, cha, keree, keree, keree, turi, turi, turi, turi. The ancestral elders call the wren the righteous one and use its songs as sacrificial invocations. They say:

Nwanza turu jam, tua jam, berena odu igu, si na nya no na ekwe nne ya, okwo nna ya, nwa sia ka nne, osikaa, nwa sia ka nna osi kaa.
Aka anaghi ehie nwa enwe na elu ma ka na nne muru nya na elu.
Nmiri ideyi puta nga ona kuru okuru
Nde na eme nke ha na eme, anyi bu umueze ji ofo eri.
Nwanza's Sacrificial Offering Songs' Translation

Nwanza perched on a palm tree frond, hopping from branch to branch singing: I am sitting on my mother's chair. If a son follows the mother's footsteps in everything he does, he will live long. The monkey does not over-reach the branch of a tree on which it wants to hang because it was born on the branch. When rain runoff water comes to its accumulation point, it settles down. Some people live by their means of livelihood, but we, princes, live by the power and effectiveness of "Ofo" (divine authority).

Nwaomia

Nwaomia is a kind of wren that has bloodless legs. It is reputed to cry very much because it is believed that its legs are afflicted with a blood-sucking disease which it calls nwaomia that keeps the legs bloodless. Nwaomioa now becomes the name of the bird known for its peculiar cry calling its nursing attendants to pay attention in applying oil to the painful spots on the legs. It would cry: Nwaomia, nwaomia, nwaomia, gbatanu oso, gbatanu oso; ona amim nga, ona amim nga, ona amin nga, ona amim nga, ona amim nga; Tem oga (oil) nga, tem oga nga, tem oga nga; ihii, ihii, ihii-e

Tortoise and His Wife Alulu Mbe (Nnambe Na Alulu (Alili)

The tortoise is a subtle, domineering husband while Alulu is a supple and docile wife. When mbe does a clever profitable act, alulu will extol and exalt him but when mbe does a shameful act, alulu will grumble about the situation with no reprimand to mbe. One day, mbekwu got one big pot and one small pot and placed them on the shore of a big river and went into the river saying to the fishes to come out and enjoy themselves in the pots:

Umu azu bianu ka anyi gwue egwu;
obele azu banye nime obele ite.
nnukwu azu banye nime nnukwu ite.

The fishes obeyed and jumped into the pots, big fish for the big pot and small fish for the small pot. When the pots were full of fishes, mbe closed and locked up the pots. When he reached home with his booty, there was a rejoicing for the family but sorrow for the fishes.

Another episode is when mbe went to a wrestling match with Nwaebuleako, the small lamb. When the contest was on, mbe helped nwaebuleako to defeat three goats but when it was mbe's turn, mbe wrestled with one Okiri (ram) without help from anyone. Mbe was defeated because okiri was very heavily muscular. Mbe was tied to a tree but Nwaebuleako came to rescue him. Nwaebuleako gave one of his goats in exchange for mbe. On their way home, mbe begged Nwaebuleako to give him one goat. Nwaebuleako agreed and did so. When he arrived home, he invited the lizard (mgwere) to party. During the party, mbe told the lizard that they would feed each other with the goat meat. The lizard first fed mbe with the flesh of the goat. Next, it was mbe's turn to feed the lizard. This time, mbe forced the goat's bones into the lizard's mouth. When the lizard objected to what was going on, mbe ran a cupful of water Into the lizard's mouth and so, the lizard swallowed the bones as mbe shouted, "Nna m mgwere lo, lo, lo, lo." Thus, the lizard was so stuffed up then it became dumb and could no longer talk. That is the reason why the lizard shakes its head and strikes the ground with its head as its way of talking. The saying is: "Mgwere ghee onuadi ihe okwu." (The lizard opens its mouth but does not talk). Alulu was not pleased but mbe treated it with levity. See Nnambe and Alulu love song:

Alulu: *Emerem nnambe gini ojiri me ihe*
Omerem; emerem nnambe gini Ojiri me ihe Omerem
NnaMbe: Tuma ugele, tuma ugele tuwa nje- nje le njeleke
tuwa nje.

*Alulu (**Alili**): What have I done to Nnambe to deserve what he has done to me?*
Mbe: Alulu please come up here and enjoy yourself.

Tortoise and the Dog (Nnambe na Nkita)

Tortise

Dog

One day, tortoise and dog bet on competition in a race; the tortoise, a slow-moving animal, claimed it would beat the dog, a fast-running animal, in a race. The dog looked down on the tortoise then they decided on a date and a target for the race. On the appointed day, the tortoise, being a smart creature, cooked the dog's food and left it on a side of the road leading to the target. They both set out. The dog ran very fast. Suddenly, the dog came upon its food left by the roadside. The dog sat down to eat, feeling comfortably that he was ahead of the tortoise. After finishing the food, the dog went on to have a nap. He slept away. The tortoise walked up to the point and saw the dog fast asleep. The tortoise craftily passed by and steadily reached the target just in time before the dog. When the dog woke up, it ran very fast but was late because the tortoise was already there at the target. The moral lesson here is that all haste without proper discernment makes a clever person a simpleton (fool). Most often, those who are in hurry make a lot of mistakes and end up achieving nothing. But those who are slow and steady achieve their goals in a slow fashion like the tortoise did. More so, Stephen R. Covey - The 7 Habits of

Highly Effective People stated:

> *"One of the most profound leanings of my life is this: if you want to achieve your highest aspirations and overcome your greatest challenges, identify and apply the principle or natural law that governs the results you seek. How we apply a principle will vary greatly and will be determined by our unique strengths, talents, and creativity, but, ultimately, success in any endeavours is always derived from acting in harmony with the principles to which the success is tied."*
>
> **—Stephen R. Covey**
> **The 7 Habits of Highly Effective People**
> **Powerful Lessons in Personal Change (Foreword p.7).**

I definitely believe that the tortoise applied this natural law principle that got him a smart success. He also used a brilliant strategy to achieve his objective. The dog was not focused; he had a divided mind that was easily distracted. In all your endeavours, try to handle one thing at a time, one after the other, with an effective strategy to thrive successfully. It is not a question of being intellectual, but being smart and creative as well as being strategic as I am. I am average but I know how to press buttons to pave my way. One of my mother's proverbs says, "Nga onye oso gbaduru ka onye ije jeduru." If you run very fast to reach the target, the one walking slowly and steadily will also eventually reach the same target in a slow approach once you plan your target well. **Become a less aggressive driver.** We are advised to take it easy in a peaceful way in whatever situation we are in.

> *"Keep silent before God. And wait longingly for him. Do not show yourself heated up at anyone making his way successfully. As the man carrying out his ideas, let anger alone and leave rage. Do not show yourself heated up only to do evil. For evil-doers themselves will be cut off. But those hoping in God are the ones that will possess the earth."*
>
> **—Psalm 37:7-9)**

In wisdom, parents admonished us to cultivate a humble, discerning, and sagacious attitude in dealing with people when in a challenging situation as follows:

1. Oje ngwa - ngwa na alaji chi (one who hurries too much to be early in doing the day's chores is always late).
2. Ota ncha - ncha na atabi ire (one that eats food in haste, always bites his tongue).

Nnambe na Agu (Tortoise and Lion, King of Animals)

Tortise

Lion

Practice being in the "Eye of the Storm" - Living a life without preparing for it is miserable, therefore, plan well before starting your program. Here, it is meant that you assume the sole responsibility of all ventures that you engage in. You must have trained for most events that you operate and must have the will and experience to endure. You must then have the flexibility to adjust and adapt to changes. You must have the operation squarely on your shoulders. You must have an advisor who is your eye in everything and also "Roll upon God your way and rely upon him and he himself will act," (Psalm 37:5). You must also have a go-between who does your wishes. You must not be afraid of innovation (neophobia) or be intimidated by the intensity of a tragedy (phobophobia).

Here is the story of the tortoise and the lion to illustrate an experience and sagacity (wisdom) needed in an engagement. One day, the lion told the animal kingdom that he was sick. For this reason, many unwise animals went to visit the lion to console him. It happened that it was a plot by the lion to have an easy meal of the animals which were foolish. The animals that went to the lion never returned. Then, their footprints went into the lion's den but there were no footprints coming back. The tortoise came to the entry point of the lion's den and saw the footprints of those going in but did not see the footprints of those coming out. In that moment, the tortoise, the craftiest and wisest of all animals, declined to go in and sent a word to the lion that he would come to see him when those who had gone in had come back. At this point, the lion knew he had been found out. Being in the eye of the storm will afford you the ability to assess the enormity of a thing and give it its appropriate attention. If you fear the storm, you will never know what a thrill it is. The tortoise used his ideal intuition to detect the lion's dubious trick. It is not a question of swim or drown; neither is it to swallow the bait and the hook; it is precision - manoeuvering of deliberations so as to detect the tumultuous centre of an event and give it its corresponding treatment. From the psychological point of view, the tortoise was in great danger and he was forced to make a drastic decision to free himself.

Kingfisher (Nkeli)

Nkeli always has shaggy head feathers, a heavy and sharp-pointed bill, blue/grey feathers on the wings and a blue-grey breast band. It makes a burrow in a steep bank overlooking a river or a lake where it dashes over the water very often when it is not fishing, swooping close to the surface of the water, uttering a rattling call. The story goes like this.

Nkeli was very rich but at one time, he sustained great losses. He decided to move to the other side of the river. He packed all his belongings into a boat, had all members of his family on the boat and sailed to the other side of the river. When he reached the middle of the river, a strong wind came and toppled his boat. The boat sank altogether with everybody and everything on board, except nkeli, who flew away. That is the reason why nkeli makes dashes into the water calling members of his family who have perished in the water. After swooping over the water, nkeli will perch on a tree on the edge of the river and shake his head. He is mourning the death of his family members and the loss of his possessions. Thus, our ancestors say, "ibu nkeli bajuru ala mana ebe akwa ka elekwe." Elekwe cries too often, so does nkeli.

Counselling/Moral Advice: Do not let your riches and love for loved ones cause you heartbreak. Likewise, do not put all your eggs in one basket. Always be careful in all your endeavours.

The Shrew (Nkapia)

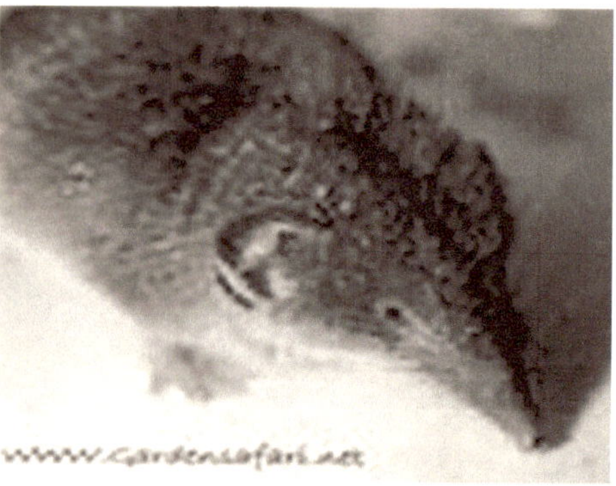

Nkapia is known for its elongated nose and characteristic objectionably offensive smell. There are two sayings about nkapia. One is: abukwana nkapia na emesu okwukwu ya. That is, when nkapia died, animals came to bury it but the animals could not withstand Nkapia's smell, so they ran away leaving nkapia to rot away unburied. Your character can attract or repel people from you. The other one is: Nwa nne nkapia na ebe ya onu. One's closest relative knows how to reduce one's excesses.

Blackbird (Nkparakwukwu)

Nkparakwukwu is a friend of the young, coming home from the stream and the farm, welcoming them by singing: uh, uh, nkparakwukwu, uh, uh nkparakwukwu, uh, uh nkparakwukwu. It also sings: ifuru umuaka ibem, oom, ifuru umuaka ibem oom, nde na ejenku oom, nde na echu nmiri oom, tata na mgbahara oom, tata na mgbahara oom, ifuru umuaka ibem oom. This means welcome, welcome, it is your friend Nkparakwukwu. Did you see my two little friends, Tata and Mgbahara, those who fetched firewood and water?

Nmasi Na Iruiju

Onwugidigidi Nwuga Aka Na Ogwu
Otanchancham Na Tabiri Ire
Obalulunu nma gbue ya na aka
Onye Kwere Nmua Ya Ekwere

"You must not swear without performing"
—Matthew 5:33.

"Be about settling matters quickly with the one complaining against you at law while you are with him on the way"
—Matthew 5:25.

"The head of every man is the Christ; in turn, the head of a woman is man; in turn, the head of the Christ is God
—1 Corinthian 11:3.

In view of the aforesaid statements, here is a story about a householder who said his wife had offended him contrary to the laws of God.

This man's name was Obieze and his wife's was Ugo. Both lived together in harmony and Obieze used to like eating ukwa meal. It was a cultural law that if a husband refused to eat his wife's food because his wife had acted ruinously against him, the wife should give a cock for a sacrifice to appease the gods and for the husband's forgiveness. One day, Ugo offended Obieze and Obieze, recognizing the misconducts, declared *"Iju nri,"* that is, refusal to eat food and demanded *"nmasi"* that is, a restitution sacrifice with a cock for *"ibusionu"* (spitting out the offensive statement). He could not eat her food until this was done, especially if he was an *ozo-titled* man. Ugo cunningly wanted her husband to connive at the offence and the nmasi by first of all cooking his favorite food, ukwa food (breadfruit). She left the ukwa food in the mortar and went into the bedroom, knowing her husband was around. Obieze, tempted, grabbed a wooden spoon (eku) and swallowed two spoonsful of hot ukwa food before his wife could get out of the bedroom. Obieze hurriedly closed his mouth and pretended to have done nothing. But his wife asked him if he had eaten ukwa before the *nmasi* sacrifice. Obieze was constrained for he had hot ukwa burning him from his mouth to his stomach. He suddenly vomited some of the ukwa food, fell down to the ground and died. The news spread. Obieze had died because he did not observe what he proclaimed - onye *kwere, nmua ekwere.* All the sayings have relation to Obieze and his behaviour. The bible said, "you must not swear without performing." Ugo recognized that, "the head of every man is the Christ; in turn, the head of a woman is man, and in turn, the head of the Christ is God." The cultural practice is in accordance with the biblical pronouncement so, Obieze consumed ukwa food (breadfruit) with "*onwugidigidi*" and *"otanchancham"* and ended up with *"obalulunu nma obue ya na aka."* A woman is conscientiously counselled about all these events before she leaves home for her husband.

He-Goat and She-Goat (Nwampi na Nne Ewu)

He-goat   *She-goat*

Nwampi wants to mate with nne ewu but he tells nne ewu to wait while he informs the god of the sky. Accordingly, he dances around *nne ewu*, kissing her left and right flanks, touching her with his left and right legs. Then he says: *mpi, mpi, mpi -mpi ee, ee, ee enigwe lekwa eze mee* while he is dancing and singing; he is watching her to see whether she is waiting in one place or she is moving away. Then he says, *mpi, mpi, mpi, mpi ee -ee inukwara ihe mgwara gi ee.* She will reply, *noronu koghasiwa, mem, mem.* Then, he will mount her and they will couple. Then, he will show his teeth again to the sky god, saying, I have done what I ought to have done. This is the reason why one always sees a he-goat raising his mouth up to the sky.

Cuckoo (Obu)

Obu, a bird with a yellow beak and reddish-brown feathers, is a sorcerer and a bad nest-maker. It is believed that obu is a **good timekeeper and a diviner**. Obumbu is the first cry for dawn of the day. Obu ibua, the second cry, is for the day break. If you want to be punctual to an event in the morning, you have to listen to the song or cry of the cuckoo. This early cry of obu (cuckoo) tallies with what one of the poets wrote in a hymn:

> *"Morning has broken like the first morning,*
> *Blackbird has spoken, like the first bird..."*
> ***—Eleanor Farjeon 1881-1965.***
> ***Celebration Hymnal for Everyone (p. 490).***

This song shows that it is not only us, the Ibos, that make use of the early first bird cry for time-keeping. Our Creator - God - has established a natural timekeeper for all nations and technology can not alter this natural timekeeper. It is always the way God set it and it cannot be stopped as long as the Creator exists. We thank God for giving our ancestors the wisdom and discernment to figure out all these timekeeping birds like obu (cuckoo) and okwa (bush fowl), and okeokpa (domestic fowl). These three birds play significant roles in our existence. Obu and okwa are also diviners. They are messengers and our ancestors paid particular attention to what they said. They always have something to reveal. In the case of obu, it is a diviner of good fortune or misfortune. For instance, if you are going to an interview and you hear the cuckoo cry on your right-hand side, that is an indication you are auspiciously favoured to succeed but if it is on your left-hand side, you are bound to fail. If you hear *uuh, uuh, uuh, cuk, cuk,* from the cuckoo, you have to be wary. I strongly believe in this assertion of the bird, "Obu," because, my mother used to tell us whenever obu cried on your left-hand side, it is a sign of a bad omen. Obu sina ike di nakpo, na akpo. Obu, the cuckoo, is proud because it says that what others fear to do, she can do. It says that as for snakes which others fear and dread to approach, it can dispatch with precision with its powerful beak though it is considered to be a weakling who starts to rot before its death. It says "different folks, different strokes," by Arnold Coleman, a threat, a rival performer of strength, is of different varieties - ike di nakpo na kpo. The psalmist who wrote this morning prayer hymn has proven the insights about this time-keeper animal.

> *"When early cock begins to crow*
> *And everything from sleep awakes,*
> *New life and hope spring up again*
> *While out of darkness colour breaks."*
> **—The Divine Office Catholic Breviary Psalter: Week 3,**
> **Sunday**
> **The Liturgy of Hours According to the Roman Rite**
> **Morning prayer hymn from paragraph two 1974, (p.**
> **266)**
> **By Collins E. J. Dwyer Talbot London Sydney Dublin.**

In days of old, the time-keeping animals played a crucial role in the lives of our ancestors. Myself as the author of this book, I am still adhering to the use of the timekeeper animals whenever I find myself in the village. Between 1 am and 3 am, when the cocks crow, I just look through the window and observe thick darkness, and then I become afraid, but once the 5 am cock crows, I feel happy and thank God that the dangers of the night have passed. I feel very confident and begin my daily activities. God is a wonderful creation.

Duck (Odugwuma)

https://www.bing.com/search?q=duck&form

The duck is a bird with webbed feet and she says, *"si na ije bu nwayo; ngaonye oso gbaduru ka onye ije jeduru."* Slow and steady wins the race. Odogwuma walks slowly and steadily to achieve her goal. So, try to achieve your ultimate goal in a neat way. Our ancestors applied duck's methodology to attain their aims and this helped them to achieve a lot and live long. We who want to fly, what is our fate? We are like what my mum used to call her children when we exceed the limit of our age standard. She called us *"Okuko eru nku akpo choghiri - choghiri"* Meaning, a chicken that never reaches its time, and starts making noise. This is like one who hangs her bag where her hand cannot reach. You should always cut your coat according to your size. Do things when they are due. Do not act prematurely. Never handle things that are beyond your limit.

The Roadrunner (okeokpa ori ububuru)

Bing.com/images/search=roadrunner&form

What to look for: silky blue long tail (*nwa nnunu ere odu*). Rough crest tuft, patch of red and pale blue behind the eye and the neck; blue on the wings and a long beak. The long-tailed, long-legged bird is very agile and fast on its feet running close to the ground, looking for insects, grubs, and caterpillars. This is what gives it its name-*okeokpa ori uburu*. It also feeds on spiders, grasshoppers, crickets, scorpions and bird's eggs. Roadrunner crows and chuckles with a cracking sound.

Horned Lark (Okere Mgbama)

https://www.bing.com/search?q=hornedlark

The news-leaker has black and yellow patches of feathers around the neck and horns of feathers on the head. It is fond of soaring sky-high in the air and then diving down singing. It is the **harbinger of dry weather or the dry season by crying**; "*kerio, kerio, chiko- chiko, okochi leyi, okochi leyi, okochi leyi okochi leyi.* It is said that if you were on the farm and it was raining and you heard the lark singing, *okochi leyi*, it means that it is summoning the dry weather to come; thus, its presence signifies the approach of the dry season, leaking the news that it will soon be dry again. Farmers use the lark as a harbinger of good weather.

The Mouse and the Trap (Oke Na Onya)

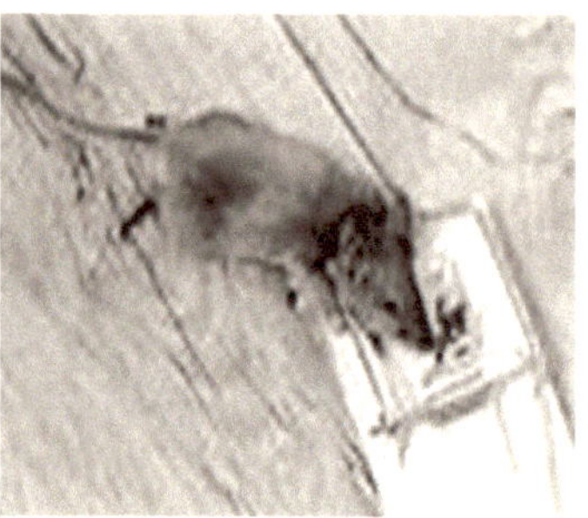

Mouse   *Mouse on a Trap*

https://www.bing.com/search?q=rat&fiorm=

The mouse was menacing in the household, eating different foods and breaking into bags of grain. As a result of this incident, the householder set a trap with meat as the bait to lure the mouse. Eventually, the mouse smelt the aroma of meat and followed the trail of the scent till it reached the trap. At once, it approached the trap and snatched at the meat. The action of the mouse triggered the trap to snap shut on the mouse, entrapping it. The mouse started to rebuke the trap saying the trap should let him go. The trap said that the meat which it had been asked to safeguard, was being taken away by the mouse. The trap ate into the body of the mouse, causing the mouse to die. It is said, "*erikwana ihe enyere ndi nmuo na aka makana ihe na aso uso na egbugbu.* Do not give way to much enjoyment for too much enjoyment intoxicates and can kill.

Oke na Ngweri (the Mouse and the Lizard)

Mouse   *Lizard*

The body of the mouse is hairy and that of the lizard is scaly. One day, it was raining and ngweri (lizard) jumped out in the rain to bathe. At once, oke (mouse) joined ngweri and made himself wet. When they came into the house, the lizard was able to shake off water from its body and dried up but the mouse was not able to shake off water from its body and was shivering with cold. This event gave rise to the saying, *"Oke soro Ngweri maa mmiri ahu koo ngweri oga ako oke?* Don't be led by the noise in any event without thinking "what if the obvious happens?" Here are some examples: It is traditionally constituted in the town that when a man and a woman socialize, they should do so with the consummation of marriage in mind. The girl must solemnize the "ikwezi" custom (ikwezi - native marriage ceremony in which the girl is fed lavishly for 7 days, after which she entertains the public with delicacies and goes to worship the goddess Obana Ezenwanyi, the wife of the land god, Ali). Otherwise, if the girl is found to be with child before the performance of ikwezi, she is considered defiled and is bound to be ostracized from the town forever while the man with whom she mated goes **scot-free,** though he would do the redemption sacrifices to the god 'Ali' and pay a token amount of money to the parents of the defiled girl. The man resumes a normal life and can get married but the girl remains outside the town forever and cannot eat with anyone in the town. Here, the man is the lizard and the girl is the mouse.

In the Moslem community, the Sharia law stipulates that if an unmarried girl is found to be with child, she should be flogged until she is exhausted but the man should go free. The same observation is detailed in the Christian Bible when a woman named Susanna, daughter of Hilkiah (cf Daniel 13:1-64) was about to be stoned to death; but Daniel rescued her by testifying against her offenders and she was freed later from her penalty. Again, according to the Law of Moses, any woman seen committing adultery should be condemned and stoned to death (John 8:1-11).

My mother used to counsel her girls with this adage: *Oke soro ngweri mma nmrir ahu koo ngweri ogaghi oke* and she would add, 'My children, if you are out there and get pregnant, carry it home and bear it and see what other women have seen' –meaning, *nwanyi ga-ahu ihe ibe ya hur).* These proverbs have helped me a lot in life; they act as checks and balances towards my life and those of the rest of my sisters. In particular, there would be certain things I would like to do, and these wise sayings would call me to order immediately. Subsequently, my fellow women, look before you leap; never look down on your parents' advice because it pays. Parents, never be afraid to advise your children, no matter the rapid effect of the Western culture in our time. Without going to university to learn it, everybody, including the blind, feels the consequence of the Western culture in our noble tradition and culture. My mother said to me, *nwa m, ngweri gbaba oso ghara ukwu osisi umuaka akpara ya n'aka* (when a lizard runs and misses its tree, the children must capture him). This is applicable as this proverb here: *Ebu juru akwu ya ogbaa.* You have to empower yourself by constantly contacting your power base. You must reach your power base before the enemy reaches you. In this context, the Western civilization has destroyed our noble tradition of family upbringing. Mama used to tell us, when you agree, your God will consent. And so, parents, never blame anybody in the upbringing of your children. As you make your bed, so you lie on it. If your children grow up in wisdom, it is to your credit, if not, it is to your discredit. Be proud to train your child(ren) well; no one has the right to stop you from doing the right thing even though he or she sends you to court as a result. Take it from me, you must surely win the court case; just try it. I urge you to read this quotation from the Bible:

"No one can hurt you if you are determined to do only what is right; if you do have to suffer for being good, you will count it a blessing. There is no need to be afraid or to worry about them. Simply reverence the Lord Christ in your hearts, and always have your answer ready for people who ask you the reason for the hope that you all have. But give it with courtesy and respect and with a clear conscience, so that those who slander you when you are living a good life in Christ may be proved wrong in the accusations that they bring. And if it is the will of God that you should suffer, it is better to suffer for doing right than for doing wrong."

—1 Peter 3:13-17
The Jerusalem Bible & Popular Edition
Darton, Longman & Todd 1974, (p. 303).

Maintain a clear conscience when doing the right thing and never allow anyone to influence you with modern shortcuts of the western ideology of nurturing their children. It is to your discredit that you let children go. 'Let go, and the child will learn when he grows.' It is not true - quote me. Our elders say, catch them while they are still young, otherwise, you lose them... children are like the yam foliage, if you fail to fix it while it is tender, you cannot do otherwise and so, there will be no good production for you. I implore you to maintain an ancestral approach and concept of raising your kids. My mother used to say to her children, (*umu m, anya agaghi agba obara, ihe oga agba bu anya mmiri*). This means, nothing would make the eye shed blood rather than tears. As a result, law or no law, nothing should prevent you from training your child well. Thus, never blame anybody for any misbehaviour of your child (ren). Children are like farm products; if you work harder on your farm, you harvest plentiful produce; if not, you will not reap any good yield. Mothers should avoid unhealthy competition that ruins their children. Jane's mother is driving a big car; in view of that, you persuade your son or daughter to buy a car for you by "any means." Beware, because this has ruined our society and a lot of children. *Isi kote ebu*, o gbaa ya. (Let wasps sting the head that touches it). If any head touches a wasp, it stings it without mercy. If you disturb a wasp, it deals with you. So, in your life, never look for trouble so that the trouble will not look for you.

House Mouse and Bush Mouse (Oke Ulo na Oke Ohia)

House Mouse

Bush Mouse

One day, the house mouse invited the bush mouse to dinner. When the bush mouse arrived, both mice went to steal food from the food store container. But each time they attempted to cut open the container (ngiga-cage), the children in the house entered the room and the house mouse shouted: "My friend, hide, for the owner of the house is coming." This harassment was frequent and so the bush mouse decided to go. A little while later, when the members of the house were ready to cook a meal, they discovered that *ngiga* (cage store) was tampered with and that much of the meat stored there had been consumed. At this moment, these two mouse friends ran across the floor. It was noticed that one of the two was rough, probably from outside the house and they said: *oke no na ulo gwara oke no na ama na anu di na ngiga*. The moral lesson, when a secret leaks out, it is the closest associate with the source that reveals it. Therefore, be guarded.

The Cock and His Fiancée (Okeokpa and Okwokworokwo)

https://www.bing.com/images/trendering?form=HDRSC2

Okeopa is a good time-keeper and a bad time-keeper respectively. When it crows at 6 pm or 3 am, it is a bad time-keeper then. At this point, it is said, it has defiled the god of the land, Ali, and is subject to be destroyed. It is killed by hitting the ground with the okeokpa. The cock, king of chickens, was intending to marry okwokworokwo and so one day, he and his people went to the home of okwokworokwo for the settlement of the bride's dowry. While the people were deliberating, okeokpa saw a woman, making soup, throw away the fibre from the palm fruits, the juice of which she used for the soup. At once, okeokpa ran outside and started eating the fibre. This cock's conduct upset everybody because the juice of the palm fruits was being used in the soup which would be served to the guests later. They did not see the reason why okeokpa should crave to eat the fibre. This attitude annoyed the bride, okwokworokwo, and she flew away forever. Okeokpa went in pursuit of okwokworokwo, calling her: Okwokworokwo – oo ooh, okwokworokwo-oo ooh - come back, come back okwokworokwo but he never saw her again. That is the reason why the cock always crows:

Okwokworokwo-oo ooh. His people sent ijimbe (fruit fly) to retrieve the crown with which they made him a king. Consequently, the cock is always fighting off the fruit fly when it grabs its cockscomb.

Lesson: Be patient and gentle.

Okeopka (Cock)

The cock (Okeokpa) is a good timekeeper too. It crows early in the morning at 4 am and at 12 noon. Our people do say; *okeokpa onu nbu ebelee.* When we were small children, my mother, on any day she was going out for an errand or market, would wake up at the first cock crow to get ready for her trip. She would then wake me up to greet her first before anyone else, because she believed that seeing me first in the mornings brought good fortune for her. Also, whenever she was going to market, she would prepare our food for the afternoon and would ask us to eat it at noon. Then, she would ask us to check our shadows to find out when it was noon. Accordingly, shadow is equally a time regulator. At noon, your shadow will be directly under your feet while when evening falls, your shadow will be very tall walking alongside you. This is the wisdom of the ancients; only those who sought for it found it. Children are advised to pay attention to their elders and parents in order to acquire knowledge. Hard drugs, TV, internet dating, Facebook courtesans, and the rest of the others will make you audacious (insolent).

Hen (Okuko) and Kite (Egbe); Duck (Odogwuma) and Kite (Egbe)

Kite   Hen   Chick

One day, Nne Egbe si nwa ya ga bute nwa okuko. Mgbe nwa egbe gara buru nwa okuko, nne okuko bido na-eti, na eti, na-achu nwa egbe ma nwa egbe burukwere nwa okuko o bu na-agba, garuo ebe Nne ya no. Nne egbe juru nwa ya ihe nne okuko mere mgbe o buuru nwa ya. Nwa egbe agwa nne ya na nne okuko tiiri mkpu fela elu. Nne egbe agwa nwa ya na nsogbu adighi n'ihina onweghi ihe ozo o ga-emeli. This story portrays the reason why up till the present time, the kite (egbe) still hunts for chicken wherever he sees it. When the baby chicken was carried away by the baby kite, the baby chicken was crying for rescue yet she was not saved by anyone. This brought about the wise saying as mama taught me, (nwa m nwasisi okuko egbe bu na eti ka uwa nu olu ya ma obughi ka ihe ji ya ha ya). One who has a terminal illness says that he is taking medicine not for healing but for formality because his illness cannot be cured. The chicken that the kite carried was crying not for relief but for people to hear her voice because her predator who was holding her could not release her.

One day, kite sent her young one to catch okuko's chick. Hence, when okuko and her chicks were basking in the sun, egbe's young one came down to grab a chick. As the scuffle raged on, okuko, the mother hen, chased and expressed words of anger and cursing the egbe's young one, but the kite's young one managed to escape with a chick anyway.

The chick was crying but no one could rescue her. In the nest, the egbe's young one told her mother how she fought to snatch the hen's chick. Then the egbe mother told her young one that the power of the mother hen had expired, therefore, she won't do anything again. The proverb goes, "*nwasisi okuko egbe bu na eti ka uwa nu olu ya ma obughi ka ihe ji ya ha ya.*

For the mother hen, egbe said that the hen's outcry and outspokenness were all she had and therefore, the hen's family should be hunted and hunted for food. The saying is*: ka onye si agba egwu ka aka si akuru ya.*

Na ubochi ozo, nne egbe dupu kwara nwa ya ka oga buta nwa odogwuma. Mgbe nwa egbe burula nwa odogwuma fela na elu, nne odogwuma emeghi ihe obula kama o lee ya anya ma gbakwa ya nkiti. Nne egbe were juu nwa egbe ihe nne oduguma mere mgbe obururu nwa ya, o si ya nweghi, nne egbe ewere gwa nwa ya ka obuchigha nwa Odogwuma azu maka ihi na omaghi ihe nne oduguma bu n'obi.

Next day, egbe sent her young one again to the odogwuma's family. When the egbe's young one arrived, the duck and her ducklings were swimming in the pond. The egbe's young one swooped down in the pond and seized one duckling and made away with it, but the mother duck did not do anything; rather, she looked at egbe's young one and decided to hatch a plan for the egbe's young one. At this instance, from that day, the mother egbe advised her young one to have nothing to do with the duck family because the mother duck, though she did not do anything, yet she had a secret weapon. Then, the mother ordered her young one, egbe, to return the duckling back to her mother. Even now, egbe (kite) never carries away the ducking but always carries the chick.

Kite *Duck* *Baby Duck*

Moral Lesson: Pay attention to what people say or do because slow water runs deep. The chicken spoke and what it said was understood but the duck did not speak and, therefore, the duck's intention was not known. Its intention could be anything. Subsequently, be vigilant.

Bush Fowl (Okwa)

https://www.bing.com//search?q=bush+fowl&form=QBLH&sp=

Bush fowl is similar to partridge and grouse with spotty black and white feathers. It is a good time-keeper too and a farmer. Okwa mbo is the first cry at 3 am. It cries again at 4 am. On the farm, you can always see where it has tilled the soil and is the first to know that yams have matured. It starts digging around yams, crying: "*Onye onyoo, onye, onyoo, onye onyoo.*" That is, it is telling her young ones to hurry up in eating the yams because the owner, the lazy man, will soon come (*onye onyoo means a lazy man*).

Wood Pecker (Otukpo Kpo Kpo)

https://www.bing.com/search?q=wood+pecker+form=QBUSH&sp=

The woodpecker has a powerful hammering horny beak, and it pecks a tree in order to create a hole in the tree where it can build a nest for storing its food and laying its eggs. It is said that one day, the woodpecker boasted that on the day its parents would die, it would commemorate their funeral ceremony by pecking down many trees. This arrogant assertion did not materialize because the woodpecker was sick with a big boil on its mouth on that day the parents died. It is good to aim high but it is not good to act high-handedly for it is all smoke and no fire. For this reason, when you are puffed up, we say, don't behave like otukpo- kpokpo. Proud people always fall. That is the reason why the wise say "Pride goes before a fall."

Spider (Udedere) and a Wasp (Ebu)

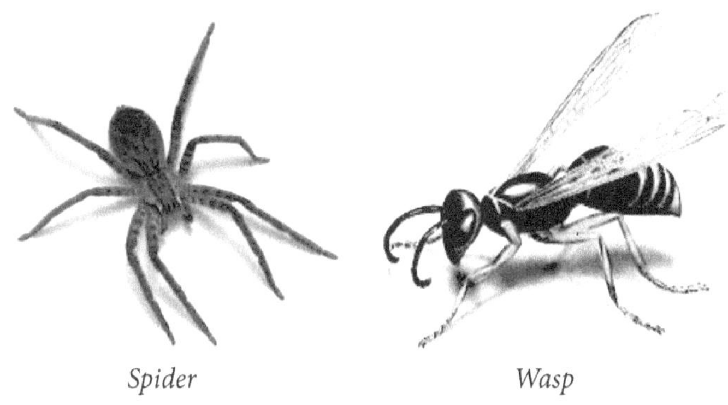

Spider

Wasp

The wasp built a nest and was ready to lay her eggs. But it has to get find prey on which to lay the eggs. As a result, the wasp found a pit dug by a ground spider (udedere). The sides of the pit were made up of freely flowing sand so that any trespasser would easily slide into the spider that was waiting at the bottom. The wasp (ebu) saw this and knew the spider was hidden at bottom of the pit. Instantly, it began to clear the sand so as to expose the spider. It was not easy but it used its wings to balance itself on the loose sand. Eventually, it reached the spider. But as it was ready to sting the spider, the spider sprang out of the pit, formed its body into the shape of a ball and quickly rolled away. The wasp was disappointed for it could not locate the spider anymore. This is a fearful threat from the wasp to the spider, which escaped by an ingeniously inborn intelligent strategy designed by its creator for deceiving its predator. There is a story between a mother-of-pearl moth caterpillar and a bird. The bird threatened the caterpillar which fell down from the tree where it was, formed itself into the shape of a green wheel and rapidly rolled away. At last, we come to the conclusion that life is programmed with intelligence and fear factors for all activities, which are preset for the survival of all living beings. The story of these animals here portrays how each of them wanted to take advantage of another to survive. This projects the wise saying of our ancestors: *ogbu agwo na azo ndu ya, agwo ona egbu na azokwa ndu ya-* one killing the snake is conscious of his life and the snake which he is trying to kill is also conscious of its life as both are in danger and thus, afraid of one another.

Moral Lesson: Everybody should be conscious of what he does because it is easy to make a dangerous mistake. This is about Theophobia - which is the act forbidden by God because of the fear of divine or spiritual retribution capable of affecting both the clan and the individual offender. According, to the original ancient orusa worship in Igboland, taboo - which is Theophobia - is practised with respect to the goddess, Ali, divine entity in charge of the land and the people. Taboo has many forms. For example:

i.   Causing a lamb to die or break a leg.
ii. Impregnating a girl before her official spiritual "ikwezi" (native cultural marriage celebration and ceremonial offering of a sacrifice to the god, Ali, and goddess.
iii. Stealing of yams (yams are sacred to the god, Ali, who gave yams to mankind).
iv. A woman in her menstruation is forbidden to go to the family shrine to eat of the food offered to the god at the shrine. This taboo can be traced to ancient Egypt and to Leviticus in the Bible. As early as 1850 BC, from the Papyrus Kahum, during the middle kingdom period in ancient Egypt, there was an inscription at the temple of Hathor (Hathor - Egyptian goddess of a number of the pleasurable aspects of life such as dance, music, sexuality, alcohol, and love), in Edfu, ancient Egypt, that contains a list of gods with specific dislikes for menstruating women. From Leviticus in the New World Translation of the Holy Scriptures, we read (Leviticus 15:19-20) 'and in case a woman having a running discharge and her running discharge in flesh proves to be blood, she should continue seven days in her menstrual impurity and anyone touching her will be unclean until the evening. And anything upon which she may lie down in her menstrual impurity will be unclean.'
v.   A hen hatching only one egg or a dog giving birth to one young one is defiled.

vi. A cock crowing too early at midnight before dawn is defiled.

vii. Anyone murdering a person deliberately or accidentally must leave the land and stay outside for a year and after that, must pay atonement to the family of the dead and to the goddess, Ali, of the land if the murdering was by mistake; if not, the person must be banished forever.

Vulture the Carrion Eater (Udele Ori Ozu)

Carrion

Vulture

Carrion is dead rotting flesh. Udele (Vulture), a bird with a long bare neck and a bald red head, is known for feeding on filth and so, its presence is an index of an unsanitary environment and a messenger of a bad omen. If someone is called udele, that person is a prophet of doom who deals in evil. Likewise, the person is always unkept. Udele has an acute sense of smell of the dead animals, and for this reason, whenever people see Udele, they say: *Udele buru ka ibu ahia azula gi,* meaning udele, let all your evil be upon you.

Fox or Wolf Ufu- Nnagwe (Nnawerede)

https://en.wikipedia.org/wiki/Fox

One day, ufu went out hunting a chicken for food. In the corner around a palm tree, ufu saw a hen eating palm fruits. Immediately, ufu chased the hen. The hen flew up and came down leaving her droppings on the ground and left. Ufu promptly ate up the hen's droppings and felt very pleased with the taste of the faeces. Then ufu, being greatly gratified by what it ate, concluded that if the faeces of the hen were so nice, then the flesh of the hen must be nicer indeed. Ufu then encamped behind the chicken house in a stealthy corner waiting for the hen to appear, mumbling to itself saying: *"Mgbe unighini di otua, unighinii oga di ufu agha."* Eventfully, when the chicken appeared, ufu pounced on her and made away with it. The owner heard the cry of the besieged hen and shouted to ufu:

> *Ufu haram okukom lee,*
> *Ufu neri okuko haram okukom lee*
> *Okpuru na akwaa.*

112

Golden Eagle (Ugo)

https://www.bing.com/images/search?q=goldern+eagles/form=

Ugo (Golden Eagle) Ugo nwa ori na nma and Ugbala Osimiri *(Cattle Egrets with brightest plumage, a follower).*

The golden eagle (ugo nwa ori na nma) is the king of birds and most stately and beautiful. The cattle egret (ugbala) is the follower of the eagle. So, one day, the eagle washed its feet with water and its feet turned golden. That caused the egret to wash itself with the same water. That also turned out to be spectacular. All the feathers of the egret became brilliantly white. Since then, a saying goes like this: *"Nmiri Ugo ji saa ukwu ka ugbala ji wua ahu."* A good follower always benefits from the goodness of the master. Ugbala now follows the cattle which arouse insects in their wake for the egret to pick up. It is also used as a way of claiming superiority over someone, such as saying, that which is my part-time is your main occupation.

Bat (Usu)

https://www.bing.com/images/Bat&qs=nsform

The bat is a nocturnal flying mammal and its body is covered with hairs. It hangs itself upside down on a tree branch by means of its talons (claws). It emerges at twilight to look for food. The bat (usu) is a mammal because it produces its young ones alive and suckles its young. We have four sayings about usu:

1. **Odiri usu mma ma ya were anyasi na aga.** Usu is partially blind during the day because its projecting big eyes have to work only in the night.

2. **Ibu usu na epu eze na afo nne ya**. Meaning, you are an unusual person with strange peculiarities. The babies of usu develops teeth in the womb but normal people develop teeth after they are born.

3. **Usu abughi anu elu nke oji abu anu ala**. Meaning, usu is not a land animal; neither is it a bird. When a person does not belong to any group, he or she is nicknamed usu.

4. **Obere ohusia ka usu ji ka anunu**. Meaning, usu does not only perch on a tree branch but also hangs upside-down on a branch by means of its claws. That is the reason why it is more than a bird. Its hanging makes it unique because birds cannot hang upside-down on tree branches.

Abughim nwa ana-ahuru aku, ma e nye m aku, aga m eri:
You cannot entice me with wealth; I am not averse to wealth but I am full of wealth.

Abughim onye ana agbakpo izu na azu:
I am not the one that can be overtaken by conspiracy.

Abum ududere anaghim akutu ulo ntara ahuhu ruu:
I am the spider; I do not destroy the house that I built with great effort.

A choba mma ekwu, a gbaa ama ihe e riri n'abali
If you are too fault-finding, you will expose what is hidden.

A du ndu na awo e rie nri na awo
If you come two times, you will be entertained two times. Meet twice, eat twice. This means you receive double merits when you perform well. Onye na eje ozi na eri ihe ozi (you earn as you work).

Ahu ekwughi n'egbu okenya; ma ekwuo anughi n'egbu nwata
An adult who sees or knows an evil but fails to expose or rather hides it, is destroyed, but the young man who pays no attention to the instruction of the adult, destroys himself.

Agbara ji ihu abua ebi n'obodo
Accurate knowledge of a situation is needed in order to swing to the appropriate side of the situation. What is the right thing to do in a complicated situation? You use diplomacy to deal with the situation.

Agbara gbuo ochia ochi, maka ihe ejiri debe ya ka omere
Gods are joyful when what they have done is what they have been asked to do. You rejoice or you are happy when you have done what you are told.

Agbaa aku otuo n'ogwe, a gbaa ozo otuo n'ogwe, o buso ogwe ka a piara aku
A shooter shoots his arrow and it falls on the tree; he shoots again and it

falls on the same tree; is that arrow made only for the tree? A particular person or group is always suffering the consequence of action meant for many, or a particular person is accused all the time; the question is, why that particular person all the time?

Agba-a nwa nnunu nneya efelaga
By pursuing a trivial matter, one loses a lot in the long run.

Agbachaa oso aguo mile
After a long-distance race, you check the mileage. You take stock of all dealings at the end of the day.

Agbakoo - agbakoo nyuo mmamiri o gbaa ufuu
United we stand but divided we fall. And so, unity is power ("Igwe bu ike") (gidi-gidi bu ugwu eze). Majority support is the grandeur of an event or majority support is the success of any event. This proverb, agbakoo- agbakoo nyuo mmamiri o gbaa ofufu, is a typical example of a role played by the mother, village men and women and the entire Orlu community in the murder case of one of our town's men in which the community teamed up and a decision carried out in affirmation. This kind of unison is what our world needs now, otherwise, things will fall apart and the centre cannot stand. In honesty, things had already fallen apart, so, we need a strong effort to revive the situation before it gets worse. I use this paragraph to commend men and women who always stand firm for peace and justice. May God reward you immensely (igwe bu ike).

Agbogho ga-atube ime, o gaghi ekwe na o na-ahu nwoke anya
If a girl never gets pregnant, she denies mating with a man. That is, pretending to be innocent but not.

Agadi nwanyi si na enweghi onye nwe ya ma gburu ama irogi ruo na ama nwoke, ga ekwu ezi okwu ma aka kpara ya
When the going gets tough, the tough get going. If you deny the truth, you will eventually come face to face with it. You said that nobody owns you, but one day, you will know that somebody owns you.

Agadi nwanyi anaghi agbara nwagbogho ukpaka
An elderly woman cannot be a servant to a little one. An elderly person cannot be submissive to a little one. But elderly person can accord respect to the little one and gives her, her right.

Agaghi m ekwo maka nna m looro mu uwa nyegbuo ya na nri
You don't spoil the child because you love him /her too much. So, never spoil the child and spare the rod.

Agaghi m enwe nkwa na-kwa aka n'afo
I cannot have a drum and at the same time be beating my stomach, thereby appearing not to have it. A typical "Ibo" man is termed to be wealthy based on the number of children he has and his land and yam barn. For this reason, our forefathers were always proud of the number of children they had; more especially, if those children were responsible children. When a man has many children but none of them is responsible, it means he has no child. Thus, it applies to the proverb above. Thus, it is better to have a child who is responsible than having many who are not. A bird in the hand is worth two in the bush.

"To be, or not to be: that is the question."
—**William Shakespeare**

Agaghi m abu usu na-abughi anu elu ma o bu anu ala
I will never be like the bat that belongs to neither the heavens nor the earth. I will neither be a man of nonentity nor bogus just like usu who is a fake animal that does not belong to any group.

Agaghi m eriju afo dachie uzo
I will not overfeed myself and fall on the roadside. Therefore, whenever you are doing anything, don't overdo it, otherwise, that action will rob you of the benefit. In all things, there must be moderation. In all, remember to be modest for any more than what suffices for the day is evil.

Agaghi m akwo aka tiere okuko aki
How can one wash hands to prepare nuts for chickens? I cannot do all that simply to please you. I cannot do this honourable thing for an undeserving person like you; it is like washing your hands to prepare meal for chickens who still feed on dirt. It is just wasting one's precious time and energy for a bogus.

Agaghi m anu ube nnawerede (fox) were okuko tupu mbara ezi
I will not hear the cry of the night fox and throw my hen outside. Literally, I will never surrender what is precious to me to someone who does not value it. I will not give up what is precious to me to someone who wants to destroy it. Do not give what is holy to dogs; neither throw your pearls to swine (Mt. 7:6).

Agaghim agbupu ga asu bia racharakwa ya
I don't go back on my word. What I have said, I have said. I do not eat my words. Maintain truth and justice.

Agha azu anaghi eri nnunu
You cannot strike a bird from the back for it will escape before you strike. But if you strike him from the front, you will get him. Evil conspiracy cannot overtake you unless you default to allow the attacks to succeed.

Agughee uzo agughee onu
When it is morning, everything gets on in earnest. When you wake up in the morning, you have to rise up briskly and clean yourself, eat food and get ready to tend to things. For it is said in Ibo: *"onye ghara nkenya ogbenye ama nya."* You have to take the lead in your life, otherwise, you will be a poor man. When you open the door, you are open to all activities and progress.

Agunyekwala akwa okuko na umu Okuko
Never count your chickens by the eggs before they hatch. Do

not take for granted the result of a project until the project has been executed.

Agu anaghi amu nwa ujo

The lion never gives birth to a cowardly cub. Whenever any of us was showing signs of laziness or fearfulness, our mother would apply this proverb. Then, she would encourage you to move on to complete the task. During farming season, anytime we saw a snake, we would encourage each other to stop working but she would motivate us to continue working.

Agu a muana okpi

One who is brave and agile has begotten one who is timid and sluggish. This is an example of a famous man of our town who was a responsible man and a successful teacher, but his son was an idiot, roaming about the streets and he became a dropout from school.

Agwaba nti ma onughi egbubiri isi nya n anti akwuru laa

One who does not regard the application of wisdom in all he does will live to have the remorse of its consequence. "The man, who knows how to lead one of his brothers towards what he has known, may one day be saved by that very brother." -Ancient Egyptian proverb. One, who does not listen will listen when the repercussion of his death hits him. Here is a short story concerning this adage. When you tell the ears and they refused to hear; when the head is being cut off, the ears follow the head. In this case, there was a young guy who joined a bad gang and everybody was asking him to come out because it wouldn't do him any good. Hence, he developed deaf ears. Behold, unfortunately for him, when his cup overflowed, he was in trouble and ended up losing his life. He was caught while performing a criminal act and he was murdered. My mother would say, "onye agwara ma ya kwe." This means things go in order if there is an agreement; things go according to plan but, if there is no agreement, things fall apart.

Agwo si umuya nwendidi na onye nona elu ferechaa odara onye no na ala

Every position has an advantage; those on the top feel safe and those on the bottom feel they are the lowest and they think that they have got nothing, but one day, those on the top will fall and the ones on the ground will catch them. Therefore, every cloud has a silver lining. No matter how gloomy anything is, it has some advantage.

Agwo nu na akereke

There is a dangerous person around, therefore, one must look out and be cautious. They say there is a green snake in a green grass. That is to say that in the night, when one is walking along a path strewn with overgrown green grass, it is advisable to have eyes and a stick in order to scare away a snake hiding in the grass. Recently, in a village, elders had selected well-trusted men to handle a matter but not knowing that one of the men was a dubious man and this diabolical individual leaked out all the secrets of the village. The elders found out though it was too late. But the good thing was that the dubious man was known and was no longer trusted among the elders. All the people in the village did fear him and distrusted him. So, he is a dangerous snake in the grass. People felt scared whenever he was around and no longer relaxed in discussing important matters in his presence.

Moral lesson: Never be a dubious fellow. Also, always be careful of whom you are associating with.

Agwo aghaghi imu ihe toro ogologo

This adage simply means like begets like.

Ahia mmadu na-azu ka o ma mgbe o ji ala

The person who attends a market knows the time it opens and closes. Literally, a dubious individual always accuses others because she thinks that others have the same behaviour.

Ahunam ihe ka ubi ree oba/Ahunam ihe kam anya ele

That is, a man looking for a treasure, finds and sells all his belongs in order to obtain it. In the holy scriptures, (Mt. 13:44-46) it is written: "The kingdom of the heavens is like a treasure hidden in the field which a man found and hid and for the joy he has, he goes and sells what things he has and buys that field. Again, the kingdom of the heavens is like a travelling merchant seeking fine pearls. Upon finding one pearl of high value, away he went and promptly sold all the things he had and bought it." Ubi is the farm where crops are harvested and oba is the barn where all reserved vital crops are stored. These crops are partly for food during "unwu" (a time when food is scarce) when reserved food is used and partly for replanting for the following year. Oba is very important for the survival and subsistence of the family. That which he has found must be so valuable that he would forego all the provisionally pressing needs of the barn (oba) and sell the contents of the barn in order to buy the treasure he has found. We say, "Ahunam ihe kam anyas ele." This means that you are so bewildered by what you see that you are held spell-bound, unable to perform intelligently. Obere uwa na agba anya nmili, nnukwu uwa eti anya kpuu. You are able to cry for a small loss but benumbed and dumbfounded when a big disaster strikes.

Ajo uka bu eghu olulo
A bad word is a return match. You have to take it back. A bad word will eventually return to the speaker. You have to be careful with your words because you may have to take them back.

Ajo okwu butere ajo osisa
A bad word provokes a bad answer or a bad word invites a bad answer. Never raise dust while walking on the road because someone will be affected and curse you in return.

Aka aja- aja na-ebute onu mmanu -mmanu
The hand that works hard brings about success and wealth. My mother would advise us saying, "My children, suffering comes before pleasure; so, no sweat, no sweet."

Aka ji anunu akwu n'ubi onye ozo

The yam stem branches that spread into the neighbour's farm. This adage applies to individuals who always engage in helping others but render little or no help to his or her family members. They are well known outside for doing well but in their families, people are dying in want of assistance. Remember that charity begins at home. Help your family and help others as well. It is good to be selfless but not in the default; you have to balance your actions.

Aka rubere ajo ohia

It is by the will of the people that a particular bush is set aside for defiled things. It is by your own desire you do things or refrain from doing them. In the olden days, a particular bush was reserved for burying bad people or dumping defiled things hence it is called "ajo ohia," "bad bush." This became a proverb that you can cut down the bush so as to cause the bush to cease being bad. That which is impossible is always possible. This is another typical example of life in a society where some people claimed to be famous through their diabolical acts and people overlooked them. Thus, one day, the entire society decided to say, enough is enough and faced those diabolical individuals squarely and got rid of their diabolical acts. In this manner, don't think that no one can handle you. Even though you are convinced that no one could, the higher beings can.

Akakpara eze udele oko mua chiri nya eze

When you come face to face with an unyielding formidable force, then you must put up otherwise you perish. One day, two men warned a man telling him that they would do away with him. He defied them. On the eventful day, they, with the help of another two men, carried him and threatened to throw him into a pit. He pleaded for mercy and even promised to do some good for them. In Igboland we say, "Ebuke be dike na onu ala okwue eziokwu." Another good example of this is a young bad boy in a village who thought he was all-powerful because he was guarded by juju and diabolical individuals, till one day, the higher force overturned him. His power was gone and none of those diabolical individuals behind him could save him. Thus, never think that nobody is above you. Mama would advise you by applying this wise saying, "iji na enweghi onye ndumodu na eso ozu ala na ala ili. This means, one who doesn't listen to advice will live to regret it. She would say, "Agwaba nti ma onughi egbubiri isi nyana nti akwuru. One who doesn't regard the application of wisdom will have remorse of the consequences; therefore, my younger ones, try to listen to the advice of our elders. Step down from following the diabolical people who mislead you. These people would offer you five thousand Naira (N5,000.00) and offer you a bottle of hot drink and give you a hammer, knife, and gun to kill human beings for them for rituals. In the end, you will be the one to suffer by being killed or imprisoned. Think twice and make the right choice of work to do. Being a wealthy fellow today and dying tomorrow is not worth it. Just think twice and mend your life; it is not too late. Forward ever, backward never. This proverb relates to this Igbo adage also, *"Agwaba nti ma onughi egbubiri isi nya n anti akwuru."* I am calling upon all the African leaders to pay much heed to these noble "Igbo" wise sayings to enable them to read the writing on the wall in order to turn over a new leaf and take precautions against the savage wolves and the international "Foxes." Beware of what happened to Muammar Qaddafi and the rest of the others. My mother would advise you, our noble African leaders, saying, *"Okuko lele etu esi abo okwa nwa nnegi"* What you have seen happening to your friend will also happen to you if you fail to learn from it. You have international opponents who seek every opportunity to take advantage of you, yet you yourselves allow that ugly opportunity to occur. This advice is applicable to everybody, including individuals, world leaders, church leaders, etcetera. Insight and guidelines for you from the Holy Scriptures;

> *"Be sober and vigilant. Your opponent, the devil, is prowling around like a roaring lion looking for someone to devour. Resist him, standing steadfast in faith."*
> **1 Peter 5:8-9a.**

My reader, "Oonye kwere chi ya ekwere." If you agree, your God affirms you. If you say yes to doom, well your chi-God will let it go as you wish it; hence he would first warn and give you some signs.

Let our African leaders not be *"Onye iberibe (onye isi na amaghi mgbe ibe ya kere nku ukwa)."* A fool never knew when the rest of the others shared the bread-fruit wood. A carefree person does not know when others are getting busy doing the real thing. He feels that everything is like that. He doesn't know that others had already done the real thing.

Aka nri kwo aka ekpe, aka ekpe akwo aka nri

When the right hand washes the left hand, the left hand also washes the right hand. When you have been assisted by someone else, you have to assist another. Mutual existence is what is advocated here.

Aka weta, aka weta onu eju

United we stand but divided we fall. Many families, institutions, individuals, and countries succeeded in life as a result of team efforts. No one is created or born with wealth. Those who are wealthy obtain it through ardent individual or team hard labour. Why can't you? Why choose the wrong way?

Ala adighi mma bu uru di nze

In a state of dispute or crisis in any land, it is the gain of the soothsayers because people will be going to them for consultations, thus, giving them the opportunity to demand money and material goods from them.

Amachie uwa george

Let's dress gaily with loincloths and be cheerful even though things are not right. Some people tend to be sorrowful when it seems the whole world is against them because of frequent calamities that are overtaking them. They have to put on a cheerful countenance to mitigate the pain.

Amaghi m ozize, amaghi m olila

My hand is clean. He or she is the just one. This means, one doesn't get involved in troublesome affairs. I do not know how to defend myself or how to escape for I am innocent. This is in a situation where one is absolutely innocent of an incident. I do not know anything about it.

A mara nwa gbogho n'ulo, a luo ya na'ama

A bad-mannered girl does not get married in close quarters but in a far-away place. Any girl who is well known in her father's community as being a noncompliant girl will find nobody near who would love to marry her. Rather, men outside her clan who do not know of her bad behaviour would marry her. As a result, it is very important for young girls to behave well. Mama would always say to her girls, "umum, kpa nu ezigbo agwa ka unu luta ezigbo di." This means live a decent life in order to get a good husband. This proverb is one of the essential analogies of the origin of family counselling. My mother, like any other Igbo mother, is the first mentor, nurse, teacher, and counsellor that children first encounter in their lives. If you have a mom who tells you dos and don'ts, you are a lucky one. I know the Western culture and the young generation would not understand this. When the girls heeded this advice, there was no divorce in marriages. Right now, the rate of divorce is high because girls have an 'I don't care' attitude to life. In some schools and after school clubs; when a child is misbehavouring and an adult corrects her, she runs into the toilet and begin to break things to vent her anger to avoid accepting correction.

A mutara ogbe nwa ka o kpagbuo ibe ya

A big child should not overshadow others. One who is an elephant should not behave like one. This is an example of a young man in a local village who wanted to live by killing others. No matter how powerful you are, live and let live because each individual has the right to exist and has a role to play in society. My mother would advise anybody like him with this wise saying, "*Ori anu madu tuo onwe nya mbo*" If hurting people is what you cherish, hurt yourself to feel the pain. Jesus said in Mathew 22:39, "You must love your neighbour as yourself." You must always use how you love yourself as a yardstick to measure your attitude towards others. What is good for the goose is also good for the gander, though one man's meat is another man's poison. Because actions have reactions, one is advised to watch what one dishes out to others, for one day, one will eat one's words.

Anaghi agba aka afu nwata eze

In ancient times, a child was not named until the appearance of the first tooth in the gum of the lower jaw for first teething was a cause for celebration. When the first tooth appeared, the parents chose an honourable, lovable person to be the first person to call the child's name with a gift (sometimes a she–goat or a hen). The parents of the child would offer a sacrifice to "ndichie" (ancestors) with a hen for a girl or a cock for a boy. The sacrificial chicken meat was used in preparing a soup with which to feed the child with yam fufu for the first time. Before this time, the child had been fed on mashed yam with palm oil "irunye oga na onu." Hence the saying that you do not declare that the child has teeth without congratulating the child with an endurable gift like a goat or a hen which will increase and multiply. The statement is good for your first attitude to a new relationship with human beings: *anaghi agba-aka afu eze. Nwanyi, anaghi agba aka eje na ihu agbara, anaghi agba ak agwo nzu.*

Anaeji ututu ama chi

This means you can never tell the day from the look of the morning. Indeed, it is not always easy to locate what is so good as to be open to it. What is, is what has been averaged from a multitude of would-be's that have been generalized to represent the truth. What is advised is to look for the truth and once one finds it, one should stick to it. Jesus says to his disciples, "Narrow is the gate and cramped the road leading off into life and few are the ones finding it." - Mathew 7:12-14.

Ana nye oji na onye mara ihe oputara

Kola-nut is given only to those who know its value. You cannot give valuable things to those who do not appreciate them.

A kpoo nkita oku, obi laa ya na nsi

Whenever you call a dog, it thinks of eating faeces. When you are talking to a guilty person in an alleged fashion, she thinks you are talking about her. When you are talking to a one-eyed person with your hand on your eye, he feels you are talking about him.

Akpia ahuru akpia nsi

Things that go together, follow together. One who has the hen, also has the eggs. Onye kpo nne nwata, Kpo nwa ya. If you have the woman, you also have her child.

Ara kata nwanyi ogbu etinye ya utu nonu

It is by doing something out of the ordinary that one, who is not aware of what is going on, comes to know it. It is by force that one who is unwilling to do things is made to do it. A young lady was just married to a family; and from the day she entered the family, she became a troublesome and very diabolical. Elders kept advising her and equally did good things for her in order to make her repent, but no way. Unfortunately, her dubious act went off-hand and elders had to speak out without minding her feelings. My mother would speak her famous figurative proverb here by saying, *"A gbaa aku, otuo n'ogwe a gbaaozo otuo n'ogwe, o buso ogwe ka piara aku?"* This means, a shooter shoots his arrow and it falls on the log; he shoots again and it falls on the log; is that arrow made only for the log? She would say again, *"ori anu madu tuo onwe nya mbo"* meaning, "she who eats human flesh should pinch herself to feel the pain. If hurting people is what you cherish, hurt yourself to feel the pain. In addition, Jesus said in Mathew 22:39, "You must love your neighbour as yourself." You must always use how you love yourself as a yardstick to measure your attitude towards others. What is good for the goose is also good for the gander though one man's meat is another man's poison. Because actions have reactions, one is advised to watch what one dishes out to others for one day, one will eat one's words.

Arusi anaghi asi ka emesia

The gods are already set for action at a special time for a certain length of time. They cannot be stopped or turned around. In anything you do, you must try to do your best in good time, for time waits for nobody.

Arusi onye na efe na egbu ya

The god that you worship is the one that can kill you or can save you. You must keep his laws otherwise he may punish you.

Arusi nwere ogbara asa

God has seven gifts of the spirit. This is true because the seven gifts are: (i) wisdom, (ii) understanding, (iii) counsel, (iv) fortitude, (v) knowledge, (vi) piety, and (vii) fear.

Ahuri anyuru n'elu ogbara iji anya ghari

Things done out of place don't have a point of location. Things without all respect are without all regard.

Afunam ihe kam anya ele

I have come in contact with a big surprise. I have embraced a devastating spectacle.

Ahunam ihe ka ubi ree oba

He has sold his treasure to obtain what he desired.

Anaghi agba nnunu nufe

You cannot shoot a bird while in flight. You cannot fight a strong person from his strong side. You have to say what you are sure of. You must dig up worms in the morning. You make hay while the sun shines. Opportunity comes but once.

Anughara odu akaghara nzu

When you change a topic, you will also change a decision. A new day goes with a new task and a new pay.

Anaghi agba Nwanza egbe, ihe anagba nwanza bu uta

It is not a useful job to waste a valuable weapon in killing a bird like a wren. It is a waste of time to use a valuable weapon to destroy a small thing.

> *"It is much ado about nothing." You must use the proper tool for the proper task. You must never kill a fly with a gun but with a fly-paper.*
>
> **—William Shakespeare.**
> ***https://www.oxforderence.com.view/10...***

Anaghi agbakpo dike izu na azu makana agbakpo dike izu agba nya ngba na ab

Never leave out an important person or thing to avoid repetition. You don't ignore a strong point (strong man) when you are gathering facts, otherwise, you will have to do it all over again. If you leave out an important person or thing in a plan, you will have to do it all over again. Also, do not treat what is true as untrue or else truth will speak for itself. Give respect to which it is due. Respect your elders in order to receive their blessings. Their blessings are as effective as those from our parents.

Anaghi e ji ihe a na-agba na nti agba n'anya

Things you put in the ear, you don't put in the eye. You cannot play with delicate matters; doing the right thing at the wrong place at the wrong time. The tool for cleaning the ear is different from the tool for cleaning the eye. Therefore, you cannot use the same tool to clean both of them. The final analogy is that you cannot play with fire and fuel. You must call a snake, a snake and a spade, a spade. There is no mixing of the two.

Anaghi ere okuko ukwu nji na no

You don't wash your dirty linen in public. This adage is similar to: "amara nwa gbogho n'ulo, a luo ya na'ama." That is, a bad-mannered girl does not get married locally but in a far-away place. If you are an evildoer, you will not do your acts in the neighbourhood where you can easily be spotted.

Anaghi m agba mmanwu a na-akwa aka

I never engage in useless affairs. You are advised not to engage in useless affairs. Engage in affairs that would be of benefit and that which you will be proud of.

Anaghi eji akpata atufuo aba ogaranya

We cannot get rich by messing up with the wealth we have at hand. Wasteful extravagance does not lead to being wealthy.

Anaghi agwa ochinti na ahia esule
You do not tell a stubborn person to repent; events will make him repent. You do not tell a deaf fellow that the war has started. A reasonable fellow knows when a matter arises without being informed.

Anaghi agwa nwata na nne ya anwua na, oga ama ma oburu na ofughi nri
You do not tell a child to cry for the dead mother; he will cry when he finds no one to feed him.

Anaghi ano na be Egbe ako ya onye anya mpia
You do not display one's disability before him, for that is not normal behaviour. You cannot dishonour somebody in his own house.

Ngwere nine makpuru amakpuru, amaghi nke afo na aru
All the lizards are lying down; we never know the one that has a stomach ache. Everybody is vulnerable to errors, so we do not know whose errors are more serious than others.

Anyi anaghi eji aku ana eji azu mmadu azu anu ohia
Do not throw your jewels to the dogs.

A si nwata saa ahu, o na-asa n'afo -n'afo
When you ask a child to bathe, she bathes only on the belly. It means, if you assign a child a duty that is above her, she would not know what to do. The child is doing as far as she knows and no more. She is innocently naïve.

Ariri egwepiara isi ebeghi akwa, o buru onye gwepiara ya isi na-ebe
The one who smashed a millipede's head cries instead of the millipede; the person who offended another complains instead. This proverb relates to a murder case of a man where the offenders never had any remorse; rather, they continued looking for another person to deal with. Live and let live! Do unto others what you would have them do unto you.

A na-ebido aka n'ikpere mana-ebili

You stand up by holding your knees. This means, you have to make a start before you achieve your goal. You do not earn by leaps and bounds but you must pay attention to steady basic specifics to win the race.

Anu abuba na eji aka nya afu onwe ya oku

Truth is self-evident and self-reliant. It speaks for itself.

Akwuru oto tuba nwanyi ime, o muo onye ara

If you want to impregnate a woman, you must do it the right way. For a woman to be pregnant, she must position herself well and rest after having conceived for her body needs a restful disposition for her fetus to have a healthy development. If you do the right thing in the wrong way, the result will be the wrong thing. Literally, anything you want to do, do it appropriately. Be focused and set your goal well before you implement it.

Anu kporo nku na-eju onu

One who is a very satisfied person fulfils his promises and is a goal-getter. A goal-getter or winner is one who is always successful and gives you the value you look for. "Sweet are the uses of adversity, which, like the toad, ugly and venomous, wears yet a precious jewel in his head."- Shakespeare. "The bee is the smallest animal but its product is the sweetest."

Another proverb applicable to this wise saying above is this; O di mkpunkpu na-eme ire (short but mighty in action). My mom called the person Gaga nogwu, anu kporo nku na eju onu; meaning, a smart fellow.

Aku fechaa o daara awo

The termite, after flying, will fall on the ground for the toad. One who works with no one in mind, will be inherited by any casual person who does not know what it takes to suffer. You must endeavour to have an inheritor otherwise your effects will go to an unknown outside person.

Akwa ona-ebe bu akwa dibia okpokoro

That cry is the empty cry of a soothsayer. That cry is the empty cry of a quack native doctor. It is a pretentious cry.

A karirigo m ozu e ji ute eli

I am no longer a small personality to be treated with levity.

Akpiri ahuri akpiri nsi

If you are inconvenienced in a thing, you have to control yourself, because if you don't, you will be in greater trouble; the reason is that things go in chains; if you cannot control the first one, you cannot control the next.

A na-asopuru isi ede alaede si o bu ya ka a na-asopuru

As you respect the head of the cocoyam, the bud claims the respect. When you are giving respect to somebody's father, the son claims that it is to him. Somebody who is pretentious claims that any good done is because of him. A disrespectful child claims the honour due to the parents.

Anya bewe, imi ehube

When it pains the eyes, it also pains the nose. When one of two things that are joined together is affected, the other must be affected too. For instance, a young man planned with his mother to kill his father in order to claim his wealth, but unfortunately, it did not work out the way they assumed. Both of them are now suffering from the consequence of their actions. Consequently, both of them are losers. Moreover, the entire family is also in horrible agony. Mother would advise us, "My children, think before you act. Look before you leap." In addition, she would instruct us, "Use your tongue to count your teeth." This means asking someone to think about the task because it is not easy. "Were iregi gua eze gi onu." She would end it by reinforcing her advice by saying, "nwam dajuu" (my child, be humble and thoughtful). The eye and the nose are joined together so that when one is affected, the other is equally affected. Those together, suffer together. Remember, no one is an island; we need each other to grow.

Anya buru egbe, a ga-eji ya agbagbu'm

If eyes were guns, men would shoot me. If wishes were wills, the lame would ride horses.

Anya m huru diochi bu n'elu ngwo

The wine-tapper is always on the job, tapping the palm tree. I always see you in the act just as I always see the wine-tapper on the top of the palm wine tree (ngwo- palm tree). A successful worker must always be busy in his job.

Anara ofu anam nma anarachana anam nile

When you attack one man, all the people are attacked. So, everybody is involved. When one person is taken away, everybody is taken away.

A hukata ogo mgbe - mgbe, a higara ya ji okpurukpu anya

Seeing an in-law too often makes one roast a bad yam for him. Too many visits from the in-law brings disregard. Too much flippancy corrodes a good habit. Frequent activity causes negligence.

A na-ama mma n'ulo mana a apu ezi

You have to be good at home before you go out. Charity begins at home.

Ana asi onye iji no na onu mechie ya, ima nde na eri iji

Do not stop him from doing what he is doing, as he may be enjoying it.

Ana awa gi ibi, afo na eto gi

The more you treat one disease, the more another develops. The more you correct an evil-doer, the more he develops a bad character. No repentance of any kind. The person hardens his heart.

Ana esi na mmiri eji akwo aka amata nwata ga eriju afo

From handwashing, you know the child that can feed well. By the quantity of water for handwashing, you know whether the host will feed the guest well. By their colour, you know them. Through people's speakers, you infer their ability and intelligence.

Anu guba m, a gaghi m aga n'okuko
Of all the meats I eat, chicken meat is not one of them. You are not the type I normally deal with. I will only assistant with responsible person.

Ana esi na mmiri eji amu nma amata onye ga akwoli oru
By the amount of water provided for sharpening work tools like machetes, you will know whether your host will be able to feed the guest workers well. Ana esi na isi ahuru anu uto nsi. Wisdom is known by its children.

Anu gbaa ajo oso, a gbairi ya ajo egbe
When an animal makes a bad run, you give it a gunshot without missing it. When an animal makes a bad run, you fire at it point-blank. You meet fire with fire. You dance according to the tune of the drum.

Anu esiri esi ona adi agu nma ma oweta nke ya orie nya na ndu
If cooked meat is good for the lion, why does he eat raw meat?

Anya mara oka karaka, nmuye nya bu asi
An experienced farmer knows when the corn is mature. On the other hand, we know who is who without being told. An auspicious character tells of its nature before the eyes of an experienced beholder. Beauty is in the eye of the beholder.

Arusi anaghi efemba awa afa
The God that you worship is the one that deals with you; he does not deal with anyone else except if that person contravenes his laws.

Aturu anaghi akpa n'afo ibe ewu/Ina acho ihe na akpa onye na acho ihe
Sheep never feed in the belly of a goat. You never hunt in the back yard of a lion for a lion is a hunter also. Never interfere in another

person's affairs.

A tuo ilu mkpuru ekete, okuko ahoro

When one mentions a covering basket, the hen thinks it is her that one is talking about. When you mention something that the person knows about, she feels uneasy. Ekwute ji onye ohi ji anugharala odu. Guilty conscience always fears accusation.

Atuoro omara -omara, mana atuoro nwa ofeke, o fenye isi n'ohia

If you advise a wise person, she understands, but if you advise a fool, he or she does not understand.

Awo anaghi agba oso ehihie na nkiti

A frog never runs in the daytime without a cause. There must be a cause for every action.

A zunye nwanyi anu abuba, onu ochi anaghiekwe ya funwuooku

When you give somebody something that he is overwhelmingly happy with, he or she finds it hard to talk. If you give a person a big gift, he or she will retort, "Is it all for me?" For he is surprisingly overwhelmed.

Azu si na ya oga no na nmiri ma ncha ekpu ya na anya

Fish cannot drown in the water because it is its environment.

Chi nyere nwata ji awom, ga enye ya mbazu o ga-eji egwu ya

If God gives you a difficult task, He will also give you the means to do it. When God created things, he also created how they were made and how they function.

Chi nyere okuku anya nyere ya ize any

The God that gave you the difficult task will also give you a method of doing it easily.

God gave you eyes and also how to use them safely.

Chuba ewu oji n'ehihie ka chi aghara iji

This literally implies, catch the child while still young before he gets spoilt. This proverb is similar to "wepu aka enwe n'ofe ka o ghara igho aka mmadu. You chase the black goat by daytime before it becomes dark. Try to prevent a matter before it gets uncontrollable. This wise saying is telling us that prevention is better than cure. Western culture believes in the intervention system, while our culture, the Igbos, believe in the preventive system. Thus, it is wise to stop unhealthy action before it gets worse. In our family counselling system, our parents push on with reprimanding us once they sense some misbehaviour. They never give us one chance until the misconduct stops. They never wait till an action is taken.

Dibe ji ozo ma ozo na egbu ya

One time, a doctor was sick, so he went on to diagnose himself and ended up with self-medication. The illness became worse. Then, he decided to go to another doctor. This time, a different routine and application were observed and the doctor was cured. In the Bible, it is said, "Physician, heal yourself; you heal others but cannot heal yourself" (Luke 4:23). dibe ji ozo ma ozo na egbu ya. Also, a native doctor doesn't know all the solutions. He treats others with one medicine but he cannot treat himself.

Dibe na agwo otoro, okobere ike ya nelu

The doctor that cures diarrhoea is not immune to diarrhoea. He who says, do not steal, does he steal? Paul said, "You can also be afflicted by the same disease which you cure people of."

Dupuga m bu ure, onye labara ghara ilaru?

Escorting me is just a courtesy, and if not, whoever intends to go by oneself will make it home. Never abuse someone as a result you are offering her help.

Ebe ariri noro nwuo bu ili ya

Wherever the millipede dies is its grave. Wherever a homeless person is, is his home. Ekele anaghi agwu ma oru agwughi: Life is a continuum; you do not count your results until the end.

Egboku adaruele ala umunwanyi aria ya elu
The unattainable has become available to all including women; so, once a tall tree falls down, women climb on it. For instance, an authentic man died and his wife started accusing him of all sorts of things because she knew that he was unable to defend himself. He was mocked and abused by the wife because he was defenseless. Hence, be careful with the dead because they are still living. Sometimes, they can do wonders. As a result, be careful.

Ebe nwata na-eriju afo ka ana-ebute ozu ya
Where a child overfeeds is where one finds his corpse. Where you do things in excess is where it is likely to find your corpse when you are gone. In other words, a place where one frequents is where she gets in trouble.

Ebe nwata na-ebe akwa na-atu aka, nna ya anoghi ebe ahu, nne ya anoro ya
When a child cries and points to a place, either the father or the mother is there. For instance, when an adult beats a child secretly, whenever that child sees that adult, he would frown and cry, which shows that the adult is an enemy to him or some how might abuse him or her.

Ebe onye oso ruru, onye ije ga-erukwa ya
Where the runner reaches, the walker reaches there too.
    Slowly and steadily the race is won.

Egbe onu
A man who cannot stop himself but keeps talking. This kind of person never knows when he contradicts himself as a result of too much talk. A man always makes a lot of promises without fulfilling them. He says one thing and does another. He is a chatterbox.

Egbe si: ghara -ghara ka eji ada oku

Once upon a time, a pack of monkeys came down to the stream to drink water while the lion was behind a tree watching. There was one monkey, the leader, which was constantly crying com, com, com, to the rest telling them to be on the lookout for the enemy was around. Therefore, monkeys changed positions and had to drink water intermittently, looking back and forth, running out of the water and running back interchangeably until the lion gave chase. They all escaped because they did not drink the water without an escape plan.

The kite enters a smouldering fire with dexterity so that it always succeeds in grabbing dead animals without being scorched and it says: ghara, ghara ka eji ada oku.

Ebu juru akwu ya ogbaa

You empower yourself by constantly contacting your power base. You must reach your power base before the enemy reaches you.

Ewu amaghi mgbe akoro na ami nya o bara gburu nya

A foolish person who is not vigilant does not know when danger is threatening him.

> *"At thirty, man suspects himself a fool; knows it at forty and reforms his plan. Be wise with speed; A fool at forty is a fool indeed."*
>
> *- Edward Young.*

"Give neither thy thoughts tongue, nor any proportioned thought his act. Be thou familiar, but by no means vulgar. The friends thou hast, and their adoption tried, grapple them to thy soul with hooks of steel. But do not dull thy palm with entertainment of each new-hatched, unfledged comrade." -Shakespeare.

Eburu ozu nwa onye ozo, odika ebu ikpochinkwu

People feel less concerned over a painful issue of others provided they are not the victims; the death of one's child is more painful than that of another's child. Other people don't feel the pain like the person concerned.

Eburu onu na-agba aja, ya na-ada ozu- ozu
When a fortune-teller performs on an empty stomach, it sounds death, death. Literally, when you are ready to consult a fortune-teller, you have to be strong and ready to bear the consequences. You must be fit before consulting a soothsayer for anything ailing to you will be like death to him.

Eburu ozu nwangwo naga, aguba ngwo nine ochiri chi ga eji
Our people say, eto ogeri obansi, esobe ka eku si kute ihe onu awa. The sayings mean, if you eulogize the dead palm wine-tapper (dingwo or nwangwo) according to his performances by counting the number of palm trees he operated upon, you will count forever because there are lots of palm trees. If you compliment a lady excessively for her performance, she will be amazed. If you swallow all that the wooden spoon (eku) puts into your mouth, your mouth will break down. Here, you are counselled to render honour to whom it is due but not to overdo your praises. Never allow the enormity of an event to overwhelm you but humbly receive the impact of every happening with equanimity of mind. "I dare do all that is becoming for a man; who does more is none," Shakespeare.

Echichanam ozom, gba ukwum njam, gba akam njam. Onye sina mu amaghichi ya chikwarakoo
I have done all I need to do; who does more is none.

Ewu na-eri ji na-ebu ebu
The goat that eats yam grows well. This means the young shall grow.

Egbe bere ugo bere, ma nke si ibenya eberena nku kwa ya
Live and let live so that you may live long. Here are some insights from Shakespeare: "Life is but a walking shadow, a poor player that struts and frets his hour upon the stage, and then is heard no more. It is a tale told by an idiot, full of sound and fury signifying nothing."
-Shakespeare. "To live long, it is necessary to live slowly." – Cicero. We must inculcate in our lives the principle of allowing for others' ways of living because variety is the spice of life.

Ewu (Goat) atalam igu nisi

This means, you and your dependents are suffering. Ewu (Goats) were supposed to be in wait in the fold for their fodder to be delivered to them but instead, they went ahead and ate it from the head of their keeper. That means the goats have been long without food. The goat- keeper had been so preoccupied with providing for himself with required materials that were hard to come by that he forgot to tend to the goats. This could also be likened to a superior person being looked down upon, neglected and therefore not respected by the commoners under him who are supposed to hold him in high esteem. In a nutshell, this is when a person bewails his suffering. So, he is suffering, his goats are suffering too. These goats literally mean people around him, whom he could not help because of lack of wealth.

Egwube odu ji nwalikiri, a ga-egwuru ya n'ala ndi mmuo

If you follow or keep digging the long tiny yam, you will reach the land of the Spirits. The literal meaning is, if you bend on recounting the bad behaviour of a dubious man or woman, you will be frustrated in life. If you persistently find faults with an incorrigible person, you will die without having done a thing.

Ele adighi ano n'obu si lewe ya aja n'isi

You don't claim to be clean when you are already in a filthy situation.

Elie ozu onuma alaa

The dead have no enemy. Once the dead are buried, everybody goes about their business. You do not bear a grudge against a dead person. If you do, you are causing yourself a psychological trauma.

Emekwana ihe ala so nso

Do not defile the sacred order of the gods of the land. For example, never shed the blood of a human being for any reason or ask someone to do it for you; it is an abomination; a taboo that is unforgiveable. It results in banishment from the land or death of the one who sheds the blood. It is absolutely a taboo in Ibo land to commit murder or commit suicide. If any married woman kills her husband, she must be sent home on Eke market day with a palm frond on her neck. She will never come back to her husband's home for the rest of her life. If she dared come back, the god of the land would torment her to death. Similarly, if a man commits the same crime, he would be banished for a year or two and will come back home to appease the gods if he committed the murder by mistake, but if it was a purposeful murder, he must be banished from his town forever. Mama would advise us, "My children, keep your hands clean. Never bring shame to yourself or to your family".

Emee ngwangwa e meghara odachi

If you hurry smartly, you pass over obstacles. If you hasten up a little, you will beat the obstacles, so, don't delay in any good thing you want to achieve; as the saying goes, "delay might be dangerous."

Ahughi nke achoro, eme nke ahuru

You have to use what is available. Someone has electrical engineering as his major but on finding himself incapable of handling the mathematical part of it, he decided to do fine arts. In life, one may have a talent that needs academic training but you have no money. Alternatively, you can switch over to trading in merchandise. Endeavour to lay your hands on what you can instead of waiting for something unattainable to you. Cut your coat according to your size.

Ehibe ogo, ehibe ikwu

When you marry somebody's daughter, you become his relative.

Ejebe uzo di ogologo owa agwu

It takes a lot of energy to make a long journey.

Aga eme aghaa mere onye oria egbule onye ya

You have to put up with it if you are terminally ill. You have to put up with it bravely till the end.

Ejirim gi ogu na ofo

I have given you enough chance to change. My innocence and clear conscience are enough to keep me from your evils.

Eji m abali luo uwa, amaghi m nga ala noro ruo

I reincarnated in the night; therefore, I never knew the crime of the land. I was born in the night. I never knew what happened in the day. The literal meaning of this is, "I do not know what is going on."

Ejule nasugbu onwenya ochee na ona asunyu oku

When a snail foams in the fire, it thinks that it is quenching the fire, not realizing that it is killing itself. It means whenever one is doing something evil, he or she is the one suffering from it; no one else is. A deceitful person always thinks he is cheating others, whereas he is cheating himself. One must learn not to deceive others for cheaters are always cheated.

Ejule kpuru isi ghoro onweya nri

The snail that is blind denies himself food. If a child is a troublemaker, he must always be in enmity with people. He will hardly win favour from people. As a result, it pays to be a good fellow but not a coward. A man has five children and this man is capable of training his children at any level of education they want. Unfortunately, one of his children chose to follow the wrong path and became a dropout from university. His dad advised him thus, *"Ejule kpuru isi ghoro onweya nri"* (one who denies himself food or good asses cheats himself.) Then, the dad stopped training him and he became a wastrel roaming about the street. Bad behaviour does not pay. That is estivation by snails. Estivation- ikpu isi ejule- is a term applied to animals like snails, insects (crickets), mammals (squirrels), frogs, and turtles, which go into a resting or torpid state (dormancy) during the dry season. This is called "summer sleep," the opposite of hibernation, "winter sleep." The animals, especially the snails, aestivate when dry season temperatures are high and food and water are in short supply. The snails (ejule) secrete mucus with which they seal their shell openings. When the mucus hardens, the snails embed themselves into the soil and remain there until the next rainy season when the mucus softens. When the snails aestivate, they become inactive, their metabolic rate is lowered and their rate of breathing reduces. The temperature of their body drops and, while on starvation, they use little energy from their stored fat reserves until their mucus seal softens at the return of the rainy season. Yes, it is true the ejule withdraws its body into its shell, seals the opening of the shell and starves, hence, the saying, *"ejule kpuru isi woro onweya nri"* likewise, when you withdraw yourself from the society of human beings, you are denying yourself the useful help and benefits that other beings can offer to you. If you do not do like the snail which conserves its fat reserve so that it can survive and consume your reserved energy lavishly, you will soon run out of supply and die of starvation. The snail denies itself food but conserves its food reserve and survives. (Ref: Encyclopedia of the Animal World by John A. Wallwork Ph.D. University of London, Westfield College (pp. 26-27).

Ejule ji ire oma aga n'ogwu

The snail traverses rough surfaces with dexterity/skillfulness. If you want to win any encounter, you have to be well-behaved, patient and tolerant.

E lelia nwa ite, o gbonyuo oku

Do not connive with a formidable person; he or she can surprise you. Do not underrate anybody.

Enwe na nwanne ya jere ohia onye mara nwanne ya eleta ma omatakwara ya

This is a mutual living in which one shares what one has in exchange for what another has.

Etinyena akwa gi niile n'otu nkata

Never put all your eggs in one basket because, when they crash, all will break. Diversify your assets to avoid a total loss.

Ewerelem eze kpe ekwore

One who is faced with survival struggles must improvise in certain conditions when the right tools for doing something are not available. A woman was returning from a meeting and remembered that she had no firewood for cooking. She then dashed to the farm and gathered firewood but had no ropes to tie the firewood together. So, she used her teeth in stripping ropes (ekwore) from palm tree fronds and used the ropes to tie the firewood. A hard life always drives people to do things in an unusual way because they cannot afford to do them in the right way. In life, one must be prepared to make the best of the materials at hand when the real things are hard to come by. Ahughi nke achoro, emee nke afuru. Ewerem eze foo ntu- use your teeth to extricate a nail from its fastener.

Ewi na upu abuo (Rabbit with two escape tunnels) na Nnambe uhe ka na ekpo (Tortoise with a red patch on the neck)

One day, nnambe (tortoise) went to the forest to hunt for ewi (rabbit). Ewi is a burrowing rodent that lives in the ground. It has two tunnels to its burrow; one for entering and one for escaping. Therefore, when nnambe found a mound of soil with a hole in the ground, he immediately knew he had found where the rabbit (ewi) lived. He started to dig up the hole in order to catch the rabbit, but nnambe did not know that ewi had two tunnels, one for entry and one for exit. When nnambe got to a recess in the ground, which was the rabbit's storeroom, full of fruits and nuts, tortoise was optimistic that the game was near. At this point, the rabbit knew that its burrow had been invaded and hurried up to the escape tunnel (upu), opened the lid, looked around for the invader and took to his heels. Nnambe saw ewi escaping and with anguish and anxiety, desperately pursued the rabbit as it climbed up a palm tree. But it was all in vain for the rabbit had gone forever. Nnambe went home empty-handed with no game for food. In the night when in bed with his wife, nnambe stuffed up the anus of his wife with a piece of cloth to ensure that the love pleasure did not escape through the second hole, then he said; "ihe upu emekarialla ya" because, his game rabbit escaped through the second hole. That's why, it is good to take precautions before any incident. The wise man says experience is the best teacher. Nnambe learnt his lesson like nwaebuleako. Nwaebuleako is the baby of the sheep who is always conscious of his environment before any danger comes his way; he is already alert and ready to handle the situation.

For this reason, be wise and attentive.

Ewu na-eri ji na-ebu ebu

The goat that eats yams grows. If you eat balanced food, you grow healthy. On the other hand, if you follow the right path, you will attain self-actualization. But if you roam about and look for a shortcut to success, you mess yourself up.

Eri ago mere nwanyi epughi afu onu

Eating and denying having eaten allows women not to grow beards. So, do not forget to say thank you for having been fed well. Always be grateful.

E shiwere onye ehihie, onye ututu aforo

First come, first served. You have to finish with the morning before you prepare for the afternoon.

Etu ariri si rinye na mbele, ya si etu ahu riputa

The path in which the millipede enters the pot, let it come out by the same path. You know how you got into trouble; you should also know how to get out of it.

E lewe osisi kporo akpo, nke di ndu buru uzo daa

While you expect a dead tree to fall, the living one falls first. While you expect the old man to die, the young one dies first. Hence, a bedridden patient will still be alive while a healthy fellow may die in the twinkling of an eye. This shows that death is not only for the sick and the dying, but also for the healthy. Just like Dr. Martin Luther King Jr. stated,

> *"That dream that blacks and whites will join hands together, that the character of a person rather than his colour will be the criterion of judgement."*
>
> **—Dr. Martin Luther King Jr.**

https://www.brainyquote.com/quotes/martin_luther_king_

jr_115056

E were ogiri gbuo mmiri oku, onye isi anugburu onwe ya

When sweet bouillon cubes are used in cooking yams, a fool will overeat. When you cook a soup with fermented melon seeds, someone sensitive to smells will be appalled. Be wise and do things judiciously.

Etu osoro anya ya diri, a ga-ele ya ele

No matter how the eye is, it must be looked at. No matter our difficulties in life, we should still strive to achieve our goals. Never give up.

Eruo ogaranya nso, a mara na onu ya na-esi isi

If you have not approached the honourable, you will not know that he makes mistakes.

Ere n'onu ehie n'obi

Sympathy on the lips but mockery in the heart. For example, when a misfortune happens to you, some people would come to sympathize with you pretentiously, but in their hearts, they are happy about your mishaps. Such people are dangerous and diabolical; they are not friends but foes.

Ejikwala ekwuruekwu kwugbuo m

Do not bring your trouble to me. Or do not talk me to death. Do not talk too much.

Ekwughim uka agam eme nsi

You better vent your anger by talking it out, rather than taking to violence.

E werekwala ukpa kunye na nkwu

Please don't take my ukpa to plant near the palm tree. This is like planting a seed among the thorns or among the stones which would never allow the seed to have a nutrient and grow well. It is just finding yourself in a difficult situation. Never plant your good seeds on infertile soil.

Ehi na enweghi odu chinya na achuru nya iji

The cow that has no tail, his God chases the fly away for him. God is the provider for those who are helpless. Jesus said, Mathew 11:28-30, "Come to me all you who are toiling and loaded down and I will refresh you. Take my yoke upon you and learn from me for I am mild-tempered and lowly in heart and you will find refreshment for your souls, for my yoke is kindly and my load light."

Ehi amaghi na odu ya bara ya uru ganya mgbe egbupuru ya odu

Those who have something valuable do not realize the importance of it until they lose it. For instance, most often, some children don't even value their parents till they pass on.

Ehi na cho nti, nti ehuchie na ya anya

One who is not satisfied with what he has got but is looking for more will lose all by looking for more. One who is not modest and moderate and is always longing for more, will eventually meet with things that will put him in a fix (dilemma).

Eziokwu na-elu ilu

Truth is always bitter. Nevertheless, speak the truth and be free. No one would punish you for speaking the truth. God will always fight for you when people are punishing you for speaking the truth. A fellow I know, always stands for truth and justice. And once she speaks the truth, she doesn't fear its effect on her. One thing is certain - the truth will always set us free. Eleanor Roosevelt, the wife of USA President Theodore Roosevelt, was asked how she handled an unjust criticism. She said,

> *"Never be bothered by what people say, as long as you know in your heart you are right. You will be damned if you do and damned if you don't anyway." (1901-1909).*
>
> **—Eleanor Roosevelt**

In the same venue, 1 Peter chapter verse 13 stated,

"No one can hurt you if you are determined to do only what is right; if you do have to suffer for being good, you will count it a blessing. There is no need to be afraid or to worry about them."
—1Peter 3:13).
**The Jerusalem Bible & Popular Edition
Darton, Longman & Todd (p. 302).**

Gaga nogwu

"Gaga n'ogwu" is a smart person whose smartness takes him through obstacles with ease. When I was in the elementary school, I saw a boy who was in the class ABC number 1. Then, in the mid-year, he had a test in which he did very well. He was placed in the class ABC number 2. At the end of the year, he had another test which he passed excellently. He was taken to class standard one. He moved up two classes in a year. That is what our elders call "Gaga nogwu." Another meaning for "Gaga nogwu" is a brave fellow; a person who strives to make ends meet come rain, come sun. He or she is also an achiever.

Ghara-ghara ka iji ada oku

You have to face the world with two fronts and sometimes you compromise. You can compromise when necessary. Sometimes, you hold on to your core value.

Gini ka a na-eme ana-enweghi ohere

What are you doing that you do not have the time for something else? My mother used to say this to anyone who was always looking for trouble. Whenever she endured the persons' indecency a lot, she decided to challenge the person. This shows that sometimes we overlook people's bad attitude and allow them to change but when they refuse to comply, react to make them feel what they are doing to others. Some people are always fussy claiming they have no time for helping other people but one day, when the tide of misfortune engulfs them, they have to have time for looking back and calling for help. Never live alone but keep on ministering to others so they can reciprocate.

Mother would equally put across this maxim; anyone who eats human flesh should prick herself. This means, *"ori anu madu tuo onwe nya mbo."* If hurting people is what you cherish and take delight in, hurt yourself to feel the pain. Jesus said in Mathew 22:39, "You must love your neighbour as yourself." You must always use how you love yourself as a yardstick to measure your attitude towards others. What is good for the goose is also good for the gander, though, one man's meat is another man's poison. Because actions have reactions, one is advised to watch what one dishes out to others for one day, one will eat one's words. Besides, she would say, *"a mutara ogbe nwa ka o kpagbuo ibe ya"* One who is like an elephant should not behave like one.

To live long, it is necessary to live slowly"
—Shakespeare

This is an example of a young man who wanted to live by killing others. No matter how powerful you may be, live and let live because each individual has the right to exist. This young man was given was ample of opportunities to change but he refused till God himself dealt with him. This is portrayed by another of my mother's proverbs; "akakpara eze udele oku muo chiri ya eze." When you come face to face with an unyielding formidable force, then you must put up, otherwise, you perish. One day, two men warned a man telling him that they would do away with him. He defied them. On the eventful day, they, with the help of another two men, carried him off and threatened to throw him into a pit. He pleaded for mercy and even promised to do some good to them. The Igbo maxim states, *"Ebuke be dike na onu ala okwue eziokwu."* Another good example of this is a young bad boy in a village who thought he was all-powerful because he was guarded by juju and diabolical individuals. One day, the higher force overturned him. Then, his power was gone and none of those diabolical individuals behind him could rescue him. Never think that nobody is more powerful than you are. Mama would counsel you by applying this wise saying, *"iji na enweghi onye ndumodu na eso ozu ala na ala ili.* One who doesn't listen to advice will live to regret it. She would say, *"agwaba nti ma onughi egbubiri isi nyana nti akwuru.* One, who doesn't regard the application of wisdom, will have remorse of his consequences. Another example of my mother's adage for treating this kind of matter is, *"O ji ofo ehibe isi, ahubeghi ajo mmuo."* This means, if you claim to be more powerful than the others, one day, you will meet with a super-powerful being that can handle you squarely. She would also conclude by saying, nwa m, jide ogu, meaning, keep your hands clean and be strengthened in everything you do. Always be sincere in all your endeavours. I borrow this aspect of my mother's life a lot. Wherever I go, I make sure I don't trouble anybody. Consequently, if anyone troubles me, I give the person the benefit of the doubts that they can change, but if he or she refuses to comply, I challenge the person. By talking sense to the person. Truly, my reader, if you keep your hands clean, nothing will happen to you. Your enemy will keep on running away whenever she sees you because you have no ills against her.

Gidi - gidi bu ugwu eze
Majority is the success of any event. Likewise, team effort brings about incredible success.

Ha gbuo kpo okpo na ohia, ha putan a 'uzo se waa
They cover up the evil they have done by pretending that nothing has happened. Those who do double-dealing are two-faced and deceptive in that they hit you with one hand and comfort you with the other hand.

Hie aka na anya ugboro asaa
Rub your eyes with your four fingers seven times (be careful in all your endeavours. Be cautious in all your undertakings). We say, "Anya saa, anya gbaa" (be very careful).

Ha bu utara, ha bu mmiri ofe
One who has the say, has the conclusion. They have got everything completely. A typical example of "ha bu utara, ha bu mmiri ofe" is in the case of four team workers who have a combined business and among these four people, one is always dominating. One day, they had a meeting to decide when would be convenient for them to be waking up in the mornings to enable them to carry on with their daily activities.

One of them suggested 7 o'clock but the domineering fellow among them said no to it and chose 6 o'clock. Then all of them were contented to be getting up at 6 o'clock. Sometime later, the domineering one couldn't afford to get up at 6 o'clock in the mornings because it was too early for him and he begged his colleagues that they should wake up at 7 am instead. His co-workers said in response, *"ngi bu utara ngi bu mmiri ofe.* Whatever you say, we will agree (one who has the say, has the conclusion). *Ngi nyuru puu ngi nyuru tee iga kwuba ogwu.* You have it all, go ahead.

Ha soro ndi mmuo gbuo mmadu, ha soro ndi mmadu gaa mgbaru

They follow spirits to kill a man and they follow human beings for condolence. They are two-faced, double-dealers. They have both hands on both sides.

Ha mara iwu otoro baa nsi

Those who make the law easily break the law. They are hypocrites, making laws that they cannot keep.

Ibu adi otutu ebu adighi anyi alu

United we stand, divided we fall. A load carried by many people never feels heavy.

Ibu usu na epu eze na afo nne ya

Are you a bad child? Ibu abuala (viper) does not wait to be born but bites through the mother's body and kills the mother. A bad child kills his parents.

Iburu onye na ekwe - ekwe iburu udara obioma

If you are too lenient, people always take you for granted. You should not be lenient; otherwise, you will become open to public ridicule. Do not be a yes-man always.

I bu anu okporo nku na-eju onu

You are dry meat that fills the mouth. One who is small but performs wonders. You are small but mighty; you fulfil the complete richness of goodness.

Ibu nkita na eri ihe ogboro

Are you a dog that eats its vomit? Be careful about what you say or do because one day, it will return to you; you will face it.

Ibu ezi (Pig)

The pig is known as a dirty animal, greedy, and stubborn. When someone is called pig, it means that the person is dirty, unkept, greedy, and stubborn. When you want to sleight a person because he behaves in an unruly, unwanted way, call himwever a pig (ezi). Jesus said,

"Do not give dogs what is holy;" and do not throw your pearls in front of pigs, or they may trample them and then turn on you and tear you to pieces."
—Mathew 7:6
The Jerusalem Bible &Popular Edition
Darton, Longman & Todd 1974, (p. 12).

I doo nku, nku doo gi, hapu ya ka o hara imeru gi ahu

If you pull firewood and it resists you, leave it alone before it hurts you. If you ask a misbehaved fellow to desist from her bad way and she wants to get you in trouble, just leave her alone or else you lose your credibility. *Hapunu onye nzuzu ka ogahieriba.* (Let the sleeping dog lie). Leave the trouble alone.

Ji ghee ofuma nda-nda eketa ka ya

When yam cooks well, the ants get their share. Aku lo ufo, oputa nwanne.

I mara asu sua n'ikwe, I ga-ama asu, I sua n'ala

If you know how to pound, pound it in the mortar, if not, pound on the ground. If you want to do the right thing, do it, but if you don't want to do the right thing, you can do anything you like. The truth will show up by itself.

Igwe bu ike (United we stand)

The Role of "Umuada" (young and elderly daughters of the village as well as married women in the villages of Igbo land) falls under the umbrella of "Igwe bu ike." "Igwe bu ike" stands for united we stand. The umuada always work in unison with each other. Their organization is a very powerful one and no one could fault them. Their union is respected and when things go wrong, umuada are called to restore order. They have one voice and one mind; no one can influence their decision. Their decision-making is a very powerful one. Our Igbo saying goes, *"nkita anaghi ata nti ha ata"* (the umuada are formidable such that any conspiracy cannot overturn their judgment). The role of umuada in society projects the attribute of the Ibo word - *"igwe bu ike."* The indigenous daughters - umuada always act in unison with one mind and one voice. No sabotaging. No government or local authorities dare to interfere with their decisions. Thus, umuada, ndi ama ala, na ndi umunwanyi (married women) behave alike in their decision-making. They have an influential voice in the society. I will include in this paragraph the actions of some different groups of women to back up my knowledge of umuada- the indigenous daughters.

Once, in a town, a man married a lady from another town. It was observed that she was having an affair with another man, hence, the husband decided to call the indigenous daughters to question her unlawful behaviour. Before umuada, she denied any such sexual encounter. Then, umuada brought kola nuts which were offered to the ancestors (the blessed dead) and broken them into pieces. A piece was given to her to chew before them. She, with effrontery, shamelessly ate a piece of the kola nut. She fell sick and died. Her sister with whom she was living went to her home town and told her people how she died. It was a cultural practice that when a young woman died, her people would come and take her corpse back to her father land. The woman's people decided to invade the village wherein she died before taking her dead body. The news of this plot leaked to the village concerned. The village concerned ran away, scattered in other towns. When the relatives of the dead lady came to the village, they found it abandoned and as a result, they decided to leave it desolate and destroyed. Nonetheless, they took her corpse and buried her. Amazingly, after a few days, her grave opened up and her coffin surfaced on the earth. Her remains were burnt and reburied. Those of her people who had come to make trouble were dumbfounded. The ancestors fought for the innocent ones; for this reason, whatever you do, keep your hands clean. The saying for this incident is: "*Ana eji ilu ata oji nsi.*" The role of umuada is peaceful but powerful. When umuada gather in a house to settle an altercation, the householder must totally resign to their will and treat them hospitably. They settle conflict, divorce, and stipulate times for "igbaoriko" or 'igbaechiri" (whole family offering sacrifice together to ancestors and eating together).

At this juncture is a short story about Aba Riot women in Nigeria –Igboland in 1929 when the White man ruled out that the women would be included in the head tax. Women, on hearing it, rallied around and took their kitchen pestles and machetes to the White man's headquarters and destroyed their property. Behold, the women's massive protest that year led to the end of women's head tax. In page 4: Reference file://A:\Igbo Traditional Rulers igbochef.htm by Axel Harnet-Sievers: Igbo Traditional Rulers: Chieftaincy and the State in Southeastern Nigeria (p. 4). This article has been published in Africa Spectrum (Hamburg), Vol. 33 No.1 1998 (pp. 57-70). But the system did not break down before the famous 1929 Woman's War which took place in large areas of Southern Igbo land and of the Ibibio-speaking areas further southeast. Thousands of women attacked native courts and besieged warrant chiefs ('Sitting on a man,' Van Allen 1972).

The Women's War made unmistakably clear the little legitimacy of Warrant Chief Rule, which since then has become paradigmatic for the errors about African societies and their traditions and rulers committed by British colonialism. The reasons behind the riots were more complicated - the immediate critical issue was the rumours that after the introduction of Direct Tax on men in 1928, women would also be taxed. At the same time, the fall in palm prices due to the world-wide recession aroused much anger and was attributed to manipulations by the European Trading Firms, the premises of which were also attacked in several places. But overall attacks on native chiefs and sieges on warrant chiefs constituted the most important aspects of the Women's Wars.

In reference number page 6 file://A:\ Igbo land Thesis June 29, 2000.htm File://A:\ Igbo Chima footnotes chima-fn.htm footnotes (6) page1. The episode of the Ahiara Expedition of 1905-1906 has been studied by Elechi (1974). The Igbo Resistance to British imperialism: The Episode of Dr. Stewart and the Ahiara Expedition in Journal of African Studies 1 (Summer 1974: 145 ff). According to Elechi's story of the incident in the book, Tradition and Transformation in Eastern Nigeria (1989), Dr. Stewart was believed to have been killed and eaten by the people of Ahiara, Mbaise. The tragic incident seems indeed to have been triggered by sad memories of British brutality and overrule. Dr. Stewart was captured in November 1905, having lost his way in route to Umuahia, mainly as a protest of the military patrol sent to Ahiara earlier in March to crush Ahiara's persistent insubordination. By December 1905, other parts of the present Mbaise and Obowo had joined the war against the British (Footnote 7).

The Women's War

In 1929, the Colonial Administration in Eastern Nigeria began collecting nominal rolls for taxation purposes following the successful collection of such taxes in 1928. Rumours spread that women were about to be taxed along with the men. Since the previous count meant taxation, the present remuneration, which included women and livestock, sparked a hostile reaction from them. Given the disturbing fall in the price of palm produce and the general rise in the cost of living, women asked how, if included, they could afford the money to pay tax. The situation came to a climax in November 1929 when one Chief Okugo (a warrant chief) in Aba division sent a school teacher, Mark Emeruwa, as his agent to compile the list of men and livestock in all Olokolo compounds. When Emeruwa confronted one madam Ojim who was preparing palm oil, passion flared. Their confrontation led to physical assault which triggered off the Women's War. The revolt spread through Aba Division to Owerri, Bende, Degema and Ibibio land. See also Mba N., (1982). Nigeria Women Mobilized" and "Heroines of the Women's War" in Awe (ed) (1982) Nigerian Women in Historical perspective, Lagos.

Another powerful role of the women was during the era of our noble Missionary-Bishop Shanahan of Southern Nigeria in 1922. Women stood tall and made a drastic decision against their husbands regarding pigs' issues. Here is the story, according to the author,

"Dr. Shanahan had one good story about the way women defended their absolute right to the koko-yam. In one district, many of the men kept pigs. They were a profitable investment, because they were in constant demand for ju-ju sacrifice. But they were also fond of daily exercise in the patches of koko-yam belonging to the women. This was very infuriating. The only certain source of female profit in the town was going towards the fattening of the pigs. The women tolerated the injustice with very bad grace for a time, while the men smiled at each other and figuratively clapped the pigs on the back for their initiative. Then a mass protest was made by the women, who declared that the pigs would have to be sold off if there was to be peace and concord in the town. The men held up their hands in horror. What! Leave odo (the ju-ju) without his blood sacrifice? Certainly not; it was regrettable, of course, but they would have to grin and bear it. The women felt very naturally that they were doing all the bearing, while the men were doing all the grinning! They decided to reverse the roles for a change. They held a meeting under their Omu (head woman) and -wonderful to relate-kept the decisions absolutely secret. That evening, the fou-fou pounders thumped out the welcome news of approaching chop as usual and the gratifying smell of smoked fish and peppered soup was wafted over compound walls into the darkness of the surrounding trees. The lords of creation sat in solitary state outside their huts, waiting to be served by their wives, for Ibo law stipulated that the men take food separately and be offered it by their consorts. It was beneath the dignity of a man to cook food or go looking for it in his own compound; that night, many men felt that dignity had its drawbacks, as delicious smells made wide nostrils wider yet with appreciation. Still, the gods were propitious and wives who could cook like that were worth having. So, the men waited, feeling that all was right with the world. Was it, though? Even as they waited, silent female figures were slipping through the darkness, with the sticky but succulent fou-fou and the fish wrapped up in banana leaves, and the peppered soup in bottles. The family meal, quite sufficient to keep a woman going for a

week, was on the move! Not in one compound, or three, or ten, but in every single compound in the whole town. It was a masterstroke, delivered at the exact moment when every man was completely off his guard, seated alone in his majesty just waiting to be fed. And, not only were the men waiting to be fed, but the small piccans (children); when food was not forthcoming, they gave tongue in no uncertain way. Soon, the whole town was like an overgrown baby farm, with hundreds of babes in arms bawling in unison for the mothers and the foods that were not. Irate heads of families tried desperately to cope with the situation. They had perforce to get down to the uncongenial and unaccustomed task of fending for themselves and the small children. No use shouting at marriageable daughters to do something; these had also disappeared, as had ever girl who knew anything about cooking. The lordly males did their best and managed to satisfy their own hunger. But they did not satisfy the babes, who scorned half-baked yam and tough stock-fish, and howled for the mothers they felt should be present.

Temporary success was achieved by pouring draughts of water down the thirsty baby throats, but the effect of that was short-lived; water was not what they wanted. It tasted better than boiled yam, but it was far from being solid baby food; they continued to howl.

After a couple of days of bedlam, the men decided to seek out the women and make terms. They found them encamped a goodly distance from the town, cheerful and well-fed, contentedly placid and happy. The men wanted peace, but peace with honour. They suggested that if the women would come back voluntarily, there would be no beatings everything would go on as before. After all, were they not good dutiful wives on whose heads great dowries had been paid? And what woman could forget her little piccan, bawling its lungs out by day and by night, especially night? Nobody in the town had managed to sleep through the uproar. Surely, they would come back? They would, the women said, when the last pig had been sold or killed and eaten. They graciously offered to join in the eating, if the men would agree to do the killing. But as long as a single trotter remained over-ground with a capacity for going underground, they would not budge. The men could choose between their pigs and their wives. If they wanted to be pig-headed, they could keep their pigs; but if they did, they would have to go the whole hog and learn all about cooking and baby welfare. They would never have wives to do such things for them again. Meanwhile, were the babies getting their morning tub and their proper feeding? They were not. And strong - the men were getting quite tired of carrying them in their arms and doing the Ibo equivalent of showing them "moo-cows" and saying "gug-gug" and "I see you!" They were tired, too, of having their fingers sucked between bouts of lusty bawling; tired above all of holding bowls of guinea-corn soup to the lips of babies who cried because they got it and cried because they did not get it. The babies apparently could keep this up indefinitely; the men could not, they were getting haggard and sleepy-eyed. After much parleying and consulting, they decided to agree to the women's demands and to do away with all the pigs in the town. It was peace at any price. Now, a society where women could stand up for their rights like that when the need arose, and in which they were betrothed and married with such display and ceremony, and in which the first wife shared in every honour and dignity that accrued to her husband, and in which a great proportion of men were monogamous, was constructed neither loosely nor immorally. It did not give women their rightful place. But it made them neither slave nor chattel. It made her subject to man and inferior to him. It needed change, especially in the matter of polygamy and divorce; it did not need total disruption. It contains much that was praiseworthy by purely natural standards and demanded spiritual sublimation more than anything else. A new and clearer vision of womanhood would purify and elevate it. That was the Bishop's view; he knew it would be difficult, if not impossible, to give it that vision except through the medium of women who were themselves living a very sublimated form of life. "

The Story of Bishop Joseph Shanahan of Southern Nigeria
A Man for Everybody
Edith Dynan, 2001, (p. 244).
by John P. Jordan, C.S.Sp.

Ife nmuo na eri ka eji efe ya

In Igboland, the lamb (sheep) is sacred to the god Ali and it is used in offering sacrifices to the god, Ani. Likewise, ebule (ram) is sacred to the deity, agwunsi (ikenga Chukwu, ike (Chukwu ji eje ogu) and it is sacrificed to him. Nne ewu is offered to nde ogaranyi (the blessed dead elders). Nkita as a symbol of set (satan) is offered to him. Okeokpa (cock) is offered to nde ogaranyi as well. Nwampi is a he-goat for aja oru - a sacrifice to the god of the farmland, Ahijioku, for protection and a successful farming season. Nnekwu (hen) is offered to nde Ada (blessed dead daughters). Ehi (cow) is offered to nde ogaranyi on irijiofu festival (new yam festival) by the king. In Ancient Egypt, the same practice prevailed. The following are sacred to their respective gods and are offered to them in real life form or in votive form:

Baboon -sacred to the god Thoth
Cow- sacred to the goddess Hathor
Lion – sacred to the god Horus (Orusa)
Bull – sacred to Mnevis Ra
Ram – sacred to the god Amen-Ra
Hare – sacred to the god Osiris
Hawk – sacred to the god Horus
Ibis – sacred to the god Thoth
Fish – sacred to goddesses Hathor and Isis
Nne Azu (fish) – sacred and offered to nde Ogaranyi.

In Christian practice, we are told that the dove or pigeon is sacred to God Almighty and the lamb is sacred to Lord Jesus. Let us look at these:

> *"Observing what stands written in the law of the Lord: Every first-born male must be consecrated to the Lord - and also to offer in sacrifice, in accordance with what is said in the law of the Lord, a pair of turtle doves or two young pigeons."*
> **—Luke 2:23-24**
> **The Jerusalem Bible & Popular Edition Darton, Longman & Todd 1974, (p. 73).**

Also, let us examine this;

> *"The next day, seeing Jesus coming towards him, John said, 'Look, there is the lamb of God that takes away the sin of the world."*
> **—John 1:29.**

The Jerusalem Bible & Popular Edition Darton, Longman & Todd 1974, (p. 115).

Moreso,

> *"As soon as Jesus was baptized, he came up from the water, and suddenly the heavens opened and he saw the Spirit of God descending like a dove and coming down on him. And a voice spoke from the heavens, "this is my Son, the Beloved; my Favour rests on him."*
>
> **—Matthew (3:16).**
> **The Jerusalem Bible & Popular Darton, Longman & Todd 1974, (p. 7-8).**

> *"To the one sitting on the throne and to the Lamb be the blessing and honour…"*
>
> **—Rev. 5:13.**

Here are more instances,

> *"And I saw when the Lamb opened one of the seven seals."*
> **—Rev. 6:1**

In the Vatican City, in Saint Peter's Cathedral, above the altar, the picture of a mighty dove was embossed, representing God Almighty. This practice started from Ancient Egypt and it is right, ife nmuo na eri ka eji efe ya- what is sacred to God is always a favourable offering to him.

Ihe ekwuru ekwerem
Ihe okuko bu nmiri acho di ya mkpa
Okuko kpara chi, kpara uke ya, mgbe oga akpa nke ya chi ejilahaya

One day, it was raining so a hen gathered her young ones together but one named Arumuka, jumped out into the rain to eat worms and the mother hen yearned for her disobedient child to come back because surface running water would carry her away. The disobedient one dared to go out and fell victim to the running water. She struggled to swim out of the water and joined the family fold with her whole body fully drenched with water. She was shivering with cold when the mother hen said, *"okwa agwaram gi agwa"*- meaning, "I told you." The disobedient young one replied, *"ihe ekwuru ekwerem."* Young ones are inclined to do their wishes without care but when the unexpected happens, it is hard to retrace one's steps. Experience is the best teacher. But we say it is not without reason that the chicken continues to feed in the rain even though there is a risk- *ihe okuko bu nmiri acho di ya mkpa* – meaning, there is a reason for the chicken's action. A chicken has three stomachs- the crop (akpiri ukwu), gizzard leko), and the real stomach (akpakwuru). When the chicken is feeding, it has to fill the three stomachs in order to be satisfied. The crop is chi ya, gizzard is ukeya and the real stomach is nkeya. This ordeal keeps the chicken busy eating even late into the night. So we say, *okuko kpara nke ya chi ejilahaya oru gara agwu, ekele anaghi agwu oru gara agwu, ekele anaghi agwu;* he who has many parts, has many functions.

Iga eshi nobi nwataa rie nobi ogaranya

If you act well while young, you will live long enough to earn good returns when you are aged. One man performed ozo title initiation while young, by the time he was fifty-five -years -old, he had become the head of the nze congregation and an honourable rich elder.

Aka chaa nwata, osoro ogaranya rie nri

If you are excellent while yet young, you can rank with blessed elderly celebrities (ihe di nma si kwute ya).

Iga na nke nwadibie, i ga ahu udele, imara aru mere na ala ndinmuo

Udele (the vulture) is a diviner of sorrowful omens and is an aide of the soothsayer (nwadibie) who consults udele for information about what the gods are planning. For this reason, udele shuttles between the living and the dead. When the gods do not want udele to reveal their odious plans to mankind, they place udele under house arrest and prevent him from appearing at the premises of the soothsayer. Then, when udele is scarce at the home of nwadibie, everyone concludes that an ominous event is at hand.

Ihe arachatara n'akukuu ite na-ala n'akuku onu
Whatever you get from the lips of the pot, goes back on the lips of human beings. Whatever is ill-gotten, will eventually become ill-fated.

Ihe anagba ose bu okirikiri ma anaghi ari ya elu
You don't spend much time doing a trifle. What you do to a pepper plant is to go around it; you can never climb it because it has no strong stem. This boils down to reason. Always take the right action from the right perspective.

Ihe nwa ewu na ebe, nne ya mara ya
The mother goat taught the baby goat to cry incessantly the way it does. This also means that your behaviours are inherited or learned from your parents. The lives of parents influence their children a lot.

Ihe egbe muru ahapughi ibu okuko
If one is a thief, his child must be a thief. However, the environment could change one to become a thief. Inheritance and environment influence behaviours.

Ihe no na be ebu no na be aghu (anu)
Whatever any man does, another can try. The story of life is generally the same everywhere because we drink the same water, breathe the same air, and eat the same foods. All peoples started off from one point and have many things in common.

Ihe mmadu na-achu di ya mkpa, o ga-agbasi mbo ya ike
To obtain your goal, you are to do your utmost to attain your highest peak. Put all your energy on the line to achieve your utmost.

Ihe nwanza buru kpute na ime akwu buru ya pua
The thing that you do obsessively is the thing that destroys you. This

adage implies, ugwumagala (Chameleon), when it is being carried by nwanza would grab the legs of nwanza and kill it and eat it instead of nwanza killing it.

Ike ejiri puta uwa abughi ike eji ala uwa
You cannot cross the same river twice. When you were born, you didn't have basic faculties; as you grow up, you acquire all skills and other faculties. When you are old, the entire senses slow down. By the time you die, you acquire all fullness of life.

Ikpu nwere isi
No matter how complex a thing may be, there must be a point of **reconciliation.**

I hu m, m hu gi
|Passu (pari passu = equal parts = evenly).

Ikuku kuo a mara na fada yi trawuza
When an upheaval takes place, then you know who is and who is not; the weak fall and the strong stand. When the wind blows, the inner clothing is exposed. When an unexpected event happens, the secret is exposed.

Ikuku kuo afu akparu ohu okuku anya
When something disastrous happens, people's weaknesses are exposed.

Ikuru oche akurum ala: Onye no na oche nwe ada, onye no na ala enweghi ada.

> *Bring them to order. In the event of the villagers' gathering, the woman stood up and said that she had done with her husband and that all she wanted were her belongings and her three children. Everyone remained calm and asked her to get her belongings. After she had obtained her belongings, the villagers asked the husband to see whether his own belongings were*

among the ones the woman had taken. The man amorously rose up and hugged his wife, saying: Nkechi, I love you; you are all I have. She, in like manner, returned the love overture to him. The villagers therefore said: Go; be doing what you have demonstrated before us. You see the woman claimed the belongings but the man claimed her. Nwata kuru oche, akurum ala - for one has the chicken as well as its eggs. The one having the chair has to ask the one having the floor where he or she will put her chair. However, the man exhibited wisdom which the woman followed suit. Divorce that never happened,

—Fr. Greg Udo Njoku C.S.Sp
Counselling Is A Community Or Village Enterprise
The Sub-Clinical Therapies In Counselling Today (An Igbo-African Perspective)
Igwebuike unity is Strength) Series First Edition 2001,
(pp. 73-74).

I lewe otu ozu dowere ihu, I begbuo onwe gi n'akwa

If you see how the corpse keeps its mouth, you will cry to death. If you look at a spoilt thing constantly, you feel sorrowful often.

I kwela ka oku agutara n'ala mmuo nyuo n'ala mmadu

Never allow the fire you got from the land of the spirits to be quenched in the land of the living. You have to run because there is a danger. So, when play or argument turns into violence, please keep off. Do not allow your treasure acquired with great painful labour to be wasted on the platter of pleasure.

Ihe okuko ji mmiri achu di ya mkpa

Whatever the hen is looking for in the rain is important to her. The hen never stops making a noise to train her young ones. Once you have a goal to achieve, come rain, come sun, you are out there striving till you succeed.

Okuko hapu kwum -kwum o ga-eji gini zuo umu
A man went out to find a treasure, and when he had found it, he went home and sold all his belongings in order to obtain it (Matthew 13:44).

Ihere anaghi eme onye ara kama o bu ndi nwe ya ka o na-eme
The shame coming from your bad conduct doesn't necessarily affect you but it does affect your family and relatives.

Ihe e jiri lie ozu di gi mma ma i ria righi (ilite)
You like to enjoy the gifts given to the dead but you don't like to die when you are sick.

Ihe i ji tunyere mmadu ka a ga-eji atunyere gi
What you wish people is what comes back to you.

Ihe onye metara sobe ya
Let what you did follow you. Curse upon curse will follow a young man who killed either of his parents.

Ihe onye metara na-eso ya
People always get a reaction from what they do.

> *"The evil that men do lives after them. The good is oft interred with their bones."*
>
> **—William Shakespeare**

https://www.bringquote.com/quotes/william_shakespeare_125015

So, whatever one does follows him/her. Good deed, good reward and bad deed, bad reward.

Ihe aki ilu dara n'onu abughi ihe o na-ato
The way the bitter kola sounds is not the way it tastes in the mouth. This bitter kola sounds nice when one chews it but it always tastes bitter. This also applies to many individuals who outwardly look pleasant but inside them, they are diabolical. When they talk, they sound pleasant,

but when they act, they are deadly.

Ihe aturu na ewu huru gba nkiti ka nkita huru na gboo uja

What a peaceful man accepts as serene, a riotous man bewails with rage.

Ike anaghi ala elu, o na-agbada ala

Power never goes up; rather, it comes down. When you are working, your power diminishes because you are tired. Ike agwu agidi- is a tool that is always working, it does not tire out. Strength in adulthood does not increase; rather, it decreases gradually until it is extinguished completely upon death.

Ikpe anaghi ebi n'otu olu

Judgement is never concluded in hearing from only one side. When there is an issue, make sure you listen to both sides before passing your judgement. Never judge by hearsay.

Ike ukwu kpia eze /eze ya di ka obara anaghi agba ya

If you endure your problems, it seems you don't have problems. If you carry a heavy load with endurance, it seems to be light.

Ikpo asi ka igbu ilu

You are better to fight your anger out and live your normal life than carrying hatred in your mind against the other person.

Ikpochinkwu anaghi eruru ikpochinkwu

Literally, you don't feed one palm tree with another palm tree. It is said that marriage is between a man and a woman. It is not between a man and a man or a woman and a woman for unlike terms attract but like terms repel. Doing so is an abomination in our noble culture.

Ijiji na-enweghi onye ndumodu na-eso ozu ala n'ili

Fly (ijiji)

A fly that has no adviser goes to the grave with the corpse. One who does not listen to advice will always be led astray and lose himself. Some people are likened to some animals; when they find food, they eat until they are overfed and die. Never get so absorbed in a thing that you forget yourself and lose your sense of proper direction. Many teens miss their track by following the advice of bad people. Many of them were deceived into absorbing the life of their parents, especially, their fathers, so as to get rich. Unfortunately, they never get rich; they lost their parents, and more so, lost their own lives and progress in life. Never be a big fly that never pays any heed to wise advice. A word is enough to the wise. As you make your bed, so shall you lie on it. Be wise and successful. Simplicity goes with wisdom. The Roman philosopher and writer said, "If you want to live long, live slowly." -Cicero. Then, in Ecclesiasticus 6:18-19, it has been stated, "My son, from your earliest youth, choose instruction; till your hair is white you will keep finding wisdom. Cultivate her like the ploughman and the sower, and wait for her fine harvest."

Ina ekwu anunu na ebubu
You are talking nonsense.

Ina ekwu chighi- chighi
What you are saying does not make sense.

Iriju oke afo na ebutere nwankita akpu otele
Too much eating causes a lot of inconvenience such as obesity, heart attack, laziness, and one's inability to function well. Too much eating makes one become fat and lazy and unhealthy and unable to reason well. It makes one vulnerable to anything.

Isi mkpi nona akpa mkp
You and your child are the same person. What you have done for your child is not lost, it is what you have done for yourself. It is all you-you. Any good deed you do, is not a waste. Its reward comes back.

Isi awo ga-ahu okenye, nya agba nwata
You always work with what is available. Some farmers wait for the rain to fall before they plant their crops but the resourceful ones use irrigation to water the soil and then plant crops. You are to invent a new condition if the desired one is not available. Grey hair is for the elderly and not for the young. Thus, let your action fall on the right spot and not on the wrong one. There was a sixteen-year-old girl in my town; she has three siblings and unfortunately, their mother passed on. She, being the eldest among them, assumed the responsibility of her mother and began to work hard to train herself and her siblings. So, she assumed the mother role.

Isi ozo buru ibu isi ozo akwapu mpumpu
Somebody who is carrying a heavy load is not feeling it; but someone else who does not carry the load is the one feeling it. That means, expectations are not always realities. You do not always get what you want. You are always doing something the consequence of which falls on someone else. Nkita na eri nsi eze na ere ewu.

Isi kote ebu, o gbaa ya
The wasp will sting the head that touches it. If the head touches a wasp, it stings it. If you disturb a wasp, it will sting you. And so, keep away

from trouble. If you do evil acts, you will receive punishment. Never blame anybody for bearing the consequence of your action. You must take 100% responsibility of your action.

Imara nga ino saa ahu gi, ije ebeahu chiri ogodo gi

You know how you got in there, accordingly, you know how to get out of it. Some people speak unsparingly without respect to the extent that they do not know when they have gone over the limit. The saying advises that you know how you scatter; you should know to gather or amend.

Ina agwa onye anya npia okwu ochee na obu anya ya ka inekwu

When you are talking to a one-eyed person, he thinks you are talking about his own bad eye.

Jide nke i ji

Hold what you have firmly. If one does well, a mother would encourage the person to keep it up. My mother always felt proud to see her child doing well in life. A good mother would never like her child to go astray. Mother encourages us to be good children. Her encouragement empowered me to reach self-actualization. This motivated me to write a book on "The Pride of My Family: A Journey of Life Fulfilment." Children, if you listen to your parents, the sky is your limit.

Ji anaghi eghe na otu akuku

Whenever you hear something about somebody, never rush to conclusions. Make an inquiry, evaluate the situation, and hear from both sides before you pass judgement. My parents always said this to us; never judge by hearsay.

Ji ofo awaa ala

A person does righteous things with authority when he offends nobody. You speak and act with authority impeccably. Hence, never judge by hearsay. Mom would advise us by saying, ori anu madu tua onwe nya mbo. This means, he who eats human flesh should prick himself to feel the pain. Do to yourself what you are doing to others to know how painful it is. Love your neighbours as you love yourself. This is moral counselling from our ancestors.

Kedu nke gbasara udele na baba

The vulture has no need for a barber because he has a bald head. One who is down need fear no fall.

Kwuba aka gi oto

Keep your hands clean. Be just in all your endeavours.

Kpoo anu i na-agba aha ka nwankelu hara igbagburu onwe ya n'oso

Name the bird that you want to shoot so that the bird - "nwankeli" will stop running. Do not belabour your point; strike the nail on the head; go straight to the point. The bird "nwankeli" is a fearful bird, any little sound and it becomes afraid. Likewise, anyone with light conscience feels guilt and becomes afraid of any unusual coincidences.

Kpara akwu bu i kpara akwu, ebukwala ogbe ya wee laa

Everything needs moderation; moderation is the key to any action; anything beyond that is evil. Do not exceed the desired expectation, for anything in excess is distasteful. Take some of the palm fruits but the bunch of palm fruits belongs to the owner.

Leenu aka m o, achoghim nsogbu

I am innocent. I have no contention with anyone. I have no axe to grind with anyone. I want nothing but only peace of mind.

Mbe adighi ako na ilulu

The wise man is never deficient in wise things.

M norokwa n'ulo ma ihe fuo, ma ya abukwala m ji ya

Let me stay home when something is missing but let me not be the one who steals it. Let something happen but let me not be the cause.

Ogara nya afuru na ulo na eli ozu nwata une

When something happens and no one is at home except you, you have to bear the brunt. It falls to your lot to do whatever is necessary. Ihe mee ma ozu anwuna.

Mgbe- mgbe mere nwa awo epughi odu

Postponing makes the frog not develop a tail. Postponing inhibits progress. Do not postpone till tomorrow what you can do today for time and the hour wait for no one. If you hurry, you surpass obstacles. In my book, "Building Up Self-Confidence - A Fundamental Way of Conquering Fear," I did emphasize much on obstacles as well as the consideration that they hinder one's progress in life. Please avoid them, otherwise, you will not be successful in your endeavours. They will help you to remain in your comfort zone forever. Challenge it, succeed, and celebrate your success.

Mgba gbakwasara nwa ite ya siri

If a pot is being supported, it stands. Always seek a firm standing base for an action. If a pot is supported on a pot-stand, it stands firmly. For this reason, you need efficacious role models in everything you do. Mirror them, copycat them, and benchmark them.

Mmebo e meboro ogaranya ka ogbugbu e gburu ya

To slander or calumniate a celebrated person is like killing the person. An insult given to a famous man is like killing him. This is an example of an honourable woman who committed an atrocity and was punished by "Umuada na ndi amala" by sending her away from her matrimonial home on Eke Market Day with a yellow foliage palm-frond on her neck and banished her forever from her lawful village. She became an outcast and has no right from her family and from the entire village as well as the entire town at large. Thus, be respectful and you will be respected too. Mama used to say to her children, *"O ji ofo ehibe isi, ahubeghi ajo mmuo,"* meaning, anyone who sleeps with a charm would one day encounter a powerful spirit who would harass him. *Okuko mmanya na-egbu ahubeghi ufu ara na-awu*, meaning, a drunk hen has never seen a mad fox. Those who think that they are more powerful than the others and do all sorts of diabolical things would one day meet with a supernatural being who would overpower them and bring them to justice. Never say you are powerful because there is a higher being than you are who would one day call you to order. Another maxim that my mother used in addressing us is this; *"Akakpara eze udele oko muoo chiri nya eze,"* meaning, when you come face to face with an unyielding formidable force, then you must put up otherwise you perish.

Madu anaghi ebu ibu na aka abua

You do not carry heavy loads on both hands at the same time. Do not over-burden yourself. *Odighi nma ibu na aka na abua kuru, nga onu gi ga elos; agbara aka na ere odu okpu nma:* Conform to the specifics of what you can do comfortably at a time. Do not overload yourself to the detriment of losing your effectiveness.

Mgbe mmiri na-ama ohu ka o na-ama onye kpo ya aga

As rain falls on the slave, so it falls on the person who holds her. Any difficult the slave you are holding encounters on the way, the same befalls on you the holder.

Ebe nwata na-ebe akwa na-atu aka, nna ya ga-ano ebe ahu, nne ya anoro ya

Any bush or place a child cries and points his finger to, either the father or the mother is there. For a punishment to endure on the sufferer, the one punishing must sustain a pain also. Both master and slave suffer. Onye Jim na ala ji onwe ya.

Mgbe o bula o na-eme mkpotu

He always blows a trumpet. This wise saying applies to an individual who speaks to be noticed. He always makes noise. He is pompous, aiming to be noticed.

> *"Take good care not to practice your righteousness in front of men in order to be observed by them."*
> **—Mathew 6:1.**

When you preserve yourself, you harvest a rich future.

Madu anaghi ata nti ya ata

A difficult person whom you cannot take for granted. One cannot penetrate him. He is unapproachable. He is not influenced by other people.

Mmuo anaghi aga ije ziriziri

The spirit is subtle; it is not one-sided; it is versatile.

Mgbada chekwaa onwe ya, ya zaa ekpuruke

When you prepare yourself, you harvest a good future. The spirit does not act half-heartedly but whole-heartedly.

Mgbede na ogidi m na agbara otuto enwere nke m lu ada ya

No matter what it is, it does not concern me. It is of no avail to toil and suffer for mgbede and ogidi who do not matter anyway.

M na ata na bu gi n'obi, gi na ata na abu m n'anya

When I chew, I spit it on your chest, but you chew and you spit on my eyes. The literal meaning of this is, when I do that which is good to you, you pay me back with evil. I cater for your uplift but you crave for my downfall. You are advised not to be this kind. Be of good behaviour.

Mmiri doro n'eju dooro nwa nkita

The water in the broken earthen pot is always for the dog. Wherever you go, you will come back to meet your problem. No matter how far you go, your problem is still your problem. It is your responsibility to sort it out.

Mmiri ju awo onu, o na-ebe woo -woo

When you are overloaded, your capability becomes zero. When you are overworked, your output is diminished. When you are filled with joy, you won't know how to express your joy.

Mmiri na ezo mkpu na afu

When something happens, some people are benefited or are blessed and some are not. The more it continues to rain, the more some benefit. The more the crisis rages, the more he is empowered.

Mara na ukwu na aga wara- wara, anya na ele zam -zam na ahu ya

Any movement made by a smart diabolical fellow it is also seen by good smart people. There is nothing hidden that will not be seen. It takes a good eye to see a good thing.

Mgbada gbata ajo oso a gbairi ya ajo egbe

When the gazelle runs very fast, you give him a fast shot. When things get tough, you get tough too in order to succeed. When it runs with a great tempo, you fire at it with a great tempo.

Mgbe onye ji teta ura bu ututu ya

When you wake up from sleep is your morning. Your day starts when you wake up. Be prompt and punctual. All things do not start at the same time and all peoples do not act the same way all the time.

Mpere adaala na obu anu ji nku ga azoro onye laa

The little brown bat has fallen into a pit, and he must escape he who has wings. But when unusual animals without wings fall into the pit, they cannot escape unless someone comes to help them. When a matter takes a serious turn, only a person with accurate knowledge knows it and has the acuity to manoeuvre it.

Mgbaoba bu ogbakwuru olua

The party is first come, first serve. Or the earlier you come, the better. *Ka onye si agba egwu ka aka si ekwuru ya. Anu bu uzo na anu nmiri oma.*

Ana esi na ulo amara mma puba ama

You have to be in good relationship with your family first before an outsider. You have to be good at home because that is where your honour lies. Charity begins at home. Never be good outside while at home, you're evil.

Anaghi eji ututu a ma njo ahia

You can never tell the day from the look of the morning. The failure of marketing is not confirmed from the uncertainty of the morning. That is to say, the situation can change to success with time.

Ndi mu na ha toro ga-ako akuko aji m gbara

My mates will tell you about my pubic hair. Those who know the identity of me will talk about my characteristics. One cannot talk about himself or herself, rather, people around you and those who know you well will do so. People are your mirror.

Ndi bi n'ulo ugegbe anaghi atupu okwute

Those who live in a glass house should never throw a stone. The well-known people are those who always live a gentle and exemplary life. The measure that you measured him by will be measured to you in equal terms. One who is prone to be hurt should not start a fight.

Ndi onya akpa eli ozu

Ndi onya akpa eli ozu are those who carry a handbag while burying a corpse. The typical example of ndi onya akpa eli ozu are the village men who are the opportunists. Once their fellow man dies, they do all sorts of things to win that man's wife and other wealth of the dead man. They are burying the dead but their minds are on what they can gain. Often, when one of our popular village men dies, some men would come forward and become the advisers to his wife and his daughters. In their hearts, these men know well enough what they want. They have no genial interest for that family, rather, what they could gain from them.

Onye isi amaghi mgbe ekere nku ukwa

A fool does not know when a decision was made against him. Consequently, anyone who does not understand, would fall victim to these men who would cheat her. So, beware of what is!

Nga ha hara zute, ha hara kee

Let those involved in the stealing, share the booty among themselves and never include those who did not participate. Enjoy your ill-gotten gains alone for it is on you that its evil will fall. The moral aspect of this is never kill someone to make your living. Never lie against someone to pave your way, otherwise, the consequences will be on you.

Nga okwugburu onweya no, omegburu onweya no ya

Where there is smoke, there is fire. Where there is a nagger, there is also a rascal,

Nga ana-ekwuokwu ndu ka ana ekwu okwu onwu

Where you plan for life, you also plan for death. You have to plan for all including death. Many people never think of making a will to their family because they feel they will live long.

Nga aka ha nwanyi, ya tukwasa ya di ya

A woman always pleases her husband by doing her best.

Nga onye oso gbaduru ka onye ije jeduru

If you run very fast to reach the target, the one walking slowly and steadily will also eventually reach the same target. In all your endeavours, plan well in order to attain your goal successfully. Follow your specifics step by step and leave room for rest; you will win the Golden Fleece.

Nga enwere ohu madu ma onweghi onye nwere ike itota nginga

In some cases, many children mean much wealth. In others, many people mean scarcity of wealth. Some are great in number but very little in performance.

Ngwugwu aga, ato -ato, anaghi atupu ya atupu

Never hurry to open a seal that will eventually be opened. To live long, it is necessary to live slowly (Cicero). Never punch a hole in a parcel that will eventually be opened. Do not leak a secret that will, in the long run, be published.

Ngwere gbaba oso hara ukwu osisi, umuaka kpara ya aka
When a lizard runs and neglects the tree, children will capture it. As an elder, never disgrace yourself before the children.

Ngwere si n'elu osisi daa, onweghi onye tooro ya, o bido towe onwe ya
A lizard fell from a tree and no one was there to cheer him up; he looked round and nodded his head, cheering himself. When people do not appreciate you, do appreciate yourself and rate yourself highly, especially when you're doing what is right. Agara akpom, akpom onwem. You must always appraise and approve yourself to uphold your self-image and integrity. "Agara etom, etom onwen."

Ngwere emela isi ka agwo
The lizard's head now seems to be that of a snake. Something that is very trivial has now become very serious. As a result, the matter is now serious. When the head of a lizard turns to be a snake, there is danger, therefore, be cautious.

Nkea a burula akaraka m: onye m mere ihe oma, ojiri ihe ojoo kwuo mugwo
It has been my destiny that whenever I do well to anyone, he pays me with evil. Sometimes, it is one's destiny to be paid back in bad coins because it is said your payment is in heaven.

Nke mkpata ka mkpata; ihem mkwuru ekwuchalam ya
I stand by what I have said. What I have said, I have said; that is the truth. This is asking us to dwell in saying the truth.

Nkirika ekete ka ana echeta mgbe ana ekwo ntu ututu
The useless basket is only remembered when removing the ash. An old overused basket is only remembered when its duty of removing ash is needed. An old soldier never dies. It shows that no one is insignificant. You are useful in certain things.

Nke onye na akwu, nke nwaekpem mana nke mbele ochichi onye na anu ya

There are people who do some things and nobody hears about them, but there are other people who can do something and that echoes everywhere over and over again.

Nke m mere ka mma

What I do is always the best. No one calls his market a small one. *Nne obi na ukwu nne*, nne bu nne. Nne bu nne. My act is always the best. In life some people always assume self-righteousness.

Nkita na-achu agu na-chukwa ndu nya

A dog that pursues a lion is pursuing his life. This is an example of a child who killed his father. He killed his father thinking that he would go free. No, he did not go free. Always be careful and think before you act. And always look before you leap. Avoid those who nicknamed you "Ok Boy." They are flattering you. When you are trapped, they will run away and disown you. Be watchful. Those who plot to hurt an innocent and powerful man are plotting against themselves.

Nkwu darue ala onweghi zi onwe ya

Make hay while the sun shines. Ownership must be responsible to be honourable.

Nkita anaghi ata okpukpo anyabara ya na olu

One does not ruin the duty for which one has been delegated. "Care keeps his watch in every old man's eye. And where lodgeth, sleep will never lie." (Shakespeare). No one does away with what he has been entrusted with. Never sell trust bestowed on you. So, when you are made responsible for a task, it is praiseworthy that you uphold the integrity of doing a nice job of it for there your honour lies. *Madu anaghi egbu onye zoro ya na -aka ebe*. You are to be hospitable to your guests.

Nkiti ka e-eji agbagbu onye nzuzu

Always ignore a fool. Silence is the best answer to a fool. No everything you will respond.

Nkita nwere ndidi na-eri anu uru

A patient dog eats the fattest bone. Labor omnia vincit (work conquers everything).

> *"He that would have a cake out of the wheat must tarry the grinding."*
>
> —*Shakespeare*
>
> https://quotes.yourdictctionary.com/author/william-shakepeare/582706

Nkita anaghi ebu isi n'ibe nti n'abuo

A dog does not carry dirt in two ears. A dog does not clean itself. No one is weak in both hands; either left or right is. No one is totally incapable of doing something.

Nkita na eri nsi eze na ere ewu

One who does something and cleans up is exonerated (freed) and one who does something and does not clean up is the one that gets the blame. Someone does evil and another earns the rebuke for the evil.

Nkita bu nsi nonu choro ka onye obuna nu isi ya

Those who commit atrocity without remorse or shame want others to feel their joy in evil (sadist).

Nke onye na-akwu nke nwa ekpem mana nke mbele ochi-chi enweghi onye na-anu ya

Those who are smart go free when they have done something wrong, but those who are not smart always get caught. Those who know how to steal get away but those who do not get caught. Avoid getting involved. There are people who can do something and nobody will hear it, but there are other people who can do something and it will resound everywhere. But it is said, let your light be on top of the hill so people can see it.

Nmiri Chukwu anaghi asapu agwa

One whose duty is to deal with indelible materials has a big problem of being clean of the materials. For example, a painter that uses acid-fast paints cannot totally clean himself to be rid of the paint. Atiti paint is still on him. No holy water can clean a bad character. We say, Ime elu me ala, nwa a holi dika nwa a holi. The leopard can never change its colours.

Nkwa na aku ka onye si agba egwu

Things happen to you according to the way you think and behave.

Nku no na mba na eghere mba nri

The local man is more active in his environment. The firewood in your environment is enough to cook your food for you. The solution to your problems is affordable and within your reach in your environment. Hence, you are comfortable in your environment.

Nne-ewu na ata nkwara, nwa ya na eleya

When the mother goat chews her cud, the baby goat watches. So, parents should be careful what they do in the presence of their children because they absorb whatever they observe the adults doing.

Nne nwata lota ahia, o dika nne ndi ozo agaghi alota

When you are fortunate, you feel nobody else is. When your mother is around, every mother is around. When your mother is absent, every mother is absent

Nne murum kporo m obubo, kedukwanu maka onye na-abughi ya muru m

If my mother calls me a bad name, how much more would another mother call me? In all you say or do, give glory to God and be positive.

Nwanne onye na-agba egwu ojoo, nku anya na-ako ya uko

When your sibling dances badly, your eyebrow itches. You always feel ashamed when your relative misbehaves in public, for his/her honour or dishonour is also yours.

Nnunu agaghi efecha, uwa aghara ihu okpuru afo ya
There is no bird that flies that the earth does not see its underside. Nothing is unseen or unknown to the earth.

Nwanne awo na azopu ya mmiri na afo
Your closest relative knows about you and he is the one that is most concerned about you. If a child does what his father does, he will pay for his father's debt.

Mmiri masaa ajo ukwu, onaghi amasa ajo okwu
Water can wash away a bad footprint but it cannot wash away a bad word. It is said that one must safeguard one's tongue against what is bad for bad words will return to the speaker and bad words stir up anger and are remembered each time the speaker is seen. Stay clear from bad words for they reflect in the memory. Likewise, bad deed. Avoid them.

Njo n'ihu ano m ya n'azu, njo n'azu ano m ya n'ihu
Whether the devil is in the front or whether it is at the back, I am on the safe side. Then, I shall not be affected no matter how the devil prevails. No matter how the evil comes, I am covered and cannot be hurt.

Noro na-egbu nwaekpe ma uriala na-eri ji gi
Stay there to prepare your barn while land ants eat your yams. These words advise us to avoid postponing our plans; rather, move on to achieve your goal. If you hurry, you pass obstacles. My mother would advise you, "My children, be prompt to harvest your yams to avoid pests destroying them." Moreso, be effective in your decision-making.

Nsi egu bu onwu ya
He who eats too much and defecates too much is going to die. Too much of everything is bad. Be moderate.

Nsi anaghi ajo njo na afo ma obu anyuputa ya nke ona ajo njo

The food is not bad in the stomach but when defecated, it becomes dirt. Nothing is bad in the offing. Not until it has progressed would evil therein show up.

Nwagbogho ga-ahu ihe ibe ya huru

A young girl will see what other women have seen. If any of us is behaving as if her own womanhood is unique, mom would put across this wise saying to the person to caution her.

Nwa agasighi ike na-eribi ukwu

Slow and steady wins the race. Slow water runs deep. Dangerous water or a dangerous human being acts unexpectedly. Slow movement makes one tired of walking. You have to be slow and steady but not so slow that you are out of time. It has to be prompt and steady.

Nwa aturu merua ala oma okwu (Olokwa) na mbara ezi

One time, the sheep soiled their pen by urinating and defecating all over the place such that they, instead of going into their shelter, remained outside in a disorderly manner. Thus, this becomes a counselling proverb for a boy who refused to obey his parents' orders. There was a time when rain was drizzling and the mother of a boy of 11 years asked him to join others who were sent to fetch cassava stems for replanting on the farm. Other boys went and returned with bundles of cassava stems but the boy refused to follow them because he said it was raining. As a result of remorse of a guilty conscience for disobeying his mother, the boy did not come home that day for dinner. He followed his friend home and slept in his friend's room. In the morning, when it was time for him to go home, he was not able to rise up for he was sweating, his feet and hands were trembling and he could not walk. He was exhausted with an insatiable hunger for he had eaten no food except for fruits for the whole day. He was carried on the back to his mother who blamed him for not coming for dinner. Before the people, his mother brought out his dinner which she had saved for him. He ate the food heartily and sprang up with strength and promptly went to the cassava farm to gather the cassava stems. He thanked his mother and promised to listen and obey her. He grew up a gentleman, having been counselled by experience. This is what psychology calls positive reinforcement in teaching a child a lesson. *Anu (bee) baa nwata, ohu okporokporo iji egwu abia ya.* And so, the saying: *Nwa Aturu merua ala oma okwu na mbara ezi.*

Nwa- nwa ogbenye anaghi awusa nkpuru ano
A poor man's child is always frugal and not lavish.

Hie aka n'anya ugboro asaa
Be careful. That is being completely cautious.

Nwa'm gbuo n'ala (daa juu)
My child, stay calm. My mom did apply this phrase when any of her children or anybody she knew was troublesome. She would advise the child in question to be at ease and in other words, to avoid trouble. She would also add, *O ji oso agbakwuru ogu, amaghi na ogu bu onwu.* This means, whoever runs towards war, never knows that the war is dreadful; therefore, avoid trouble and listen to your elders and respect them. She would then say, okro anaghi aka onye kuru ya, meaning that the okro plant never grows taller than the person who planted it. In other words, a child is never above his parents, no matter his status in life. He must be loyal to his parents. This is in terms of loyalty, otherwise, average parents in Igbo culture always wish their children to do better than them in life in progressive aspects. According to H.R.H. EZE Edmund Osuagwu 1992, ***"No one ever prays that his or her child be greater than him or her. It is the mark of a civilized society to make progress."***

Therefore, we always pray and hope for a greater and better tomorrow. Subsequently, in Igboland culture, it is the wish of parents to see their children performing far better than them. Parents feel fulfilled when their children are excelling. Also, parents never wish to see their children misbehaving; that is the reason why the Igbos put up the proverb above. That is, be careful or calm down.

Nwa'm, jide ogu" na ihe o bula i na-eme
My child, whatever you do, keep your hands clean. Always be just in all your endeavours. Be sure you are on the righteous side in everything you do.

Nwa'm o bu isi ozo buru ibu, isi ozo kwapu mkpumkpu?
One head carries a load, and another head forms a hunchback. One does a thing; another person suffers the outcome of it.

Nwa'm meghee anya gi
My children, open your eyes, that is, be wise.

Nwa'm kwuru na ukwu gi
Be yourself, stand on your word and never allow anyone to influence you to anything that your mind does not accept.

Nwanne nkapia na ebii onu
The person who knows you is the one who can deal with you or knows your weakness and strength.

Nwa'm kwaa efe nga oga-aba gi
My children, cut your coat according to your size. Do not overestimate or underestimate your talent.

Nwa agbogho ara juru na obi abughi nwata
A girl with full breasts is mature, so, you have to act like a responsible fellow.

Nwa'm, anya ruo gi ala:
My child, be vigilant.

Nwa'm, i ga taa ahuhu mana-eri uru
My child, you have to suffer before pleasure. When you suffer first, you will earn the fruit of your labour.

Nwa nhuho gara na ohia horo okasi
It was an intelligent man who was able to recognize okasi vegetable as edible. Okasi vegetable is very rare and small in size in the forest and it was said it was a wise man who was led by the spirit that recognized the vegetable as edible. It is used in making African soups and it has a high level of ***vitamin C and antioxidants*** (*chemicals that capture free radicals that cause illnesses*). It is an important vegetable in Nigeria's daily meal, especially in Igboland.

Nwa nnunu si n'ala benye n'okpuru mkpu, nokwa ebe o no
The bird that stands on the ground and perches on the anti-hill is still on the ground: One, convinced against his opinion, is still of the same opinion.

Nwa ofo diadi si na nkwa ejiri akpukpo madu kwoo, nde na agba egwu ya bu nwa madu that is nwa ofo diadi
This assertion is made by Ibos today but it came from time immemorial. Here, we are saying we are the living replica of the original Being. The Egyptians were familiar with this statement as far back as 1550 to 1295 BC, the Egyptian eighteenth dynasty when a Pharaoh (Egyptian King) was named Tutankhamen (1336 to 1327 BC). This name means "living image of the god, Amun (Amun was Egyptian King of all gods whose name later changed to Amen-Ra from which the Christian Amen was derived). This statement was again mentioned in the Old Testament in the Bible, (Genesis 1:26), and God went on to say: "Let us make man in our image, according to our likeness." Genesis was written by Moses who departed from Egypt (Exodus) in 1250 BC. He must have known this saying from the Egyptians.

Here is an Ibo Creation Poem

Eburu ukwu aru atokwasara ukwu aru abua
Eburu ukwu aru atokwasara ukwu aru ato
Eburu ukwu aru atokwasara ukwu aru ano
Eburu ukwu aru atokwasara ukwu aru ise and so on iri.

By adding one to the old number, a new number with a new character is created. This is in line with the modern science discovery of how the ninety-two natural elements were created. By adding one proton (P) and one electron (E) to hydrogen (primary substance containing one proton and one electron), a new number of 2P and 2E is created, giving us helium with a new character. If we add one proton and one electron to helium 3E, it gives us lithium with a new character and so on to 92 elements. This idea came down from Egyptians who said God of wisdom taught them these things. Therefore, we conclude that our ancestors knew how we were created for we are a "living image of God" by multiplying one number into many folds "eburu ukwu atokwasara ukwu aru abua."

Reference: Our history is principally oral, not from archival records, hence, stringent attention is paid when counselling our youth so that they stick to the application of the right protocols before they fall out of grace rather than counsel them when they have fallen out of glory. Here are the books: Treasures of Tutankhamen by editors: Katharine Stoddert, Joan K. Hott and Sara Hudson, (pp. 127-141); Tut=image, ankh= living Amun=of Amun, King of all gods. Sources from Ancient Egypt by Helen Strudwick (pp. 9, 80); History's timeline by Jean Cooke, Ann Kramer, Theodore Rowland Entwistle (p. 11), Molecular Biology by C.U.M. Smith (p. 65). The Treasures of Ancient Egypt (pp. 17-19). New World Translation of Holy Scriptures by WatchTower Bible and Tract Society (p. 8).

Nwanza nuru na akwu, odika oga aka nne ya, Nwanyi ga ahu ihe ibe nya huru, Okuko nmanya na egbu ga ahu ufu ara na awe
The chicks of nwanza (wren) are usually bigger than their mother because they are well fed by their mothers. But when they are grown up and are on their own, they have to work hard to find food and by so doing, they become lightweight like their mother. Likewise, young women, when under parental care, are well equipped with all their needs such as good food, fashionable dresses, cosmetics and good education. But when on their own, they meet with obstacles and hard nuts they have to crack in order to reach the meaty stuff. They learn

how to plan strategies for reaching a goal whether in the house or at work. They exercise restraint in all expressions in order to be on the safe side. All these things the parents have been doing for them, they now have to do for themselves. All these involvements make them busy, consciously thinking about self-preservation. Eventually, when they get into the child-bearing stage, a whole new arena ushers in many unknowns. What has been taken for granted becomes obvious, demanding solvable answers. If you have been critical of your mom, that she has been defaulting when she should not, then you know it is your turn to deliberate. Now, you see what she has seen. Nwanyi ga ahu ihe ibe nya huru. Okuku nmanya na egbu ga afu ufu ara na awe. Do not be too intoxicated with too much rejoicing; otherwise, you will be destroyed by the evil therein. I, the author, cite myself here; when I was growing up, I used to hear from my mother and other women discussing their problems and each time, I kept wondering what they could be. Moreover, I did say within myself that these moms were always talking rubbish. I then asked myself what was that problem all about. Behold, when I found myself in the USA as a missionary, student, and as a worker, I came to the realization of what that problem they used to discuss was all about. Then, I pitied them and learnt from them. More importantly, this experience helped me to handle all my affairs well wherever I find myself. I urge you, children, do listen to your parents and pay attention to what they are saying because you will be able to acquire a lot of wisdom from them. Here is a biblical quote to assist you to seek the wisdom that can lead you to self-actualization.

> *"Wisdom is bright and does not grow dim. By those who love her, she is really seen, and found by those who look for her. Quick to anticipate those who desire her, she makes herself known to them. Watch for her early and you will have no trouble; you will find her sitting at your gates..."*
> **—Wisdom 6:12-16.**
> **The Jerusalem Bible & Popular**
> **Edition Darton, Longman & Todd 1974, (p. 882).**

Nwanza kpa nku odika ya aka nne ya
When you are in the youthful stage, you tend to be greater than your parents. When a girl is growing up to maturity, she develops a strong character equivalent to those of her parents. So, she begins to claim equality with the parents. She declines to do what she used to do in the house. That is, she declines to do household chores.

Nwa nza ga –agba obara nga oha
A small bird bleeds according to its size. Literally, it means that one has to do things according to one's capability.

Nwa nza bu eze n'akwu ya
An Englishman said every man is king in his castle. No matter how little you are, you are very important in yourself because no one is insignificant. Be fulfilled for what you are.

Nwa nagum ma obughi nke onye agba
I want children but not from a sick woman.

Nwa Okuko egbe bu na eti ka uwa nu olu ya, ma obughi na ihe ji ya ga aha ya
A troubled person complains not because they will hear and release him from his troubles, but that people should hear his voice and be aware. One who is sick is telling people about it not for them to cure him because the illness is incurable.

Nwata gbakaa ute ya, o hie n'ala
If a child destroys her mat, she lies on the floor. Always have a reserve to take care of a rainy day. Cherish what you have.

Nwanyi ga afu ihe ibe ya furu (devise)
Referring to the attitude of a young girl towards her mother; she claims she would do this or that better than the mother but the fact is, she will grow into motherhood to discover what mothers have seen.

Nwanyi ihere na-amugbu nwa

A shy woman delivers her child dead. A shy person does not perform well because she suffers psychological inhibition.

Nwanyi si na ya amaghi afa di ya, oga ekwu afa ya ma aka kpara ya

When a woman refuses to say her husband's name, she will do so when she is mistreated. If you deny the truth, you will accept the truth when it is due.

Nwata kuru oche m kuru ala

The one on the chair is the one that has to fall, but the one on the ground cannot fall. If you claim the chair, I claim the ground; therefore, you have no place to put your chair. So, my claim is greater than yours.

Nwata gbere egbere suo m oku, m gbere egbere sogwara ya

If you play ignorance and burn me with fire, I will play ignorance and burn you with fire; sometimes, life is tit for tat.

Nwata na enweghi nne na nna na esi na ndumodu ndi nwere nne na nna amata ihe

A wise fellow learns from the mistakes of experienced people. A certain man lost his father when he was a day old for he was born the same night his father died. He grew up under the auspices of his grandfather who imparted elderly wisdom to him but he lacked fatherly affection. When the grandfather died, he lived with the man who remarried his mother. He had to fend for himself with regard to understanding things and how things worked. His new foster parent was not paternal enough, so he had to seek good advice from those who were brotherly and elderly. These people showed him his father's estate, property, and land and also taught him how to recover all these things. Step by step, one by one, day by day with these people's assistance, he gradually took over his father's properties. It was not without difficulties that he succeeded. He paid a huge price for daring to be in his estate. Assassination was attempted on him five times but he escaped unhurt and lived to be 120 years of age, enjoying all the privileges of a king, head Nze, head Urasi; head Dibe Afa, Head Owu. He signed an agreement with the

British Royal Niger Company, now the UAC Ltd of Nigeria, to stop the slave trade and endorse trade on palm oil and palm kernels. He received three royalty payments from the Royal Niger Company and won the court case on the title of the land of the town. He was revered as *"Nwamereonwa, nwa mere onwa"*- The redeemer of anyone in trouble.

Another man lost his mother when he was three months old. So, an old woman suckled him till he was able to eat solid food. There was in the family another childless woman whose hair was so unkempt that children did not eat her food because of her loose hair. This was an opportunity for this man for he had no competition for her food and so he attached himself to her. When the woman started cooking, the man would sit around till the food was done and he would receive his portion with gratitude. When he went to school, he lived with another woman who had only a child, Ossai. Ossai's mother treated Ossai and the man equally just as if they both were her children. The man and Ossai were obedient and dutiful. He learnt how to listen to moms, how to do household chores and how to learn in school. He grew up a giant of a man, loyal, expedient, diligent, truthful, effective, and adept. Twice, he represented his father in village cases by interpreting his father's statement to the lawyer handling the case and also by interpreting the lawyer's statement to his father. His father won both cases and so his father appointed him the head chief of the town to replace him. As a head chief, he resigned from his Local Government Division, as his Clan Court Judge too. He then became his Clan's Local Councillor and his Town's Divisional Councillor as well as his Local Town Divisional Financial Committee Member; also, he became a Government Contractor. He built schools, maternities, dispensaries, courthouses and churches. This noble man also became his Town Head Chief known as "Second Head Nze." He was adept in judicial sagacity in the adjudication of his local markets. As a result of his nobility, he was revered as *Nna Oma, Echimkini, Abiazie enu odika ananana, ma abiagharia uwa odika naa echirine.*

Nwata namu elu nne na nna ya n'amu akwa
If a child is displaying a bad attitude, the parents should practice how to avoid future disaster. Never allow your child to practice a dangerous

act for it is you who will regret the future disaster.

Nwata anaghi ata mkpisi aka na enye ya nri aru
You do not hurt your source of livelihood. You do not ruin your source of livelihood.

Nwata rie ihe nna ya riri, anya ya emeghee
When a child eats what his father ate, his eyes open. When a child matures as his father, he begins to do things like his father.

Nwayoo -nwayoo ka-eji aracha ofe di oku
Slowly, slowly, you sip a hot soup. Step by step, you tackle a difficult task. When you are dealing with difficult things, you need to be very careful, otherwise, you will get hurt and lose the thread of things.

Nwata gahie ozi, o gaa ya ugboro abuo
When a child does a bad job on an errand, he has to do it again. You are advised to be accurate in doing your duties.

Nwata gaa ajo ije ya kpata nku
When a child fails to do what he is expected to do, he fetches firewood instead to cover up his misdeed. When a child has done something wrong, he or she does some good deeds to cover up the wrongdoing.

Nwata kwochaa aka o soro ndi okenye rie nri
If a child washes her hands well, he eats at the same table as the elders. When a young person becomes prosperous, he qualifies to share with the elders. In other words, when you excel in great works of life, you at once become a member of the elders' society. Subsequently, when a young man attains excellence, he joins the elders.

Nwata bulie nna ya elu, ogodo ekpuchie ya anya
If you attempt to do what is greater than yourself, you will be instantly defeated. Therefore, do not attempt to contend with a person significantly greater than you.

Nwata mee ihe nna ya mere, ya kwukwaa ugwo nna ya ji

You have to be like your father in all good respects, endeavouring, enduring and prospering and paying your father's debts.

Nwata fu onye ona egbu ike na adu nya

When one sees an easy task, one is willing to do something.

Nwata ga-eto eto wara ogodo, ifufe fee ya bulie ya

When a child is not matured and begins to wear a wrapper, when the wind blows, it blows him away. One has to attain maturity before engaging in certain responsibilities. You have to be mature enough for things before you can handle them.

Nwata jee egwu onwa fu enyi ya nwanyi osi na egwu onwa agbaka

When you find what you cherish, your joy is consummated. When you find what you cherish, you feel fulfilled.

Nwoke bie ezi ndu obanye n'agba ndichie

If man lives very well according to accepted traditional rules, he becomes a member of blessed ancestors.

Obara anaghi atu asi

Blood does not tell lies. The blood of the son must reflect that of the father. Like begets like. This proverb portrays the fact that if one of the parents is a thief, it is a must that one of the children will be a thief. No doubt about it. Also, DNA is a powerful bond between the parents and their children.

Obi bu akpa; onye o bula nya nke ya

Everybody knows herself better than anybody else. The heart is like a bag; everybody carries his or her own.

O bu ahu uzo a si muta oku?

You do not need a light when you see clearly, but you need light when it is dark. If you do not know the truth, you have to research to find it.

Obu aru na nne na nna ini nwa ha

It is unusual for parents to bury their child though it happens sometimes.

Obughi nani onye nwuru anwu ka a na-edozi olu

It is not only the dead man whose neck we strengthen but the living also. We not only pay attention to the dead but also to the living. When an elderly is missing the track, he will be corrected.

Obiara ele'm omugwo na-ele eke'm

One who tends to me when I give birth to a baby uses that advantage to know my private part. One very close to you is the one who is supposed to know your weak point.

Obughi mmadu gbachaa ejiaku, anya ato ya n'akwukwa

Even though he is through with his cooking, he still remains by the fireside. Why should one still continue flogging a dead horse? Do not belabour your points.

Oburu ibu emeghi ogu

This applies to someone who is big for no reason or empty like a vessel that makes most sound. My mother, whenever anyone was quarrelling, would call the person "oburu ibu emeghi ogu" – meaning that, that person could only scold and talk but won't do more than that. This corresponds with what William Shakespeare said a long time ago about when we are confronted by fearful obstacles. He said to the ghost of a murdered king flashing its eyes, "***There is no speculation in those eyes; it is the eye of childhood that fears a painted devil.***"

Again, William Shakespeare described a man as, "A tale told by an idiot, full of sound and fury, signifying nothing." However, we are also unique and different and there is something else we do not understand. We have become aesthetic (loving beautiful things) and have a strong ardent desire for happiness in all things. When in a congregation of people, we should not feel stage-fright or fidgeting (feeling nervous restlessness), especially among those people who mostly sound their power only on their lips; summon up courage and never fear them.

Obiara egbum, gbue onwe ya/Njo emena njo emena ka anyi la
Let your evil be on you and yours and not on me and mine.

Obiara be m abia gbulem onaba mkpumkpu apula ya n'azu
Let me be hospitable to my guest and let him pay me back with the same coin.

Obughi taa ka m huwara Awusa na uta
I have been here for a long time; everything that has passed by, I have seen them all: I have been seeing Hausas with bows and arrows for a long time, therefore, nothing perturbs me.

Obu anu ehi n'isi ma were ukwu na-akpi adam
A greedy person always craves that which he has already got in great quantity.

Oburu na nme nya imara na anama eri adu Orlu na Amike sonso
It is the impossible thing I can do because I can never eat adu which Orlu and Amike abstain from eating.

Obu onye laba nka ya na-aku ukpa?
When one is old, the person should not plant ukpa, because he will not live to eat it. When you are old, you do not need to continue working or doing things impossible for you.

Obu onye kpara nku ahuhu si ngwere biara ya ura
Once you collect firewood that has a lot of ants in it, the lizard will visit you. My mother used to say this proverb to any of us when the person got into trouble. She would say that if you never look for trouble, trouble will never come to you. A good example of this is the story of a woman who planned the murder of her husband and in the end, the umuada- that is, the daughters of the land - punished her by sending her back to her fatherland on Eke Market day. Mama would say, do not trouble trouble until trouble troubles you. She would end up her wise saying by putting across this adage: *O jig ofo ehibe isi, ahubeghi ajo mmuo;* this means, one who sleeps with charm under his pillow

has never seen a powerful ghost. Thus, the fact that people keep quiet doesn't mean that people cannot act. The literal interpretation is, if you think that charm is your power, don't be surprised when one day, your charm will not save you. Anyone who thinks he/she is more powerful than everybody will definitely meet a superior being one day. Never think that no one can handle you; just watch out for the fullness of time to come. Then, you will be powerless and regretful. For this reason, mellow down.

O bu onye okwu biri n'onu

He is the one that has the veto power. He is the kind that says the last word and whatever he says, goes. He has the last word.

Onye ji ngwere hapu ngwere na ngwere abughi anu ana eriri

Whoever is bothering me should leave me alone, for I am no problem to anyone.

Ochu nwa okuko nwe ada

You will fall many times if you pursue a hen vainly. The one chasing an innocent person is the one that has to fall and get hurt. Whoever pursues an innocent person will always be the one that falls into trouble. Never deal with an innocent fellow because God hears the cry of such a person.

Ochichara mere ihe e boro oke

The cockroach did what was termed to be the rat's deed. One, who does something wrongly in a covert way, always escapes being blamed but one who does the same thing as an extrovert, gets blamed for something that someone else has done. One must always tidy up one's works and not leave behind a trail of what has been done. When it is known by the public that one is always untidy in behaviour, any time a sloppy act is observed, people attribute the act to that person.

Odi mkpunkpu na-eme ire

Short but mighty in action. Literally, this kind of person is the type people look down on, but when she performs, you see the effect of her power.

Odika ihe mee ma ozu anwukwana

Let anything happen except death.

Odighi mma i hu isi gakwaa kpuo isi

Do not see a danger and willingly let it hit you. Be careful that you do not fall prey to a trap that you are aware of.

Odiri usu mma ma nya were anyasi na aga

The bat is a nocturnal animal because it has bad eyesight; it cannot come out during the day. The female delivers her young ones alive. She suckles her young ones. This makes her a mammal. We could also call bats a bird because they fly. If it has been all right with you, you should be doing what you are doing.

Ofo na eji ogu ere onaghi egbu ninye

One in authority must have a good reason for his action to be effective: Ofo is the emblem and symbol of justice and truth and must act with righteousness. Ofo does not act in absence of guilt. You cannot act offensively without a good reason. Ofo does not act in default but with clear justification.

Ofo

Ofo ma ofojue akpa na ebu akpa ikpo onyinye Chukwu di aso

A greedy person always ends up with nothing. He is Jack of all trades and master of none. Jesus said that sufficient for the day is the evil thereof. In being vigilant toward the achievement of a goal, one is to be very thoughtful not over-zealous in activities which can spell a disaster. Here is a little story about this wise adage - *ofo ma ofojue akpa na ebu akpa ikpoala.*

Moral lesson it imparts

One day, two blind men were walking down a path. The one in the front stumbled over a goat's horn which had been fashioned into a trumpet. He bent over and picked it up. Realising it was a trumpet, he blew it. Fortunately and magically, his eyes opened and he began to see. He called on the second blind man and narrated what had happened to him by blowing the trumpet. The second blind man beckoned to him to give him the trumpet. So, he gave it to him and he blew it; likewise, his eyes opened and he could see. At this point, the first blind man, wanting to be better than his friend, recovered the trumpet from him and blew it again. This time, his blindness returned. Being frustrated, he asked his friend to blow the trumpet again but that one, knowing what had happened, refused to do so. Hence the saying, *ofo ma ofojue akpa na ebu akpo ikpo ala* - one who waits until he has got it all will eventually go empty-handed. Here is a lesson of punishment for abuse of divine privilege in being greedy. The horn was divinely sent. The one with modest intention received help but the one with inordinate ambition was helpless and dispossessed. Fr. George Udo Njoku, C.S. Sp. Counselling Is A Community or Village Enterprise 200, (pp. 8-9).

Ofu nne na-amu ma ofu chi adighi eke

This means, that even children of the same mother have their individual 'chi' or personal guardian spirit and so, each has a unique charisma. The children would be differently gifted in their intelligence, their tastes, and interests. They could have different temperaments and utterly opposed views on certain things.

Ofu anya bebe, nke ozo esoro ya ebe

When one of the two people who are together is affected, the other one must be affected too. The two eyes are joined together in function and in pain, so two people who go together, suffer together.

Ofo bu nti nmuo ji anu ihe

The spirit acts through ofo. Ofo is the authority symbol of elders. It is the instrument of calling upon God. It is an instrument through which God blesses you.

Ofo na Amen

Whenever elders bring their ofo out in any ceremony, and after their invocation, everybody will say "ofo oo" that is, Amen or "iseee" in affirmation. So, in the Christian denomination, when priests or chief celebrants pray, everybody affirms it, Amen. These affirmations show unison and oneness of people. As a result, ofo is the centre of unity and the staff of office of the elders in Igboland of Southeastern Nigeria.

Ogbu opi na-ezi imi

The person who blows the trumpet should blow his nose. Literally, a person who works harder gets the reward. One who has time for work also has time for rest. There is time for work and time for rest and refreshment.

Ogeri luo di abuo ya horo nke ka ya nma

When a woman marries two husbands, she chooses the better one. One who has two has a choice but one with one has no choice.

Ogaranya afuru na ulo na eni ozu nwatakere

Whoever is found at home can bury a dead child. In our culture, when a woman delivers her baby and is nursing the baby, the husband takes over her domestic functions and cooks for her. Sometimes, her mother or a close relative does the domestic chores for her. Whoever is available at home can bury a dead child. Usually, it is the young men that bury a dead child but when the young men are not around and only the elderly man is home, he has to do it.

Oguru negbu nde, nde afuwo oguru nara

Our mother used to express this proverb whenever we were lavishing food; while there are people who are abundantly drunk, there are also people in the same surrounding area who are longing to drink but have nothing to drink. In the world, some people have more to spare, while others can just scarcely make ends meet.

Ogologo abughi na nwa m etoola

A child that is tall does not mean that she is mature. She may look big and beautiful but cannot make decisions or handle responsibilities.

Ogbu agwo na azo ndu, agwo ona egbu na azokwa ndu ya

One kills the snake for his dear life and the snake which he is killing fears for its life too. Egwu ekweghi nwata gbue orira, egwu ekweghi orira nyara anwu. Fear that prevents a man from killing a snake is the same fear that prevents the snake from basking in the sun.

Oha gburu akwukwo jere inweta ihe ofe

The oha (green plant) that sheds old leaves wants to get new ones used in soups. This means when you change your behaviour, you develop a better one. If a bad fellow stops the old lifestyle, he will change to a better life.

Oji ofo ehibe isi, ahubeghi ajo mmuo

One who sleeps with a charm under his pillow has never seen a powerful ghost. So, the fact that people keep quiet doesn't mean that people do not act. The literal interpretation is: if you think that charm is your power, don't be surprised when one day, your charm will not save you. Anyone who thinks he is more powerful than everybody will definitely meet a super being one day. Never think that nobody could handle you; just watch out for the fullness of time to come. Then you will be powerless. This is a typical example of a young man whose mission was killing people until God said enough is enough. This young man was arrested and put to death. Don't think that no one will deal with you. My mom would say, "aka rubere aja ohia." It is by the will of the people that everything is done. It is we who say that this forest should be saved. However, the fact that people keep quiet doesn't mean that people cannot do react.

Oji oso agbakwuru ogu, amaghi na ogu bu onwu

One who dares to embrace danger doesn't know that danger is death. Avoid putting yourself in danger.

Oje ngwa- ngwa na-alaji chi. (Onye ngwangwa lara n'afo asaa)

One who hurries too much to be early in doing the day's chores is always late because she spends much energy in hurrying but little for work, thereby, staying late at the job.

Ojiri agbara ghara njo

By acting smartly, you cover up the weak points of what you are doing. It is said that everyone is vulnerable because to err is human; to forgive is divine. We must act upon our task with dexterity so that the brightness of our actions overshadows the darkness of our faults.

Oji onyike egwu ala nacho onye uka na apu n'onu

One who does a provocative act invites criticism. It is said that doing the right thing in the right way with a desirable result invokes people's admiration, but doing the right thing the wrong way with the wrong instrument elicits people's condemnation.

Oji na ano ose na ano na ahia na ano ubo na ano

It means you will give me whatever, according to the complete ordinance of the gods.

Oji onye wetara oji wetara ihe oma

Kola nuts are a symbol of peace, love, unity, goodness, blessing, and offering. Our elders do say, he who brings kola nuts brings life.

Oke aha na-egbu nwa nkita

Too much assumption of a big name kills a dog. Literally, too much self-importance ruins a man.

Okenye no n'ulo, ewu amuo n'omu (n'ogbu)

To allow a goat to deliver her young one while being tethered is a wrong practice for an elderly person. A goat should not be harnessed while in labour and delivering her young one. That is to say, you are to be blamed when you see a preventable act but do not stop it. You failed your responsibility as an elder.

Okenye ji akwukwo eke nsi, ya luo uwa ya lokwute ya

An elderly fellow who wraps faeces in paper will meet it again when he reincarnates. This proverb has become a reverse because our ancestors pose the punishment on the person right there. For example, there are some disobedient parents that give birth to disobedient children. When the parents say one, the children talk two; I am an eye witness. On the other hand, the evil that men do lives after them. The disobedient one will suffer the karma of all the evils he does when he reincarnates.

Okenye ana-egwu ala n'azu ulo ya, egwuchaa ala, onye ka aga-atunye na ya Ogaranya aruru mala

If an old man keeps quiet when a hole is being dug in his back yard, who does he expect will be thrown into it? Don't ignore the prevention of evil act of any kind because you never know who it will affect.

Okenye na-eme anya mpia

Elders do not say a word about everything they see. They are always reserved.

Okenye ekunyere nwa osi na ya enweghi eze, asi ya rie nwa ahu?

If you are made responsible for a thing, that does not mean that you have a chance to ruin it.

Okee mebiri mmiri ofe

Never be an elderly person who spoils fufu soup. An unwise elderly person who doesn't know his worth; he is supposed to do the right thing and set a good example, but he is the one who misbehaves. Thus, he doesn't know his authority.

Oke osisi furum na ama jijiji, oke ifefe buru ya

If you have animosity against me, you will be consumed by your animosity. If you make a fist at me, you will meet a fighter on the way.

Oke no n'ulo gwara oke no n'ama na azu no na ngiga

The rat in the house tells the rat in the bush that there is meat in the basket. It is always close relatives or friends who release the secret.

Oke ochicho butere oshi

Too much ambition brings about stealing.

Oke soro ngwere maa mmiri, ahu kochaa nwa ngwere, o gaghi akocha nwa oke

When a rat follows a lizard to swim, the lizard's body will dry but the rats' body will not dry. Do not join in a project that militates against you. Our Nigerian famous musician- nwafor Igbo sang, *"Oke soro ngwere maa nmirii ma ahu kochaa nwa ngwere ogagi akocha nwa Oke..........O nwannem elu uwa akweghi nghota, onye iwe na ewe, ewezina (Osadabe).*

Oke na ohia ngwere n'uzo (rat in the bush and lizard on the road)/ Ukwu na ohia, ukwu na uzo- walking aimlessly higgledy-piggledy like a drunken man

This means by hook or by crook, that is to say, one who has no aim in his actions. Not doing things in order. That is, everyone is doing what he likes his own way but not according to the general rule.

Okenye jiri ahuri ke nsi olo uwa oga alokwute ya

Shakespeare said, *"The evil that men do lives after them, the good is oft interr'd with their bones."* In the Vedic scripture (Indian scripture), it is said that whatever one does here will reappear in one's body when one reincarnates. This is the law of karma. Simply put, in whatever condition one quits his present body, in his next life, he will attain to that state of being without fail," (Veda p. 143). In Igboland, *we say, "ihe ojoo bu nwa- nwa lo uwa olokwuru, ihe obuna i na eme bu uwa tu uwa."* In this world, those who are handicapped and disabled, when they die and reincarnate, they earn good bodies and good health and those who lived like dogs will take on dogs' bodies and reincarnate as dogs. Another saying goes, *"ihe bu ugba gbara nwa nkwu ya na ya wu laba ali."* If evil dwells in one, that evil will follow that one to the grave. Thus, it is advised that one should tailor one's behaviour to conform to the high ideals that are approved by God so that at the end, one can receive a good body and a good destiny.

Okirikiri ka a na-agba ukwu ose, anaghi ari ya elu

You only walk round the hot pepper plant for you cannot climb it. In life, there are certain things that are impossible for one to do. You only look at them and carry on your way.

Okwo nke o na-eme anaghi ekwe nwa ya gaa egwu onwa

He, who knows evil never allows his children to go out in the night for moonlight play. That is, he is always suspicious of others. A capricious man does not trust you because of his own disposition.

Okuko kpakwara akwa ya kpashaa nke ibe ya

People protect their own interests and ruin the interests of others. My mother would say to us, "Do not do unto others that which you would not allow others to do unto you. If you don't like people to gossip about you, don't gossip about them. If you're the one that loves to kill others but you love your own life so dearly, please refrain from doing so. Therefore, live and let live.

Okuko anaghi-akpo ibe ya onye ohu akpala

A hen that calls the other hen dirty anus. This proverb is like a person calling another a sinner. All of us are sinners; there is no doubt about it, though, it depends on the gravity of the sin committed. That is the pot calling the kettle black. All chickens have a dirty anus; that is, all peoples are equally placed in life.

Okuko nile bu akpara na ike

Everybody has dirty linen in the closet. Therefore, it is he who exposes himself that will be called dirt because he calls himself dirt.

Okuko richera ihe no n'ukwu nkwu, ya kpara ete rigoro elu ya

When a hen finishes eating all the food around the surrounding palm tree, she will use rope to climb up. One has to manage what one has. That is, you have to be economical, not finishing what you have too quickly. Just have self-control and be moderate. Eat cautiously. Do not eat greedily so as not to be forced to do the unexpected because of lack of food.

Okuko lele etu esi abo okwa nwanne gi

What you have seen happening to your friend, will also happen to you. Be vigilant to learn from the mistakes of others. Our parents give us honest and sincere counselling by examining all aspects of life so that when one fails to heed their advice, and face its consequences, others can learn from it. Here is a practical example of *okuko lele etu esi abo okwa nwanne gi:* A married woman has been unfaithful to her husband; she was having a love affair with other men. One day, people found out about it, including her husband; she was warned to stop it. She developed deaf ears yet, her husband overlooked it and forgave her. Still, she hardened her heart and in addition, plotted to kill her husband with rat poison but unfortunately, she was caught. She went to the extent of bringing her brothers to beat up and kidnap her husband but the man was rescued. Finally, this diabolical woman succeeded in arranging with her son to brutally assassinate her husband. Thus, as my mother used to put across her wise saying, *umu m isi kota ebu ogbu ya*, meaning that whatever one does will affect her. This woman was given a proper punishment by indigenous tribunals of ndi umunna (the indigenous men of the land) and ndi umuada (the indigenous women of the land). The most significant part of this punishment is that no government or law enforcement could overturn the ruling sentence. And so, it was agreed by ndi umunna na ndi umuada that this dubious woman should be sent back to her parents on a practical market day called Eke. Eke is one of our local market days. The uniqueness of Eke is that any married woman sent home on Eke market day with a yellow palm frond, must never come back to her husband's home again, in life or in death. In our culture, it is rare to see anyone being sent home on that day. Accordingly, everybody is afraid to commit any crime that would lead to this kind of punishment. It is taboo or an abomination to shed blood in our culture. Thus, if anyone dares commit such a taboo, no mercy is shown to that person. In my final analogy, our people never feel any remorse in giving punishment for this kind of atrocity. Our ancestors' adage says as my mother taught me, *umu m, ihe onye metara ga eso nya,* that is to say, any wrong one does, follows him/her. Shakespeare in his insight said the evil that men do lives after them. Their bones are interred with their good. Proverb is the oil that smoothes the words. It makes the word more explicit or vivid. At this juncture, our wise men and women say, *a gwa nti ya ga-anu, e gburu isi, ya na nti akwuru laa.* When you tell the ears and they refused to hear, when the head is being cut off, the ears follow suit. Live and let live (onye biri ibe ya biri). The case of this wicked woman is a big lesson for other women in the village because, if anyone does what this woman did, they would be ostracized. The justified punishment given to that lady is a sort of check and balance for the remaining women who would dare to attempt such an action. More so, the punishment is a stop sign for any evil conspirator.

Okuko mmanya na-egbu ahubeghi ufu ara na-awu

A drunken hen has never seen a mad fox. Those who think that they are more powerful than others and do all sorts of diabolical things will one day meet with a supernatural being who will overpower them and bring them to justice. Thus, do not say you are powerful because there is a higher being than you are, who one day, will call you to order. Okika kporo, kpokwa onye ji gi mma.

Okuko gara mba ohuru, na-eji otu ukwu aga

When a hen goes to a foreign country for the first time, she walks on one leg. That means when in a foreign land, walk cautiously, taking time to observe all events so as to make a correct discernment before any step further. Do not row in with the excited crowd for the crowd may know the details but you do not.

Okuko nyua ahuru, ala achu nya oso

He who does something wrong runs away even when there is no one pursuing him. Actually, animals, like humans, know when they have done wrong and can show a sense of shame by running away.

Okuko isi opine anaghi atupu onwe ya ihe n'isi

One who has an infirmity in his body does not do anything to hurt it. Bad behaviour has the effect of stinging the conscience of the evildoer such that he feels guilt at seeing people looking at him. A young man killed his father and tried to cover it up. When the elders gathered together to examine what had happened, they tried to check whether the man had been murdered or not. Immediately, the son who killed him began to run even though no one said anything to him. And so, in this case, he portrayed himself and people started chasing him and caught him. This young man is also like a fat meat that fans itself. Therefore, when a man does something wrong, he feels guilt. Biblical wisdom states, "The wicked man's oracle is Sin in the depths of his heart; there is no fear of God before his eyes." Psalm 36:1.

Okuko anaghi echefu onye furu ya oku na udu nmiri

One good turn deserves another. No one forgets the hand that fed him. Animals don't forget the one that feeds them. Train them with a particular call, then, when they hear it, they run to you.

Okuko eru nku akpo choghiri -choghiri

That the chicken never reaches its time and starts making noise. This is like someone who hangs her bag where her hand cannot reach. You should always cut your coat according to your size. Do things when they are due. Do not act prematurely.

Okuko egbe buruna na eti ka uwa nu olu ya obughi na ihe ji ya ga ahupu ya

One who is in trouble should let others know it, even though that action would not relieve him of the pain involved. The typical example of this is my late elderly brother's murder case. All of my siblings and relatives are still lamenting and talking about the circumstances surrounding it but the fact is that he is dead and he will never come back to life. However, one thing is certain, the killer and his mentors hear our lamentation and feel the "guilt." "Sin speaks to the sinner in the depth of his heart."

Okuko hapu kwum -kwum, o ga-eji gini zuo umu

The hen never stops making noise to train her young ones. If parents stop daily striving, they won't be able to train their kids.

Okuko anaghi anyu akpana na akwa ya

One does not do anything that will eventually hurt him. No one does evil in his own household; it is an abomination.

Okwu eji ofo kwu n'eru ihu Chukwu

The dealing on truth goes direct to God, for God is truth. The words with ofo go directly to God.

Omepuru onye o diri nke ya luru (altruism)

This is a person who takes care of others' problems rather than her own. Altruism – selflessness is a virtuous attribute of human beings.

This is the story of an altruistic bird, Abiri Nachu Egbe. (Abiri is a harrier and Egbe is a kite). A selfless bird, Abiri is the size of a sparrow but is capable of harassing egbe which is much bigger than it and it is able to stop egbe from taking chickens at the expense of its life. This is true because egbe can kill abiri. But abiri is so undaunted and persistent in stabbing egbe with its beak and fluttering and perching on egbe's wings that egbe cannot continue hunting for chickens. Here, abiri puts his life on line for the sake of saving the chickens. Jesus recommended altruism - (self-sacrifice) as the highest quality of a man when he said,

"No one has love greater than this, that someone should surrender his soul on behalf of his friends"
—John 15:13

Onwa nato mere onye arafu erile nri

It takes three months of hard work to produce plenty of food but the sluggard will not endure the hard labour involved in the cultivation of land and so, he will be hard up and hungry at the time of harvest.

That is why it is said,

> *"So work the honey-bees; creatures that by a rule in nature teach the art of order to a peopled kingdom"*
> **—Book of Familiar Quotations (Shakespeare)**

> *"Even bees, the little alms-men of spring bowers, know there is richest juice in poison flowers"*
> **—Keats.**

Onweghi onye na kpo ekeya nwaogbodo eke
Rank yourself first in everything you do. You stand supreme in your eyes. Call yourself number one.

Onwere ihe mere ede ojiri bee nwuu
There is always cause for alarm. Where there is smoke, there is fire: There is some truth in every allegation.

Onweyi ihe anya huru gbaa obara ihe oga agba bu anya mmiri
Nothing makes the eyes shed blood but tears. Water always seeks its level, no more, no less. No pain is beyond endurance. No matter how great a disaster may be, it can take its toll and die down.

Onweghi onye ga-anwu, e jiri nwa ya lie ya
No one would be buried with her child. Death is natural; it does not require that anyone should be bled to fulfil its rites.

Onwu gidi -gidi na-awunye aka na ogwu
One who rushes unwittingly always falls into a trap.

Onwu bu oke, onwu adighi aso anya
Death is already ordained; it's no respecter of any person.

Onweghi ihe ka nwanne n'ihi na nwanne di uto
Blood is thicker than water and brotherhood is very sweet.

Onye bi n'ulo ma ebe o na-eshi mmiri
He, who lives in the house, knows where it leaks. One, who carries a load knows where it aches.

Onye isi amaghi mgbe ekere nku ukwa
A fool does not know when decisions are made. One who does not know, does not know when he gets to a limit.

Onye ajuju anaghi efu uzo
If you ask questions, you will not make mistakes. Correct direction means accurate execution.

Onye nwere ihe nabu na eri oke nabu
The one who has two shares has two rights.

Onye maa atu, okwue ihe odikaya (ikwue na ihe na ato uto, ikwue ihe ona ato ka ya)
If you are saying something about a thing, you must give an example of it. Also, if you say something is sweet, you must say what it tastes like. If you give an instance, you must give an earmark by which it can be recognized.

Onye ama na agbaram, anam aso ya aso
I fear a tale-bearer. Most people fear one who always has his neighbour's names in his/her mouth; peering into people's privacy and spreading bad news about them. Do not be a tale-bearer or a tell-tale.

Onye mkpumkpu kobe akpa ya ebe aka ga-eru ya
A short fellow should hang his bag where his hand can reach. You should act according to your ability.

Onye oma data aku oputa onye ojoo
The fruit of good works of a good person benefits the good and the bad. When a person builds a roadway, everyone, good or bad, passes along it. So, the goodness of a good person benefits everybody. The sweet palm wine is the product of the labour of the palm-wine tapper.

Aku shie nne, oputu nwanne.

Onye ji ahu amaghi ihe onye ibi na nahu
Those who have, do not know the pain of scarcity.

Onye nne ya di ndu amaghi ihe onye nne ya nwuru anwu na nahu
Those whose mothers are alive do not know what others whose mothers are dead go through.

Onye nne ya di ndu were ogbo nnu gobara ya ofo maka na nne di uko
You have a lot of sacrifice to make to sustain the life of your mother because mothers are precious.

Onye nwe nkwu legide ya anya mgbe okwuru akwuru, odarue ala onwewadi onye nwe ya
You have to pay proper attention to your property for if it becomes public, you cannot lay claim to it. Rights are to be preserved to be deserved.

Onye nwere madu ka onye nwere ego
Mmadu ka aku: Human worth is more valuable than material wealth. They say, if you go to war with people more numerous than you are, you will run out of reinforcements while they have more people to engage; for this reason, one with greater number will run you over. Madu ka eji ekwu obi bu aku.

Onye juru inye okenye ihe ruru ya, okenye agaghi eru ya aka
Give elderly people due respect so that when it is your turn, you will be honoured.

Onye Chineke nyere anya abuo ya tufuo ya obiri n'uwa ozo o ga-alo
If you have been given ample opportunities and you miss them, rarely will you get those opportunities again. Here is an example of a guy whose parents and relatives made every effort to raise him up well, but he chose the wrong path that led to his destruction. He roamed

about going after women, stealing, taking hard drugs, and murdering vulnerable men and women. His life was useless and hopeless. He ended woefully. Mom would say in her wise saying, Okuko, lele etu esi abo okwa nwa nnegi. If you are a bad fellow, you end up like this fellow. Avoid being wander about. Be responsible to gain self-actualization.

Onye ji nna ya n'ala ji onwe ya

He who holds his father on the floor, holds himself. Do not ever struggle with or overpower your father because you are strong. Never dare to contend with your father. He is your God who created you.

Onye a kwo n'azu amaghi na uzo di anya

The one whom you always carry on your back never feels that the journey is too far. He who is always being served takes everything for granted.

Onye gbakaa ute ya, o hie n'ala

If you spoil your mat, you lie on the floor. Value your precious jewels. In the situation like this, Mama would go on and on issuing proverbs to us, her children. At this juncture, she would say, "*O ji ofo ehibe isi, ahubeghi ajo mmuo.* This means, if you claim that you are so powerful, one day, you will meet with a more powerful being that can handle you squarely. She would also say, *"atuara omara, o mara, mana atuara ofeke, o fenye isi n'ohia."* Her final word for this matter would be this; she would again sing her famous song to remind the person. It goes like this; *"ihuna ihe mere onwegiee, ihuna ihe i mere onwegie, ihuna ihe mere onwegi-nwatakiri ifuna ihe imere onwegi public assault na okporo kokota na ama achara."* Mama Monica used to sing this a lot whenever any of the children disobeyed and had been punished by our father; when the person began to cry, our mother would sing this rebuking song to them. "Do not waste your talent but preserve it for, *'oma nma ghara nma ya orusia'* if beauty loses its gloss, it becomes slip-shod or shoddy."

Onye ara na aga na ezi, obu mmadu nweya

That thing you call useless belongs to somebody who values it. No matter how you appear, you belong to someone who cherishes you.

No person is insignificant.

Onye anya ruru ala na atuta ihe furu efu

One who is very observant is one who finds what is lost. A good observer is a good informer.

Onye na-amaghi anya a na-ele ya, si huru ya ahuru to ya

If a person sneers at you and you do not understand, you will not know when he plucks out your eyes. The wise fellow understands any movement one makes around him. You should be aware when a row is against you. Be sensitive to your environment.

Onye na-anoghi nso, ji ya na-ahu n'agiga oku

When you are not around, people make decisions against your wishes. This is just like the man who has made a will and when he dies, the living remake his will the way it would suit them. This is literally out of sight, out of mind. *(Diji rubaram anaghi aruta ogbo ji)*. When you hire a farmer to farm for you, after the harvest, he will give to himself big yams and to you, small yams. When you are not around, your lot is left out.

Onye kwere chi ya ekwere

If you agree, your God consents to you. *Vox Populi, Vox Dei (the voice of the people is the voice of God)*.

Onye iwu na ama bu onye biara Eke Orlu

One who is most involved in doing a thing is the one who gets the most blame.

Onye a na-agbara aja, ya were anya ya lekiri, werekwa nti ya gere

The person whom a fortune-teller makes a sacrifice for should use his eyes to see and his ears to hear. Let one who has eyes see, and the one with ears hear. One day, the hen went to a soothsayer to find how to escape from the fox. While the soothsayer was consulting his spirit, the fox arrived to find out how to catch the hen. The soothsayer put the hen under cover of a basket while advising the fox. As the soothsayer spoke to the fox, he would repeatedly strike the basket reminding the hen to listen because what he was saying to the fox applied to her. Hence, the saying: *Onye ana agbara afa, were nti ya gere.* The way the fox will go is the way the hen will escape. The thief is praying that he will not be caught and the owner of the house is praying that the thief does not dare to come.

Onye iberibe (onye isi) amaghi mgbe ibe ya kere nku ukwa

A fool never knows when the others shared the bread-fruit wood. A person who is too carefree does not know when others are busy doing the real thing. He feels that everything is like that. He doesn't know that others had already done the real thing.

Onye iberibe amaghi mgbe agafere ama ndi ogo ya

One who is too light-headed does not know when he is involved in a real insidious task.

Onye ji nna ya n'ala ji onwe ya

He who holds his father on the floor holds himself. The way a child treats his father is the way he will be treated by his child. Therefore, children, respect your parents because any treatment you render to them is what you will receive.

Onye ji ihe nwata welie aka ya elu, aka fuwa ya ufu, owetuo aka ya ala nwata werekwa ihe ya

Anyone who holds a child's belonging and raises up his hand, when his hand starts paining him, he will bring it down and the child gets his possession back. Many a time, people scramble for what does not belong to them. But in their hearts, they know that, that thing does not belong to them. Mom would say to us, "never take what does not belong to you, my children. But if people take your own, God will always fight for you." She would also say, "never mind, what is hot will eventually cool down." Finally, if you take that which does not belong to you, when your conscience pricks you, you will give it up. Well, the question is: do we have a conscience a living nowadays?

Onye si o bu mu na ya, ya gakwuge ndi ike ya na ha-ha
He who says it is me and him, will meet those with equal strength to fight hand to hand.

Onye na-anoghi ebe eliri ozu na-esi n'ukwu abo ya
Anyone who was not there when the corpse was buried always dug the corpse out by the leg. In other words, if you are not there when a decision is made, your argument will be illogical.

Onye ajuru anaghi aju onwe ya
Yourself is more preferable to you than others, even if others are better.

Onye ria elu oji, ya kpatachaa nku ya makana anaghi ari oji ugbo abuo
Whoever climbs the iroko tree, should try to fetch enough firewood because he will rarely climb it again. This means make proper use of the opportunity you have. Never waste your time for no reason.

Onye kpu miri na onu anaghi afu oku onu
The person who has water in their mouth does not blow fire. When you are occupied with something, you have no time for another. You have to be focused.

Onye si m noro, ya norokwa
Whoever wants me to be, let that person be too. This proverb is like wishing someone what the person wishes you. So, wish people well and they will do the same.

Onye ahu bu ukpala fuka-fuka
The person is one who pretends to be strong but he is not. He is always an empty vessel. An empty vessel makes the most noise. A powerless being will always make people notice him and fear him or her.

Onye obi ojoo na-ebu onye arisi uzo anwu
One who is hard-hearted dies earlier than one who has offended the gods. Hard-heartedness causes melancholia which results in the

psychological disorder of depression, mental and physical apathy. Intense hatred can cause white blood cell antibodies to fight against the body's own tissues causing injury such as hemolytic anemia which can cause death. Therefore, if you are always angry and depressed, the white blood cells that fight antigens keep on dropping to fight, and get weakened; they would be unable to fight for you, and then you die. Beware of being upset all the time.

Onye nzuzu, ihe kweere ya bu, I gbachi ya nkiti (Nkiti ka eji agbagbu onye nzuzu
Silence is the best answer to a fool. Ignore them and move on.

Onye eze ya putara elu ala, obu ya ka-ana akpo onye eze nkotonko
One whose acts are known, is not tacit enough in comporting herself. You are asked to be reserved in that you present to the world your good self and keep within you your conflicting self, for Shakespeare said, "It is the loud laugh that spoke the vacant mind."

Onye buru uzo shibe ite na-enwe nkpokoro ite
The person who begins cooking early, will soon have an old pot. The first to be born is the first to be old. The longer you live, the more fragile you become. The earlier you are born, the earlier you get old.

Onye o bula a muru n'uwa nwere uru o bara
No one is born insignificant. Everybody is important and useful for something.

Onye nzuzu amaghi na nwanne ya bu obia
A fool never knows that his little brother is his guest. Be hospitable to both your brothers and brethren.

Onye atuoro ilu, kowara ya, ego e jiri luo nne ya furu ohia
When a proverb is given to you and explained to you, it means that the dowry paid on your mother is a waste. Usually, when you make a statement, it must be clearly stated for *Akoziere ofo, ofo ere.*

Onye nwere madu ka onye nwere ego
The worth of a man is much more than the worth of money. That is the reason why our ancestors name their children *madu ka aku.*

Onye bute chi ya uzo ogbagbue onwe ya na oso
If you overtake your helper, you become helpless.

Onye ya na nkita ya na-egwu egwu amaghi na nkita ya na-ata ata
The person who plays with his dog never knows that it bites.

Onye mee ka oke, ologbo achuwa ya oso
If you behave like a rat, the cat will pursue you.

Onye ujo amaghi na ogu di uru
That which is hard is also useful. That which is hard has some benefit.

Onye bu uche n'obi kwere aturu ndewo
One who is overwhelmingly occupied by a problem, mistakenly takes a sheep for a man. He is so subdued by his pain that he does not know his left from his right.

Onye ulo ya n'agba oku ya na achu oke
He is pursuing the little matter while leaving the important matter undone: The English adage says, penny wise, pound foolish. You are too concerned with little things but you are careless of big matters.

Onye njija ogu ka onye olulu ya
One who empowers you to fight is better than the one who is fighting with you. The one you do for yourself is better than the one somebody is doing for you.

Onye kwue okwu nna ya kwuru, nya kwukwaa ugwo nna nya ji

King JaJa of Opobo was born in 1821 at Umuduruoha Amaigbo, Nkwerre, Orlu Local Government Area, Imo State, Nigeria and kidnapped into slavery at 12 years of age. His real name was

Jubo Jubogha, contracted to Jaja na Ubani (Ubani meaning Bonny) by the Ibos but called JaJa by the Europeans. He was sold as a slave to chief Iganipughuma Alison of Bonny who, finding him insubordinate, made a gift of him to an Ibo ex-slave, Chief Madu (Maduka), a man of rare ability, religiously dedicated to the service of the monarchy, who had been elevated by King Opubu of Bonny to head the Anna Pepple House of which the King was the head before his ascension to the throne. At the time of King Opubu's death, his son and successor, William Dappa Pepple, was a minor; consequently, Chief Madu became a regent. During his headship of Opubu House, Chief Madu, by his industry and efficient administration in developing trade in palm oil, made himself the wealthiest in the land. Chief Madu was succeeded by his son, Alali, who also became a regent and the head of the Anna Pepple House. In this House, JaJa rose from slavery to freedom and made an exceptional career in the palm oil trade with British merchants. Later, Alali died, leaving the Anna Pepple House without a head. Head chiefs held successful repeated meetings but the coveted honour did not tempt any of them, though by right they were senior and men of wealth. They shirked the responsibility of being the Head after the late Alali who had been a great trader but owed the Europeans, 1000 to 1500 puncheons (Puncheons =wooden barrels for holding palm oil) of palm oil, the value of which was £10,000 to £15,000 sterling. Not one of the chiefs felt able to settle such a huge debt which was heavy with bankruptcy and meant a downfall for the late Alali's successor. JaJa was the youngest of the chiefs but he had been a very good trader, respected by the European traders for honesty and dependence in adhering strictly to any promise he made regarding trade matters. When all chiefs declined to be elected, JaJa was unanimously elected to fill the office of the head of Anna Pepple House. Though he hesitated to accept the offer, finally, he accepted the Headship and solemnly pledged himself to maintain the high ideals of the founder and the integrity of the House. The chiefs unanimously congratulated him and promised him their unrelenting support and loyalty. JaJa knew the characters of the leading political leaders, studied the

Bonny scene and made up his mind on his future line of action. Knowing that the source of Niger Delta wealth was in the palm oil markets, he made himself 'persona grata' (adorable acceptable person) with the chiefs of the hinterland and popular with the European merchants. He perceived that the Europeans were eager to capture the hinterland trade and made his plans accordingly. He was elected in 1863, seven years later; he was the greatest African living in the east of modern Nigeria. During the first twelve months, from the ex-regent's (Alali's) deputy officers, JaJa had selected twenty young men of proven ability and elevated them to positions of trusteeship. He helped them to trade on their own account, bought canoes for them and took them to the European traders who gave them franchises with JaJa as a guarantor. Within two years, the debts owed by his predecessor, Alali, were paid off. From this time on, JaJa never looked back, becoming the most popular chief in Bonny and the idol of his own people. Here is the application of the saying that if you would speak like a chief, you would also pay the chief's liabilities. No chief dared to act as a successor to the indebted late chief of Anna Pepple House because of the outstanding debts to be paid but JaJa summoned the courage, spoke like` a chief, acted like a chief, and paid a chief's debts. Is that not something to be applauded?

Trade Winds on the Niger by Geoffrey L. Baker pp.76 to 113: Trade and Politics in the Niger Delta by Kenneth Onwuka Dike pp. 182-202.

Onye aghugho nwua, onye aghugho ibe ya elie ya

When a crafty (cunning) man dies, a crafty man buries him. Another interpretation of this is, "*Chukwu kee ajo nmadu owere ajo nmuo doso ya*" (*When God creates a bad man, he creates a bad spirit to watch him*).

Onye dunyere nwata ga nwute nkapia ga enye ya nmiri oga eji akwo aka ya

If you induce a person to do something wrong, you will also help him or her to correct it.

Onye kpuru isi aburula onye nwuru anwu

My mother used to say that a blind person is already dead. Today, disability is no cause for alarm. A blind man can perform. Therefore, never assume that you cannot do it. Here are some moral upliftments:

"Motivation is a very important issue and an integral part of achieving your personal best."
—Marc Woods

Personal Best How to achieve your full potential (p. 41)

"Promise me you'll always remember: You're braver than you believe, and stronger than you seem, and smarter than you think,"
—Christopher Robin to Pooh
A.A. Milne

Oria na egbu onye na ebu uche n'obi

One who keeps his illness to himself, does not have anyone to console him or to show him how to get free from the illness. To be relieved, one has to get help from others.

Orimara butere akpiri Udele

Too much eating causes a long throat like that of a vulture. A greedy fellow fall into trouble.

Oru Mbiri: Aka nri kwoo aka ekpe, aka ekpe akwoo aka nri

In the "Igbo" villages in Nigeria, young girls practice "*Oru Mbiri*, that is, they join together in groups of 4-6 girls to help each other in the farm work. On the day that is allocated to a girl, that host girl will prepare sumptuous meals to entertain the guest girls. Usually, the mother prepares the meal. When they arrive in the girl's house, they are taken to the farm. The guest girls will spend the whole day doing the farm work. It can be weeding, planting cassava, or "*ikwo ubi*"(clearing the farm by gathering all weeds and piling up the trash). They are entertained with food in the farm and when they return home from the farm, they are again entertained and they come back in the evening again for entertainment by the girl's parents. The girls' mothers always took a lead in preparing the food such as ukwa (breadfruit food), rice, and fufu. Their father bought palm wine to entertained them. This is a great show of solidarity among young girls and I was among those who participated in this act of farming. This brought peace, love, respect, and unity among the young girls and their families. In turn, each girl gets a day allocated to her. It is their parents' farms that they are cultivating. It is a cooperative labour-sharing opportunity as well as a kiwi social get-together. So, the saying goes: *Aka nri kwoo aka ekpe, aka ekpe akwoo aka nri* – the right hand helps the left hand and the left hand helps the right hand. This proverb is also applicable when parents rear their child and, in turn, the child grows up and takes care of his or her parents. Likewise, in other aspects of life, people do return good for good. This also brings us to the wise adage that one good turn deserves another.

Osisi no n'uzo na-ebu apa mma

A tree by the roadside always receives knife-cuts. A public servant always receives frequent criticisms.

O si ya anaghi eri oke, mana were eze na-ekere ya umu aka

This is a pretentious being who always claims to be righteous but underneath, he or she does diabolical acts that one could not imagine. Fear such a person because he or she is more dangerous than a serpent. My mother would put her proverb across this way saying, *ochichara mere ihe eboro oke.* (The cockroach did what the rat was accused of. In other words, a cunning person does something that he cannot be blamed for).

Osisi na-ami ego

This means a machine or a tree of wealth; a money provider. This is my mother's nickname which showed that she delivered many children. In our culture, it is believed that anyone who has many children is greater than the one who has money. Hence, in my culture, my parents were wealthy as a result of having many responsible children.

Osisi ukwu daruo ala umu nnunu agbafuchaa

When a big tree falls, the birds will fly away. When the head of a family is not there, his family is always in disorder. When the head of the house is dead, the family affairs are in disarray.

Oso ndu agwu ike

Life's race is never tiresome. You are never tired of working hard as long as you are alive.

As long as you have an ultimate goal to attain, keep working assiduously.

Osisi kwuru, nnunu ebere ya, ma na odaa na ala, nnunu amaghi ebe ya

If things happen normally, the result will be normal, otherwise, the contrary will be the case.

Otu aka gi na atu onye ozo, mkpisi aka ano ana atu gi

When you are finding fault with your neighbour for a little error of his/hers, whereas your own errors are double. On the other hand, you're finding fault for one error but there are four errors in you.

Otu aka ruta nmanu orue aka ndi ozo

One bad apple spoils the broth. In a family where one person is a thief, it affects other members of that family. Therefore, beware of what you do so that you will not discredit your family like that boy who killed his parents. It doesn't pay to be a bad person. Food processors are always strict about not using bad raw materials because you cannot make a good quality product from bad materials.

Otu onye siere oha, oha ga-erichali mana oha siere otu onye, ogaghi erichali

If one person cooks for a whole group of people, they will finish the food, but if the people cook for one person, she won't be able to finish it. One person cannot fight a whole group. Two heads are better than one.

O tara amu ebele ji ibi ugwo
When one does something wrong, one is bound to have a recoiling consequence. If you are a killer, what do you expect would be your reward? If you are a young girl who goes about accepting gifts from the boys, what would you think would happen to you? *O ta ncha- ncha na atabi ire*. One who eats food in haste always bites his tongue.

Otele onye ozo na-aka akwa
It is only the buttocks of another person that tear the clothes. Everybody regards his own thing as superior. On the other hand, no matter if your mother is a thief, you will regard her as a good person. You can see her weakness as weakness as usual. Yours is always the best.

Otu onye anaghi eri nri bara ora
It is not only one person that eats the left-over food. All must eat the left-over food because everybody has developed a fresh appetite. If a negative reaction has occurred on the food, by being shared by many, the danger will be less felt.

Otiti abali tie, onye nurunu kwuo si egbule, o jinu haa, maka amaghi onye e ji nke ya
When you hear in the night 'kill, kill', respond with, 'do not kill' because, you never can tell who the person is; he may be yours. Literally, mercy is required always.

Otu mkpuru okwu ezugoro onye ma ihe
A word is enough\sufficient for the wise.

Owu ruru ala wuru na ji
Anything that affects the land also affects things planted in it. If it is too hot, things planted would be affected by heat and they could die off. This proverb is a typical example of a woman who planned and murdered her husband in order to enjoy the husband's wealth by herself. Hence, what she expected was not what she saw. She neither has her husband nor has the proposed wealth. She lost everything including her freedom. One, who fertilizes the land, also fertilizes

the yams planted in it.

Oze for all- live and let live
Onyee kanyi ga na ukwu oze
Onyee kanyi ga na ukwu oze
Oze ukwu daram -daram
Oze nta daram -daram
Anu ukwu kpara rie kpara rie
Anu nta kpara rie kpara rie
Ogele titingu tingu

Ogho kanyi ga na ukwu oze

Oze is a fruit tree and its fruits fall abundantly when ripe and people and animals are free to go to the tree and gather the fallen fruits. They are free for all. Sometimes, the fallen fruits are so many that there are always many left over uncollected. Thus, the saying goes that if you want something free, go to the oze fruit tree which is liberally available to everyone, man and creatures. A generous fellow never lacks.

Taa ahuhu mana eri uru

Suffer before pleasure. Sweat before sweet.

Ubosi ajo njo

The day is always full of many events which people have to engage in for survival. Every day is busy with everybody doing something gainful, aimed at helping oneself and others. At the end of the day, everybody goes home to come back the following day, doing the same thing, hopefully for beneficial results. *Ubosi ajo-njo-* the day must provide useful outcomes, no matter what.

Udele buru ka ibu ahia a zukwana ngi

Let all your evil be upon you.

Uga atalam ake

Old age or suffering. *Nti apuanam ika, Nti atalam ake* means owing to long suffering and old age, I have now lost all my youthful glamour and I am now a mere remnant of my previous self. Some people supplement their foods by eating a lot of palm nuts and kernels with roasted corn or ukwa. When they get old, "*oke itita*"-frequent chewing of hard nuts, gives rise to loss of teeth and collapsed cheeks, thereby giving the impression of a person of lost glory. When a person says *nti apuanam ika*, he means to say, I have been long doing this agonizing thing that wears and tears me down to smithereens; For example, a truck pusher who, day in day out, is on the job of loading his truck with people's goods and pushing the truck to its destination. His is hard labour. "*Nit apuanaya ika.*"

Ugboguru zeere m zere nwunye dim, ka aririo ghara igbu nke m
Let my vegetables grow and others' vegetables grow as well, so that begging will not destroy my own. The goodness that happens to me, let it also happen to others so that they will be merry as well.

Ugwu bu nkwaghi -nkwaghi
Respect is reciprocal. Respect others and they will respect you too.

Ukwu nku akaghi ihe lara n'ohia
A bird in the hand is worth more than many of them in the bush. The bundle of firewood is not greater than the things wasted in the bush. It is better to hold onto what you have rather than desiring something you don't have.

Ukwu na aga wara -wara, anya na ahu wara- wara na ele ya
One who always goes astray invites the eyes of a curious, interested person. When one raises dust in his wake, that also raises curiosity about what is going on. Therefore, there is nothing hidden that cannot be seen or known.

Ukpala okpoko gburu nti shiri ya
The one who does not take heed from warnings will suddenly be hit by a dangerous warning encounter. A grasshopper that is caught by a noisy bird is deaf.

Ulo chere ihe
There is a lot going on under the roof. Every man's home is his castle in which he is free to do what he likes. No one knows except him and his household.

Umu m, ana ajugbu -ajugbu ma na eri
You have to kill before you eat. You must study your subject well. You have to procure the prerequisites before you prosecute. You have to make sure that all actions are correct and complete before you conclude. You must cook your yam before you eat it. You keep everything in order before conclusion.

Utu hu onye ona aragbu ogelie
When a man sees his girlfriend, he feels sexy. When a person sees the one he is stronger than, he feels like fighting him.

Ihe onye metara na-eso nya
People always get a reaction from what they do.

> *"The evil that men do lives after them. The good is oft interred with their bones."*
>
> **—Shakespeare.**
> https://www.poetryfoundation.org/poems/56968

Consequently, whatever someone does, follows him/her.

Anaghi ekpuchi afoime aka
My children, one cannot cover up pregnancy with palm.
Truth always surfaces sooner or later.

Onye gburu nne oke anaghi ekwe umu ya saa anya
One who kills one's parent will also be very aggressive to the young ones. That which is on the top of the mountain cannot be hidden. One, who hates one's parents, also hates their children.

Welite ukwu elu

Be smart, walk fast, and hurry up; do not delay. Be up and doing. Be energetic in all your undertakings.

Nke afo a ebughi ibu, nke aka ga-aka

Next year will be more prosperous. This was my mom's good wishes and encouragement to us whenever we were in desperation. She would encourage us not to worry for that moment. She would advise us to be hopeful and resolute for future prosperity.

Umu m, anaghi m alu ogu ihere

My children, I never fight a shameful fight.

Arusi anaghi efe mba agba afa

The Spirit cannot go to a foreign country to operate. It does if the worshipper is abroad but if the worshipper is not in that particular country, it won't be effective.

Egbubie n'ututu otunwuo n'ehihie

If one cuts in the morning, it withers in the evening. If one cuts grass in the morning, in the afternoon, it dies. That is, what evil you do in the morning will show up in the afternoon. Furthermore, the evil done in the dark often reveals in the day light.

Anaghi amu aka ekpe na nka

One does not start learning to use his or her left hand in old age. My mother used to say this a lot to us when she counselled us about life and how to handle situations at an early stage before it gets late.

Eriela m ariri

I have endured a lot of anguish. One has to endure many pains in many undertakings in order to, appreciate life and have equanimity of mind in facing the world.

Ajo nnunu si, onye si ka o nwuo, ka o nwu o, ka onwu o

Bluebird (ajo nnunu)

The bad bird says, he who wants to die, let him die. If you want to follow the right path to life, you can do so, if not, you have to bear the consequences of it and have yourself to blame. This is message of the bluebird. The bluebird is one of the diviners.

Ego si nnukwere ya

Poverty makes one complain. Money speaks loudly. When money speaks, people listen.

Anaghi ezi onwu onye o na-egbu

Death has no discrimination. It does its work at will with no respect to any person or anything.

Unu emekwala omume nke imewo anya

Do not do eye service but be diligent always.

I puo n'ogbo ikpe, kwuo eziokwu maka na ihe onye kpetara ka o ji ala n'ulo ya

During the village deliberations, always speak the truth because the judgement you pass is the judgement you will take home. When you speak the truth, nothing will happen to you. Even though people are against you, God will always be on your side.

Anaghi m ebi ikpe n'ihe m nuru n'akuko

Never base your judgement on hearsay. Rather, judge according to what you observed, so that you will not make a mistake and God will bless you for your truthfulness.

Abughim nwa aga-edobe n'ulo dobekwe onye na-eche ya

I am not the kind you will keep at home and keep a guard to guide. I am not a bad person that you keep at home and keep a guard to watch over.

Ihe uwa eju afo

This world is an unfulfilled world. The world is full of unfinished plans. If you try to fulfil and satisfy the world, you will lose your life. Only try your best and keep your hands clean. Things in the world are not totally fulfilling but one has to say, *"egbiri nde ogu nde ogu alaa."*

Unu ejikwala onu unu ekwu erie

Never use your mouth to talk about unhealthy things. Whenever my mother advised us on this, she would add this proverb, *"Ajo uka bu eghu olulo" (A bad word will eventually return to the speaker)*. You have to be careful with your words because you may have to take them back).

Usu (bat) si, ya ma na ya joro ajo njo mere ya jiri were abali na-akpa

Bat (Usu)

The bat says that she know how ugly she is, that is what makes her move around in the middle of the night. This proverb is similar to the ones about cutting her coat according to her size or one hanging her bag where her hand would reach. Most often, one aims higher where he/she could not cope with. Always attempt what you are able to achieve. Here is a story following this: A young boy wanted to get rich overnight. He joined a cult and he was asked to get the head of his mother and his elder sister so that he would be rich. This boy foolishly went and killed his mother and his sister but unfortunately, he was caught and put to death. This young man's life and future were ruined forever. Now, where is his wealth and high ambition? He lost his father and ruined his future. Whatever you do, think before you act.

"To live long, it is necessary to live slowly." -
—Shakespeare

Odiri usu nma ma ya ejiri abali nakpa

Is it all well with the bat, that it does its business in the night? The bat does not see well during the day but navigates well in the night. It is he who says it is all right, yet, there is a stumbling block in his pride.

Ikwu amaghi ibe ezi ya

It is common practice that if one does not know how to do things, others will show him how.

Unu eberekwala n'elu

Do not stand on the surface. Don't stand on the fence; be inside. This means you have to belong. Whatever others are doing that is good and peaceful, do it. All the things my mother used to say helped me a lot wherever I found myself.

Eziokwu bu ndu

Truth is life. Always stand by truth and nothing will happen to you.

Unu emekwala ndi muru unu ihe buru n'obi

No matter what happens, never go to the extreme with regard to your parents. Never do anything to your parents that will make them feel very bad. Respect your parents in order to get blessings and live a long life with prosperity.

> *"Honour your father and your mother, as God has commanded you, so that you may have long life and may prosper in the land that God gives to you"*
> **—Deuteronomy 5: 16.**
> **The Jerusalem Bible & Popular Edition**
> **Darton, Longman & Todd (p. 194).**

One can see that our ancestors' proverbs, most often, match the teachings in the Bible even though they did not read the Bible or go to school. They had wonderful knowledge which God and nature instilled in them. We are blessed to be their children.

Unu ejikwala nganga aba n'osu
Never use pride to be an outcast. Most often, someone might out of pride involve himself in trouble.

Onwu adi otutu n'anwu adighi atu ujo
Death is literally for everyone. There is no need to fear it. It comes to everyone.

Unu amanyekwala okenye aka n' onu mgbe o na-ekwu okwu
Never interrupt your elders when they are talking to you. Listen attentively.

Werenu nri rijuo afo, ann abughi nri
Eat regular food except meat. My mother used to say this whenever any of her children were crying for meat instead.

A buzighi m ozu katon
I am no longer a worthless somebody. My body is worthy of good attention when living and when dead.

Unu mara ihe, unu ga-eji otu aku gbagbuo nnunu abuo

If you are wise, you could use an arrow to catch two birds. In other words, make proper use of the little things you have. If you pay attention to little important things, you will harvest good results. The English adage says, "Penny wise, pound foolish."

Juanum ajuju, esim Oru

Ask me and learn from me; I have experienced much in struggling for life. My mother went through many obstacles before achieving her goals. So, whenever any of us was complaining, and expressing her sufferings then my mother would say to that person, "ask me, I am from Oru." She would say to the person in question, "when you go out, you will meet with people whose anguishes are greater than yours." Therefore, you are not alone. Have patience and look for solution.

Story: In times past, people went to Oru (the coast) to buy fish. They had to cross some rivers. They, at times, had to walk barefoot on clay slippery places and they had no protection against mosquitoes. Though they were treated fairly, it was not like what they had back home.

After that entire rigorous journey, they returned home with the fish they bought and took a breath of relief. Thus, they had a lot of stories to tell. And so, they say, "ask me, I am from Oru."

Abum ajuala, anam aguzu- aguzu mana atu

I am like the Viper; I give a due warning before I bite. It is just like a chicken that gives a number of strikes before it eats the victim or the prey (eji ogu).

Inwereike ijiri inyinya ga na nmiri ma inweghi ike imanye ya ka onuo nmiri

One man can take a horse to the spring but twenty men cannot force it to drink. It is only when you are willing to do a thing that it is possible. It is not possible if you are not willing. Our parents had shown us and yet have been showing us good pathway to follow; it has left for us alone to follow their good examples.

Ura ga-eju onye nwuru anwu afo

The dead will sleep forever. This means you will have plenty of time to do what you want. It is your choice to make proper use of your time.

Utara sirike onye na eri bu ebelebe

The fufu is hard and the eater is more sophisticated. That means, both ways, things are even. When things get hard, everyone gets tougher.

Usu abudi anu elu nke oji abu anu ala

The bat does not belong to the bird family because it has no feathers and does not lay eggs. It cannot walk as a land animal though it delivers her young ones alive. Usu is like somebody who does not belong to any group. As a result, he resembles nobody. He has his own character. It means that such a person is a strange (queer) fellow.

Ozu sibe isi, enyi alaa ma nwanne eburu

A friend in need is a friend indeed. When a dead man starts to smell, some brothers stand by, while others go. No matter what you do, never forget your people.

Were ire gi guo eze gi onu

Use your initiative to understand what is going on. Watch how you speak. That is, watch your pronouncement. Research your conscience and mend your life.

Wepu aka enwe n'ofe ka o hara igho aka mmadu

It is very crucial that you start early avoiding trouble. If you're following bad guys, start now to withdraw yourself, knowing that you may end up dead in the near future. Here is a short story.

A young man began to follow bad boys and take hard drugs to get high. His boys praised him for being powerful and fearless. Do you know what happened to him? One day, when his cup was full, he acted and killed someone. He who kills by the sword, dies by the sword. This handsome young man was arrested and put in jail by the law enforcement agents. Now, his life is useless. One could ask where his power is. Where is his highness? Where are his friends who misled him? He is suffering alone and his friends and those who deceived him are still living and enjoying themselves. My mother would advise us and say, "a word is enough for the wise. If you know how to pound, pound in a mortar, if not, pound on the ground. She would add, if destroy your mat, you lie on the floor." Then she would sing this song for you and me; "have you seen what you did to yourself on the express road? See how you disgraced yourself publicly." Finally, she would end it with this proverb: *"iji na enweghi onye ndumodu na eso ozu ekpu na ili"*-meaning one who does not have an adviser, always goes astray.

Ya wuru ma tabiri tasa eze, ya noro n'oku fee oku
Instead of giving something grudgingly, you better withdraw your gift.

2.2 Igbo Proverbs, Body Sign Language, Metaphoric Sayings, and Songs

In the Ancestral Family Counselling, nonverbal signals are very essential in the upbringing of children. In my own case, my mother used all aspects of nonverbal language to train us. She was an expert in the usage of nonverbal cues in communicating to her children. These nonverbal cues include eye contact, body posture, personal stance, gestures, and facial expressions, tone of voice, inflation of voice, vocal volume, and timing. Also, she used other variables including smile, head-nodding, and appropriate animation. When we were growing up, Mama used facial expressions a lot to reprimand her girls especially when one was not sitting well as a woman. She would swing her hand and twist her mouth to signal the person to sit properly. If one failed to get the message, she would use the head of a broom to punch that person between the legs.

Eye Contact: Mama used this nonverbal cue a lot to disapprove or approve certain behaviours. Whenever she rolled her eyes towards the left side, it meant disapproval but whenever she rolled them on the right side, it meant approval. Such disapproval is like when a visitor came into the house, and she did not want any of the children to be around, she would roll her eyes left, asking the child to leave the scene. Hence, if she wanted you to stay to listen to their conversation, she would roll her eyes towards the right asking you to pay attention too.

Tone of Voice: This is another of my mother's crucial cues. Whenever she was not happy with our behaviour, her tone of voice would portray it. We would then keep our distance. Likewise, when she was happy, we also realized it from the tone of her voice. Really, we were connected with our parents and ancestors then, unlike the children of this present time, who would even moan when their parents look at them or make any non-verbal signs to them. Some would say to her mom or dad, "why are you eyeing me?" The Western child would even add to it, saying his parents were silly for making non-verbal signs. Before you know it, she claims abuse.

Metaphoric sayings are part of home counselling. Like our mother, when any of her children was conveying her to market or somewhere else, she would say, "lift up your legs." This means move faster. She used to say it a lot to me because I was slow walker then and she would say to me, *nne m Rosa, (welita ukwu gi elu)*. Then she would say, uzo too *ogologo atukwasaya ukwu odi mkpu- mkpu*. (When the road is long, the fast on it make it shorter). Our parents use body sign language a lot in the education of their young ones. And all the children who paid much attention towards these non-verbal cues are great men and women in society, of which the author is one among them. They are easily adjusted in any society. They are also always sensitive to their environment. They always know how to signal and when one signals, they understand it immediately.

Body Language Signs

Eyes: Eyes blinking with twisting mouth means rebuke with disapproval. Eyes blinking with head thrown forward means come or approval: forward and backward means approval. Eyes blinking with head thrown side to side (left to right) is a mark of disapproval. Eyes opening widely with tongue out means rebuke with disgust.

Fingers rubbing across eyes mean be cautious. Eyes opening widely and steadily means surprised. When the eyes along with the head are thrown to one side, it means they are disgusted with you.

Nose: Making nose at means sneering or jeering at.

Mouth: Licking the mouth and smacking the lips means very pleasant flavour. Twisting the mouth means looking with disapproval. Wide mouth with huu sound means why did you do this? Closed mouth with hissing sound means shut up. Finger on the mouth means do not talk any more.

Head: Nodding of head forwards and backwards means in conformity with the speaker.

Ear: Turning left or right ear from side to side means intently trying to understand what is being said.

Hand: Wave of hand with palm down means go down; and wave with palm up means come up. A show of hand with fingers crossed means very good. Two open hands up means I have nothing to hide. With open hands down means hide it or hide yourself.

Leg: Stamping or shuffling the floor with a foot while someone is talking or doing something means disapproval.

Breast: Tapping your chest with your fingers means is it me? Or have mercy on me.

Tongue: Wagging your tongue at anyone means he is talking too much.

Breath: When you release your breath with a sigh it means dissatisfied. When you cat-call anyone, it means you are ridiculing him. When you are making a speech and your mentor waves the two palms up, she is telling you to keep it up.

Egwu Onwa Song
Chukwu nuru olu anyi, Chukwu nuru olu anyi
Nuruolu anyi Chukwu nuru olu anyi
Onwedi mgbe ike mmadu ji akaria ike Chukwu
Onwedi mgbe ike mmadu ji akaria ike Chukwu
Chukwu nuru onye kere uwu nuru olu anyi
Chukwu nuru onye kere uwa nuru olu anyi.

(a) Anieze -Anieze Chineke kanyi ga eje,
      Kanyi ga eje, kanyi ga eje Chineke,
      Chineke kanyi ga eje, kanyi ga eje
      Kanyi ga eje Chineke, Chineke kanyi ga eje

(b) Anieze -Anieze Orusa kanyi ga eje,
      Kanyi ja eje, kanyi ga eje Oruas,
      Orusa kanyi- kanyi ga eje, ka ga eje,
      Kanyi ga eje, Orusa, Orusa kanyi ga eje

(c) Anieze -Anieze Chileke kanyi ga eje
      Kanyi ga eje, kanyi ga eje Chileke
      Chileke, kanyi ga eje, ka ga eje, kanyi
      ga eje Chileke, Chileke kanyi ga eje, kanyi ga eje,
      kanyi ga eje

(d) Anieze -Anieze Chineke kanyi ga eje
      Kanyi ga eje, kanyi ga eje Chineke
      Chineke, kanyi ga eje, kanyi ga eje
      Kanyi ga eje Chineke, Chineke kanyi ga eje.
      Umu Chineke jikerebenu
      Anieze Chineke adigo nso, jikerebenu -jikerebenu e-e
      Odigo nso jikerebenu- jikerebenu
      Umu oma nulibanu,
      Anieze Chineke adigo nso, unlibanu, nulibanu ye- ye
      odigo nso nulibanu, nulibanu
      Umu agozili -agozi nulibanu
      Anieze Chineke adigo nso ye- ye

Odigo nso nulibanu, nulibanu
Umu Chineke nulibanu
Anieze Chineke adigo nso, nulibanu -nulibanu ye -ye
Odigo nulibanu, nulibanu.

2.3 Mode of Life - (a) Housing (b) Food (c) Health (d) Farming (e) Industry (f) Trade (g) Wealth

Housing

Before the White man brought zinc corrugated iron sheets for roofing, our people built their houses by making the walls with red earth brick blocks and the roofs with thatched mats made from raffia palm leaves. The construction of houses is the duty of men; thus, boys are instructed how to get palm leaves and make palm mats. A house has two roof frame-works made up of palm frond rafters running from the top to the bottom and from side to side as beams. On these rafters, palm mats are thatched. Boys must learn how to do all these things. They must learn to dig a hole in the soil if there is not one already made, to reach where the red clay earth is. They mash the red soil until it is pliably soft. Then, they make bricks blocks from it and allow them to dry. They must learn how to lay the brick blocks in making the walls.

Food

We have a variety of foodstuffs from which to make foods. We have foodstuffs like yams, potatoes, cocoyam's (taro), cassava, maize (corn), onions, garlic, beans, rice, bananas, plantains, carrots, tomatoes, peppers, pumpkin (anyu), fluted pumpkin (ohi), breadfruit (ukwa), melon (ogiri, egusi), ugba" (ukpakala), mangoes, "ube", "achara", oranges, pawpaw, avocados, and vegetables (ugu, okasi, oha, inene, anara, olugbo, ahihiara, ogbolo, ororo, okro, egusi). Our foods are yam, rice fufu, cassava fufu, aribo (yam flour), acica (dried yam fufu), garri (dried grated cassava), ikpa (junk cornmeal), moi-moi (soft fabricated black eye bean), akamu (corn porridge), agidi (semi-solid corn flour), akpakpa (corn meal), aturuatu (half-sifted cornmeal), ibibe (cassava chips) ukwa meal, anyu meal, ohi meal, beans meal, rice meal, and junk yam meal. See nutrition and medical uses. There are elaborate indigenous ways of preparing these meals. The preparation of the food is the duty of women and girls who are counselled how to make good meals by their mothers. In the house, you must have a hearth (fireplace), a pot-stand (okeigwe), firewood, pots, water, foodstuffs, and condiments for cooking them.

Pot-stand (okeigwe)

Obogu (plantain and Dayflower)

These are commonplace weeds which cause despair to farmers, gardeners, and lawn tenders because whenever they are cut into pieces, each piece persists and starts to grow into a new plant. A new whole appears a day or two after the plant is cut to the ground. These weeds are valued by some people for their tasty and nutritious foliage which is richer than spinach in iron and vitamins A and C. Some use them as a remedy for cuts, sores, burns, and insect bites. It is a symbol of self-confidence and immortality for we call them *"anwuanwu"* because they never die; they are everlasting. We gather the weeds and put them in a heap where they can be controlled.

Nchanwu

African parsley, rich in iron, vitamins A and C and minerals. It is good for gravies and yam pottage. It is also used as a remedy for sores, cuts, and stomach pains. We sing *"nchanwu na ato uto ma etinye ya na ofe ma ona afu ufu ma etinye ya na onya"* This means it is sweet in the soup but painful on sores.

Health

Boys and girls are groomed how to keep their bodies and minds healthy by proper use of toilet articles and proper application of cosmetic materials. They must eat well and enough and must not be greedy and gluttonous or be awkward while at table. They must do dishes after meals. They must report any pain in the body so that the proper attention can be paid to it. They must wash their clothes as often as necessary so as to be always neat before people for cleanliness is next to godliness. The native medicine person is always consulted with respect to getting protection from the god because we believe that the well-being of our lives depends on the gods.

Farming

Farming is a must for everyone, male and female, in the community because the community is the bread basket of the clan. Everyone must learn how to farm and endure the rigours of food production. You start to cut the bush down in the month of February and allow the green leaves of the cut trees to dry up. In the month of March, towards the end of the month, the dry cut bush is set on fire. Then, we wait for the first rain in April before preparing the soil for planting the crops. Men and women join together in every step. When planting, mixed planting is used. Yams are planted first, then maize, melon, pumpkin, fluted pumpkin and vegetables, then cassava comes last. While yam vines are trained on stakes of plants, women will go on cultivating the soil to loosen it up to allow water and manure to penetrate into the soil and to remove weeds and new outgrowths of plants. By May, maize is growing to maturity. Pests like grasshoppers, crickets and caterpillars are sought and killed. Maize and vegetables are the first to be harvested. It takes three months to labour in the farm before harvesting starts. It is always with hardship that you have to labour in the sun and in the rain. And so, children must be drilled, coached and encouraged to be hardy in their farm work. On a farm work day, boys sharpen the farm tools - hoes, knives, and "mbiribas" and the girls cook food that will be eaten on the farm.

Industry

There is a saying in Iboland which my mother taught us: "*Ibughi onye Oru iburu onye Oku.*" That is the general policy that you have to learn to be an artisan craftsman or a farmer or both. That time, everyone was fully employed. You could be a blacksmith, a tailor, a carpenter, a bricklayer (a mason), a builder, a hairdresser, a machine repairer, a trader, a harvester of palm fruits, a palm wine tapper, a native engineer, a native psychologist, a native doctor, etc. You could not afford to be idle, otherwise, you would be suspected of evil-doing. People lived within their means. There was no ambition to be rich through greediness or manipulation. Everyone was studied in order to assess his/her capability. This process was the origin of our modern schooling system. Though people did not learn how to read and write in English, yet technically, they were educated in the native cultural technology. No university taught the palm wine tapper how to do his occupation or how to use the yeast in the air to produce a typical palm wine. No school taught my people how to process the indigenous foodstuffs in order to produce edible foods. It was by local counselling that professional trades were passed on from generation to generation. They designed and made the instruments they used for any process. All our hoes, knives, spades, mortars and pestles, wooden plates, musical instruments, clothes and buildings were designed and made to custom by our people and the relevant information was given by oral counselling. Thus, illustrious nobles and ladies have been produced as a result. We had the famous farmers who celebrated the abundance of harvested yams annually. We had the "*omenkas*" who were known for all sorts of products ranging from jewelry, artistry, clothing machinery, etcetera. The present-day technical artefacts are copies of those ancestral technical initiatives.

Trade

We produce foodstuffs and sell foodstuffs. We raise animals mainly for domestic use and sacrifices to gods. Originally, we started the use of gold as a means of exchange because we had gold in abundance.

In ancient Egypt, gold was a noble, royal, and divine metal and so, it was the means of exchange. The Chinese, because of the bulkiness and the scarcity of gold, invented paper money for exchange. Today, gold is the world's standard of exchange. Yet, this was the case in Africa some three thousand years ago. Africans first started using the bellows in metal smelting and they are still using them in metal works. Our women wear bangles, necklaces, anklets, and bracelets of gold and even use marble and gold chips for playing games. There were men and women traders and they had to be counselled in the know-how. Our people traded in farm produce, fish, animals, clothes and products of the blacksmiths and craftsmen in exchange for commodities from outside the clan. Men and women were attached to those who were already experienced in trading as trainees who were taught all it took to run a trading business. Men would deal in clothes and animals and animal products while women would opt for trading in fish, foodstuffs, foods, and women's apparel. They exchanged gold for salt from North Africa. We made our clothes.

Wealth

There was a traditional way of showing that you had wealth. Men were initiated in the "*Ozo*" titled "*agbalanze*" society. You had to be very strong before you could take the "Ozo" title. You were to show that you were a man of high esteem by worshipping at 21 shrines of 21 gods with a lot of expenses of money and materials. At the initiation, you are counselled on what you eat, on what to abstain from, on how to behave, on your rights, your place in the community, and how to worship the gods every day and every four days. When you have finished the initiation, you are now "*Nze*" (*Ozo* initiate and exemplary, truthful, righteous one, free from defilement and ridicule) and you are given (1) *arunze* - a gold spear (a sign of power), (2) an elephant tusk (*oduenyi*) (greatness), (3) an eagle feather (a symbol of truthfulness), (4) a portable throne (okobe) (a symbol of royalty), (5) '*ikolobibi*' feather (*igoloma* feather) (saying you are doubly truthful), (6) a crown-like cap (you are like a king), (7) your title name, for example, *Nnanyelugo* - my father made me a king. Egyptians would say, user – maat -Ra - the beloved of Ra, the justice of Ra. You can now wear anklets of gold and lion's teeth meaning that you are a nobleman *(ogaranye)*. You are given a sceptre (*okpipikpa of ofo*) and onyima of ofo (spiritual power).

For women, they take "*Ekwe*" title. They spend a lot of money and material and are initiated in the *Obana Ezenwanyi goddess shri*ne, where they dip their fingers in the big pot (*nneoku*) of all goodies (*imanye aka na nne oku*). They are given a staff of gold. The *Ekwe* women become powerful in that they speak up when there is controversy or an important discussion in town. They settle cases among women. Young girls from rich families wear "ija" (many-coiled anklets of gold or brass) and bracelets made from elephant tusks. For saving their money, they use big wooden casks or they organize an *"Isoso"* lending society in which they contribute money every month and give it to one of the members in rotation. Each has to have her turn for receiving contributions. Men celebrate *ikwaji* and women celebrate with dancing orchestras. All these display a show of wealth, peace and unity in the society.

CHAPTER 3

3.1 Outline of the Marvels of Folk Tales, Their Psychological and Moral Merits on the Children.

Mother's Advice Song to a Troublesome Child that Disapproved of Bad Behaviour (Ozo Mgbim, Mgbim -Meaning, stamping)

Ozo mgbim- mgbim, ozo mgbim-mgbim (stamping)
biko azogbukwana nwaewu ocha nwa -nwa Igodo
Aanunu werere iya nwa ololo anunu werere Orie nnem osoro bia
Anunu werere iya nwa ololo anunu werere Afo nnem osoro bia
Anunu werere iya nwa ololo anunu werere Nkwo nnem osoro bia
Anunu werere iya nwa ololo anunu werere Eke nnem osoro bia.

This song means: you, who is stamping along, please do not set your foot down on the white goat belonging to Igodo. This advice is being addressed to Anunu Werere (a dullards).

Anunu werere, you of dull mind, you see Orie, the good one of my mother's?

Did you see Afo, the good one of my mother's?
Did you see Nkwo, the good one of my mother's?
Did you see Eke, the good one of my mother's?

This song is showing the disappointment of a mother over one of her children, that is to say, a bad child who is a trouble-maker, and is being consoled with the rest whom she calls by their names. Orie, Afo, Nkwo, and Eke - these are her well-behaved children and sources of her consolation. So, it is not good to be stubborn and troublesome. Never give your parents a hard time because it does not pay. (Deut. 5:16). Umu'm, were nu otu obi na eme ihe, olu onu buru out, unu atukwana asi. This means be united and carry out all your activities in unison and with one mind and one voice. Bear with one another and never lie.

Mother's Protection over Her Child (Anu Ukwu Eburu Le Nwa Gi Naba)

Nne totuo udo-o, totuo udo, anu ukwu abiana eburu nwa gi naba, totuo udo.
Anta abiana eburu nwa gi naba totue udo.

This means, mother, drop down the rope for me to climb up for a big wild beast will carry me away. Please drop the rope, mother, drop down the rope for me to climb up for a small wild animal has come to take me away; mother drop the rope.

This is a mother's protection over her child and childlike confidence in her mother as well as his/her parents at large. A mother animal left her young one at the foot of a tree and climbed up the tree. For this reason, a big wild beast and small animal saw her and threatened to take the young one away. The young one cried out to the mother to let down the rope so that the young could be pulled up away from harm from the wild beasts. This is also teaching us to have trust in our parents. And good parents always protect their young ones. It is only a bad parent who misleads her child.

Children should always heed to the advice of their parents.

An Orphan Lamentation Song (Nwa Enwe Nne-Orphan)

Agaba oru unee, asikpo nwa enwe nne unee.
Echube miri unee, asikpo nwa enwe nne unee.
Esibe nri unee, asikpo nwa enwe nne unee.
Ma esicha nri unee, achupu nwa enwe nne unee.
Nwa enwe nne unee, afusienam anya unee.
Ifufusienya unee ifufusienya ka onwu unee.

English Translation

When there is need to work in the farm, the orphan is made to work in the farm.

When it is time to fetch water, the orphan is asked to fetch water.

When it is time to cook food, the orphan is called in to cook the food.

When cooking is done, and eating is on, the orphan is left out.

Oh! Orphan, I have suffered a lot, such that my suffering is more than my beingdead.

Here, we are urged not to maltreat any orphan or under-privileged people.

It doesn't pay to be wicked. A wicked fellow receives his/her reward the same way.

Seven Cult Girls, their Stories, the Lessons, and what they Teach

Umu-Ogbanje Nasaa

Omunkwu na Omungwo, imirima ngbawara eze,
Afu ara anwua imirima ngbawara eze,
Afu ezi anwua imirima ngbawara eze,
Alua di anwua imirima ngbawara eze,
Aturu ime anwua imirima ngbawara eze,

Amuta nwa anwua imirima ngbawara eze,
Anyi na abia-a imirima ngbawara eze
Anyi na ala-a imirima ngbawara eze (Iho dei).

Seven Ogbanjes with Seven Predestinations

Seven persons who are predestined to die young, The first two answered Omunkwu and Omungwo as their guy names. So, once someone outside their cult group calls them these names, they would die. Here are the predestinations of the rest.
The third one is predestined to die once she develops breasts.
The fourth one is predestined to die when her first menstruation appears.
The fifth one is predestined to die when she gets married.
The sixth one is predestined to die on her first pregnancy.
The seventh one is predestined to die at her first childbirth.
The sooner they come, the earlier they go back.

When our mother narrated this story to us, she advised us not to follow a bad group and not to make bad promises. It doesn't pay to join a bad group. Always follow people who would influence your life in a successful way.

Relevance Song of Old Basket

Nkirika ekete mgbe ana ekwo ntu ka ana echeta ya,
Nkirika ekete mgbe ana ekwo ntu ka ana echeta ya.
Oh, old basket, you are remembered only when you are to be used for removing the firewood ash.
Oh, old basket, you are remembered only when you are to be used for removing the firewood ash.

This relevant song of old basket reprimands and disapproves of the action of a child that disobeys the parents when asked to do some chore and he or she refuses but comes back to the parents in times of need. Mama used this to reprimand any of her children that disobeyed and came back to her asking for food or anything. This song calls one back to one's senses. Avoid disobeying your parents because they have the final say to you. You have to obey their words in order to earn their blessings. The wise man says,

> *"Fare hard and work hard while you are young and you will have a chance of rest when you are old."*
> **—Michael Chijioke Nduka**

Another Joyful Song of our Mother

> *O lee ndi nwe ngozi uwa, ndi Orlu nwe ngozi (x2)*
> *Ngozi Chineke nyere Orlu nwafor mba were ego bia izu ngozi*
> *Ana eji ego azu ngozi uwa, Orlu nwe ngozi.*

English Translation

Who owns the blessing? Orlu people own it.
The blessing which God gave Orlu people the children of nwafor but another neighbourhood came to buy it;
Can blessing be obtained by buying it?

Sorrowful Song of a Sick Child (Akwa Ariri)

> *Onye riabara di nma o -o nwa kere,*
> *Onye riabara di nma o -o nwa kere*
> *Nne mu aburu na nne dim oma o -o nwa kere*
> *Nna mu aburuna nna dim oma o- o nwa kere*
> *Nwa nnem nwoke aburuna dim mara nma o- o nwa kere.*

Whoever has sustained a long illness - Oh a little child
Whoever has sustained from a long illness - Oh little child
My mother has become my mother-in-law - Oh a little child
My father has become my father-in-law - Oh little child
My brother has become my husband - Oh little child.

Wedding Song (Amara Chukwu du la kwa anyi ulo)

Amara Chukwu du na kwa anyi ulo,
Chineke bi na igwe du na kwa anyi ulo
Amara Chukwu du na kwa anyi ulo.

We are here praying that God's watchful, enduring guidance will protect the newly married couple in every endeavour they undertake. Mothers here do show their solidarity, praying, wishing, and encouraging the couple for the new life they have undertaken.

Birth Song (Egwu Omungwo)

In Ibo culture, our mothers especially value the newborn baby and her mother so dearly. Whenever a newborn is returning home from the maternity, our mothers will dress up gorgeously and the family of the newborn baby will produce a big jar of powder for all the women to put on their faces or necks and on everyone else who visits the baby. Hence, our mothers would go to the maternity to welcome the child and his or her mother home as they sing their joyful songs which I learnt from my own mother:

O nuru ube (akwa) nwa bia o, bia o, bia o, bia, oo o
Obughi otu onye nwe nwa na uwa
Oha nile nwe nwa oo

English Translation

Whoever hears the cry of a child should come
It is not only one person who owns the child
The whole world owns him/her.

Another Egwu Omungwo) Birth Song

Sakara, sakara, ihe anyi gbatara n' utee
Sakra, sakara, ihe anyi gbatara n' utee

Sakara, sakara, ihe anyi gbatara n'utee

This means the love between husband and wife has given rise to a healthy bouncing baby. Also has brought a blessing and happiness to the family and the entire community.

Agam ekpere Chineke ekpere oma-a,
Agam ekpere Chineke ekpere oma-a,
Kpeere Chineke kpeere ala Orlu si ogodo kwere ibem atukwanam-o.

With this song, the mothers ask God for the blessing to give them the necessary things that others have such as children like other women. This is a song of a happy mood when a good thing happens to our mothers; when a new child is born and when any of their grown-up children bought some gifts such as clothes for them. Thus, whenever a new child is born, mothers anticipate future hope of gifts and wealth from the child.

A Happy Mood Song- A gift from Child to Mother (Agana Ma Nwa, Onye Ga Enyem)

Agana ma nwa, onye ga enyem,
Agana ma nwa, onye ga enyem.

They sing it several times, shaking their big buttocks.

This song means:

If I have not had a child, who gives me gifts,
Who else could have done it otherwise?
If I have not had a child, who gives me gifts,
Who else could have done it otherwise?

Parents receive rewards from their children through the assistance they render to them, like the children buying clothes, gold, shoes, etc., for their parents and giving them money. Such help makes parents, especially mothers, sing these songs. Thus, it is their happy mood on receiving a gift from their children that elicits this song. It is also an appreciation song to their children on receiving the gifts and a welcome song for the newborn - their future hope.

Onye muta, ibe ya amuta, ihe eji nwa eme buru ibu ooo

Then they would make this sound several times:
Eh, eh ey ee h, eh, eh, eh, eh, eh, eh, etc.
They would feel happy and joyous, blessing the baby and the mother. They also ask obu gini oo? That is, what is it oo? They respond in affirmation, obu nwao, that is, it is a child oo! And then some ask nwa gini oo? What kind of child oo? Some answer back nwa nwoke, nwa nwanyi oo, that is, the child is a boy or a girl; depending on the sex of the child. There would be eating and drinking. Jubilation would fill the hearts of everybody around. One could see oneness and the solidarity as well as the bonding of the women. The way the mothers feel when the newborn arrives, grows, and progresses is also how they feel bad when the child is not doing well. The concern of a mother is a concern for all the mothers in Igboland of Southeastern Nigeria.

Onye ihe oma di mma bia juo anyi ilola. Onye ihe oma na dighi mma ala gbaa ya ose n'anya. '(3time)

Let every good person come and say welcome to the newcomer. Anyone who does not like good things should be peppered by the land. In other words, when a newborn arrives, or someone makes a great achievement, everybody is requested to come together and rejoice with the person. Subsequently, the jealous ones are being discouraged by the norms of the land.

Song for inu omungwo for celebrating a child's birth)

Okwaegwu: *Anyi je oru, anyi ejeghi oru*
Chorus: Anyi jegbu ji nma nisi
Okwa: Onye weta onye weta
Chorus: Onye oriri pom -pom nonu

Okwa: Onye muru nwa jide nwa
Chorus: Egwu ali peteri, peteri, peteri
Egwu ali peteri, egwu ali peteri.
Okwa: Anyi je eri -eri
Chorus: obughi ubu.

English Translation
Main Singer: Whether we work or do not work.
Chorus: We must eat yams.
Singer: Everyone, bring all the delicacies.
Chorus: We will be eating and carousing.
Singer: May child-bearer enjoy childbirth.
Chorus: We dance to your well-being.
Singer: We are going to eat and drink.
Chorus: Happy entertainment on dainty foods.

Lesson of Virtue of an Orphan Song (Udaram –pue-pue-pue-pue nda)

Udaram pue nda,
pue, pue- pue nda
Puere nwa enwe nne – nda
Puere nwa nwe nna – nda.
Nwunye nnam gara zuta udara n'ahia - nda
Rachaa -rachaa -rachaa - nda
Rachakwu nwa enwe nne - nda,
Rachakwu nwa enwe nna - nda,
Elu uwa bu olili - nda,
Onye nochaa ola ba - nda.
Nwata ibem nda
Jiri udara kom onu - nda
Udara bue nda,
Bue-bue - nda
Buere nwa enwe nne - nda
Buere nwa enwe nna - nda
Nnwata ibem nda jiri udara kom onu - nda

Udaram mia - nda
Mia-mia-mia nda,
Miara nwa enwe nne - nda
Miara nwa enwe nna - nda
Nwata ibem nda
Jiri udara kom onu nda
Udaram chaa nda
Chaa-chaa-chaa nda,
Chara nwa enwe nne nda
Chara nwa enwe nna nda
Nwata ibem nda
Jiri udara kom onu nda
eluwa bu oriri nda,
Onye puta oghoro-nda-a.

The Story of an Orphan (Nwa enwe Nna)

It happened that an orphan went to a family which had an Udara fruit tree (Apple – a West African fruit). The orphan was disappointed for he was told to go and eat his mother's udara fruit. Knowing full well he had no parents but God, he decided to plant an udara seed and called on God to help his udara seed grow into maturity. He sang for it to germinate, grow, blossom, flower and develop into ripe fruits. God heard him and made him a big udara orchard. He called everyone to come and rejoice with him. This is a lesson of virtue.

This is the hopeful song of an orphan. He trusted that his hope would be fulfilled. He was a generous and compassionate individual even though he was denied getting apple from his neighbour, yet, he has an open heart and pleaded for his chi to make his apple grow so that others in need would get it from his own. This equally shows that through a difficult experience, we learn how to forgive. When you forgive and have a good thought of others, God blesses you. Therefore, avoid being wicked.

Broom and Green (Aziza Na Inene)

Aziza oo, Aziza yana nwanne ya soro jee ohia nku, aziza agbaghara inene, inene oma-o olo ogho inene oma-o efuonem inene oma-o.

This is a story of Broom and Green (two sisters) who went to fetch firewood in the bush, then Broom left Green and went home. This story is teaching us not to desert our sisters or brothers in times of difficulty; so, comfort the sorrowful and help the needy. Always be compassionate and kind-hearted. No one is an island. We need each other to grow. We are called upon to care for one another. Aziza (Broom) did not care about her sister, Inene (Green) with whom she went to fetch firewood because Inene was weak and not as smart as Aziza. She left her behind and went home but when she was worried because Inene was nowhere to be found, Aziza cried in vain when it was late. Never forget to help the weak ones; encourage them, and uplift them. United we stand, divided we fall. Always try to pull your sister or brother along with you. If you are educated, never neglect those who are not educated. All of us have unique talents and unique work to do to enhance one another. Therefore, team effort is the ultimate goal for success and progress.

A Story of a Man Who wanted to buy a Shotgun (Egbe cham- Shotgun)

Nwoke si ya ga-azu egbe cham, nwa ya nwoke si nna ya oburu na a zuta ya, a ga m-ebu uzo gbaa ya mata ka o si ada, nna ya were mma mapu nwa nwoke a isi, nwa ya
a nwua ma na o zughikwa egbe cham, o jighi nwa ya.

Our mother used to tell us about a shotgun story. A man wanted to purchase a shotgun and his son said he would test it first. Then his father got upset and cut his son's head with a knife. Consequently, he lost his son and did not buy the gun. Mama, after telling us this story, would counsel us not to be upset because it can cause one to overreact. She usually told us this story whenever we were struggling for something that was about to happen. She would also add this maxim by saying, umu m, onye obi ojoo na-ebu onye arisi uzo anwu. One who is hardhearted dies earlier than one who has offended the gods. As a result, she would also instruct us, "take away anger in your heart." At this juncture, one can infer that what she applied here was ***anger management skill***. This is the reason why I firmly say that counselling originated from our family setup and our elders do counsel us ahead of the time, not when something goes wrong as parents in the Western World do. Our parents arm us before an event happens instead.

Mother's Happy Song Showing Love and Unity

Enyim Cletus, Cletus enokwa ngala o, o, ogho,
Enyinwanne ka nma o, o, ogho,
Enyinwanne lee, o, o, ogho.
Enyinwanne lee a gam akporo onye ghara onye, o, o, ogho
Enyinwanne ka nma o, o, ogho,
Enyinwanne lee, o, o, ogho.
Enyim Onwuemenyi, Onwuemenyi enokwa ngala, o, o, ogho,
Enyinwanne ka nma, o, o, ogho
Enyinwanne lee, o, o, ogho,
Enyinwanne lee agam akporo onye ghara onye o, o, ogho
Enyinwanne ka nma, o, o, ogho
Enyinwanne lee, o, o, ogho.

When my mother passed on, I visited Mr. Cletus, the man my mother used to sing this song for. I began to sing the sing to him; he and his wife started weeping and asked me to stop reminding them of their good times with Mama. The couple expressed that they could never experience such good times in their lifetime. Enyinwanne told me good stories about Dada Ojukwu - my mother. Enyinwanne said to me, "Sister, your mother was a symbol of unity and a treasure to our community." I then shed tears of joy and responded she really was.

A Happy Song of My Mother Showing Love and Unity

Happy Song of Entreaty

Onyenyem- onyenyem mbele ejum aka
Onye agaghi enyem onya ama ya.

This means that by receiving from everyone, I am full of gifts but if anyone does not give me something, that one will be at a loss. This is a wishful demand from anyone when one wants to get favours from others. When this is sung, people willingly offer that person what they have. When our mother wanted us to give her what we were eating, she sang this song. Then everybody would give her what we were eating, such foods as rice, peanuts, meat, fish, bananas, etc. This teaches a sense of sharing.

Okenya ona erikwa ihe ooo

Mama's funny mood - she would tell us to go outside our house and shout "does elder eat?" This was whenever we finished eating our own food and expected her to share her own food with us.

My mother's immediate junior used to sing this song for my late elder brother whenever he was crying when he was still a child:

Ofojiogu o, Ofojiogu o, Ofojiogu nnemu nuu Ofojiogu o
Agala ma onwu ndu na-ato ka nnu koo koo-koo -koo.

Immediately after this song, my late elder brother would keep quiet and be pleased. I learnt this song from my mother. This portrays the effect of the family members' team counselling on the children. All the family members join hands in the upbringing of the children. Anybody can reprimand any child when he or she misbehaves. After reprimanding the child, that person who reprimanded him or her would receive a 'thank you' from the parents of the child being reprimanded. It is never an abuse to call a child to order in Igboland of Southeastern culture. The whole village has the right to discipline a child because it is believed that not only one person has the child, rather, the whole village. This belief affirms thus:

"It takes a village to raise a child."
—Hillary Rodham Clinton 1996.

Egwu Onwa Egwu Oyo

Anyi abiana, anyi abiana na obodo
Anyi abiana, anyi abiana na obodo
Umuaka ibe anyi, anyi abiana,
Anyi abiana na obodo.
Umu nma jiaku, anyi abiana, anyi abiana na obodo
Omanma odenigbo kanyi naa nu
Omanma Nwanyi nma kanyi soo nu
Omanma oji- oji eri ka je gwu
Oma nma nwa mama kanyi naa nu
A, a, a, a.
A, a, a, a; a, a, a, a; sokoto nwa mama
Anu soro nwa enwe omajie olu
Nwa baby, onye nwuru ozurikee
A, a, a, a onye nwuru ozurike
A, a, a, a onye nwuru ozurikee

This is a song of justice which our village men sang for a man who suffered an injustice by his neighbours. In Igbo culture, people are being reprimanded through songs, proverbs, and sign languages; this is to disapprove of their ill-behaviour.

Most of our ancestors still left that bad legacy of scrambling for people's land behind their children. Today, young men in the villages are still scrambling for lands that do not belong to them. They lie against the rightful owner in order to acquire the land that never belonged to them.

I urge you to avert yourself from this practice because it never favours those who practice deceit. Never hurt your neighbours in order to get wealth. Remember, the cry of the oppressed reaches the ears of God.

"Atu puo ala ahu mmuo"

This is our mother's nickname for an inquisitive fellow or fault-finder or a person who delves deeply to find facts. If you go into the deep, you will find the treasure at the bottom of the sea.

Ofeke: (Neckname for a Fool)

Our ancestors always discourage the young to avoid being "ofeke" (a fool or bogus). During the slave trade, any child that proved himself or herself to be a fool would be sold into slavery then. Here is a song our ancestors did sing for fools.

> *Ofeke nupu mmanya- mmanya egbuwe ofeke ya kwuwe ihe*
> *soro ya, Okidoki inukwa ihe uwa si na chi.*
> *A drunken man is always senseless. A drowning man clutches*
> *onto straw.*
> *Ifuna ihe imere onwegi-e,*
> *ifuna ihe imere onwegi-e,*
> *ifuna ihe imere onwegi Nwata kere,*
> *ifuna ihe imere onwegi na okporo achara.*

This is a reprimanding song which our mother used to redirect any of my blood sisters when something happened that they had been instructed to avoid. Mother used to sing this for the one to claim the consequence of her actions. At this point, our mother would give out this proverb; if you tell the ear and it refuses to hear, then when the head is cut off, the ear will follow. In other words, an elderly person rebukes an erring child for misbehaving on the road. It is a cultural thing to guide a young girl how to behave in public, how to eat food at a gathering and how to handle herself when together with other people. Old people get annoyed when they see a young girl doing something of which they disapprove. At that instance, they sing this song which sounds the note of disapproval. Our mother used to call any of her children "Gaga nogwu (alika ife –ife)" a smart person who used his smartness to win even though he or she doesn't look like they can win. When my mother wanted to tease you, to get you to do some works for her, she would call the person "Gaga nogwu (alika ife-ife)" to win. She will also call you Agu nwam (lion) to melt your heart. These words of praise uplift children; even though that person did not want to do the work, he/she would be motivated to do it immediately. Encouragement is necessary to empower children. My mother was good at empowering her children and other children as well.

Mother's Folk-Tale to a Proud Fellow

Otukpukpo (woodpecker), very adept in pecking wood with its strong beak, once upon a time, prophesied that no tree would be left unpecked until the day its parents would die. It happened that it had a big boil in its mouth on the day its parents died and so, it could not peck a tree. It is said that if wishes were horses, the lame could ride. Hence, never brag too much because you never know what will happen next.

Funeral Song: The Night has come
> *Chi ejiele loo, chi ejiele loo, chi ejiele lo;*
> *Onye ekwele ka okika uwa kpo ya na ukwu.*

This means it is now night; one has to be careful in order to avoid being hurt by the stump on the road. You are warned not to stumble on the stump, the difficulties of this life.

Ajo anunu si onye si ka onwuo, ka onwuo ka onwuo
The way you make your bed is the way you lie on it.

Ikwikwi si ozu ijikwa okpu gi-ohoo (the cry of an owl is a sign of bad omen)
The owl is advising the man who is preparing to die, whether he has put everything in order for the journey.

For the living, you have to be prepared before you start your encounter. On other hand, fasten your belt.
Advice to Students by the Bush Fowl (Okwa si ejeje- College -ejeje College)

Ikwikwi (Owl) iga eje College, igukwara ABCD, igukwara ABCD

Do you have the prerequisite for going to College? So, before you intend to go to college, be ready to face all odds.

Akidi kiridim-kiridim,
Na ndidi ka eji eso uwa,
Na nwayo ka eji eso uwa
Onye soro uwa nike ola nmuo.

Slow and steady wins the race.
If you live fast, you die young.
"If you want to live long, live slowly."
—Shakespeare

Complaining Song

Onye muru nwa nebe akwa,
Egbe muru nwa nebe akwa
Weta uzuza weta ose,
Weta amara ngologo ofe
Ka umunnunu Racha ya…

A child that cries a lot does not benefit from all the nourishment the parents give her.

Story of Nwaebuleako

Mama used to tell us a story about an animal called Nwaebuleako. Nwaebuleako is a baby lamb. She said that this animal is a wise animal that anticipates danger ahead of time and plays an effective strategy to handle the situation. Therefore, before danger approaches him, he has already set out a strategy to combat it. After telling us this story, she would advise us to be like Nwaebuleako. This story from my mother was a source of inspiration to me in the USA. In the USA, I was like Nwaebuleako; I always anticipated danger and armed myself. Honestly speaking, this was a major key to my success in the USA. Mama, thanks a lot and may you rest in peace - Amen. At this juncture, I cite the story of this famous animal, Nwaebuleako, to back up my stance.

A lion planned to eat one of the sheep's young ones. The lion begged the sheep to allow one of her young ones to baby-sit her young cub. The sheep agreed but told the lion to wait for her in the night. Then, the sheep summoned all her little ones to find out who was *astute* enough to maneuver the lion so as to escape if the lion tried to kill and eat her up. She located Nwaebuleako, the youngest, who said that he was alert so much so that before you thought to kill him, he was already aware. For this reason, the sheep sent him to the lion at night. The lion planned to kill Nwaebuleako in the night by making him to sleep on the left-hand side which was the lion's powerful hand. At that moment, Nwaebuleako worked out his own strategy by putting the lion's baby on the left-hand side when the lion was deeply asleep. In the middle of the night, the lion woke up suddenly and quickly grabbed the one sleeping on the left-hand side, killed it immediately and began to eat it. There and then, the lion discovered that it was her baby that she had killed. She became angry and devastated, and started searching for Nwaebuleako. By that time, Nwaebuleako had already slipped away and had run home. Nwaebuleako played smartly here. It is good to be smart when you are in a danger zone; if not, you cannot sort yourself out and escape from a trap. The lesson here is that dealing with a lion is scary and fearful but the sheep, honest and harmless, decided anyway to take a plunge. She, however, depended on her past experience to come up even with the lion, a formidable and fierce animal. Never plan evil against anyone. Again, look before you leap. Also, never think you cannot do it, yes you can. Never look down on anybody because no one is insignificant. However, if you are the kind of person people have ill notions of and look down on, show them you're able; that you can do what others do to succeed and your ardent effort to succeed depends on your will-power. I call it "surprise-surprise." Surprise anyone who doubts you; do not be afraid. Show them that a short man can perform wonders as David did to Goliath. Hence, I am not asking you to do as David did; rather, show your ability through paving your way successfully on your life career. Also, show that a slow deep-running stream is always more frightening than the fast-running stream. The Igbo wise saying puts it this way; 'odimkpukpu na eme ire' –small but mighty.

In the United States of America, I set a goal, and I was always fearful of one thing; that is failure. Being afraid, I set a strategy to protect my goal. The strategy I set was to keep away from every person that I knew would be an obstacle or a distractor to my ultimate goal. I hid my phone book inside my box where my hand could not reach it easily to call anybody. I disowned anyone who would tell me distractive stories. I maintained only those who motivated and influenced me positively. This worked for me and I succeeded amazingly. It will work for you too. Fear is a two-edge sword; if you do not know what to do, you mess yourself up? The key to your success is thoughtfulness. It is said that if wishes were horses, men could ride. "***Eneji ututu ama chi?***" Meaning, you can never tell the day from the look of the morning. Very much so, it is not always easy to locate what is, so as to be open to it. What is, is what has been averaged from a multitude of would-bes that have been generalized to represent the truth. What is advised is to look for the truth and when one finds it, one should stick to it. Jesus says to his disciples,

> *"If you make my word your home you will indeed be my disciple; you will learn the truth and the truth will set you free"*
> **—John 8:31-32**
> **The Jerusalem Bible & Popular Edition**
> **Darton, Longman & Todd 1974, (p. 129).**

This is important for it is said in Igbo proverb, "*idide ji ofo awa ala,*" that is, the earthworm has no tool but its head for penetrating the soil because it has the power, authority, and know-how to do so

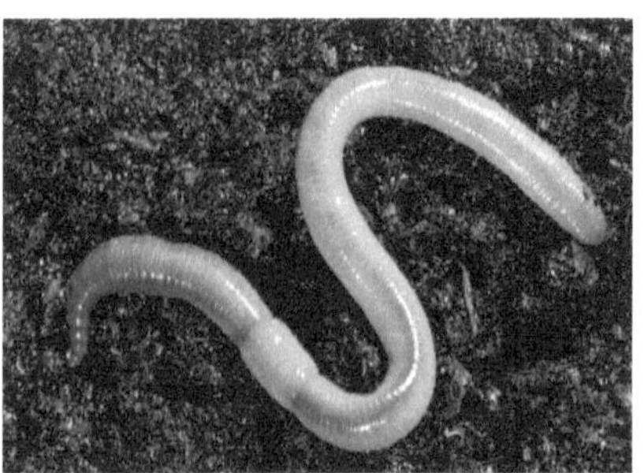

Earthworm
https://www.bing.com/search?q=

Another Christian maxim says,

> *"Keep on then seeking first the kingdom and his righteousness
> and all these (other) things will be added to you"*
> —**Matthew 6:33**
> **New World Translation of the Holy Scriptures.**

You must first seek to find the truth for then it is easy to know how to proceed in order to reach the goal. If we must harvest a good apple, we must know how to plant a good seed and grow it. When you know the truth, stick to it, for it will set you free.

Story about the Tortoise and the Dog

The tortoise and the dog bet in a race competition. The tortoise, a slow-moving animal, claimed it would beat the dog, a fast-running animal, in a race. The dog looked down on the tortoise, then, they decided on a date and a target for the race. On the appointed day, the tortoise, being a cunning creature, cooked the dog's food and left it on the side of the road leading to the target. They both set off. The dog ran very fast. Suddenly, the dog came upon its food left by the roadside. The dog sat down to eat, feeling comfortably that he was ahead of the tortoise. After finishing the food, the dog went on to have a nap. He slept on. The tortoise walked up to the point and saw the dog fast asleep. The tortoise craftily passed by and steadily reached the target just in time before the dog. When the dog woke up, it ran very fast but was late because the tortoise was already there at the target. What is the lesson here? All haste without proper discernment, makes a clever person a simpleton (fool). Covey stated thus:

> *"One of the most profound learning of my life is this: 'If you want to achieve your highest aspirations and overcome your greatest challenges, identify and apply the principle or natural law that governs the results you seek. How we apply a principle will vary greatly and will be determined by our unique strengths, talents, and creativity, but, ultimately, success in any endeavours is always derived from acting in harmony with the principles to which the success is tied."*
>
> **—Stephen R. Covey**
> **The 7 Habits of Highly Effective People 1989, (Foreword**
> **page 7).**

I definitely believe that the tortoise applied this natural law principle that achieved a smart result for him. He also applied a wonderful strategy to achieve his objective. Moreover, the dog was not focused; he had a divided mind for this reason, he was easily distracted. In all your endeavours, try to handle one thing at a time, one after the other, moment by moment with effective planning and strategy to actualize your goal successfully. It is not a question of being intellectual but being smart and creative as well as being strategic. So, think, plan and actualize.

The Story of the Tortoise and the Lion to Illustrate an Experience and Sagacity (Wisdom), Needed in an Engagement

Once upon a time, the lion told the animal kingdom that he was sick. For this reason, many unwise animals went to visit the lion to console him. It happened that this was a plot against them by the lion to make the foolish animals an easy meal for the lion. The animals that went to the lion never returned. Therefore, their footprints went into the lion's den but there were no footprints returning. The tortoise came to the entry point of the lion's den and saw the footprints of those going in but did not see the footprints of those coming out. In that very moment, the tortoise, the craftiest and wisest of all animals, declined to go in and sent word to the lion that he would come to see the lion when those who had gone in had come back. At this point, the lion knew he had been detected. Being in the eye of the storm will afford you the ability to assess the enormity of a thing and give it its appropriate attention. If you fear the storm, you will never know what a thrill it is. The tortoise used his wonderful intuition to detect the lion's dubious trick. It is not a question of swim or drown; neither is it to swallow the bait and the hook; it is precision maneuvering of deliberations so as to detect the tumultuous centre of an event and give it its corresponding treatment.

From the psychological point of view, the tortoise was in immense fear and danger and he was forced to make a drastic decision to free himself. Henceforth, always be focused on your task. Thinks before you do anything. I did so when I was a student in the USA and that enabled me to succeed hugely. Therefore, always apply effective methodology towards your success. Don't be like the dog but be like the tortoise. Play smart.

Story about Lizard and Rat

The lizard and the rat agreed to swim but the rat forgot that she has a hairy body and went to a river to swim with the lizard. At the end, the lizard's body dried up and the rat's did not and she died of cold. Its adage goes, *"oke soro ngwere maa mmiri, ahu kochaa nwa ngwere o gaghi akocha nwa oke."* From now, never get involved in anything you cannot do. This story reminds us of the adage that goes, cut your coat according to your size or hang your bag where your hand can reach. When the rat joins the lizard to swim, lizard's body will dry but rat's body will not dry. This is shown in daily life when people do things because others have done them without finding the approach they applied to succeed. In other words, they fail to assess their capability before embarking on a task. Never jump into a task without preparation, otherwise, it results in failure. Just like cultic individuals; they know the way, pave their way and those who do not know the trick, get trapped on the way and mess their lives up forever. Look before you leap so that you will not make mistakes. Mama used to advise us not to point accusing fingers at others. She also used to say, "*otu aka na atu onye ozo, mkpisi aka ano ana atu ya*. You are guiltier of the offence that you are putting against the other person. Here is a similar case as Emeka George Ekwuru portrayed on his story about Rat, Fish, and Trap. According to him,

> *"One day, a rat saw some fish and, being of a covetous disposition, he immediately planned to steal them. In his eagerness, he did not observe that the fish were in a trap and, consequently, he was caught in the trap too. He cried out to the trap, "Why are you treating me in this manner? I know of no cause of a quarrel between us." "Oh," replied the trap, "it is because you came to steal what was in my possession and so I caught you also."*

—George E. Ekwuru
Igbo Cosmology and the Ontogeny and Hermeneutics
of Igbo Sculpture – Studies in African Ethnoaesthetics
2009, (p. 123, no.3.2.5.)

The actions of the rat and the trap here explain the wise saying that says, *ugwo na ugwo alala*. It is eye for an eye (*eme emegwere*). The literal meaning is retaliation for retaliation. It also indicates the proverb that says, *ihe akputara na akuku ite na ala na akuku onu*. Ill-gotten goods always are lavished in vain. The story of this rat applies here again. The adage reads, o*gbu agwo na azo ndu ya, agwo ona ogbu na azo kwa ndu ya-* which means, with respect to life, everybody is anxious to live.

Obu nani gi ga ebi (one who preferred to live alone)
In the world, you specialize in one thing and others specialize in other things; you give them what you have and they give you what they have

too. Therefore, you cannot live alone. Mother used to call a selfish child a nickname (nani gi ga ebi). Then, she would reprimand the child for being selfish. She would also make every effort to discourage the person and encourage him or her to be generous because she believed in sharing.

Uwaezuoke (ihe uwa eju afor)

The world is full of hazards; therefore, it is not complete harmony, and as a result, nothing is fulfilling. It is not possible to fulfill all your wishes; you have to get some and let some go.

Asking for Forgiveness and Feeling Remorse

Nne m, ite ijiri chu nmiri awala
Ukwu m gbachapuru ite mbu n'isi were kuwa
Mere m ebere, nne'm oma.

Mother, my water pot, with which I used to fetch water, has broken.
By mistake, my leg slipped and my pot fell and broke.
Please mother, have mercy on me.

This is teaching us that we should be sorry whenever we break something.

3.2. The Nature of Social Organization-Indigenous Democracy and Rights to Land, Language, and Political Representation

Indigenous Democracy

The community is organized according to age groups made up of men born within a period of three years and each age group has a name such as "Ubani," Asagba, *ubianko* for the purpose of sharing any common assets and administration. The community is further classed into three hierarchies, namely: (1) Chieftaincy Eze hierarchy (head chief and sub chiefs), (2) Nze hierarchy (Ozo titled men), (3) Ohani Amala (elders and young men). Women (titled women) are brought in when discussions become controversial because what is being discussed is mainly men's duty and these women are involved as a result of the privilege accorded to them by their title. If the community has a project like building a roadway into the farmlands, a gathering is held in which a number of age groups are appointed to do the work of preparing the roadway and one senior age group is also appointed to supervise the work of building the roadway. If two families are quarrelling about the boundary between their plots of land, the three hierarchies will sit on the case of the matter about the boundary. When women are involved, they have an equal say with men. If a general levy of money is to be made for the installation of pipe-borne water, men and women sit together to assess the levy. By the way, women also are organized into age groups according to the number of women married within a period of three years. There is no opposition party as is the case with European democracy. The subject of discussion is paramount and all participate inclusively. Stealing and killing of human beings are violations against "Ala"- goddess of the land. The people sit to deliberate on apportioning blame to the culprit. All festivals have their days of observation. There are market days. Violations of laws of the community are reported by the age group appointed for this purpose.

Right to Land: Land is shared according to;
(1) families,

(2) age groups, and
(3) community heroic achievers,
For example, those who fought for the ownership of the land.

Right to Free Speech: Freedom of expression is engendered in the law of the land. Slander and false accusation are not allowed.

Right to Political Representation: Whether for spiritual, judicial, social, or political gatherings, representation is according to the three hierarchies as mentioned above as the saying goes, "efee eze, eze efee okpala." The order is Eze to Okpala, and then Amala.

CHAPTER 4

4.1. The Effect of Good Home Training on the Children and Society at Large

Good home training brings about good quality personality formation. Your parents, especially mothers, give their children that good quality personality formation. If he/she doesn't get this from his/her home, forget all about it. Here are issues on personality types by Taber's Cyclopaedic Medical Dictionary (P. 1273). Personality is the unique organization of traits, characteristics and modes of behaviour of individuals, setting the individual apart from others and at the same time, determining how others react to the individual. Personality refers to the mental aspects of an individual in contrast to physique.

Personality Types

1) **Antisocial Personality:** This is concerning a person whose outlook and actions are socially negative and whose behaviour is repeatedly in conflict with what society perceives as the norms; he disregards the rights of others.

2) **Compulsive Personality**: Inability to express warm and tender emotions. His perfectionism makes him concerned with trivial details, rules, orderliness, organization, schedules, and indecision because of fear of mistakes.

3) **Double Personality**: This is also called dual personality, which is the mental dissociation in which and individual alternates between

two different personalities, for example, bipolar.

4) **Extroverted Personality**: This is a situation in which activities or libido are directed to other individuals.

5) **Histrionic Personality**: In this case, the individuals are active and dramatic, drawing attention to themselves, prone to exaggeration and irrational angry outbursts.

6) **Inadequate Personality**: Here, the individual is ineffective and is physically and emotionally unstable, unable to cope with normal stress.

7) **Introverted Personality**: In this case, activities or libido are directed to the individual himself.

8) **Multiple Personality**: Here, three or more personalities alternate in the same individual with each personality unaware of the others.

9) **Neurotic Personality:** This is characterized by behaviour intermediate between normal and that of a neurotic person.

10) **Obsessive-Compulsive Personality:** Same as compulsive personality.

11) **Paranoid Personality:** This is characterized by a continuing and unwarranted suspiciousness, mistrust of people and hypersensitivity.

12) **Passive-Aggressive Personality**: In this case, individuals resist demands for adequate performances in work and social situations.

13) **Psychopathic Personality**: See Antisocial Personality. In early childhood, the signs are lying, stealing, fighting, truancy, and disregard for authority. In adolescence, they are aggressive sexual behaviour, excessive use of alcohol, and use of drugs of abuse. In adulthood, these behaviour patterns continue with the addition of poor work performance, inability to function responsibly as a parent and inability to accept normal restrictions.

14) **Schizoid Personality**: This is characterized by shyness, oversensitivity, seclusion,

15) dissociation from close interpersonal or competitive relationships, eccentricity, daydreaming, inability to express hostility, and aggression in situations that would call for such reactions.

An Alchemy of Mind by Diane Ackerman says,

"Since both individuals and their adventures varied, they evolved personal strategies, emotions, beliefs, habits, and preferences. This combination of rigid behaviour on the one hand and adaptability on the other hand, is why all people are alike but everyone is different. We call this personality."
"We are gifted generalists. We sample. We analyze. We learn. We form opinions. We change our minds. We avoid danger. We bend to pressure. We persuade others. We are persuaded. We take risks."

—An Alchemy of Mind
by Diane Ackerman (pp. 140-141).

Terrie Moffitt and her team studied the chemistry of MAO A and B (monoamine Oxidase A and B) and serotonin on personality. The serotonin gene exists in three versions: two long copies of the gene, one long and one short copy of the gene, and two short copies of the gene. People with two long copies were able to bounce back after some traumatic events. People with one long and one short copy were subject to mild depression but people with two short copies were worse off with severe depression. Two thirds of human beings do not have the high-risk gene. A lucky 30 per cent had two long, 50 per cent balanced one long and one short and 20 per cent, the most depressed, had two shorts.

Effect of Environment on Personality
Genome by Matt Ridley P. 161-172

We all experience stress; we all have genes switched on and off by external events but each of us is unique: Some are anxious, some others risk-seeking; some are quiet, others loquacious; some are confident, others shy. Personality has a strong genetic component but the right kind of parenting can alter the innate personality. The right way to breed a good strain of fox is to pick the darkest pups in the nursery and train them to be tamer than their parents. A good upbringing matters a great deal. But biology determines behaviour as well as society.

Mood, mind, personality and behaviour are indeed socially and biologically determined. Social influences upon behaviour work through the switching on and off of genes. Extract on Personality from Alchemy of Mind by Diane Ackerman (P.143-150). Nature and nurture are not rivals; nor are they conjoined twins but both contain innumerable fates and processes, jostling membranes so dense, that they work together to create us. Ultimately, personality springs from both nature and nurture: experiences of all sorts and our genetic heritage, influencing everything including deeply personal idiosyncratic traits (some inherited, some shaped by family life, some thanks to the vulnerabilities all humans share). Today's bag of tricks will create a personality but tomorrow's will differ a little, depending on sleep, work, food, head-to-tail therapy, sex, fresh air, viruses, prolonged periods of cuddling, a surprise in the mail or just an innate streak of perversity. Our genes determine talents, temperaments, general intelligence, and susceptibility to alcoholism, depression, and diseases but these traits are expressed, ameliorated or stressed or inhibited or promoted or warped by life itself. We vary in many ways but especially in five ways:

1. *Extroversion or introversion,*
2. *Antagonism or agreeableness,*
3. *Conscientiousness,*
4. *Neuroticism, and*
5. *Openness to experience.*

Children's brains are plastic for years, enabling to learn lessons which the brains emphasize, modify, and so influence the birth personality.

Child Psychologists have shown that the Genes and Upbringing Design Personality

All learning affects the brain. Mothering affects the brain. So, do talk therapy religion, cognitive (learning) behavioural therapy, and teachers.

We adjust ourselves to each person we meet and each situation we are in and so, yes, peers, culture, and nature influence our lives. Parents must start early in the careful mothering of their children so as to have a good reward of having adorable grownup children who bring home happy results in the future. I brought happiness to my family. Do you?

4.2 Cultural Issues Regarding (a) Language (b) Myth (c) History (d) Religion (e) Art (f) Psyche (g) Education (h) African Culture in a Global Perspective

Language

It is generally accepted that there is a genetically rooted linguistic relationship between the Ancient Egyptian language and modern Negro-African languages. For example:

Ancient Egyptian Language-fa-akhu –to kindle fire,
Ibo Language- fu-oku-to kindle fire.

The four major languages in Nigeria- Ibo, Yoruba, Hausa, and Fulani - are linguistically related in reference to their original root from the Ancient Egyptian language (Ibo ogwugwu or Ogungu, Yoruba - Ogun, Hausa - Argungu,

Egyptian - Agu - god,
Ibo Agu - god. Afor - third day - god of four-day Ibo week,
Egyptian Afau = a god of one of the seasons of the year,
Ibo – Afa = god of war;
Egyptian -Afa = a class of divine beings; Egyptian; Asar = the great Ancestor - god of the dynastic Egyptian; Ibo Orusa - the great Ancestor - god of Ibos;
Yoruba - Oluwa – great Ancestor - god of Yorubas.

The manner of expression shows this relationship. In Ibo, we say, I am speaking from my heart. In Ancient Egypt, the heart is the centre of motivation in which all thoughts and deeds are stored; hence, the content of your heart becomes the amount of truth in you which is weighed against the truth of God when one is dead. In Ibo, what is called "omenala" is simply the way to say things nicely, avoiding obscene words, how to address seniors (dede), how to address authorities (nna muo), how to speak of spiritual matters with reverence and faithfulness; how to tell a visitor to join you in eating (bia rie nri) even though the visitor has not been invited for food, not to speak too openly about sex or how to speak courteously to people and be quick in apologizing when at fault. Boys and girls are orally counselled to speak in pleasantly decent ways.

Map of Orlu

Source: https://www.google.co.uk/search

Myth

Orlu is a town in Igboland of Southeastern (Nigeria) and it is made up of ten villages called Orlu Gedegwum; meaning the Orlu origins. According to historians, Orlu's Igbo name is "Olu." The ten villages are made up of Orlu Gedegwum: Aboh, Eluama, Ndiowerre, Umudiato, Umudihe, Umundele, Umueleke, Umuire, Umuafor, and Umuokpara. The ruling council is Eze Igwe of Orlu Gedegwum. Orlu has a small stream called "Mgbede River." This river joins another river, the Orasi, from Mgbee that make their way towards the Atlantic Ocean. My siblings and I used to fetch water from Mgbede River and also, caught some crabs for domestic use. Our ancestors have high regards for this river. She has a boa called Eke-Mgbede. It is a big python which is also regarded as a sacred snake and no one touches or eats it. The boa is a harmless and friendly animal, according to our ancestors. There is a mythical story that goes like this.

In the ancient time, the goddess of the river, Mgbede, told the indigenes of Orlu town not to eat the boa because it is a spirit animal from the river that protects the land. The boa is taboo, set aside as sacred to the goddess. If anyone is caught killing it or harming it, that person is subjected to a fine and a sacrifice to the goddess. This myth is still observed today by the traditional men and women. There are other animals such as the sheep and ediabali (The African Palm Civet), that are sacred to the god of the land and should anyone hurt them, that person is bound to perform a redemption sacrifice to appease the gods. Young people are counselled on the truth about these myths and how to observe them. Whenever we were sick, our mother would ask us to go to the Mgbede River to bathe so that the goddess of the river would wash away our ill-health. Our ancestors believed in this goddess curing ill-health and it worked for them.

Orlu Gedegwum is the mother of the other towns in Orlu senatorial zone, such towns as: Orsu, Isu, Njaba, Nwangele, Nkwerre, Ideato North, Ideato South, Oru East, Oru West, Ohaji Egbema, and last but not least, Oguta. These towns are the heart of Igboland. Oguta has a lake that produces big fishes of every kind.

Orlu Gedegwum, Umuna, Owerre Ebeiri and Amaifeke are in the heart of Orlu Local Government Area in Imo State. Orlu is one of the largest cities and second in position after Owerri, the capital of Imo State. Orlu Gedegwum is said to have a population of around

420,000. According to our famous historians, the inhabitants of Orlu senatorial zone number about three million (3,000,000). Orlu is also highly blessed with men and women of different calibres; that is, people of all walks of life.

Orlu Gedegwum has four market days, Orie, Afor, Nkwo, and Eke. Eke is a sacred day and our ancestors keep it holy. They don't farm on Eke market day. Any child born on this market day is a special child, as applied to me, the author of this book. This is the reason why my mother named me "Nwamgbeke" and my parents made me a special child. Now that I have found myself in the convent and become a reverend sister, it enabled me to believe in the significance of this name. Also, in our culture, any married woman sent home on Eke market day will never come back to her husband. I am an eye witness to this about a woman who planned and killed her husband; she was sent home on an Eke market day to her motherland. Orlu people rightly condemn evil-doing.

Orlu town is surrounded by many primary schools, colleges and secondary schools. We have Ojike Memorial Secondary School, Bishop Shanahan Secondary School, and former Bishop Shanahan Teacher's Training College, Orlu. We have maternities, hospitals, local businesses, other amenities that keep life going. At the present time, Bishop Shanahan Teacher's Training College has turned into Imo Polytechnic Orlu.

Orlu is made up of Christians and non-Christians. We have Holy Trinity Parish Church and Holy Trinity Cathedral, Orlu. The Cathedral was erected in isi Obiukwu Gedegwum. Our late Bishop emeritus was Rt. Rev. Dr. Gregory O. Ochiagha. Rt. Rev. Augustine T. Ukwuoma is his predecessor. Orlu Gedegwum has a lot of priests and religious leaders, both indigenous and non-indigenous. I discovered my congregation – The Holy Family Sisters of the Needy - on the 29th November, 1980 during the erection of the Holy Trinity Cathedral, Orlu. Sisters from this congregation, HFSN, attended the installation of the Bishop emeritus of Orlu when my eagle eyes set on them; then, I began to inquire about their life. Here I am today as one of theirs.

Before the erection of the Holy Trinity Cathedral, the late Eze Igwe of Orlu, Patrick Acholonu, declared to all the natives of Orlu

Gedegwum to go to the hillside to collect stones for the building of our Cathedral. Igwe was there in the site supervising the work. My mother, my god-daughter and I were among those who were collecting the stones. My mother, the late Mrs. Ojukwu Monica Konye Nwadike, was still a pagan then but participated in gathering the stones for the building of our Cathedral. My god-daughter, Mary Ajidike, helped in collecting my mother's stones. My ultimate fulfilment is that Mama later became a baptized Catholic, worshipped and buried as a member of the Catholic Church. I am pleased that I am still witnessing and enjoying the rites of this noble Cathedral.

The Eze Igwe of Orlu loved and cherished our traditional heritage. He Christianized most of paganism traditions into Christian traditions, such traditions as Eriji, the new yam festival, cultural dances like Okorosha, Ebuebu dance, Ayoroyo, Ayoroyo dance, Keleke dance, Okonko dance, and other masquerade dances. Other autonomous communities have their different dances that used to make everybody in the community happy. Orlu Gedegwum gave birth to about thirty (33) autonomous local government areas. Some of these local government areas are as follows: Umuna, Owerre Ebeiri, Okporo, Eziachi, Umudioka, Obor, Ugberuru, Umuzike, Umutanze, and Obibi ochase and Ihitte Owerre etcetera.

Orlu is a stable and peaceful town. Her sons, daughters, and wives are happy and hardworking beings. All the Orlu senatorial zone are in unity and unanimous in helping one another whether in joy and sorrow.

In the pictures that follow, distinctive Orlu Gedegwum people as well as Orlu Senatorial Zone join in celebrating with their daughter and sister, Rev. Sr. Chinedum Joachim Konye Nwadike, HFSN, in the United Kingdom on April 10, 2016 for her Silver Jubilee Celebration of First Religious Profession in the United Kingdom (UK).

My people are always around for you whenever you need them. Long live the Orlu Gedegwum; long live Orlu Senatorial Zone. I am proud of you; may the Good Lord continue showering His blessings on you and your children's children - Amen.

Legend

Here is a legend of one town in Orlu senatorial zone in Imo State called Mgbidi. There is a river called "Obana" River, the fish from which all Mgbidi people must not eat. There is a mythical story that goes like this:

In the ancient times, the goddess of the River Obana, Ezenwanyi, ordered the people of Mgbidi town not to eat fish from the river if they wanted to bear children because all the children they would bear would be the reincarnated spirits of the fishes. The fishes are taboos, set aside as sacred to the goddess. If anyone is caught fishing in the river, that person is subjected to a fine and a sacrifice to the goddess. This myth is still observed today and it caused inter-village wars in the past. There are other animals, such as the sheep and boa, that are sacred to the god of the land, Ali-Mgbidi, and should anyone hurt them, that person is bound to perform a redemption sacrifice to appease the gods. Young people are counselled on the truth about these myths and how to observe them.

History

Our history is oral, mostly, as opposed to archival history. The Oru clan community in Oru West Local Government, Imo State, Nigeria originated from the ancestor called Oru (the wife) and Oma (the husband.) They both came from the river of Ime Oru (the sea coast region) and prohibited all their children from eating fish from a special river. The ancestors controlled the access to the Ime Oru coastal area and no one was allowed to go to the coastal area for trade without first passing under the watchful eyes of the people and paying homage to royalty. Sometimes, some venturesome party would want to pass by with effrontery and that party would be dealt with severely. Laws were made regarding religion, festivals, farming observations, social events (community dance association), marriage, and social behaviour. The young people are admonished on the proper adherence to the upkeep of all social matters in the right perspective in order to grow up as admirable and respected gentle people.

Religion

My people believe in the god of the land. Ali, and in God Almighty, Chukwu Okike Abiama, and small gods, the divine deities like Ogwugwu (Ogun-Yoruba), Agwunsi (Afa-Dibe), Anyanwu (Sun god), Urasi, Obana Ezenwanyi, Chiagu, Ndeada Nde Ogaranye. Our ancestors believe there is by his own volition. They offer aja ekwensu (exorcism sacrifice) to him to avert his perturbations. They also offer bread and wine, goats, rams, cows, hens, and cocks, and even yam fou-fou and soup made with sacrificial animal's meat to God Almighty. With respect to life and death, they believe that when you are born, there is someone dead whose spirit reincarnates in you and that spirit agu (agau-Egyptian) is always with the one guiding and teaching the person what to do like guardian Angels in haven. That spirit gives one his predestination. It is God Almighty who organizes the Chiagu and the predestination. One's life will be lived towards the realization of one's predestination and at death, his spirit will give an account of how the person's life was spent and how much good has been realized. The burial ceremony and offerings are meant to cleanse the dead person's soul and give it a good standing before the gods. Young men and women are taught these things because, in the future, it will be their turn to conduct and practice them. The observation of religious principles is mandatory since the gods are benevolent and auspicious when they are placated graciously.

Discussion

Omenala bu Obueme- meaning spiritual initiation is a must for every person, idonmua for men and ikwezi and ikpunzu for women. Jesus said (John 3:3-5) to Nicodemus, "Most truly I say to you, unless anyone is born again, he cannot see the kingdom of God." Nicodemus said to him, "How can a man be born when he is old? He cannot enter into the womb of his mother a second time and be born, can he? "Jesus answered, "Most truly I say to you, unless anyone is born from water and spirit, he cannot enter into the kingdom of God." The traditional spiritual induction into the kingdom of gods is what we are talking about here and is what Christians call baptism. This spiritual traditional culture is a must for everyone for without it, one cannot officiate here on earth nor can he/she be allowed into the kingdom of gods hereafter. He is neither here nor there. When one is born, he/she gets named and gets fed solid food the first time by "irunye oga nonu." By the time the male child is five years old, parents prepare to perform idonmuna for him, that is, initiation into the kingdom of god for gods' protection. The practice goes like this: He is taken to the shrine by the elders after all required ceremonial dues have been given to the community. There, the elders wash the child's face with water to cleanse "njo aloluwa" (sins of previous reincarnation) and offer a sacrifice. When the child grows up into a man, he can offer sacrifices to gods and ancients. This he cannot do without Idonmua. Without idonmua, he has neither place here nor place in the spiritual world. The girls get the first initiation at sixteen years when they perform ikwezi at the point of getting ready to marry. Without ikwezi, girls have no place here or in the spiritual world. When they marry, women must perform ikpunzu (decorating the body with chalk solution-nzu). The husband must give the ceremonial dues to women of Nzu society and the elders will offer a sacrifice to urasi goddess. We must remember that baptism with water was in practice before Jesus. John the Baptist poured water over the head of Jesus and so Jesus was baptized. Here, the traditional culture is shown to have been given another name, baptism, by Christians.

—Oral narrative by an anonymous.

Ibo Social Obligation - Onye Aghana Nwa Nnne Ya

We say in Ibo, "*Onye aghana nwa nne ya maka alulo uwa.*" It is social justice to share your fortune or misfortune with others. We say, "*Ngbaru le ya akwa or njem kele ya maka ihe merenu.*" We share our joys and sorrows with each other. If you offer a goat or palm wine to the gods and ancients, it is social justice to share the sacrificial offerings with others, that is, your elder and umunnadi.

A story goes like this: One day, two brothers went to the farm. one had a calabash jar of water (mbele used for palm wine), and the other had nothing. During the heated period of the day, the brother with water went to the shade to drink and rest. The other brother with nothing assumed that his brother would call him to come and drink palm wine for he believed what was in the mbele was palm wine. It was water instead and his brother did not invite him to drink. When it was evening, the brother with nothing approached the other brother, rebuking him for drinking palm wine alone contrary to omenala. Before his brother could explain that what he had was water instead of palm wine, his brother knocked him down and rushed to the mbele to drink palm wine. He was disappointed for what was in the mbele was water. Looking back, he saw his brother still lying down. He rushed to him, but it was too late; he had killed his brother for the sake of drinking. He, bewailing, shouted, "Oh, I have killed my brother foolishly for the sake of not drinking palm wine." He apologized; he was sorry. Neighbours gathered to hear him. He confessed it was in error.

There are two lessons to be learnt here. The victim, the brother with water who was killed, forgot to be socially brotherly in not calling his brother, "*Bia rie nri*" *(ikponri)-* as it is a customary in Iboland. It is socially bad manners in Ibo land to be called "*onye njo iri*" (one who eats alone). The other lesson is that the killer brother, the one with nothing, should have taken it easy in not being covetously greedy. His uncontrolled craving for palm wine led him to commit murder of his brother. Eating and drinking should not be so valued as to cause one to go off limits. In Matthew 4:4 it says, "Man must live not on bread alone but on every utterance coming forth through God's mouth."

Maintain modesty in all expressions. If you deny your brother food (*riwo nwanne gi nri*") while he is alive, when he dies, he will reincarnate in your house and will make you pay a retribution for your misdeeds. We say, "*Ngi na nwa nne gi meme ihe, chetakwa alulo uwa.*" That is, remember never go to the extreme when dealing with brothers for you will all come together again in reincarnation.

Eke Asaa Orie Asaa, Otutu Aja, Ogba Ghari, Ughanmiri, Omadi Ezi Omadi Ulo

Eke asaa Orie asaa – point of no reconciliation or recognition- crossing deadline, otutu aja - a cross-road where all sacrificial offerings are placed for all gods, a place of no man's land, it is considered to be sacred to be frequented by all gods. Ogba ghari - a point of helplessness and hopelessness, the point of no return. Ughanmiri- deepest part of the river where there is an under-current that whirls round and round so that any canoe going in there will sink. *Omadi ezi omadi ulo*- a person of nonentity, *a persona non grata*. He is *eke asaa orie asaa, ogba ghari.*

Urioma

> *Urioma dele- dele urioma. Urioma dee dele - urioma*
> *Onye na nwanne ya gara ikpa nku na Alaeze - urioma*
> *Nwa nne na nwa nne jere ohia nka na Alaeze - urioma*
> *Okpuchuu nku ghuru nwanne nke ya - urioma*
> *Okporo kporo iji biara nga anyi na echi eze - urioma*
> *Ndi eze anyi jiri ejiji bekee - urioma*
> *Onye na nwanne ya kwuru gawa egwu atuo ya - urioma*
> *Agamefu adighi mma n'aju unu anuna - urioma*
> *Dede - urioma dede urioma.*

This means, never abandon your brother, sister, or friend, no matter what happens. Be your brother's keeper.

Ofo
Ofo is a symbol of authority and seniority in the community in Ibo land, kept by the oldest man of a family. His entitlements are:

1) "Mpoanu" (middle part of a goat together with kidneys, heart, liver, and lungs).
2) First share of anything that is shared.
3) He wears the crown if his father was a king.
4) He is the judge of the family.
5) He is the high priest of the community; meaning, he recites the sacrificial incantations.
6) He has a veto power over all judgmental rulings.

The Ofo emblem staff is obtained from osisi-ofo (a sacred plant) and is blessed by a man's mother's family. The procedure goes like this: if a man wants to take the ozo title (the loftiest entitlement a man has to undertake in order to join the top hierarchy of the society), he has to go to his mother's family for the ofo ozo. His mother's family tells him things he has to bring in order to obtain the ofo ozo. Then the mother's family will go to the sacred plant (osisi-ofo plant) to obtain a branch of the tree. The branch is then chiseled into the shape of ofo. When the appointed day for the handover of the ofo has arrived, both the father's side and mother's side of the man's family will offer a sacrifice with kolas, peppers, palm wine, a goat, yams, and nzu (chalk) to the gods and ancestors to bless the ofo. This is the symbol of his ozo title. He will kneel down to receive the blessed ofo staff. When he dies, his oldest son will take the ofo. Thus, the ofo will pass from hand to hand according to age and seniority. As a high priest, the keeper of ofo will perform "*innuokwukwu*" every four days with kola, pepper, palm wine, and nzu to the gods and ancestors at the family's altar.

Oje

Fashioned from oja-a, woman's name. This woman was beloved by her husband and she died while delivering her 7th child. And so, the husband buried her and fenced in the grave. But after some days, a tree grew out of the grave and produced kola-nuts. Thus, the elders and the ancestor called the tree "Oje," after the woman's name. They used oje in offering sacrifices to the gods because it is manna from the gods, signifying love. It is a symbol of love and unity among the Ibos, even among Africans.

Ogu

The symbol of ogu is the palm frond (leaves) which stands for the symbol of an offer of peace; it is like the olive branch which had a similar meaning in Europe. If a man from village **A** kills a man from village **B**, then the village A man will send some palm leaves to village **B** appealing for peace. If village **B** refuses to accept the peace offering, then village A will say "anyi ejiena ogu." Then, if a commotion arises out of the man's death, the village **A** people will say, anyi ji ogu, anyi ji ofo na ogu" that is to say, we have the authority of righteousness and respect for the village **B** people in this matter. We need not fear - "idide ji ofo awa ala."

Art

Women decorate their skins with black indigo (from uri seeds), brown indigo (from nkasiala corms) and red indigo (from uhie wood) - dyes derived from plants that have skin-lightening agents. The artistic women will design the art forms that they paint on their female clients. The effect of these indigo dye decorations is to make the women's bodies well-cleansed and plump. They look flushed and pleasing to the eyes. The indigo dyes have a sun protection factor that filters out the dangerous part of sunlight, thereby preventing the radioactive power of the sunlight. This dye decoration has the same effect as the Europeans' sun-blocking creams and sun screens. Women undertake these decorations during festivals and during fat-rooming conducted in a marriage ceremony. Men do some carved forms out of wood, stones, bones, and metals. The art forms can be of human forms, animal forms and spirit forms. Examples are *Agwunsi,* a bronze figure of ancient king of Benin.

Psyche

It has been mentioned earlier that when a person is born, the person is accompanied by the spirit of one who reincarnates in the person. In Ibo land, this spirit is called "*Agu*." Compare Christ Jesus. Jesus said to them:

"You, though, who do you say I am?" In answer, Simon Peter

said, "You are the Christ, the son of the living God." In response Jesus said to him, "Happy you are, Simon son of Jonah, because flesh and blood did not reveal it to you but my Father who is in the heavens did."

—Matthew 16:15-17
The Jerusalem Bible &
Popular Edition
Darton, Longman & Todd 1974, (p. 26).

When you grow up, you have to be initiated into the cult of the ancestors called *"Idomuo"* and have to erect a shrine to your *"Agu"* whom you have to invoke occasionally by hitting a wooden (ekwe Agu) or metal (ogene Agu) gong designated for him and leaving some food for him. Then, you go on to be initiated into the worship of all gods. The elders and members of the cult conduct all the proceedings. All these are for men. Finally, when you deem yourself rich enough, you take the "ozo" title by once again being initiated into the cults of seven spirits of God and then erect a shrine to the Almighty God (Ihuchukwu). Now, you take an ozo title name, example, *"Ogbuehi Akunwata."* Annually, you worship these gods one by one from the beginning of the year to the end.

Education
Education is received through oral instruction by either an experienced artisan or an elderly person. I was taught how to farm. My tools of farming are the machete, a hoe, ube, mbiriba and mbazu. We start farming on February 2nd by cutting down the bush (Ikpu oru) which has been left fallow **for six years**. The fallow condition is to allow the land to replenish itself with manure. I was educated in the ways of cultivating the land for raising crops: labour, tilling, planting, caring, weeding, and harvesting. It is very interesting to be a farmer. *"Nwata chue miri, nwata nua miri."* Work hard and eat well.

African Culture in a Global Perspective
Now, our population has grown. Therefore, we need better ways of doing everything, including farming chores. We have bush-cutting

machines, tilling machines, cultivating machines, and harvesting machines. Manuring is done by using NPK fertilizers made up of Nitrogen (N), Phosphorus (P) and Potassium (K = katium) in the proportion of 5 parts of nitrogen, 10 parts of phosphorus and 10 parts of potassium (NPK: 5:10:10). Since we are living in a world renamed a global village, all good things for mankind have got to be pursued together and conscientiously with no bias, bigotry, fanaticism or discrimination against anybody's culture or mannerism. In this light, whatever is good in any culture can be inculcated in all other cultures. We in Africa are faced with Muslim culture, Christian culture, European, and indigenous cultures. The way to do it is to use the African indigenous culture as the centre-piece of all other cultures and then grow a new cultural construct from all the cultures as of modest necessity. It is ruinous to abandon African traditional culture for any other culture out of a sheer assumption that the new culture is more civilized than the local one. In terms of religion, the African religion is the first and the core of all religions. Take for instance, the seven-day worship of Christians originated from the African four-day worship (*Eke Ukwu, Orie Ukwu, Afor Ukwu, Nkwo Ukwu*). These days are set up to be sacred to the gods and one has to abstain from work on these days. The Jews were not as religious when they entered Egypt as they were when they left Egypt. Our clothing is perfectly designed to suit our climate just as the Europeans put on coats and trousers because of their cold climate. I think the best idea is while in Rome, behave like the Romans. One has to tolerate all religions and all cultures while practising one's own choice. Democracy is a five-fingered entity with the five fingers of different sizes performing together in a task. Each democracy is designed according to each country's culture with a special allowance for global fundamental human rights and dignity.

CHAPTER 5

5.1 Traditional (Omenala na Iwuala) and Moral Guidance on Children

Role of Religion, both Traditional and Christian

In the traditional way of living, the civil role and religious role are integrated and the rituals are orally enunciated and passed on from one generation to the next. For example, a family wants to offer a sacrifice to God through the ancestors. (Compare Christians saying rosary to our Mother Mary for her intercession, and invoking the Saints to pray for us). The members of the family will gather in the shrine where the altar of their fathers is with a basket of four yams, a dried fish, a cock, a 2-gallon jar of palm wine, four kola nuts, a dried alligator pepper, and a small mortar of crushed nzu (okwanzu). Why a basket of four yams? Why three kola nuts? Our ancestors believe in the importance of the figure **"4."** Four means we have come to stay or I have come to stay. That is the reason why we have four market days. The three kola nuts signify **love**, peace, and **unity;** while in the Christian ethos, **"3"** signifies the "**Trinity**." The head of the family will sprinkle four lines with nzu (chalk) before the altar (if untitled) or eight lines (if titled) (compare Christian sprinkle of incense and holy water). He will anoint the face and chest of anyone present with the nzu (chalk). Then, he will bring out all ofos of the ancestors and lay them on "*omaku*" (a wooden square board) (compare Christian altar stone). The elder will sprinkle water and nzu on the ofos. He will sit on his "okobo" (chair) and start the sacrificial incantations calling Chukwu Orusa olua oha in the names of his ancestors and, at every beat, all present will say, **"*ihia*" (*isee*)**, meaning, (let it so happen) (compare Christian Amen). When he concludes his invocations, he will blow his elephant tusk horn (if titled). He will then break the kola nuts into pieces and give one piece to the ancestors and the rest to all in attendance. He will conduct the libation of palm wine to God Chukwu Okike (The Almighty God), and offer the cock by killing it and splashing the blood on the ofos. He will then touch the chest of everyone with a yam saying *"Ndu Gi"* (good life to you). Children will take the slaughtered cock away and defeather it. The mother of the house will take the yams for preparing yam fufu. All will drink the palm wine and cut the carcass of the cock into special pieces - the lumbar portion, the kidney portion, the drumsticks, the thighs, the two breast portions, and the rib portion. The neck, the liver, and gizzard are roasted, and cut into pieces and given together with the dried fish to the elders. What is paramount here is that when all these are going on, the boys and girls are around watching, listening, and collaborating as I did during my father's time of sacrificing. The children do all chores necessary for each step (compare Christian mass servants). There you go. The teaching of morals and the traditional cultural practices have already been passed on. The respect for Almighty God, the elders, ancestors, and everybody else has been exemplified, exhibited and passed on to the next generation. In the sharing of the sacrificial meat, the eldest gets the lumbar portion, and *abibanu*, the next to the elder gets one drumstick and *abibanu*, the third man gets one *thigh*, and *abibanu*, the owner of the household where the sacrifice is offered, gets one whole leg (drumstick with thigh), one half of the two breast portions, head, and feet and *abibanu*. The Amala group gets one half of the breast portion and the rib cage. The kidney portion is given to the eldest man but in some Igbo culture, they give it to *"Ada"*, the eldest daughter.

In the evening, the housewife prepares yam fufu dinner and oha vegetable soup with the chicken meat and brings these sweet-smelling delicacies to the husband who will then sprinkle some crumbs of fufu dipped in soup, and some pieces of meat to the ancestors and gods. The whole family will then feast on the food and soup. The young play a part in material handling and by so doing, get inculcated in the tradition. Tradition and culture define morality involved when they are expressed. Good traditional and Christian sacrifices are the same before God. What the Christian religion is doing is not different from what the traditional religion is doing. Rather, the traditional religion is the original in its aspect. Possibly, the good traditional religion advocates mutual love, unity, compassion, and socialization of the human race and through traditional religion, I obtained my Christian faith. My parents, through their traditional worship, came into Catholicism.

The Christian first commandment says,

"You must love God, your God with your whole heart and with your whole soul and with your whole mind. This is the greatest and first commandment."
—Matthew 22:37-40).

The second, like it, is this: You must love your neighbour as yourself. On these two commandments hang the prophets and the entire law. Here, Jesus is teaching love for God and man on which everything else hangs. The traditional religion uses the sacrifice as a love sample to God and blessing to mankind. The sacrifice extols God and asks for blessing from *Chukwu* Okike Abiama (Almighty God). The lesson is this, that young people learn how to worship God, learn how to respect elderly people and learn how to obey the law and order in society. This is most exemplified in the sharing of the sacrificial animal meat. The young get the least share because they are at the bottom of the honour ladder, the top of which they will attain by growing up with age and wisdom. All these activities spell out love for God and humanity. By the way, the Old Testament is a replica of the traditional religion practice. Morals are not specifically self-styled but are derived from standard value points set for behaviour in all aspects. For example, one can be rated a good student because one has scored high points in the examinations set for assessing one's intelligence capability. Christian morals are set in written laws but traditional morals are set in the practical observation of the norms of set rituals, containing the elements of love, respect, and holiness. The people, rather than reciting laws, do acts of law by living up to the laws in their lives and by doing things of God. In the centre of these activities and sayings are the children who must be fashioned to carry on doing them in the future. To further understand the traditional guidance on children's behaviour, let us define the six dimensions of culture which are passed on from generation to generation in systems of learned ideas and behaviour: (1) Technological, (2) Economic, (3) Political, (4) Institutional (social), (5) Aesthetic values, and (6) Belief-perceptual.

(1) **Technological Dimension of Culture**: It is its capital, its tools, skills, and ways of dealing with the physical environment. It is the interface between humanity and nature: our hoe helps us cultivate the soil (nature).

(2) **Economic Dimension of Culture:** It is its various ways and means of production and allocation of goods and services (wealth) through gift-giving, obligations, and exchange of goods, market trade or state allocation. We do what is called "ilibe ewu," that is, giving someone a goat so that when the goat multiplies in number, those concerned share them. We practice traditional credit rotation of collected money to be given to members in turns. My father used to give money in exchange for land as well.

(3) **Political Dimension of Culture**: It is its various ways and means of allocating power, influence and decision-making in a society. It includes types of governments and management system. Our government is by Ndi eze, Ndi Nze na Ozo, and Ndi Ichie, and Ohali including titled women and young women. They confer to deliberate on projects.

(4) **Institutional Dimension of Culture:** It is composed of the ways people act and interact between each other and expect each other to act and interact. It includes marriage, friendship roles as a mother, father, children, rituals of the ozo title, ekwe title and dances. Ozo title takes a whole year to perform and it takes a lot of

material and money. The ozo title performer, from time to time, will celebrate to show to what extent he has performed.

(5) **Aesthetic Values Dimension of Culture**: This is the structure of ideas sometimes paradoxical, inconsistent and contradictory that people have about good and bad, about beautiful and ugly, and about right and wrong. We hate igbaemu (backbite) and extol otito (praises). We have moonlight dances to enjoy ourselves. We love good clothes, food, ornaments, and fashionable ways of doing things.

(6) **Beliefs** - Perceptual Dimension Culture: This is a structure of ideas that people have about the nature of the universe, the world around them, their role in it, cause and effect and the nature of time, matter and behaviour towards the ultimate creator and the owner of all created entities. Our beliefs are rooted in our sacrifices: one for blessings, one for thanksgiving, and one exorcise, rituals - ikwezi, festivals - irijiofua, igbuchiahu (spiritual initiation).

(7) All these aspects of culture are passed on to children in activities that entail them. The fact is when they are executed in their intrinsic values, the children respond in beautiful outcomes.

Here is biblical reflection on the above stated facts:
Standard Ways of Doing:

> *"Let these words of mine remain in your heart and in your soul; fasten them on your hand as a sign and on your forehead as a circlet. Teach them to your children and say them over to them, whether at rest in your house or walking abroad, at your lying down or at your rising. Write them on the doorposts of your house and on your gates. So that you and your children may live long in the land that Yahweh swore to your fathers he would give to them for as long as there is a sky above the earth.*

—Deuteronomy 11:18-21
The Jerusalem Bible & Popular Edition
Darton, Longman & Todd 1966, 1967, & 1968, (p. 200).

Discipline and Security in Igboland

These two principles are attained by the Igbo communities by instituting the following cultural ordinances:

- Ikwa arusi na ahu (Igbandu)
- Idu isi ala- when it is not easy to ascertain the truth and justice
- Igbaehiri – family togetherness
- Igba asara urasi – slander and false accusation
- Ogulano agwunsi-
- Ikpara ali unwu-
- Ikpara mgbeba unwu-
- Ahiajioku-

Though Igbo communities have *Ogbo na eche obodo* (community watchmen) who go about sniffing the air to detect wrong-doing anywhere by anyone, yet a general session of the people is annually held for the invocation of the gods and the ancestors upon anyone who would violate or desecrate any of the taboos, totems and ordinances. The ancients would drag the violators to death in order to cleanse the defiled land, but later, this action was dropped for a new order which ordained that either a penalty is levied or a curse from the gods be invoked on the culprit. This observation enables everyone to feel free and safe anywhere, to eat anywhere with people and keep one's yams anywhere without any fear of theft.

Prohibitions

a) **Stealing** – especially
   (a) yam theft,
   (b) Adultery,
   (c) Physical poisoning (putting poison in one's food) and spiritual poisoning (paying a native doctor to curse any human being or bringing into the town an outside destructive godly fetish against anyone) – ime nsi, (d) Igba asiri- slander and false accusation (iboibonsi na igba emu),

(e) Homicide (igbu ochi na imebi afa mmadu),

(f) Ime ihe ala sonso:

    i.   having sexual intercourse with a girl before her "ikwaezi,"

    ii.   killing of a boa constrictor,

    iii.   giving a person food he is forbidden to eat like 'ona,' wara - wara (iguana), akwu Ojukwu,

    iv.   fighting or quarrelling or failing to abstain from work on a holy day of obligation failing to pay a penalty for one's violation of the ordinances,

    v.   Iya nwanyi akwa (unclothing a woman),

    vi.   Ifu nwanyi na oto ebe ona asa ahu (peeping into a woman's bathroom),

    vii. Iga ada obi mana imara nwa agbogho tupu okwaezi (hugging but not sex is allowed),

    viii. Iga agba ba omu ma ima edo arusi nkwo okporo. Omunkwo (palm leaves) on a fruit tree means you can ask for a fruit but cannot take it by force with effrontery. Nkwo Okporo is a forbidden destructive spiritual fetish), and

    ix.   Ikwu onye nze uze - to sleight a titled Nze man with a howling noise is not allowed.

(b) Ikwa Arusi na Ahu (Igbandu): Every year, at the end of the Isu Olila Festival (final Okorosha dance), all the people gather together to decide cases of violations of prohibitive ordinances and levy penalties and to bind over all the people with a general oath of oblation, placing all under legal mandate to observe all ordinances regarding things prohibited as listed above, then all elders with their 'ofos', all Nzes with their 'ofo,' together with the head of Okorosha Cult pronounce blessings for the observation of all cultural statutes and curses for the violation of the traditional orders.

Stealing

One time, a man called Boyi stole a hen which had been restrained from moving out too far with a harness (egbenku) on the wings and he threw away the harness. In the night, the owner noticed that the hen did not come home and began to tell the villagers her chicken did not return and she would be grateful if anyone who had seen it would let her know by sounding a wooden bell (ima ekwe). She said: Aku ulo efuele. By custom, if anyone had seen it, that one would say: *Ono ebaaoo*. Thus, someone who saw Boyi (a lazy man who had no occupation) defeathering a chicken, called on the oma ekwe to Boyi about it. In the following morning, some people, with the owner of the chicken, went to Boyi to inquire if he had seen the chicken. Luckily, the owner saw the *egbenku* with which she had restrained the hen by the side of Boyi's house. Boyi denied he knew anything about the chicken. They requested to see the soup Boyi had made the previous night. Boyi hesitated. Subsequently, they rushed into his house and recovered a whole chicken in a pot of soup. The people took the egbenku, the pot of chicken soup and Boyi to the chief's house. Immediately, more people gathered to decide the case of the chicken theft (ochi okuko). Boyi was arraigned before the people. Boyi requested that he be allowed to use the lavatory. He was allowed and he used this opportunity to get out of the chief's house and hurriedly ran very fast into the bush and escaped. Those who saw Boyi running came to the chief's house to inform the audience in the chief's house that Boyi had escaped. They thought Boyi would come home one day but he never came home till today. That is the story of a chicken thief. Never exhibit a nonchalant attitude in a serious matter, otherwise, the wise one will trick you and find his way.

Idu Isi Ala: When a prohibitive act has been committed but it is not clear how to determine the culprit, then "idu isi ala" is approved for locating the guilty one. All the people - the high priest, chiefs, elders, nzes, and amalas gather at the god Ali shrine together with the contending parties for the swearing to the god Ali by the party which claims to be innocent. The effectiveness of the oath lasts until the end of the year. The panel for deciding who is right keeps watch over the swearer of the oath. This story here will explain the whole procedure.

Once, two people processed their palm fruits for palm oil at one palm oil press mill; they normally kept their palm oil at the oil press mill station. One day, one of them complained that his drums of palm oil were missing and so he accused the other fellow, his partner, of being responsible for the theft. The one accused sued his accuser for defaming his name because the accused man was a titled nze man. The community found it hard to find out who was telling the truth, so, it was agreed that the accused should take an oath, the effectiveness of which should last for a year. All the people gathered at the god Ali shrine and after the cultural ritual, the accuser took an oath. At the end of one year, the accused was vindicated and exonerated for he did not suffer any illness or any mishap during the whole designated year. The rule says that when the accused is freed, the accuser should pay for the cost of the celebration of vindication. The truth was that the palm oil was taken not by the accused but by the accuser's brother who ran errands for him. This was revealed by an oracle who was approached by the accuser's brother when the accuser's brother was very ill. The accuser's brother was told by the oracle to confess his crime before his brother before it was too late. The accuser's brother confessed but he later died. It was normal to take your brother's property with his permission but not to do so by force in stealth.

Igba Ehiri: Annually, members of families gather together at their family shrines to offer gifts of goats, cocks, hens, fishes, wines, and yam fufu to their gods and ancestors. Each family unit prepares a meal to be eaten by all. The elders bind them over to observe all the ordinances and bless them all to be fruitful and prosperous.

Igba Ehiri Dance Song

> **Family Head:** *Egwu Ali Peteri, peteri, peteri, egwu Ali peterim*
> **Family Head:** *Onye muru nwa, kuru nwa*
> **Oha Lile:** *Egwu Ali, Peteri, peteri, peteri, egwu Ali peterim*
> **Family Head:** *Onye muru nwa zua nwa*
> **Oha Lile:** *Egwu Ali peteri, peteri, peteri, egwu Ali*

Peterim
Family Head: Onye muru nwa rie nri
Oha Lile*: Egwu Ali peteri, peteri, peteri, egwu Ali pe-*
terim
Family Head: *Chiaku bute aku*
Oha Lile: *Egwu Ali peteri, peteri, peteri, peteri, egwu*
Ali peterim
Family Head*: Chi omumu kpota omumu*
Oha Lile*: Egwu Ali peteri, peteri, peteri, egwu Ali*
peterim
Family Head: *Ezi na ulo ezue onu ma uma*
Oha Lile: *egwu Ali peteri, peteri, peteri, egwu Ali pe-*
terim
Family Head: *Mkpukpu, mkpukpu*
Oha Lile: *Mkpukpu, kaa nka*
Family Head*: Ndebe anyi eriele aku*
Oha Lile: *Ndebe anyi umu aku emela aku yom- yom*

- **Igba Asara Urasi**: Every family has 'Ofo Urasi' with which to offer sacrifices to the sea god, Urasi ezeugo oshimiri, every year. The Urasi god is clothed in white apparel and its symbol is chalk (nzu). The god allows women to conceive easily and also can prevent women from being pregnant or having a peaceful married life, hence the worship of the god to appease him. Women are consecrated to him and men are initiated into the urasi cult.

- **Ogulano Agwunsi***:* It is believed that the spirits of people transmigrate into the animal world yearly by becoming different kinds of animals. A general sacrifice is offered to the god *Agwunsi* (war power of God) to bring home from the brush, back to human community, the spirits of those who have transmigrated (*ogulano*). Only cocks, one for each male, are offered according to the number of male members of each family. Also, okasi salad, made up of okazi, roasted corn, ugba, and palm oil, is offered to the *Agwunsi* god who is powerful in causing the transmigrated souls to return.

Ogulano Incantation

> *Family Head:* *Ogulano na nwa; ogulano na Nwanyi; ogulano na ji; ogulano na ede; ogulano na nde kpuru ohia; na ndeputara uzo, na nde yiri ezi; na nde yiri agu; na nde yiri ozo; gbanwata nihu; gbanwata na azu; nchari nehu; nnuri nehu; na akpoku onye ihu; na akpoku onye azu si na ohia puta na afa nde mbo nde egede.*

> *All People:* *Oho kapok oho kapok ooo (that is: Hurray let it so happen to us).*

- **Ikpara Ali Unwu:** Annually, on the day of Isu olila (final Okolosa dance), elders gather at the Ali shrine (god of the land) to offer some harvest produce, especially four cobs of corn and a 2-gallon jar of palm wine to the god Ali. The high priest will receive all the gifts and will entertain the elders with cornmeal and a soup of 'atuma' fish (catfish). At the end, they will all denounce with a curse those who contravene the ordinances and bless those who live according to the regulations.

- **Ikpara Mgbeba Unwu:** The day before *Isu Olila,* elders gather at the Mgbeba god shrine to offer some farm produce, especially four cobs of corn and palm wine to the god which protects households. The elders are entertained with a meal. At the end, they curse those who act contrary to the orders and bless those who walk in the way of the ordinances.

- **Ahiajioku:** This is observed annually after the harvesting of yams in a sacrifice to the farm god, *Ahiajioku,* by each family, thanking the god for protection during the farming period and for causing an abundant production of crops. When a family is large, members are reminded of the observation of farm ordinances, namely

 a) no yam or crop theft is allowed,
 b) women in menses should not go to the farm or yam barn,

c) no one farms on a holy day,
d) 'Ona' (dioscorea dum etorum) should not be planted in the farm or near someone who is forbidden to eat ona;
e) No lighted firewood (owa) should be taken to the yam barn.

If a male and a female child are born, a cock and a hen are offered to *Ahiajioku god*. Yam fufu meal and yam mashed with palm oil (abubu) are also offered to the god.

5.2 Latest Development - Modern Trend of Affairs - Modern Integrated Cultures (a) Indigenous (b) Christian (c) Islam (Muslim) (d) Judaism (e) Hinduism (f) Socio-Economic Structures

Trends of Affairs in Infrastructures

(a) Indigenous Cultures

We are witnessing a success story in this sector. There are now state and national cultural organizations which stipulate occasions when annual exhibitions of cultures of different ethnic communities are staged. In these organizations, there are groups of people who lay down rules of operations and how to award points on the degree of excellence of their performances. The topmost performers are awarded trophies that signify the best performances. In the past, there used to be a practice by means of which people of the community went to learn how to perform a certain dance from another community. All members of a community participate in the dances.

(b) Christian Culture

In the past, Christians used to denounce local people and local social events. Such an antisocial attitude has been disallowed because Christmas Day and Easter Sunday and all Sundays are observed by all, irrespective of religion. Everyone has respect for God. Both the Old Testament and the New Testament talk about the same God.

(c) **Islam Culture**

During the feasts of Ramadan, all people participate with the Muslims in the celebrations because the Muslims offer rams to the one God in commemoration of when Abraham nearly sacrificed his son as an act of faith in the one God. God gave Abraham a ram instead. This sacrifice embraces the Jews, Muslims, and Christians. It is also what our elders do when they offer rams, goats, cows, and chickens to Chukwu Okike Abiama – The God Almighty.

(d) **Judaism**

Judaic practices are copies from Ancient Egyptian texts and therefore, should be no wonders to any Africans. The seven branched candlestand of menorah, the incense, and the offerings are all African in origin. All are united in one God.

(e) **Hinduism**

Some of us are members of the Hare Krishna Confraternity, called the International Society for Krishna Consciousness. One on the Pharisee versed in the law asked Jesus:

> *"Teacher, which is the greatest commandment in the Law?" Jesus said to him, "You must love the lord your God with your whole heart and with your whole soul and with your whole mind." This is the greatest and first commandment. The second like it, is this: You must love your neighbour as yourself." On these two commandments, the whole law hangs.*
> **—Matthew 22:34-38**
> **The Jerusalem Bible & Popular Edition**
> **Darton Longman & Todd 1974, (p. 34).**

> *"I am the father of all living entities. Surrender unto Me."*
> **—*The prophets Krishna***
> ***Vedas (Indian Scriptures),***

> *"All that you do, all that you eat, all that you offer and give away, as well as all austerities that you may perform, should be*

done as an offering unto me."

—*The Indian scripture*
Bhagavad-Gita 9:27 P. 159)

"*therefore, whether you are eating or drinking or doing anything else, do all things for God's Glory.*"
—1Conrinthians 10:31

Here, we are told in the New Testament to love God with our whole self and in the Indian New Testament of Hinduism, we are told to surrender to God. Christ's and Krishna's teachings present a healing touch of reconciliation and spiritualization in inter-religious relationships and so, we should embrace all spiritual matters with open-mindedness and brotherly love.

(f) Socio-Economic Structures

The social structures that are of importance are electricity, industry, the postal service, telephone, transportation facilities like railways, roads, rivers (these involve trains, buses, vehicles, ships), schools, agriculture, communication systems, and global modern culture.

The modern global culture in these facilities is acceptable to all and therefore, should be acclimatized and acculturated or domesticated. We can now send money, mail, and packages anywhere, at any instant, and can instantly receive the acknowledgement of their proper reception. It is a global culture.

Telephone

Before the telephone, messages were relayed by people carrying the information from the point of dispatch to the point of designation. Today, we are connected not only by wires but also by air, sea, and light. There are computerized satellites in the sky which transmit messages anywhere. We can talk to each other in a matter of minutes, anywhere, anytime. We can organize, instruct, and even work online. Furthermore, all other things done by other facilities have now been taken over by the worldwide web networks.

Transportation

In the near distant past, our ancestors travelled to distant places on foot and by boat. What a tedious journey! In 1854, a British man named Dr. William Balfour Baikie, whose name caused Ibos to call all Europeans ***"nwa" Baikie***, as a British Consular agent, after Beecroft, undertook to go first by steamship to Hausa land from Onitsha to Lokoja and then walked 250 miles on foot inland to Benue because his steamship ran aground. Dr. Baikie was the one who tested the use of quinine in treating the African fever, malaria, which bothered Europeans and Dr. Baikie was popular among Nigerian people because of the use of quinine as a prophylactic or preventive. In those days, from 1912 to 1916 and 1922 to 1927, there were two railway lines, one from Kaduna to Port Harcourt and one from Kaduna to Lagos. The scant land road system had what were called "dust bowls" in the dry season and veritable quagmires of potholes in the wet season. The movement and transportation of goods were stifled. But today, a railway line beltway going around the country of Nigeria has been planned and is being constructed in some parts of the country. Modern highways and an array of road networks have been created. The Niger River is being dredged from Baro in the North to Forcados in the South and many river ports created in some parts of the country. The roads are so drivable that trips to and from Lagos are partially achievable within a short time. A new shuttle vehicle that takes people from the market to their homes has been invented. This vehicle makes interconnecting trips to villages and towns. We are in an era of an enhanced way of living.

Schools

Before, there were only two universities but in the present day, we have about three universities in each of the 36 states. School facilities are adequate but the curricula have to be structured to teach students how to initiate and invent a new technology by improving indigenous equipment such as "*ikwo.*" This sort of origination brings about a new facet of technological procedures and consequently, a new industry. For example, we have earlier mentioned "*nkasiala*" corms culturally used by young women to create a lighter skin colour and flushed sheen rated so much and incorporated in making a skin cleansing cream. Today, education has liberated boys and girls so much that they behave not according to the native culture but according to the modern school culture of liberalism. They now know the truth and the truth has set them free. The old-fashioned way is dead and a new culture with its entrained peculiarity of lasciviousness has arrived. That is why a professional counselling therapy has been instituted to discourage the newly acquired behaviours and orientate the active person to a normal behaviour.

Agriculture

Modern agriculture is designed for mass food production to feed the teeming population with standardized nutritional diets. In this case, fast and convenient foods have been created. Now, we have instant mashed potatoes compared to the old-fashioned "aribo" or "alibo." The old-fashioned aribo is yam flour which is greyish because the discoloration chemical was not destroyed, and it is packaged in an open-air environment, thus making it vulnerable to an enzyme reaction and attack from yeasts and moulds. The mashed potatoes have been produced in a scientifically technological fashion in that potatoes are peeled and then they are cooked and mashed with an antioxidant added to retain the white colour. They are then dried to 8 per cent moisture and packaged in a vacuum or in an inert gas environment. This practice creates a wholesome intact product that is tamper-proofed until it is ready for consumption. The vacuum packaging or an inert gas environment packaging creates a condition which keeps air and yeasts and moulds out.

Communications

In this aspect of life, the culture is integrated so much that right now, new appliances in computer technology are evolving. In this information age, people do not need to move to socialize. They use worldwide web networks to e-mail, to converse, to send money, to apply for a job, to download music and enjoy music or to receive news about anything, anywhere, anytime. We are even being connected to the stars in that we now know what stars are made up of and what is happening in them. The uneducated can use a cellular phone to talk to relations. We are in the midst of information super highway networks which connect individuals, households, businesses, governments, social agencies and institutions. The universe has shrunk into a global village in which long-distance telephone services, communications satellite channels, mobile radio and television networks are brought into homes in an instant. Travellers commune with the office network as fully and easily as if they are sitting at their desks; workers with computer will transmit video, voice, data, and images to their faraway colleagues. Here is one world, one culture.

Global Modern Culture

Here, we are talking of the new trends in behaviour as compared to the old-fashioned way. Some people are abandoning their native religion for any other religion blindly because they say they have found a new religion. They do not know that the new religion is nothing but the old one dressed in camouflage. Some denounce their native titles to become a knight of Donatus. Some do not respect local words of wisdom or local festivities because they have found a new mannerism. But we have actually found a global culture. When you travel, you encounter a global culture which embraces everyone everywhere. When you attend a seminar, the manner of doing business is adopted by all without question. The way schools are conducted is the same everywhere but the language of instruction may be different. We are the world.

Electricity

Today, we are now familiar with street lights, office lights, house lights, light power-houses and a variety of things that are powered by electricity. The culture is the same everywhere.

Industry

The modern systems are mechanized and technologized such that what used to be culturally done by hand is now industrialized and commercialized. The result is the emergence of different work systems and different classes of workmen. Here and there are scattered institutions for manufacturing, fabricating, instruction, merchandising, and commercialization. To be up-to-date and culturally involved, one has to get oneself trained skillfully in the modern work culture. The culture is the same everywhere.

Postal Services

In the past, messages and dispatches had to be dealt with culturally by manual labour. At the present time, it is so organized that the government handles all forms of dispatching letters, packages and messages and much more. We are witnessing a new era of an explosion of technological gadgets and applications. One can now send money, mail and messages anywhere, at any instant and can instantly receive the acknowledgement of their proper reception. It is a global culture. In the final analyses, our ancestral manual ways of doing things are gradually giving way to the mechanized way of doing things.

CHAPTER 6

6.1 Family Team Counselling and Upbringing of the Children on Positive Thinking; a Conflict with the Western Methodology of Raising of Children

Eight Words that can Transform Your Life

The right choice of positive thoughts will put us on the right road to solving all problems. The Roman emperor said in eight words,

> *"Our life is what our thoughts make it."*
> **— Marcus Aurelius (161-180 AD)**
> **Roman emperor**

If we think happy thoughts, we will be happy. If we think miserable thoughts, we will be miserable. If we think fearful thoughts, we will be fearful. If we think sickly thoughts, we will be ill. If we think failure, we will fail. This is a philosophy of thought. Always try harder to have positive thoughts. I believe what the Roman emperor, Marcus Aurelius, said; I use myself here as an example. When I was student in the USA, I always maintained positive thinking about my academic pursuit; I always said to myself, come rain, come sun, and come snow, etc., I must make it a huge success and I did. What you believe works for you. I believed and it worked for me. According to the discipline of the Scriptures, we should "discern the sayings of understanding, receive the discipline that gives insight, righteousness, judgment, and uprightness, and give to the inexperienced one's shrewdness (intelligence), to a young man knowledge, and thinking ability." (Ephesians 6:11). "Put on the complete suit of armor (truth) from God that you may be able to stand firm against the maneuverings of the devil."

Children Need Modeling and Prototyping in Order to Grow; Good Consciousness

The foregoing statement is a preamble to what comes next. The theme says that collective family counselling is the way of African teaching. The principle of positive thinking is used in all upbringing practices. A child is made to be a good listener, a good follower with a 'yes sir/ madam' attitude in good faith. This makes for easy understanding and consequent easy practice. Children are taught to pay attention, emulate and become perfect. This means all hands on deck. When the parents send out two brothers, one senior, one junior, to fetch the goats' vegetable fodder from the bush, it is the senior who shows the junior what vegetable the goats eat. The senior executes the parents' commands and the junior follows suit. The instruction should be smart and positive. The execution will follow through; in togetherness, we fetch fodder, firewood, water, and cook meals. We are made to bear the brunt of doing household chores.

In the African family of old, the young are put at the front of all operations so as to afford them the chances of seeing things as they are, of experiencing the rigours involved in getting things done and of participating actively in solving problems. They are not pampered but are safeguarded. For example, they fetch water with vessels according to their ages, a big vessel for a big one and a small vessel for a small one. When they bring yams home from the farms, it is a big basket of yams for a big one and small basket for a small one. When the parents are in the farm, they are also there. This is a contrast with respect to the Western methodology of raising children. In the West, in a typical family, both parents work. Children do not work (child labour) until they are of age. The parents leave the kindergarten children (2-4 years, 4-6 years) in the nursery school and leave the rest (6-12 years early adolescent; 12-18 years adolescent) to take care of themselves after school. When they all, parents and children, return home, they hurry over their meals and go to sleep. Everyone is tired. There is no room for family associative dialogue and discussions. This is called "too busy to be present." What the kids have is the **teacher's personality and the subject matter personality.** The parents' part is lacking, and kids fill that parental gap up with peer pressure mentality. The moral issue is out of question since your high-grade status can speak for you. There has to be time for moral construct in the lives of men. The 'end justifies the means' is not moral. If you want peace, prepare for war; this is not moral. Greedy ambition to be rich is not moral or divine. Social construct built in social activity is moral.

Westernization and African Decay

The ancestors of Africa are angry. That is the reason why things are not working in Africa because there are some Africans who do not believe in the ancestors. For such people, Edmund Burke, in his Reflection on the Revolution in France (London 1790) works (London: World's Classic Edition 1907) Volume IV, (P. 109), said,

> *"People will not look forward to posterity who never look back to their ancestors."*
>
> — ***Edmund Burke.***

For such people, the ancestors had pronounced a curse and now such Africans are hearing the ancestral voice in these terms by Chinua Achebe, Nigerian novelist, in his novel, "Things Fall Apart" (London: Heinemann Educational Books, 1958; New York: Astor-Honor, 1961):

> *"Warriors will fight scribes for the control of your institutions; wild bush will conquer your roads and pathways; your land will yield less and less while your offspring multiply; your houses will leak from the floods and your soil will crack from the*

drought; your sons will refuse to pick up the hoe and prefer to wander in the wilds; you shall learn ways of cheating and you will poison the kola nuts you serve your own friends. Yes, things will fall apart." The sins of such people are (1) the compact between Africa and the twentieth-century Westernization (2) an attempt to "modernize" without consulting cultural continuities and an attempt to start the process of "dis-Africanizing Africa, hence a remarkable pace of cultural dis-Africanization and Westernization.

—Chinua Achebe.

Franklin Delano Roosevelt, 32nd President of the USA (1933-1945), said to Americans when they were faced with the economic crisis of the 1930s,

"The only thing we have to fear is fear itself."
—Franklin Delano Roosevelt

But Ali A. Mazrui, Kenyan author of "The Africans, (p. 11-21)," said, to fellow Africans facing a series of severe political, economic, social, and cultural crises in the 1980s,

"The main thing we need to change is our own changeability." Africa is at war between indigenous Africa and the forces of Westernization. It takes the forms of inefficiency, mismanagement, corruption, and decay of the infrastructure. This is the curse of the ancestors, a warning calling on Africans to rethink their recent past, their present and their future and to turn again to their traditions and reshape their society anew, to create a modern and a future Africa that incorporates the best of its own culture."

—Ali A. Mazrui

What Has Been Done to Africa?

This is how African culture was destroyed:

1) It started with the slave trade which dragged free African labour into the emerging global capitalist system and enriched the coffers of the West. The kidnappers and enslavers of their fellow human beings were not stabbed by any pangs of conscience. From their own records, we infer that they considered themselves to be very pious people. The first Englishman of importance to engage in the slave trade was John Hawkins who was later made a knight by Queen Elizabeth I and appointed Admiral of the Navy. Hawkins started out with a fleet of eight ships, the flagship of which was christened, 'Jesus' and his motto was "serve God daily and love one another." It was estimated that the total number of African slaves imported into the English colonies of America and the West Indies was at least 40,000,000. Livingstone estimated one slave out of three was killed in the raid and also slave merchants lost one out of three of their human cargo.

2) It dragged Africa into an international community whose rules and culture were drawn out of European diplomatic history and statecraft originating from international ideologies such as liberalism, capitalism, socialism, Marxism, communism, and fascism.

3) It made European languages the Lingua Franca in African states, for example, English, French, and Portuguese.

4) It involved African states in international law which is Eurocentric, contrary to the African way of living. The African culture is the cultivation of peaceful pursuits of ways of life; equality between the sexes is observed; the fundamental approach to life is the pursuit of utmost good; religious beliefs are idealistic in form and the concept of sin is conspicuous by its absence.

5) It is true it brought African states into the West's technological and scientific system but there was little or no European industry in Africa except a few establishments which served the colonial interests.

6) Africa was faced with a moral dilemma arising from the Western forces of colonialism and with Christianity on the one hand and ethical moral order on the other hand. There are questions like: Can a man have more than one wife? Is female circumcision

morally legitimate? Is there such a thing as an illegitimate child when the father and the mother are known? Where is the morality in accepting the children of a polygamous marriage and rejecting their mothers? Where is the morality of having the Bible and cross in one hand and having a shotgun in the other hand? There are many more questions about the rejection of the morality of the African indigenous cultural principles and accepting of the European Christian dogma.

7) Western consumption pattern tastes were acquired without the corresponding production establishments and skills available locally. The capitalist profit motive, greed, was transferred without adequate capitalist discipline for profit distribution. The rich get richer; the poor get poorer. They took our oil and minerals without creating local processing industries.

8) In Africa, urbanization was created without industrialization which should be its cause. In the Western world, the growth of cities occurred in response to fundamental changes in industrial production or agrarian/agricultural transformation.

9) The materialism of Western civilization, the superiority of Western science and technology at their home base, the declining moral standards in at least certain areas of Western culture (production is done by all but the managers and the chief executive officers get the lion's share of the profits), the glitter and temptations of Western lifestyles have all combined to pose a significant threat to the African younger generation.

Recommendation

Two principles should influence and inform social reform in Africa in the forthcoming decades. One principle is the imperative of looking inwards towards ancestry and the other principle is the imperative of looking outward towards wider humanity. The inward feature requires more systematic understanding of the cultural preconditions of the success of each project, of each piece of legislation, of each system of government. Feasibility studies should be much more sensitive to the issue of cultural feasibility in consulting our ancestors. The world is becoming a village and so Africa's opportunity for fundamental social, economic, and political changes should include sensitivity to the wider world practices of the human race as a whole.

313

CHAPTER 7

Time Consciousness (Sensitivity), and ItsEffectiveness among Igbos

7.1 General Concept of Time Among Nations

From northernmost Greenland to the southernmost South Africa, people greet the moon with enthusiasm as a time for singing, praying, eating, and drinking. The Eskimos of Greenland spread feasts; they extinguish lamps and exchange women. The South African Bushmen (Khoisan) chant a prayer, "Young Moon, Hail, Hail Yong Moon. In Nigeria, Igbos pray: "*Onwa leyi onwa leyi, Iga echem, chekwam ka ichekwuruiche, echekwanam ka oke -oke na eme ochekata oturia,*" (oh young moon, watch over me as a preserver like the hoarder ant but not like the mouse which eats the food that has been placed under its care). At this juncture, the psalmist recognizes the moon and the sun as being the timekeepers when he was praising the Lord; he said,

"You made the moon to mark the months;
the sun knows the time for its setting,
when you spread the darkness, it is night
and all the beasts of the forest creep forth.

*The young lions roar for their prey
and ask their food from God.
At the raising of the sun, they steal away
and go to rest in their dens.
Man goes forth to his work,
to labour till evening falls."*

**The Divine Office, Volume II
the Liturgy of the Hours according to the Roman Rite
The Office of Readings, Catholic Breviary Lent and Eastertide
By Collins 2006, (p. 389).**

Everywhere we find relics of mythical, mystic, and romantic meanings attached to the moon (for example, moonstruck - distracted with romantic sentiment) and it is regarded everywhere in ancient service as the first universal measurer of time. What the ancient farmers and hunters did was to use the moon to form a calendar of seasons for a way to predict the coming of rain or snow, of heat and cold, how long before the planting time and when to expect the heavy rains. The cycles of the moon corresponded with the menstrual cycles of women and as such, pregnant women expected her child after 10 moon-months.

7.2. How Ancient Egyptians Started Time Reckoning in 4241 BC Through 1600 BC

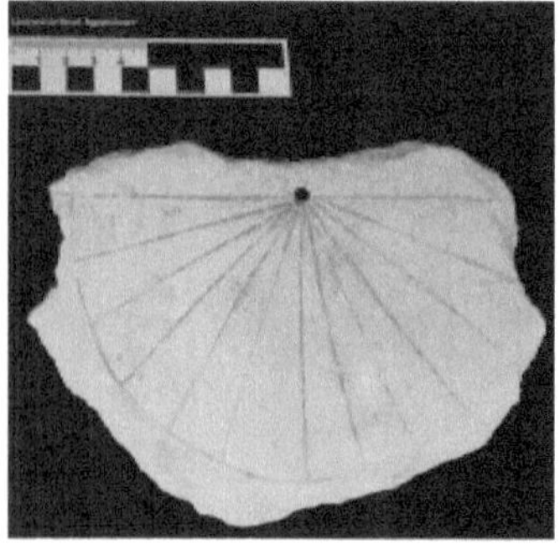

Above are samples of Ancient Egyptian sundial timekeeping since c. 1500 BC, from the Valley of the Kings, used for measuring work hours. Daytime was divided into 12 parts.

https://en.wikipedia.org/wiki/History_of_timekeeping_devices_in_ Egypthttps://en.wikipedia.org?wiki/History_oftimekeeping_devices_ inEgypy

It was said that Ancient Egyptians were one of the first cultures to widely divide days into generally "agreed-upon" equal parts using early timekeeping devices such as sundials, shadow clocks, and merchets (plumb lines used by early astronomers. The Obelisks are used by reading the shadow that it makes. The citizens could divide the day into two parts, and then into smaller hours. The Ancient Egyptians were the first to discover the length of the solar year and to define it in a useful, practical fashion by developing a Calendar - a time schedule for organizing events and activities. The measurement of the solar year at 365 days was close but not exact. However, two more precise measurements for the year were made:

1) the solar year measured from solstice (June 21) to solstice (June 21) of 365.241 days and

2) the Sothic or sideral (star) year of 365.25636 days. This latter measurement for the year was obtained by Egyptians watching the stars. Every year, the New Year (Egyptian – Wep -Renpet - the Opening of the Year) was celebrated when the Dog Star Sirius/

Orion (sopdet/Sah) – the brightest star in the sky, was sighted on its heliacal rising. That is to say, Sirius appears on the eastern horizon just before dawn at the summer solstice (June 21st) with the sun at the same time. This rising of the star Sirius is significant in that

i. It marks the start of the New Year.
ii. It gives a signal that inundation of the Nile is close and
iii. It ushers in the preparation for the start of the farming period. The coincidence of all these events left a profound impression on the minds of the early Egyptian astronomers who made Sirius the herald of the sun, the announcer of the flood and the harbinger of the New Year.

Egyptian Star Sirius

The ancient Egyptians rounded off the length of the "tropical year" to 365 ¼ days, an exact mean between the Solstitial and Sothic years. This meant that the civil calendar used by the Egyptians differed from the true year by ¼ day per year. This difference hardly bothered Egyptians and it was not corrected until the Ptolemaic period when the notion of a "leap year (one extra day every fourth year) was introduced by Ptolemy III, Energetes (246-222 BC), dating the New Year from August 29th. The "Civil" year or "Nile" year of 365days began to be used by the Egyptians as early as 4241 BC and the 360 days per year was taken from the zodiac (a band of celestial sphere of 360 divided into 12 constellations of Stars) of the Temple of Hathor (goddess) at Dendera (Egyptian city) erected around 3200 BC and rebuilt in 1600 BC. This is the history of our Egyptian calendar. This Egyptian calendar served so much better than any other known at the time that it was adopted by Julius Caesar in 45 BC to make his Julian calendar. It survived the Middle Ages (476-1453 AD) and was still used by Copernicus (1473-1543 AD), a Polish astronomer. It is still being used today.

7.3. God, Thoth, Taught Ancient Egyptians How to Do Everything

The Egyptian god Tehuti or Thoth represented the divine intelligence which, at creation, uttered the words that were carried into effect by the gods Ptah and Khnemu (compare John1:1, "In the beginning was the word, and the word was with God and the word was God"). According to Egyptian belief, he was self-produced and was the great god of the earth, air, sea, and sky and he united in himself the attributes of many gods. He was the scribe of the gods and as such, he was regarded as the inventor of all the arts and sciences known to the Ancient Egyptians; some of his titles are," "Lord of writing," "master of papyrus," "maker of the palette and the ink-jar," "the mighty speaker," "the sweet-tongued." He was the god of right and truth, wherein he lived, and whereby he established the world and all that is in it. As the chronologist (arranger of events in time) of heaven and earth, he became the god of the moon, and, as the reckoner of time, he obtained his name, ***Thoth,*** that is, the measurer of time.

Ref:www.Sacred.texts. Com/edgy/ebod/ebodog.htm.

In Ancient Egypt, the god Thoth, the reckoner of time, was symbolized by the baboon whose cry before dawn kept time for Egyptians, just as cock-crow or Obumbo or okwambo kept time for Igbos. For this reason, the first efforts to divide time and measure the passing of the sun across the heavens used the baboon as a symbol of time.

Baboons; a symbol of time in Egypt.

Symbol of Time in Igbos

Here, we are describing the first human device, the sundial, shadow clock or sun clock used by Pharaoh Thutmose III (1479-1425 BC) to measure time. The sun clock or solar clock is a device made up of two slabs of alabaster (tinted fine-grained gypsum mineral), one vertical casting the sun's shadow, the front of which is surmounted with a statue of a baboon, the symbol of the god, Thoth, the Lord of time measurement, and one slanting behind the vertical one, graduated in one-hour segments for measuring the sun's shadow. In the morning, the device was set with the vertical facing east. When the shadow of the front slab was cast on the slanting slab, the end of the length of the shadows was noted. When it was noon, the shadow disappeared and the device was turned facing west. By taking hourly records either way, the device was calibrated to read 1ˢᵗ, 2ⁿᵈ etc. hours for a whole day. The Ancient Egyptians also discovered that they could measure the passage of time by the amount of water that dripped from a pot and so they designed what was called the water clock for measuring time in the night when the sun had set.

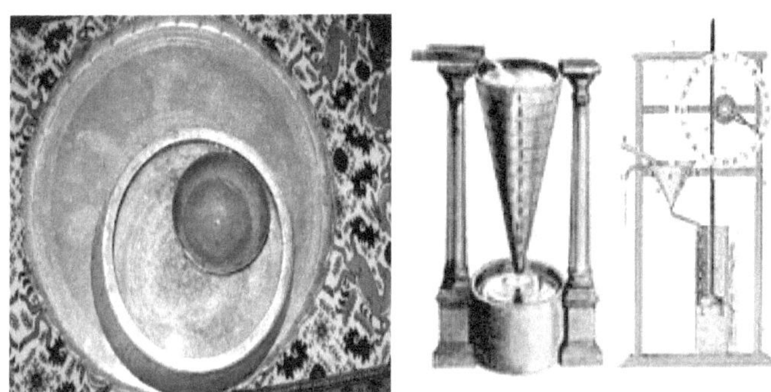

Samples of Egyptian Water Clocks

The water clock was a stone container which tapered towards the bottom where a small hole was inserted to allow the water to drip. The interior of the water clock vessel was inscribed with 12 rings, each representing the passing of an hour as the water dripped. The tapering at the bottom of the vessel was to keep the pressure constant in an hourly fashion. Thus, the Egyptians used the sundial shadow clock during the day and the water clock during the night. Igbos used the shadow by putting up a tall wooden pole, about 6 feet high, in an open field where it was easy to follow the sun and read the length of the shadow of the pole. This gave rise to important time periods of *owuwa anyanwu* (6 am), *oge nri ututu* (8 am), *anyanwu noro na ubu aka nri* (9 am), facing north, *anyanwu buru n'isi* (noon) shadow disappears, *anyanwu noro na ubu aka ekpe* (3 pm), *anyanwu efe na ogwugwu nazu* (before 6 pm when you must leave your farm for home for you will not be able to see enough light after that time).

In Ancient Egypt, the feast of "opening of the year" was celebrated when the dog star Sirius was seen on its heliacal rising; the heliacal rising means that Sirius rises at the same time as the sun and is seen in the eastern horizon before dawn. This happened shortly before the flooding of the River Nile; hence it is called the heralder of inundation (flood), the beginning of farming. The Igbos uses the sighting of this Sirius star as an indication of the time for the start of farming. It is called three Stars of Orion, "*Okoronato.*" Orion made up of four stars is the consort of Sirius made up of three stars. When they appear, they embrace each other forming three stars, the fourth being hidden. Egyptians called Sirius the goddess Sopdet and Orion, the god Sah. Igbos call both of them **Okoronato**, and harbingers of farming.

7.4 How Igbos keep Time with Cock-Crow

"The cock that is the trumpet to the morn, doth, with his lofty and shrill sounding throat, awake the god of day."
—Shakespeare

Igbos Time-Keeper (Cock-Crow)

Okwambo, and Obumbo, with shadows cast by the sun and with the appearance of the Sirius-Orion Stars known as **Okoronato.** As soon as my parents would see the Okoronato stars in the sky in the evening, the time the stars appear brightest, they would hurry to offer sacrifices "ajaoru" to the god of the farmland. My father offered a he-goat and my mother offered a hen. They ordered new farm implements (machetes, hoes, mbiribas). My parents and we their children join hands in cutting bush down in preparation for farming. My parents never contracted anybody for farming; hence, they always had free labourers like my native young man Evaristus Okereke, and our relatives. All preparations, including food, water and palm wine, are scheduled for the appointed day. On that day, our natural time-keepers **Okeokpa-cock-crow, ube obu, ube okwa**, all herald the approach of the day. Between 7 am and 8 am, all interested persons have assembled for breakfast at our home. As soon as meals are over, they are taken to the farm. From a distance, you can hear their farm songs. When the shadow disappears, it is midday and the workers are fed on yam pottage and ukwa meal with palm wine for lunch. As the sun leaves the left shoulder dropping down to the horizon, *obu* (Cuckoo) will cry "*anyanwu efe na ogwugwu nazu,*" meaning it is time for you to leave for home. At once, all workers will leave for home. At home, my mother would feed them again on cassava fufu with fish-vegetable soup for supper. My father would offer them wine and kola nuts. This farm work setup is repeated every two days until bush-cutting is complete. Because bush-cutting is done during the dry season, it takes about eight days for the cut twigs of trees to dry up. On a bright, sun-scorched day in March, that is, "*izunato*" from completion of bush-cutting, all the cut bush farms are set on fire (*isu ohia oku*), getting ready for the first rains. Farms are ready for the tilling and planting of crops. My parents would engage the same workers for planting season. Mama supervised the planting of corn (maize), ogiri, cassava, anara ogiriahu, beans and vegetables (*inene, ugu, ohi*). Papa organized the planting of yams and *igbu aruru ji*. After planting, farm crops are left for some time to germinate and grow. When the yams are ready, our people come home to celebrate Okorosha and traditional dances during new yam festivals. Everybody felt good and uplifted.

7.5. How Ancient Egyptians Determined the Time Divisions of Seconds (hat), minutes (at), hours (unut), days |(hru), months (abet) and years (renpit)

The Ancient Egyptians combined the observations of the lunar months of 29 to 30 days and the annual agricultural cycles of the River Nile flooding in a solar year to fix 360 regular days of their years of 12 months, 30 days per month, supplemented by 5 additional days called "days upon the year," the holy birthdays of the cosmological deities viz-14th July, Osiris; 15th July, Horus; 16th July, Seth; 17th July, Isis and 18th July, Nephthys, to come up with 365 ¼ days of the solar year. They also marked off 360 degrees in a circle according to the yearly circuit of the sun. Sixty, being one-sixth of 360 (360/6), the natural subdivision of the circle, became 60 subdivisions of the hour (unit). Next, the first 60 subdivisions of the hour became the first minute (at) and the second 60 subdivisions became the second (hat). Thus, they had 365 ¼ days per year, 24 hours per day, 60 minutes per hour and 60 seconds per minute. This is what we inherited from the Ancient Egyptians.

The Egyptian Nile Calendar, according to the Annual Cycle of the River Nile, had three Seasons of four Lunar Months each as follows:

- **Akhet The flood season**

Month	Days
1st Thot	19th July to 17th August
2nd Paophi	18th August to 16th September
3rd Athyr	17th September to 16th October
4th Sholiak	17th October to 15th November.

- **Peret** — **The growing season**

Month	Days
1st Tybi	16th November to 15th December
2nd Meshir	16th December to 14th January
3rd Phamenoth	15th January to 13th February
4th Pharmouthi	14th February to 15th March.

- **Shemu** — **The harvest season**

1st Pashons	16th March to 14th April
2nd Payni	15th April to 14th May
3rd Epiphi	15th May to 13th June
4th Mesori	14th June to 13th July.

- **Plus, Five Extra Holy Birthdays**
  14th July – Osiris, 15th July - Horus, 16th July – Seth
  17th July - Isis, 18th July - Nephthys.

7.6 Igbos Fix Time

Onwu Ututu Gbogbo (6 am, East), anyanwu nuru na ubu aka nri (9 am, East), anyanwu buru nisi (no shadow -12 o'clock noon), anyanwu nuru na ubu aka ekpe (3 pm, West), chi rube isi na mgbede anyasu (6 pm, West), chi nri anyasu (9 pm, West), anyasu ada na ura (12 o'clock midnight), Obumbo (4 am) Okwambo (4 am), Okeokpambo (5 am), izu ekwe (4-day week), izunato (12-day 3 week), izunasa (28-day, 7 week moon-month), 12 moon-months for a year of 336 days, ohu = 20, ogu =200, nnu = 400, nnu kwuru nnu = 400 x 400, Ebebe =1000,000, nnu ebebe = 400,000,000.

1 = ofu, 2 – abua, 3 = ato, 4 – ano, 5 = ise, 6 = isie, 7 = asaa, 8 = isato, 9 = iteghete or itenani, 10 = iri.

In Igboland, every town has its own security guardsmen known as *ogbo ji imeofo (obodo)*, an age group in charge of operations in the town. When it is sunset at 6 pm, the head man of the guardsmen beats a wooden tom-tom (*ekwe*) to alert those concerned to take up their positions at 7 pm in the four locations designated as their beats for duty. They keep watch over the city until the first cry of *Okwa*, (African Grouse), *Okwambo* and *Obumbo* at 4 am, when the tom-tom bell strikes four times. They wait till the cock crows at 5 am (*Okeokpambo*). From this time on, the watch is over but they come together to report any incidents at 6 am and then go home. Igbos use the moon and the sun for timekeeping. The moon gives the 28 days for a moon-month from *onwa opupu* to *onwa nlakpu* (appearance to disappearance of the moon) but the sun gives the days from *owuwa anyanwu to odida anyanwu* (from sunrise at 6 am to sunset 6 pm daytime and from sunset 6 pm to sunrise 6 am nighttime and the year is reckoned from *ikpoahu to chioha* (from New Year to the celebration of the festival of the god that closes the year). Igbos have four days per week, namely *Eke, Orie, Afor, Nkwo*, each day is a god worshipped on every eighth repeat of the day; for example, *Eke Ukwu mbosi Okwukwu* (holy Eke day for worship). We have Izuekwe = 4 days = 1 week, 28 days = 7 weeks = 1 moon-month. Onwa neri na abua = ofuaho =12 moon-months = 1 year.

Igboland Numbers:

1 11 111 1111 11111 111111 1111111 11111111 111111111 1111111111

1 2 3 4 5 6 7 8 9 10

Ohu = 20, ogu = 200, nnu= 400
Nnu kwuru nnu = 400 x 400
Ebebe =1000,000
Nnu ebebe = 400,000,000

Igboland of Southeastern Nigeria has feast days and festivals (*agwunsi* is a feast day and *ogele or aranumu* is a festival) as attached. We also have the Igbo calendar for December 2011 and January 2012 as attached. After the *Ikpoaho* marriage ceremony, *ikwezi* starts from January to March every year. The onset of farming begins in February with the clearing of bush. The planting of crops starts in late March to April and sometimes in early May. The worship of gods is shown in the festival list. Those who perform *ozo title* initiation and *Ekwe Nwanyi* undertake doing so in stages, one stage every month.

Typical Time Schedule of Igboland of Southeastern Nigeria like that of Mgbidi Traditional Festivals 1988. Mgbidi is a Town in Orlu Local Government Area Imo State

1.	Itummanyi Owu Uzinumu Mgbidi	11-5-88
2.	Mgbada Obana Mgbidi	25-5-88
3.	Nkwo Ude	26-5-88
4.	Eke Itu Amachi Osele Uzinumu	27-5-88
5.	Owu Uzinumu, Ugbele, Umuabiahu	28-5-88
6.	Owu Imeoha, Ihite	1-6-88
7.	Owu Umorji, Okwudo, Umuehi Umuokpara	5-6-88
8.	Ika Achichi Owu	12-6-88
9.	Owu Eziani	13-6-88
10.	Owu Ahichi Mgbidi	28-6-88
11.	Itoihenani Nkwesa	14-7-88
12.	Itoihenani Duru	18-7-88
13.	Itoihenani Ogbara	22-7-88
14.	Isaire Ndinze Duru	26-7-88

15. Isaire Ndinze Ogbara	30-7-88
16. Ijenaho Duru	9-8-88
17. Ijenaho Ogbara	13-8-88
18. Asara Urasi Ogbara	14-8-88
19. Ikpara Ali Unwu	16-8-88
20. Isu Olila Uzinumu	17-8-88
21. Agwunsi Duru	11-8-88
22. Agwunsi Ezike	15-8-88
23. Agwunsi Uzinumu	23-8-88
24. Ogele-Irijiofu of His Highness Iyasara Nnowu Ezeugo Eleberi	17-9-88
25. Ogele Ogbuehi Odu Na Ogbuehi Kezie	21-9-88
26. Ogbodo Arisi Mgbidi	21-9-88
27. Ironmuo Duru	28-9-88
28. Ironmuo Ogbara	2-10-88
29. Ibu Izege Ndinze	26-10-88
30. Imanye Ukwu Nanmili Ndinze	18-11-88

31. Igbuwaji Duru Na Uzinumu	24-11-88
32. Nkekwu Obana Mbata	24-11-88
33. Urasi Uzinum	26-11-88
34. Aranumu Mgbidi	2-12-88
35. Ahijioku Mgbidi	11-12-88
36. Obana Opupu	8-12-88
37. Ikpoahu Mgbidi	27-12-88
38. Chioha Mgbig	19-1-89

DECEMBER 2011

Sunday	Monday	Tuesday	Wednesday	Thursday	Friday	Saturday
4 Eke	5 Orie	6 Afor	7 Nkwo	1 Orie	2 Afor	3 Nkwo
11 Nkwo	12 Eke	13 Orie	14 Afor	8 Eke	9 Orie	10 Afor
18 Afor	19 Nkwo	20 Eke	21 Orie	15 Nkwo	16 Eke	17 Orie
25 Orie	26 Afor	27 Nkwo	28 Eke	22 Afor	23 Nkwo	24 Eke
				29 Orie	30 Afor	31 Nkwo

January 2012

Sunday	Monday	Tuesday	Wednesday	Thursday	Friday	Saturday
1 Eke	2 Orie	3 Afor	4 Nkwo	5 Eke	6 Orie	7 Afor
8 Nkwo	9 Eke	10 Orie	11 Afor	12 Nkwo	13 Eke	14 Orie
15 Afor	16 Nkwo	17 Eke	18 Orie	19 Afor	20 Nkwo	21 Eke
22 Orie	23 Afor	24 Nkwo	25 Eke	26 Orie	27 Afor	28 Nkwo
29 Eke	30 Orie	31 Afor				

7.7 Why Time-Keeping is Essential

This is necessary for fixing the time for expecting heavy rains or snow, heat or cold, how long until planting time, for household use by the husband and wife expecting a baby, for fixing times for festivals, feasts and sacrifices, for holding people together for common agreements, for harvesting of crops, commerce, delivery of goods and everyday needs and keeping records of events and architecture.

Ancient Egypt was called **"the gift of the Nile"** by a Greek historian, Herodotus (483-420 BC) because without the River Nile which irrigated the South and North of Egypt and so made agriculture possible, Egypt would be a huge desert. Around 5000 BC, climatic changes turned the Saharan grassland into a desert and the nomadic hunter-gatherers living there were forced towards the Nile valley's rich fertile soil created by flooding.

Here, they developed viable farming and domesticated animals brought down from the interior of Africa by the River Nile flood. They enjoyed a lot of fish swept down by the flood. Thus, stable communities grew up and the booming economic conditions led to the creation of the Egyptian civilization which lasted for 3000 years. The Egyptians totally depended on the majestic Nile for the annual flood which replenished the soil of the field with rich silt and supplied fish, water fowl, papyrus for writing, reeds, grass for baskets and matting, and mud for pottery and bricks. The Nile was the main artery for communication and transportation. The Egyptians deified the annual flood or inundation as the god Hapi. Because of all the importance of the Nile, Egyptians created the Nile Calendar. Hence, they had 365 ¼ days per year, 24 hours per day, 60 minutes per hour and 60 seconds per minute. This is what we inherited from the ancient Egyptians.

The Egyptian Nile Calendar, according to the annual cycle of the River Nile, had three seasons of four lunar months each as follows:

Akhet – the Flood Season

Month	**Day**
1st thoth	19th July to 17th August
2nd paopi	18th August to 16th September
3rd athyr	17th September to 16th October
4th sholiak	17th October to 15th November

Peret- the Growing Season

Month	Day
1st tybi	16th November to 15th December
2nd meshir	16th December to 14th January
3rd phamenoth	15th January to 13th February
4th pharmouth	14th February to 15th March

Shemu – the Harvest Season

Month	Day
1st pashons	16th March to 14th April
2nd Payni	15th April to 14th May
3rd epiphi	15th May to 13th June
14th mesori	14th June to 13th July

The Five Days Upon the Year`

This myth occurred during the time of creation when the cosmological deities were coming into being. The sky goddess, Nut, was pregnant by Geb, the earth god, her consort, and this incidence threatened the sun-god, Ra, who felt that more gods and goddesses would be a great risk to his supremacy if he did not take any precaution and so he cursed Nut, preventing her from giving birth on any day of the year (which at that time was 360 days).

Luckily for mankind, the lunar deity, Thoth, decided to intervene. By beating the Moon in a chess game, Thoth succeeded to win enough light to create an additional five days each year (referred to by the Ancient Egyptians as "days upon the year"). These five days added to 360 days gave us our 365 days of the year. This is how Egyptians did it. Nut was able to give birth to five of her offspring each on consecutive days, namely 14th July, Osiris; 15th July, Horus; 16th July, Seth; 17th July, Isis; 18th July, Nephthys.

In chapter 2a above, I mentioned some timekeeper birds as *Obu* (Cuckoo), *Okwa* (Bush Fowl) and *Okeokpa* (Domestic Foul). These birds played an important role in timekeeping. I say so because, in the present time, only a few people are still paying attention to these timekeeper animals. In the olden days, my parents used these time birds a lot to regulate their daily plans. I could remember my father waking up at first cock-crow to tap his wine. My mother would also wake up and prepare for market or for an errand in the nearby village. At 5 o'clock, after the last cock-crow every morning, my mother would knock at my door for me to greet her first before another person saw her face. She believed seeing my face first in the morning brought good fortunes for her. Time is necessary in our lives; if you are a good planner and effective timekeeper, you will be a great achiever. My parents trained me to be a good time manager. When I was a student, I was able to manage my time effectively. I always combined my academic pursuits with work and church activities. It was not easy but I could make ends meet. To reinforce the importance of the time in one's life, here is a study time management instruction given to students of 2011 Cambridge Open College for their study tips.

Manage Your Time

"Time is a scarce commodity. There are a fixed number of hours in a week and you have to learn to make the most of them for your studies. The hours you waste idling around doing unproductive work cannot be brought back. Time management is a crucial skill that students have to learn if they wish to succeed in their studies. For managing your time effectively, you should be very clear about what you are trying to achieve. Once you have decided your goals and priorities, you should divide your time between studies and leisure accordingly. For this, you should first conduct a time audit of your day-to-day activities. When do you wake up? When do you sleep? Are you spending some time in unproductive work? You should keep a detailed log of your activities for a week to get a good idea of how much time you spend on which activities. Doing just 20 minutes of study during your work lunch break each working day adds up to nearly two extra hours a week. The next step is to review and evaluate your time expenditure and compare it with the goals and priorities that you have set for yourself. You have to find the best fit that gives most of your time to preparing for what you are trying to achieve and drastically cut down on every activity that is irrelevant to your goals. An effective way to take control of your time is to create a fresh but realistic weekly schedule that focuses most of your energy and number of hours on your studies but also some flexibility built in for unexpected tasks that may crop up."

—Cambridge Open Study Tips

CHAPTER 8

Afa Itu Afa Ma obu Afa Ikonu- Igbo-Diminutive Names or Nicknames - Names that either Belittle a Person or Endear a Person

When elders call you "orima obuo" meaning, you're eating too much and it makes you too fat, they are trying to deter you from eating too much. It is an indirect way of teaching good manners at table to youngsters. Fools always go with this name because they eat too much as they have no mental work to do. They just eat and grow big. When they label you with an unpleasant name with contempt or derision, they are counselling you to stop the attitude which gives you that name. When they attach an endearing or an affectionate name to your name, they are reinforcing and encouraging the trend of action in which you always excel. For example, *"Agu, oleke gara taa"* meaning brave and lionhearted one, where and what are you successful at today? Parents get loyal and obedient responses from children by using sweet little names that uplift and make them feel enriched, happy and needed and gives a sense of belonging. All the same, when a child does something wrong, they will equally call him/her by the act to make him/her feel the remorse of conscience. For example, Oluoha imefokwara emefo taa (Mr. Destroyer, how much harm have you done today?). Most of the time, these good new names replace the actual names. A person was the first-born and was named *"Amaeze"* but parents later nicknamed him '*Nwokoro*' (little pleasant boy); people knew and called him *"Nwaokoro."*

The List of Pleasant Nicknames

Nicknames and Praises
Nwa iheukwu na anyi aru: Oh, grand and illustrious one, welcome.

Nwa ioha ukwu: You are an honourable prince; well done.

Nwa utughutu na eme eke: You are the protector of all beings.

Nwa eke na ehiwu ala: You are consecrated as the boa constrictor is to the earth god, Ala.

Nwa okata ekweghi ekwe: You are unshakeable and relentlessly engaged in doing a good, great thing.

Nwa Imo ori onye ofuru ukwu ya: You are one who deals squarely with any intruder.

Nwa ogbulua akwughi ugwo: You are one who is exempt from reparation for wrong-doing.

Nwa apiti uzo oru onye sorochaa otere: You are one who is indispensable; no one can avoid you and survive.

Nwa idigiri riri ji nwata were mpi chere ya: You are a formidable devourer without compensation.

Nwa elilia ite ogbonyua oku: You are the stone which the builders rejected, and which has become the head of the corner.

Nwa oku gbarue ala eree: You are one who when you get the grasp of a task, you consume it.

Nwa mgwogo osimiri: You are as great as the ocean.

Nwa oporocha: You are sweet as shrimps.

Nwa onunu ji: You are very young and tender and need attention.

Nwa eze na eri ij: You are noble, your meals are of yams, you eat good foods. You are well-born.

Nwa anya saa anya gbaa: You are one who is cautious and takes one step at a time to ensure precise execution of a project.

Nwa ese- ese: You are slight and fulfilling.

Nwa ukwa achi na aka na agba neju: You are one who readily works very fast and achieves quick results.

Nwa igirigi: You are one who, when you are around, evil-doers find it hard to do their havoc.

Nwa urukpu na eri onwa. You are the black cloud that engulfs the moon.

Nwa igwe oji na eri onwa: You're the dark cloud that swallows the moon.

Nwa Agu anaghi eri akwukwo ohia: Lions eat no vegetable but meat. In reference to people, we encourage the youths not to do anything unbecoming of them but do things that exalt them.

Nwa okpu: You are the original one.

Nwa ngaji ola: You are born with a silver spoon in your mouth.

Greeting: *Ike odikwagi?* Are you ok?
        Ee, ikedi: Yes, I am ok.

Mbosi ajo njo: Everyday events always result in the affirmative. You are given this name if you are always a successful winner in your endeavours or a hunter that always comes home with game or a student that always excels in examinations.

Damirida: Always prevailing fiercely like a lion on the hunt for food. When you return from hunting, carrying in your bag a gazelle, your wife will address you. Damirida, olea, nta di anu- go-getter, I think we have meat for dinner.

Okpokii: Small and stirring. This name is taken from *"okpokii onwe"* which is small old monkey but keeps every other monkey on edge when it is around. Likewise, a man is called okpokii when he is small and old but drives others to zestful uneasiness.

Nwanyi ji: Very satisfying type of yam that gives one one's fill in food. A woman is called '*nwanyj ji* if she is satisfying as a useful woman.

Nwa ayia -ayia: You are small as crayfish that serves as a big fish for poor people-very small, very important.

Nwayo bu ije: You are the one who does things quietly and gently (a peaceful and serene fellow). Very reserved fellow and always focused.

Anwuru na eme na anya: Very disturbing, when you are making everybody unable to concentrate, you are '*anwuru.'*

Anwuru gele - gele ruru igwe: Smoke that funnels up slowly in a gay manner. When a person progresses in a slow and steady manner in achieving his/her goals, he or she is called *"anwuru gele- gele."*

Onya bele -bele na egbu Agu: A supple, simple trap that catches a lion. The literal meaning is a fellow who uses a simple device to entrap a giant. It is a man or woman who is very resourceful; a great achiever.

Nwa agada aga okenku: You're great and effective at your aim. When you successfully complete a task and being entertained for this reason, the task master will address you as '*agada aga okenku.*'

Nwa anya kopi - kopi: Fat small eyes; that is, you have eyes like the Chinese eyes. Your mates can make fun of you by calling you "*anya kopi- kopi.*"

Nwa akwara bu ike ahu: Strong man. If you have just cut down an iroko tree (oji), your consignor for the job will praise you by calling you "*akwara bu ike.*"

Isi okponku: Very intelligent. If the result of my midterm examination arrives, showing that I have four "As" in four subjects, my father appraises me by calling me "*isi okponku.*" That endears me to his heart and reinforces me.

Ogbaka Nwanyi: Feminine man: A man who wears a wrapper (loin cloth) like a woman, he is called Ogbaka Nwanyi.

Nwa ulari eji eke isi: Very tender beautiful girl who looks beautiful in a silken dress. Mothers address their daughters as "*nwa ulari*" to show their appreciation of the beautiful way they dress. Daughters are pleased greatly.

Aka na agba mgbada: A hunter with precise shots. Renowned hunters who hunt lions are called "Ogbuagu." They celebrate "*aka igbuka*" every year and are so honoured.

Mgborogwu: Good remedial medicine and also the statue of a spirit put up in front of the house to guard the household. Ancient Egyptians called it the Sphinx. If you are "*nyiri nmuo nyiri mmadu*", you are mgborogwu: That is, you are indefeasible spiritually and physically.

Akata aka kwere ozo dimgba: A man can wrestle with a gorilla. He is a tough man for a tough job. This is praise for a hardworking man that motives the person.

Nne meri opuru ogu alughi ogu: (*Okwu n'onu emeghi n'aka*)
A braggart or a shirker - a man full of words with no actions - a soldier who runs away from fighting.

Atu epi*:* This represents one who is very reproductive and very viable. A woman is *atu epi* when she is readily impregnated. She is then called "*ezi agbogho.*"

Okwuru ukwu erughi nne: There are yams that produce a lot of leaves, but they cannot produce big yam tubers. There are men who are very big but cannot do work according to their big size. People are advised not to be *okwuru ukwu erughi nne.*

Obu uzo ogu: One who is always in the forefront of any event. He is the one in the eye of the storm, taking the brunt of all eventualities. He is onye njija ogu.

Nwa igbelu: You are fragrant like the pleasant-smelling pomade. Again, mothers used this name in appraising their daughters. You are a box of sweet cosmetics.

Ngalaba ji ulo: The bread-winner of the house. Fathers admonish their sons to act their part well because on them, the whole weight of the house lies. They cannot fall shy of their duties, nor grow irresponsible by not having a gainful occupation. Successful ones are always called this name.

Abum oku mgbam - mgbam: (Ihem fue na ahu, achom ya na ahu). He said, he is like the great land slug which stays in a moist place during the day and emerges at night to feed. Slugs belong to the snail's family, but they have no shells. He is saying as it takes slugs one day to find food, so, it takes him one year to look for his lost property. In other words, he forgives but does not forget. Be docile like a dove and sharp like a serpent.

Nwa eresi: Peaceful as a dove. This is an admonition to one going abroad. We say anyi jebe mba, anyi achokwala okwu ma okwu choro anyi - do not be aggressive or offensive but defensive.

Nwa mgboyi or Nwagbo: A fledgling girl. This is the feminine equivalent of masculine, Nwokoro, used by mothers to make their children enthusiastically endearing.

Nwa nsikoro agwo atu nsiko: This is a ritual initiation song for protection against all dangers sung by "dibias" (native spiritual doctors) when a person is being initiated into the cult of agwunsi.

Nwangworo lee oghoyi song: (Song of one crippled in both legs and hands - quadriplegic). The master of the crippled man calls him for various events:

Master: Nwaawo (nwangworo) bia je kpata nku
Cripple: Ukwu adi, aka adi
Master: Nwaawo (nwangworo) bia chute nmiri
Cripple: Ukwu adi, aka adi
Master: Nwaawo bia rie nri
Cripple: Obu onye akporo oku ogaghi aza, obu onye akporo oku ogaghi aza.

Explanation

Master: Cripple, go and fetch firewood
Cripple: I have no legs, I have no hands
Master: Cripple, go and fetch water
Cripple: I have no legs, I have no hands
Master: Cripple, come and eat food
Cripple: Since I have been called to eat, I will go and answer the call.

This is the name given to a person who has a non-committal attitude towards doing the chores of the household except being good for meals.

Nwa Okwo Anya: One who withers another with a glance or one who makes eyes at another with belittlement. Some people have eyes like those of a dog and when they look at you with a snarl they tend to be saying, "Why did you do that?" It is not a compliment when you are called "nwa okwo anya."

Nwa agugo or nwa esi ma gugo: One who always argues and is unwilling to take orders readily. A child who is stubborn and unwilling to go on errands for the benefit of the household is always nicknamed "*nwa agugo.*"

Nwa aturu ocha: An albino who hates to be in the sun because he is uncomfortable. Albinos are adversely afflicted by sunlight and sun heat so much so that they detest being in the sun. They do not do farm work very often because they develop painful scabby sores on the skin. When you are called this name by an elder, he is sympathizing with you because of your unavoidable condition.

Nwa aru gburu agu: One who is very good at accurate aim and precise catch. If you are a marksman as a hunter or a goal-getter as an athlete, you can be given this name. It's another form is *"ogbuagu"* - a lion killer. You must be very daring and precise if you want to hunt a lion. It is an honourable name in recognition of one being a marksman hunter.

Nwa onuma juru: You are named thus because by the time you were born, there have been young ones who were born but did not survive but you survived. So, you are a consolation to the family.

Ogugua: The child who comes to comfort and stop the parents from crying for dead children. Parents might have been bereaved of the first two children but the third child comes to stay. The child is named Ogugua. (comforter).

Oda-aku: Born at the time of prosperity. When some children are born, propitious fund-raising circumstances prevail, making adequate money available for expenses and entertainment. They are called "Chibuaku" – God that provides wealth. One of my sisters had this name. My mother gave it to her because, when she was born, my mother received a lot of gifts and money from friends and well-wishers. Also, my father was very prosperous that year.

Jeremiah: The coming of this child was prophesied by one of our ancestors, and everything said about him happened and so he was named as the prophet Jeremiah. He grew up to be very spiritually inclined, being able to prescribe healing recipes for the sick.

Ofo ji ogu ere*:* Ofo is the authority of the elder which he wields in execution of his duties. When he pronounces you blessed because you have righteously performed a duty, you are blessed, but if you have become vindictive, you will not receive a blessing but a curse. If you are given this name, you are commissioned to live in truth all your life, for in truth, you will prosper effectively. If you are assailed or persecuted by an uncontrolled evil-doer, you will escape unhurt because evil does not afflict one who is guiltless.

Ikejiofo: The authority of Ofo goes from elder to elder according to seniority and when ofo comes to you, whether you are well-to-do or a pauper, the authority of ofo makes you grand, respected, and revered. When you are an ofo-holder, you receive homage gifts; all family sacrifices are offered in your shrine. You receive the first share of the meats of all sacrificial gifts. Family squabbles are settled in the senior's house. All the offering gifts, homages and the keeping of law and order make the ofo-holder powerful and well off. If the ofo-holder is an ozo-titled man and wealthy, he has sway of power over the community, hence the naming of a person as Ikejiofo - with the power of ofo, he is reigning and he prevails over matters. My elder brother, being the first child of the family, was named Ikejiofo by my father, knowing that he would take after him in holding the family staff. As his name implied, he tried and lived good life.

Ibu damirida, ibu anyi damda*:* Damirida, Obu Mgwomgwo - Damirida is called the firefly or glow-worm when it is in the larval stage. It is a drab-looking insect of the beetle family, famed for carrying queer dusty particles all over its body as a camouflage against predators during the day, and in the night, it becomes luminescent, flashing light for mating. As a glow-worm, it flashes light in the night and is called nmu- nmu owa because of the way it emits light like *owa* -firewood. If you carry a lot loads of assorted quaint articles, you can be called *Ibu anyi danda*. If you are jack of all trades, you are *Ibu anyi Danda*. If you hoard a lot of strange articles, you are called *Damirida obu mgwomgwo*. If you have an assignment which is very exacting, demanding all you can afford, you are carrying *Ibu Damirida*. This is the wisdom of old. Our ancestors were wonderful in their thinking and reasoning.

Oganankpa: One who is always present when his craft is ever in need. We say "a friend in need is a friend indeed." He is also an indispensable person in any successful venture. He is admirable and a good goal-scoring man.

Ngaamaeme chupu gam ezi: This means if I fail to satisfy you, discard me. This is a woman who has vowed to do good so that if you engage her in a job, she will give you a guarantee of good performance. She always delivers a successful task.

Akpa aka egbe atua: That is, one who is very beautiful, inviolate, and cannot be tampered with. When a child is the only child of the mother, she calls him *nwa akpa aka egbe kwuo or nwa nnaghi eji aro nro*. The child is precious, sacred, and cannot be traded for anything; neither would one give him up without unrelentless fight.

Agwunihu onaghi agwu n'obi: We say, "The Irish forgives but the Irish do not forget" and in Igbo we say, *Oke ahuru ahu ma obi ya di ndu.* "That is, when we socialize, my friend appears forgiving but in his/her mind, he or she harbours revenge for wrongs done to him/her. In other words, the person does a good lip-service in front of people but does backbiting when out of sight.

This can be put this way: i*to uto nonu or oke ahuru ahu ma obi ya di ndu or ina agba nja nma.* All these mean putting up a false pretext that covers the real thing. It can mean one who does lip-service and it is used to label one who is notorious in playing with false words and actions before people. By this name, people are warned to beware of a man or a woman of this ilk.

Ukwudiya: A name given to a woman who does all the chores of the husband. Another version of this is *"Omasiridiya."* An adorable woman, who is conscientious about all affairs of the husband, earns this name. This name endears her to every heart.

Mgbeke: A woman born on Eke day. This can be a real name or a nickname. Eke is a market day and Eke is a sacred market day. Accordingly, a child born on an Eke market day is a sacred child. Any married woman sent home on Eke market day will never go back to her husband's house again. That is the end of her marriage with him. Thus, it is a taboo to send any married woman home on Eke market day. If this happens, it means that the woman has committed an atrocity which is an unforgivable sin.

In Igboland, we have freedom of choice and execution of rules and regulations while in good faith. This is expressed by Jesus in the scriptures,

> *"Tell you solemnly, whatever you bind on earth shall be considered bound in heaven; whatever you loos one earth shall be considered loosed in heaven. "I tell you solemnly once again, if two of you on earth agree to ask anything at all, it will be granted to you by my Father in heaven. For where two or three meet in my name, I shall be there with them."*
> **— (Matthew 18:18-20).**
> **The Jerusalem Bible & Popular Edition**
> **Darton, Longman & Todd 1974, (p. 28).**

Chirim Borom: Another version of this name is *"Onye na agba emu."* That is, when the person is dealing with you, the person keeps you busy, fully engaged with you until he/she leaves you. Usually, it is a woman who buys fish on credit from a female market vendor. Usually, they do "chirim bororom." That is, they use intrigue or tactics and intimations to enthuse their fellow women while they buy fish on credit.

Uloaku, Agunkwo: That is, she is resourceful and as smart as a hawk. When you beget a beautiful lass, you give her a name that suggests that men will spend a fortune to get her. Usually, men give a high bride's price to get married to her. The lion is a flawless hunting go-getter who has never come home without game, so if your parents call you *"Agunkwo or "Agu,"* they are extolling you as an unfailingly successful person or as an always-must-win person.

Ogo Amaka: This is a name given to an in-law who is a good man to his father and mother in-law. He is a worthy in-law to have.

Daddy ihuru (ifuru) Nma'm Nwasos Nsoso: A child who always follows the mother and is frequently asking people about the whereabouts of her mother. If you follow your mom very often you are called '*nwansos.*'

Ahubere Olenga: This is a name given to a child of great importance. A baby that looks very beautiful whom people admire so much; she is a special child to behold. So, the name applies to one in town. No comparison anywhere.

Ihe ama nga oru: My treasure is always handy to me. This name is given to a girl whose parents consider a treasure that is in reserved order. She is trustworthy so much so you need not doubt her good intention.

Onumanyi turu obasi: One who drinks so much that he is carefree and unconventional in his attitude. He allows his cup of wine to be filled to the brim so that the wine overflows. They say she drinks wine like gods whose wines always overflow.

Utara na enye obara: You are as pleasant as luscious and delicious yam fufu that nourishes the blood. When you do pleasant things, you are likened to sweet-smelling food. Mama and my elderly sister used to nickname each other with these names. Mom called my sister utara na enye obara. They used these names when they were in a happy mood. They used to amuse (entertain) us whenever they were calling us these names.

Ikegwuonu (Ikegwuoha) or Onukwube: This name means you are beyond compare. Your destiny is to excel.

Oriede: One who loves eating *ede* (taro). Ede is a tropical food plant that has starchy corms that serve as food to the people. When you eat too much of it, people label you with the name oriede.

Nwaisi Okem: You have a head like that of a mouse. Some people are born with small skulls and so that feature of your head gives you a name.

Ogba Egbe: A hunter as marksman. Some people are gifted precision shooters and when they are on hunting expeditions, they always come back with some game- '*nta di anu.*'

Ero epukwana na ala adighi: When you are counselling a girl or a boy to behave, you use this stern statement: 'Do not do it for there is no room for its existence.' They will understand you very well.

Ukwa ona adagbu ala puru ya: When you are boisterous with an 'I don't care' attitude, someone must remind you of the duty you owe to your procreators whose legacy you must uphold with care. While children are born to be greater than parents in knowledge and possessions, they, at the same time, must revere the parents and the legacy they hand down to them; hence you are not greater than your parents.

Nwa oka owuru: One whose words and actions are efficacious. His intelligence pinpoints the truth which he uses in making things happen. He is also revered for this matter.

Nwa awuru bu nma (ochonma): She is beautiful because of costly fashionable dresses and cosmetics. When a girl is of age, she grooms herself beautifully to make herself attractive to a would-be intending suitor. But sometimes a girl overdoes the beautification such that her cosmetic decoration stands out on her body. They call her 'ochonma."

Nwa oji nma eri: She is naturally beautiful and is fond of showing off her beauty to advantage. She smiles, baring her good teeth appealingly, hoping to take advantage of the person concerned.

Nwa di na emere: When a man performs "Ozo lolo nwanyi and Ekwe" titles for his wife, the woman is called *Lolo di na emere*. She must also be reproductive and very successfully courageous.

Nwa izu agbaforochi: This man is very formidable, popular and subtle and cannot be taken for granted. Thus, those who want to confront him must spend a lot of time plotting their specifics to engage him and defeat him. He is ingrained with wisdom and strength, capable of understanding a conspiracy. As a result, his assailants spend a whole night musing about how to grapple him.

Nwadiogo: One with prestige devoted to doing good works.

Nwunye nzu: Born on the day the mother performed nzu title rituals *(ipunzu)*. She is a respected lady.

Nwa Urashi: Born on the day the god *Urashi* was worshipped. She is also respectable. *Nwa Urashi* is like *Nwanyi*-Sunday, a female child born on a Sunday.

Nwa ochoma okwaa: *Gbuerem onwa mam tibe ka onwa-* A rebellious replacer or over-thrower. He is a pretentious character, pretending to have goodwill for all but in reality, he is acting in concert to supersede an authority. People are warned not to be subverted by or in the company of a subversive man. He is a saboteur.

Nwa akapuru: Ancient people used their charming amulet to survey the way for a successful venture. If the expedition would be successful, the charm would pull the man forward when he thrust his right hand forward. There is a saying that '*akapuru ya.*' If you are a hunter and you point your amulet in your hand forward and you are pulled forward, you will kill big game in your hunting expedition.

Oreere gi or aka apukwala gi: If a man is working against you in an evil way, you can curse him by saying to him *oreere gi or aka apukwala gi*, which means, you will not succeed in your bidding.

Nwatata: Little sweet child. Your parents can call you this name, showing how they are pleased to have you. On the other hand, if an adult is behaving like a little baby, the parents will also call the one '*Nwatata*' to disapprove of the action she is exhibiting.

Diji ruorom anaghi aruta ogbo ji: When you hire a farmer by giving him money to raise yam crops for you, at harvesting, he usually keeps big yams for himself and gives you small yams. That means, if you desire big yams, you have to do the farming yourself. When you send someone on an errand, do not expect him/her to do exactly what you want.

Nwa amiri: Slender tender girl. Friends and parents call you this name because you are young and delicate. The way she does things and the way she walks seem to say she is fragile.

Nwa eruru: Plump and fat like the pupa of a beetle. She is delicate and does not do hard things. She is petted for this reason.

Oku dara ala oree: When you are fully engaged, you become active. You are called this name when you are a man who is a novice in an enterprise and who has to acquire all the details of playing a role before deliberating. You are given orientation in which you are shown how to do things. Then, when you are fully versed in what to do, you go on blazing your way like fire which has gained ground, raging furiously.

Nwa udo na atu nwa ewu: Tough man, *ikiri jide ahaghi-* What I have, I hold. Udo is a plant, the fruits of which have sticky prickly spines that adhere to the body of a goat when it goes amidst the plants to eat their leaves. If you walk through the plants, your clothes will get a bunch of the fruits stuck to them. If you are tenaciously holding onto a project until it is consummated, you are *udo na atu nwa ewu.*

Nwa okpoto eji tuchie uzo: Elders use *okpoto* stems in *"idoarusi."* That is when *okpoto* stems are put across a road or a fruit plant like an orange tree; it means no one is to pass through the road or pluck fruits from the orange tree because they have been handed over to the gods to look after. If you are called this name, no one should fight with you or hurt or curse you for you are now under the care of the gods.

Nwa ewu okwa: This name is given to one who is afflicted with a motional disease. If a man walks like one who has this disease, he is named nwa ewu okwa. Sometimes, if one is walking about aimlessly or helter-skelter, he is called this name in addition to *'onye nzuzu.'*

Nwa akpiri: A child who is attracted by the presence of food, craving to have a bite. Children who are parentless or who are deprived, crave for food, and if they grow up with this attitude, they will always exhibit this behaviour.

Nwa aka schichi: A stingy person who spends reluctantly even in need. He may go to a cheap market for cheap articles. In an economic crisis, money becomes scarce; it might be wise to economize by reducing expenses.

Nwa aka nsikoro: A person with crooked hands like a crab. Sometimes, some people are born with this deformity or they get this feature as a result of an accident. If you are turbulent and have crooked hands, people call you *nwa aka nsiko.*

Akaramaka na etiri agu aki: A sturdy, fearless person capable of feeding the lion face to face. In other words, he can hold the bull by the horns. One who does hard things with ease. Martin Luther King Jr.is regarded as a person of this character, delivering his dream message in face of all confrontation of hate, threat, and imprisonment. Another person with such character is Mazi Nnamdi Kanu – the leader of IPOB. Everyone desires to have a child like this.

Nwa lara ahia: One whose character, like a commodity, is not saleable. One has to be up and doing in respect to application to work, behaviour and realization of the desired results. Play your part well for there your honour lies. Everyone is good for something. Do not surrender to complacency. Values are made, not inborn.

Ugo bere no oji ka anya na ele: One who is on top of the iroko tree is seen by all. When you are in a high place, all eyes are on you; it behooves you to play your card well so that people may admire the good works you do for there is no hiding place therein.

Onye eje nlele anaghi eru ntu: One who is going to be a paragon of beauty, a showcase spectacle of excellence, must conform to the demand of this condition in order to satisfy the curiosity of the interested people. He/she must not be negligent of the necessity to appear desirable and enticing. To be the opposite of this paradigm is regrettable. People in high places must be clean inside and outside and must show a devout intention to do so.

Gbue dike gbue dike, ewepu dike obodo ajua oyi: One who is not comfortable with the influence of a strong man will be much less comfortable if the strong man is taken away and his influence disappears. There is need for a man with influence. Do not frown at the manifestation of power for it is meant to be the cornerstone of human edifice. Do not reject a man of strength for there is an occasion for his specialty.

Onyiri dimgba: One who dismays a strong man so that he cannot deliver. He is known as an indefeasible man to deal with.

Otokwu otie ebeghi: A young cock that is trying to crow but cannot because it is not yet mature. A man can be called *otie ebeghi* if he deliberates with no result. He is *'aki oforo.'* That is, he has growth with no yield. He always fights and always loses.

Atakata eloo: That which you chew for some time and because it cannot be broken down into pieces; then you have to swallow it piece-meal. Some people are *atakata eloo* because you try your best to mould them into your desired form but they cannot yield, so you take them as they are. If you cannot beat him, join him.

Ejebe ekwuru: One whom you must not by-pass but always embrace. He or she is indispensable and unavoidable, always sitting on your way. He is *apiti uzo oru onye sorocha otere.*

Abum nmiri nri anuokuko, agbaram onwem sogorole: Chicken soup is always light, not thick. Therefore, when you are the chicken soup, you are very simple and blamelessly clean. This is what people say when they are denying an allegation that they are culprits in certain bad events.

Nicknames with Negative Characteristics which are given to Those Whom Wewant to Redeem from Their Bad Attitudes

Omekome, Ome kwuruma - Kwuruma: One who does havoc; he creates chaos amidst serenity; he rouses a sleeping barking dog to anger. He is called this name which he does not accept and that shows he is aware of the fact that he is a bully but is unwilling to retract from being projected as such.

Nwa nkita na awa ohia or awaka ohia: One who runs here and there sniffing the air, searching for something to crop up. He is also restless so that people feel uneasy when he is around. This name is to calm him/her down.

Nwa piki - piki: One who short-changes money when dealing with people. This is dishonest and the name labels him with bad conduct and warns people to take care when in business with him.

Nwa egbu-kere mpi: You look like an owl. We use this name to belittle a person in the way the person appears, especially if he comes out at night.

Nwa olunabu: You are ambiguous and double-dealing. You cannot be trusted. This name makes a person aware that he is unreliable and should change.

Nwa ogbanje: One who has been predestined to die young. If you behave very hurriedly just as if you are going to die soon, you are ogbanje. This is to advise you not to act as if you will not see tomorrow.

Nwa utunku: You are like the wood-borer: Small and ugly and destructive. This is a beetle that bores holes into wood and then lays its eggs. When the eggs hatch into larvae and pupae and then adult beetles, they eat up the plant to death. If you are small and harmful you are '*nwa utunku.*'

Nwa nkpukpo: You are like the noisy cricket that eavesdrops in the house when the husband and wife are talking. This is what the cricket cries out: *Urighiri arina urighiri arina. Urighiri arina Urighiri arina:* It says they are discussing romance; they are acting romantically in the night. For this reason, if you are an eavesdropper, you are 'nwa nkpukpo.'

Orimaobue: You eat too much and you are too fat. When you are huge and obese, people call you this name, discouraging you from eating too much. A person with this name is always seen as good for nothing.

Nwa mboli: Shallow small plate that contains a small amount of water.

This person is short with small bodily parts. He talks with suppressed breath and does little work. The man's body features give him this name.

Nwa titiri igba: Clean, tough child with sinewy body that seems to be unafraid. If you are like the child, you are *titiri gba.*

Nwaofeke: You are uninitiated. It is one who has got no title in anything. Some people, because of poverty, cannot attain the capability of being consecrated to any god. They are *ofeke, opuru ogu alughi ogu, ngwere oluoto.* 'Nwaofeke' is riffraff, a fool, a bogus or disreputable person, "good for nothing man or woman."

Ihu mpi or ihu okiri: You have an aggressive face. You look war-like. Most men look hard-headed but there are some that have a high degree of hardness on their faces. He speaks with grimaces.

Nwa ora nra: You are an instigator. There are people who indulge in coercing the private lives of others by inciting one person against another. They do not see any good in some people and they go on telling others to feel like that. They make two people fight by highlighting the offence of one against the other. They are pessimistic.

Nwa agu na eri akwukwo ohia: You are no longer a lion because lions eat the flesh of their prey but you eat leaves and yet are a lion. When one has become somebody else other than who he really is meant to be, he is said to have become *nwa agu na eri akwukwo.* One who joins an evil gang and begins to practice evil, he has gone out of his real self and has assumed a different personality.

Nwa dube - dube: A sluggish fellow. He or she is *okuko udunmiri.* That is, he is always sick and always looks morose. You can say he/she looks '*dio - dio.*' Some people are born like that.

Nwa ojionu kam: He is a boaster whose wealth and talent lie only in words, not in the reality of hard cash. He is called "*oji onu egbu oji*" *or ojionu karaa umunna ya.* He can say but cannot perform. We have this kind of fellow in every village. He is known as a trouble-maker. He or she always instigates trouble and causes friends to turn away.

Onye arafu or onye arori: This is a name given to a lazy man or woman. He or she is sick in the farming season but well during the harvest time. When the sun's scorching heat is raging or when the rain is coming down in bucketfuls, drenching the skin, this person fakes sickness, rubbing all medicines on the body and lying down near the fireplace shivering. This person sobs while lying down, basking in the fire to arouse people's sympathy. But it takes only three months for intensive farm work and then comes the enjoyable harvest time.

Orichara mkpukuru chere oba: This is a name given to an insatiably voracious eater. This person has a bulky stomach and when he/she comes to work for you, you better plan to cook a lot of food for if he is not satisfied after finishing the food you have given him, he is going to ask for more. Your best bet is to initially supply enough food.

Odumisi ayiaghayia: One with slovenly dress and bushy unkempt hair. He or she is sloppy. This name makes the man feel that he needs to be better than he is. There was a particular man that used to be like this. His relish (enjoyment) is to spoil your meal and so, if you see him coming while at dinner, you had better hide to avoid being embarrassed.

Nwa otankiri: You are as hurting as thorns of the palm leaf frond. There are people who always tend to insult you with some hurt when you have dealings with them. Your best action is to avoid them. They are like a green snake in the green grass.

Nwa oforo ube: An immature person - exhibiting less than normal maturity. There was a man who said the coins that he recognized and wanted were the ones with holes in them. That is, he wanted only pennies and farthings. These he could count. When he did a job for someone, he would request that he be paid in pennies. And so, some people cheated him by paying him less than he had earned. He was an adult but his mind was that of a boy. That is, he was a man of feeble mind. He was not fully developed.

Nwa asiri: One who goes from person to person gossiping. He or she is a tale-bearer who goes meddling with people's lives, exposing their infirmities to other people. She is detestable; no one wants to engage in conversation with her otherwise, she will carry bad gossip to other people.

Nwa ogo apu ezi: One who is stingy, finds it hard to give gifts and when he or she gives out something, he gives very little. He does not give freely and unreservedly.

Nwa isi opioro: One whose head has a shape like a mango. He is said to be brainy. This name is complimentary in that it gives a credit to one with 'isi *opioro.*'

Nwa ogiri ahu: One with pleasant attitude as compared to a sweet flavour. *Ogiri ahu* is used in making a sweet soup. This person is of a desirable nature, very likeable.

Nwa imi nga anya nga: One with squeezed head and twisted face. This is a congenital defect. This feature stands out as an ear-mark for identification. There was one Aguobi who had this feature but he was also brainy.

Nwa aziza na aza ulo: One who cleans the trash left around by others. He is the handyman that bears the brunt of all labour. He is called "*danda.*"

Nwa ebubere mefu: Useless man who loiters and lounges around while people are busy doing useful work. If he is a boy, he is punished by letting him have less food - negative reward. This action keeps him in check.

Nwa aku ekwoba: This is a fellow who exhibits his wealth so that people can extol him. He shows off, bragging about his performances. On fund-raising occasions, he gives big cheques (checks-American) of money. In Igbo culture, naming is part of counselling. Our parents give us names that uplift our spirits. These names make us feel a sense of belonging, being in good rapport with one another, and welcomed in the society.

Ero epukwana na ala adighi - nwaokuku haa nmiri, nmiri ama ya: This means that you do not try to do that for which there is no fertile ground for it to flourish. A man planned to plant yams in the flood plain. He was worried but he did plant yams anyway. When the flood came, all the yams were submerged in the flood water which was very deep. Nobody could reach the yams and they were a total loss. So, we sing *"Ogbuji egbukwana ji na idemili makana ido ga ebu ji ana mgbe ebiri tiwa ugbo na nmiri."*

Ija amu nwa mua ukpa, amukwana ukwa makana ukwa daa odawasia, ma ukpa daa odawaa ala: The late American actor Arnold Coleman said, "Different folks, different strokes." There are different people with different talents. *It has been said in the scripture, for example,*

> *"To one there is given through the spirit speech of wisdom, to another speech of knowledge according to the same spirit, to another faith by the same spirit, to another gifts of healings by that one spirit, to yet another operation of powerful works, to another prophesying, to another discernment of inspired utterances, to another different tongues, and to another interpretation of tongues."*
> **—1 Corinthians 12:8-10.**

Though some talents are very beneficial and some are just vague, yet, they are all gifts of the spirit.

Burukwa ihe eji ama atu, abukwana ihe eji akonu - Iga ebu ka oji, buo ka uzi: Counselling is hereby given to the young about becoming a role-model in different aspects of life. It is advisable to live an exemplary life so that those coming behind you can emulate you. Be like an iroko tree *(oij)* or mahogany *(uzi),* which is a remarkable landmark that stands out above all trees.

Nchiko ede abughi okuko, nkpacha a kpacha aku nricha ericha ya: Here, we are advised to be moderate and not to be overzealous in grabbing everything, for he who fights and runs away, will live to fight again. This is so because *"dike anaghi alu ogu makana isi dike enighi eru ala, okoro na aja."* Do not gulp all your drink at one go, but sip it a little bit at a time for *"ofoma ofojue akpa na ebu akpa ikpo; esobe ihe ekukuter, onu awaa."* Let not your enthusiasm be of great remorse to you but handle every task with zest and reservation, knowing that enough for the day is enough indeed.

Irikwana ejule na nkikere ya: You are advised not to be like a fish which swallows hook line and sinker. You are also advised not to do your work by hook or (by) crook but do it methodically to obtain a fine final result. If you do it anyhow, you will need to come back and redo the same thing all over again. If you make a clear distinction between what is bad and what is good, you can distinguish the desirable good quality and be eager to procure it. Do not muddle your way so that you may not slip and fall. Do not eat the whole snail but the fleshy meat in the shell.

Igba kwara ikpu - ikpu (lika-lika) ka onye ana egbu aruru n'ihu oru ya? You are asked whether you have done all it takes before giving up. The expression is to explain that after you have planted yams, you're to get stakes for training the yam vines and if you obtain the stakes from another man's bush, he will confront you for taking his property. Therefore, for a peaceful co-existence with your neighbour, you are to consult him before taking his stakes. You're to strive to do the right thing, otherwise, you will be prevented from having your way.

Chukwu ke ajo mmadu, okee ajo nmuo du so ya: This means when a bad person is created, there is also a bad spirit to watch over him.

There are trees that have thorns and thistles around their stems to keep those who molest them at a distance. Porcupines (*obiogwu*) have long sharp spines to keep their pursuers at bay. Some caterpillars *(ububara)* have stinging poisonous spinners to keep predators away. God created poisons and also antidotes to counteract the poisons. They say, after thunder, comes rain. A wicked person always has a deterrent to keep him from being overbearing.

Oso nwa mgbada ejila chi, Mgbada gbata ajo oso, agbonyere ya ajo egbe: Once, mgbada (gazelle) was besieged by a number of hunters and a hound. The gazelle, being a good runner, galloped from corner to corner as the hunter shot at it aimlessly. It managed to escape unharmed, so much so that it ran non-stop relentlessly out of its territory till it was dark. It has survived but by its own smart effort and therefore, it can settle for anything. When you exhaust yourself in struggling to live, you can settle for what is left over and say *osomgbada ejila na chi.*

Anaghi ekpuchi afo ime aka: Pregnancy is so self-expressing and conspicuous that no one can hide it. But usually, young girls in the early stage of pregnancy deny that they are pregnant until their stomachs start to be inflated. This has become a proverb in that when a young girl is hiding her body, the symptoms of pregnancy will betray her. She will be sleepy and will spit too often. She might even show some feverish exaggeration. When you are hiding something which everyone knows, we say *"ina ekpu afo ime aka."*

Okuko eji ekete kpuchie no na nsoro: One who is under cover can say he is safe. When a chicken is newly bought and is to be domesticated, it is first put under a basket and is fed therein. By so doing, it is out of reach of a thief or a predator. Therefore, it is safe. Children are at times told to confine themselves to the house and stop loitering around. This is to ensure their safety. Those who go out too often encounter troubles.

Nwa oburu uzo hum, nwa anya kwari - kwari, nwa mgbogo: One who is too smart in dealing with people; some people are so smart that before you speak, they already know how to answer you. They have ready answers for your questions. You may be taken aback by the way you were overtaken. This smart person blinks several times as he speaks, making you off guard. He sings his words and rattles over his expressions so much that you have to concur with all he says.

The Psychology of Right Name and Wrong Name

Umum, unu abakwana umu unu afa ajoo makana ona enwe ire. Ihe si na afa eme: Igbos give names to their children or take names in title initiation in order to cause the one named to have the support of the meaning of the name in his life-time. Bad names inflict a bad influence on the receivers of the names and likewise, good names invoke the attraction of good spirits to the named. This is not a mere statement but a living truth which has been evidenced in the lives of people in the past.

It is also a good attitude to call someone a good name. Jesus said,

> *"If you ask anything in my name, I will do it."*
> **—John 14:14)**

By giving good names, you are asking God to give the destinies of such names to the individuals concerned. Listen to what Jesus said on his ascension to heaven;

> *"Truly I say to you men, whatever things you may bind on earth will be things bound in heaven and whatever things you may loose on earth will be things loosed in heaven."*
> **—Matthew 18:18**

That is to say, if you give bad names, bad names are registered in heaven and if you give good names, good names are also observed in heaven. Also, as Jesus was passing along, two blind men followed him, crying out,

"Have mercy on us, Son of David" and Jesus asked them: "Do you have faith that I can do this?" They answered: "Yes, Lord." Then he touched their eyes, saying, "According to your faith, let it happen to you." And their eyes received sight.
—Matthew 9:27-29

According to your wish and faith, if you give your child a bad name, he is cursed and if you give him a good name, he is blessed. One man was named Onwudiwe (death is angry). This man became mysophobic and divorced his wife as a result of this attitude (mysophobia - abnormal aversion to dirt). He did not remarry and had no child. His line became extinct. Another man, Obodoiwe (angry town, angry people) always wore his loin cloth like a woman. He did not prosper until his peers gave him a new name Obodoma (good town, good people). He started at once to see good fortune smile on him. He got married and had a baby girl. The girl was very beautiful, in in effect, the parents named her Nwaesuruma (beautiful as a coral bead necklace). When she became marriageable and beautiful, many suitors came to ask for her hand but she turned them away. Her parents pleaded with her to be reasonable but she would not listen. Thus, one day, a good spirit wanted to teach her a lesson. The spirit transformed into a handsome rich man and approached her in courtship. She was charmed and she consented. The man wanted to see her home. She took him home and introduced him to her parents. A day was chosen for his second visit. On that day, he came in a big praiseworthy way. After entertainment, he asked her to have a walk with him. They were talking and laughing along. The road they were walking on began to change with bewilderment. The man changed into a spirit person. The girl became ecstatic and cried aloud. The spirit caused her cry to be heard by people who came to her rescue. The rescuers knew her and took her home. The parents remarked that they knew something was in the offing. The lesson here is, too much praise destroys a child, (*Oke aha na egbu nwankita*). You should never pride yourself on your esteem or virtue but should be humble, reserved and discernible. The principle of a good name works but anything excessive ranks in disorder as a misdemeanor.

Circumstances Surrounding Naming a Child at Birth

Parents name their child (ren) based on the circumstances surrounding the parents during the child's birth. For instance, when my mother was conceived of me, the author of this book, she had been sick and her doctor told her that she might lose her child. Fortunately, she delivered me safely; though, I was too skinny and too light. When her fellow women came to visit her, each person would ask: what kind of child is this? Then my mother answered, '*Nkechinyerem*' meaning God's gift. My elder brother was given 'Oforjiogu' because of maltreatment my father went through from his neighbours.

Good Wishes

Onye nwannem tutubele, bele, bele tutubele,

Agnes nwannem tutubele bele, bele, tutubele,

Onwu nne anwuna gi tutubele ya anwuna gi, ya anwukwalamuo tutubele

Onwu nna anwuna gi tutubele ya anwuna gi, ya anwukwalamuo tutubele

Onwunwanne anwuna gi tutubele ya anwuna gi, ya anwukwalamuo tutubele

Onwu enyi anwuna gi, tutubele ya anwuna gi, ya anwukwalamuo tutubele

Child Curse

Ebu gba nne gi, gba nna gi, gba nwa na ekuru gi nwa – This means, may the wasp sting your mother, your father, and your babysitter. So, this is an evil curse and a bad wish that children cast on their comrades.

During our childhood, if one wanted to quarrel with another child, he/she would start singing this evil wish to the other child. Once the person mentioned the child's parents' name, the fight began because it is disrespectful to mention one's parents in children's affairs. Thus, wishing evil to strike him/her and the parents is a serious offense. Subsequently, if one is strong enough to face his/her opponent, one has to be ready to fight, but if one is not too strong to face his/her opponent, one has to be ready to run as he/she sings along.

> *Chi nne gi do gi nkwoko*
> *Chi nna gi do gi nkwoko,*
> *Aju anunu be na ini gi, kwo, kwo, kwo, kwo.*

You wish his parents' god to shake him to death and let the bird that cries doom, cry over his grave. Children take these curses very seriously and they always fight as a result of mentioning their parents.

Wish for Prosperity

- Ji ghe ofuma, nda, nda ekete nke ya.
  When the yam is well done, everyone eats their fill, leaving the scraps to the ants.

- Aku lo ufo oputa nwannem.
  When wealth is surplus, it flows to relatives.

- Ala di nma agadi nwanyi aturu udo, ga re na ahia.
  When there is peace, the poorest person's (old woman's) trade sells well in the market.

- Nkwu gbajuo na elu, oputa onye no na ala.
  When the wine cup is over-filled, the surplus flows to the ground.
  In the Bible, a Phoenician woman said to Jesus,

> *"Yes, Lord, but really the little dogs do eat of the crumbs falling*
> *from the table of their masters"*
> **Mathew 15:27).**

- Nmiri na ezo mgbada ana amu nwa na ohia.
  When good rains fall, the gazelle (mgbada) gives birth to goodly young ones.

- Oriri dakwa ma ogu adana, oriri pom, pom na onu. When goodies abound, everyone takes life easy.

364

- Oriri dakwa ma ogu adana, oriri pom, pom na onu. When goodies abound, everyone takes life easy.

Chapter 9

The Importance of Greetings in Igboland

Greetings are signs of respect, unity, and oneness in Igboland and in Nigeria at large. A child would never pass an adult or his/her elders without greeting them first. It is a taboo for an adult to greet a child first; it is disrespectful if a child fails to greet an elder first. Any child who shows a lack of respect is termed irresponsible, a good for nothing, and would be regarded as an unreasonable fellow. A child who shows disrespect to the elders will be disciplined by the elders. Any adult without the concept of his or her parents could discipline the child when he/she displays a lack of respect. This is the evidence of what Hillary Clinton said, "It Takes a Village to Raise a Child." Our parents permit other parents to discipline their children whenever they misbehave. So, respect and greeting are part of family counselling in our clan. I had a big culture shock on my first day in class in the USA when the students came in without greeting their teachers. More so, I had a great shock when they addressed their teachers by their names, like Mr. Joe, Ms. Mary, etc. I couldn't believe it and I found it difficult to adapt to that system. I maintained addressing them as sir or madam till I finish my studies. What I am trying to impart here is that we have a wonderful culture and we should not let our noble culture fade by imitating the one that is not in accordance with our culture as a result of Western civilization. Imitate their good ones and let go unimportant ones.

Different Greetings in Igboland

In Orlu, my own town, for instance, Nwangele people say "anwunao" meaning, don't die o! Nna or Nne ibolachi - good morning. Umidoka greets *Nna or Nne nmaa.* Mgbidi greets for good morning, afternoon and evening: nna nnuo, Nne nnuo, dede nnuo.
Good night: Nna kachi foo, Nne kachi foo, Dede ka anyi bochi.

Before meals- Father or mother blesses the food by taking a portion of it and scattering it to the ancestors, gods, and God and muttering these words: Anyi ayio unu ndu, Nwanyi, nwa, aku, isinka onurue uwa ezi na ulo ofooo.

Afternoon meal: Everyone says nna nnuo, nne nnuo, dede nnuo.
If you are going to the market, we say: lo gboo ta nna, nne, and dede.
Home from market, we say: nnuo, ilotala nna, nne, dede.

Going aboard: we say: nna, nne, dede ijeoma or siriri werere.

To a friend: kedu ka idi, idikwa nma, ijikwahu?

Greetings in obioru na imo (igbo in general)

Oru (Mgbidi) - nna nnuo, iyaanuo
Oru (Oguta) - didim doo, iyaa nnuo
Oru (uli) - nnaa nmao
Oru (Awomama) - nnaa a nma
Orlu (Nwangele) - nna iboblachi
Owerri ndaa ilola, isanachi, unu anuola
Onitsha - nna ndewo.

Igbo decorum in greetings is expressed in a manner that shows respect to people and to gods and also thanks God Almighty for your success in your venture.

In the ancient times, every aspect of activities had either a good or bad outcome. Henceforth, whether you were eating, working, journeying, hunting or doing anything at all, you were expected to end up with success. In view of that, when you return from an activity, you were greeted with *nnuo* - happy welcome from your venture. *Consequently, nnuo* permeates all well-wishing attitudes toward receiving you back from any encounter. Africa has fabulous culture please cherish it.

CONCLUSION

This book, "*The Ancestral Legacy of Family Counselling*" is trying to re-establish and strengthen the fast-fading family ethics which the Western culture is seemingly affecting. In my other book, "*Building Up Self-Confidence – A Fundamental Way of Conquering Fear,*" I emphasized much on fears that undermine our capabilities to perform various tasks. Today, in our present time, Western civilization, culture, and its rules and regulations are deeply imposing fear into our own noble African culture and family upbringing. This creates fear in our modern parents who are now afraid to raise their children according to the norms and African culture. As a result, any child could do whatever he/she wants without caring and subsequently, if the parents re-direct him/her, those parents would be punished by the law. Hence, the child in question could rise up against his parents or beat them to death, thereby creating a quick job opportunity for newscasters and story-bearers. This book is urging, empowering, motivating, and encouraging you, all African parents, never to pay heed to Western principles while raising your children according to the rightful standards of our noble culture. Our noble culture taught us that we have to suffer first before pleasure, but today, the Western culture is teaching us pleasure first before suffering. I say this because, in the Western schools nowadays, little children are being taught about sex, the usage of condoms, contraceptives, and abortions. They are being taught how to contact 911 for Americans, and 999 for British for police assistance when their parents discipline them. However, there is different between discipline and abuse. Abuse is not allowed. Anyhow, you and I have seen the effect of these on our world that is, lack of discipline. Today, you can see the rate of teen pregnancy and the rate of dropout boys and girls from the schools and subsequent impact in our peaceful societies. Are you happy about these? Are you proud of your children, brothers and sisters, or relatives? After reading this book, if you have already walked away from our noble family values, please endeavour to make a U-turn. Then, let us join hands to restore and redirect our noble family morals and norms which breed pride to all the citizenry. My parents were uneducated according to conventional education, but they gave me standard home training which today, aids me to produce this book for all of you. I am proud of my parents and they were proud of me too. Are you proud of your own? In the past, our parents lived very long but nowadays, they die prematurely because of heart attacks, or high blood pressure which their children cause them. Is this a credit? Please, hold back Western regulations that impose confusion in the manner of raising our children. If you intend to raise respectful and responsible children, maintain our traditional way of raising them. Most of the children are behaving like wild beasts. They could devour you at any time or could run crazy, out of control because they know that the elders are afraid of so-called law enforcement. Parents, you have alternatives; either you discipline your children or you let the government and the so-called law enforcement discipline them in their massive jails or correctional facilities. I assure you, no one could punish you for doing what is right, therefore, never be afraid to raise your children according to the norms and standard culture.

In the olden days when there was no organized schooling, the traditional culture became the teacher of all things, how things were made, how they functioned and how people applied the regulations and laws that governed those activities as contained in anecdotes, sayings, idioms, figures of speech, names, worship, and entertainments. The traditional culture became imbued with all that was necessary to up bring youngsters in the required standards of performance. The ancestral legacy of family counselling is the embodiment of all mannerisms Igbos have designed for raising their children so that they grow up respected and respectful of others and systems dedicated to the welfare of human beings and to the worship of Almighty God (Chukwu Okike Abiama).

The question is: who are we, the Igbos? We are the Igbos in

Southeastern Biafra living inside Nigeria. The biblical records emphasized the Jews and things of Jewish nature and were blunt about other nations because Jews spent 400 years in Africa and this length of time had made them Africans, mixing with Africans, including Igbos. But the Ancient Egyptian records were very efficient in the records elaborated on peoples of Egypt, things of Egypt, systems of Egypt, technologies of Egypt, modes of life of Egypt, Egyptian worldly relations and relationships, and they called the land of Egypt "Khem, Kam or Ham", literally meaning, "Black land" and called the inhabitants Khemi or Kamites or Hamites meaning "the black people." The English Poet, Gerald Massey, in his book, A Book of the Beginnings, said, in 1881, "Egypt is often called Kam, the black land, and Kam does signify black; the name probably applied to the earliest inhabitants whose type is the Kam or Ham of the Hebrew writers" (African Civilizations by John G. Jackson p. 153). The West Africans (Igbos, Hausas, Yoruba, Bantus, Ghana, and Senegal) were in Egypt until 500 BC when they departed and came to the present location. They emancipated empires of Ghana, Mali, and Songhay until the 15 century AD when the Europeans, on hearing of abundance of gold and minerals which the Kingdoms manifested, took to their heels to arrive in West Africa about 1481 AD. In case there is anyone who is not conversant with the self-evident notions of an African Garden of Eden or out of Africa, here are facts to reflect on. There is genetic, archaeological, anthropological, historical and linguistic evidence to show that man and mankind were begotten in Africa and the present Africans are the original representatives of our ancestors.

Genetic

Genes with most variations are in Africa. The African mtDNAs diverge from each other by an average of 0.057 per cent, making them by far the most varied and therefore the oldest. R.L. Cann enunciates that the common ancestor of all surviving mtDNAs of all surviving human beings lived between 140,000 to 290,000 years ago in Eastern or Southern Africa (present samples are Khoisan of the Kalahari Desert, South Africa and Twa Pygmies of Rwanda Eastern Africa). Do races differ? Not really, DNA shows (by Natalie Angier, Culture/Society

News.
Source: New York Times, 8/22/2000 FreeRepublic.Com "Conservative News Forum).

Archaeological

Fossil and skull bones of earliest humans found in Africa have been dated 150,000 years old. No fossils of modern humans of this age have been found anywhere else in the rest of Asia or Europe (Christopher Stringer, an English anthropologist of the Natural History Museum, London.

Refer his book: The Origin of Modern Humans: A World Survey of the Fossil Evidence. P. 51-135).

Anthropological

Anthropologically, of all forms, shapes, and colours, the black colour is the oldest. Other colours evolved from black around 50,000 to 40,000 years ago due to extreme environmental conditions. Dr. J. Craig Venter, Head of the Celera Genomics Corporation in Rockville, Maryland USA, said, "We all evolved in the last 100,000 years from the same small number of tribes that migrated out of Africa and colonized the world." (Free Republic.Com "A Conservative News Forum New York Times by Natalie Angier 8/22/2000).

Historical

Gerald Massey, the 19th-Century English socialist, poet and antiquarian said, "We can track the common psycho-mytho-historical thread of African culture in global society." In Massey's words, "thought were things:" ideas were concrete and symbols at the same time and derived from man's intimate experience with nature.

The beginning of Egyptian dynastic history, which is also the beginning of modern human history, was put at 5500 BC. This is as translated by Manetho, an Egyptian high priest commissioned by Pharaoh Ptolemy II Philadelphus (286-246 BC) to write into Greek the history of earliest Egyptian records from the temple archives. Thus, ancient Egyptian wisdom, activities and all the developmental paraphernalia were interpreted into Greek around the third Century

BC. What was Egyptian then was now Greek and from that point into Roman.

There is another historical record that is worth mentioning - the Rosetta Stone Decree of 196 BC. Public announcements (deeds and decrees) were set up in three scripts, namely: hieroglyphic Egyptian, demotic Egyptian (cursive script version), and Greek. In 196 BC, to commemorate the coronation of Pharaoh Ptolemy V Epiphanes (205-180 BC), a decree was issued and written on a basalt stone slab in three different kinds of writing, viz - Greek, Egyptian hieroglyphs, and demotic (Cursive script version of hieroglyphs). This basalt stone writing was done in the town of Rosetta, hence the name Rosetta Stone and the three scripts were written by the Egyptian Priests of Memphis bestowing special honours upon the Pharaoh Ptolemy V Epiphanes for his services rendered to the temples and Egyptians. The Rosetta Stone Scripts became the key to the understanding and decipherment of other Egyptian records like the Turin Papyrus, Abydos Papyrus and Palermo Stone.

Religion

Ancient Egyptians configured that there were 36 decans (gods) who moved 10 degrees each in turning the universe round every year, thus covering 360 degrees from which they recognized 360 days in the year. To 360 days they added five days for five birthdays of five gods (*Osiris, Isis,* Seth, Nephthys, and Horus to come up with our present 365 days for a year.

According to creation records of Heliopolis (present day Cairo, capital of Egypt), before anything existed, there was darkness and endless, lifeless water divinely personified as Nun. A mound of fertile land emerged from the watery expanse. Then, the self-engendered creator, God, Atum ("the All" or "the Complete One") appeared upon the mound. Then, Atum gave life to Shu (male) and Tefnut (female), both personifications respectively of Air and Moisture. This male-female god pair then produced Geb, the earth god (male) and Nut, the sky god (female). Both Geb and Nut gave birth to Osiris, Isis, Set Nephthys, and Horus. The religious observations of Ancient Egypt formed the core values of the present-day religious values and beliefs.

The altar, the shrine, the bread, and wine, the incense and the holy water of present-day practices were taken from Ancient Egypt.

Natural

Egypt was said to be the gift of the Nile River and it can be rightly said that Egyptian civilization, which lasted for three thousand years, was the gift of the land of Egypt. Nature endowed the African lands with food and materials abundantly so much so that by following the natural trends of affairs of life, it was possible to develop what happened in Egypt; plant life and animal growth were favoured by the tropical clement climate. Egyptians went to the Nile River not only to catch fish but also to catch the wild birds and water animals. Egypt was reputed to have given a gift of grain by Pharaoh Merneptah to the Hittites during a famine and Egypt was Rome's granary during the Roman imperial times. The Egyptian agriculture was far more secure and productive than any in the Near East. Natural abundance gave rise to complacency in Africans, yet, to a great extent, creating a technological society which could make its tools and technical practices which were the basic starting points of all modern practices. Bellows invented in Africa for iron smelting are still in force and are fundamental for modern iron furnaces. Everyday life was and is still natural in Africa.

Ethnological

Origins of culture and factoring culture were first established in Africa. Bread-making and eating of bread and making and drinking of wine were practised in Africa as archaeological finds in tombs and temples have borne witness. The African cultural norms as symbolized in our greetings give rise to Africans' hospitality and friendliness to other peoples. Our proverbs, songs and poems praise the achievements of men and the glory of God. For example, *Nwa ogbulie akwughi ugwo and obana Ezenwanyi olum na ekele gioo* - meaning a man who does not pay compensation for his errors, and Obana Goddess, the musical rhythm in my voice, is greeting and praising you. All African tribal clans were in existence before the advent of the Europeans. They are as they were in ancient Egypt where the country was organized into 42 nomes (states) ruled by a monarch (governor). This is the nucleus of today's municipal setup.

Linguistic

Writing is the legacy of Ancient Egypt to modern societies and the concept of languages came from record-keeping. All African languages have their roots in the Ancient Egyptian languages. For example, "I am speaking from my heart" was passed onto the rest of the world (the Bible says the word of God is in his heart). Egyptians regarded the heart as the organ that contained all the deeds of a man. The Egyptian word, "mer" that is love, came from the English word Mary. The ideas of traditional behaviour of culture and traditional counselling are one and the same for they purport to create a personality that is self-sufficient in knowing the nature of things and how best to behave and act in a situation demanding attention so as to come up even with the status quo and deliver a successful outcome. It is not that a man has fallen out of grace and needs a therapeutic counselling to redress the errors; rather, it is from the growing point where foundations of what it entails in life are being laid down to teach it right by means of examples, samples, words, actions, proverbs, and all that are necessary for right action. This is what ancestral tradition is all about. Bless your day when parents teach and you listen and act accordingly for it is a double blessing that makes you live happily and for a long time.

Chapter 1.1

In a conventional counselling practice, a forum is organized for the counsellor (moderator). The moderator has a behavioural remedy recipe to be set before the troubled client for resuscitating his ailing character. That is character correction intervention. But in the African Igbo original family counselling, what is intended is the family implanting the good behaviour regimen in the young as early as possible, possible at 5 years old, so as to serve as prevention before one falls out of grace and becomes subject to therapeutic counselling. This family counselling induction is spread out in all aspects and activities of life such that as one grows in knowing and doing things, one gets initiated into character-moulding formation and refinement, the end result of which is a champion of a role model of game of life. This family counselling is educational and cultural. It is educational because the practice is the origin of the present-day school system. It is cultural for the reason that it embraces all aspects of people's life as culture is defined as a system of inter-related values, active enough to influence and condition perception, judgement, communication and behaviour in a given society.

Chapter 1.2

In the genesis of man, all Africana - those living on the continent of Africa, and those living outside the continent, are related to one another in our genetic makeup, 99.999 per cent homogeneous resulting from one African Mother (by Dr. Eric S. Lander, a genome expert, Whitehead Institute, Cambridge Massachusetts, USA www.freerepublic.com/forum/a39a2e66d/d//.htm. We are all related in colour of the skin because the same chemical molecule responsible for colour of the skin is in all of us, making different colours as a result of the affectation of different climatic conditions. Our civilization and technology arose from Ancient Egypt in Africa because there is nothing we have today that was not practised in Ancient Egyptian Civilization in its aesthetic form, be it food, medicine, clothes, machines, money (Nubian gold), cosmetic fashion, construction, etcetera. The Greeks, Romans, Jews, and Asians (Middle East) made their copy-books from Ancient Egypt and then remodelled them. For example, our present–day alphabets were formulated from Ancient **Egypt hieroglyphics** (writing system of Egypt) by Phoenicians (present-day Lebanese) and then the Greeks and Romans copied and refined them. We in the African continent, the original children of the Paradise of Eden, have common relics of originality of Adam and Eve in our culture, language, modes of life, blood, and an abundance of natural wealth. For example, the Ancient Egyptians drank palm wine, bouza beer, and millet wine, and we also in Nigeria, Ghana, Senegal, Benin, Ivory Coast, Sierra Leone, Mali, Guinea, and Cameroon drink palm wine, pito beer, and burkutu beer (millet beer). Ancient Egyptians wore loincloths or wrapper (ogodo) made by them and we also wear loincloths or wrapper. Our languages have a common root. In Ancient Egypt, *fa-akhu* means to kindle fire.

In Igbo, *fu-oku* means to kindle fire. In Ancient Egypt, the heart was the centre of consciousness where all the deeds of man are recorded, hence the spiritual notion of the truth of God when one dies. In Igboland we say, *echerem na obim* (I am thinking with my heart). The heart is the centre of consciousness in Igboland too. Psalm (37:31) says, "The law of his God is in his heart." In the whole world, the first three original gene markers are contained in the entire three African gene groups, namely (1) Mbuti Pygmy (Central Africa) (2) Khoisan of Southern Africa, and (3) the Western Africans (Nigeria, Ghana, Ivory Coast, Senegal, Guinea, and Cameroons Bantus of Southern Africa). The Egyptians (North Africa) came next in fourth position because their genes have been diluted by mixture with other races. Egyptian religion was the same as that of Igbos (indigenous religious). They both use herbal medicine; both have the spiritual initiation and title initiation names. In Ancient Egypt, the throne title name of Egyptian Pharaoh, Ramses II (1279-1213) was User-Maat-Ra (Justice of God Ra is Powerful). In Igbo, Igbo title names are *Osadebe* (Power of God Orusa is with me) *Ezebuenyi* (the King is as great as the Elephant). Ramses' Queen's name was Nefertari, Merit-n Mut= the most beautiful, the beloved of goddess Mut.

Chapter 2.1

As mentioned earlier, the cultural instructional regimens are contained in Igbo folklore, rituals, festivities, and activities. Folklore · Proverb instruction - *obiara bem abia-gbulem, olaba mkpumkpu apula ya* (you have to be hospitable to your guests who will pay you back in the same terms). During the native dance celebration, friends from village **B** are invited and entertained by friends from village **A**. Likewise, those friends from village **B** will stage a native dance and invite and entertain their friends from village **A**. Thus, hospitality is reciprocal.

Proverb: *Oko aghakwana nwa dibie maka ofeke achigbue ya ochi* – meaning a doctor's child should not be infected with craw – craw for such an infection will be a laughing matter for non-medical children.

Lesson: Let us be clean in manner and mind to avoid being a public laughing stock. When you are invited to any occasion, you have to put up all your best to earn the praises of all.

Event: Mgbokwo danced so rhythmically during the *iri ji ohuru* festival that many gave her a lot of gifts of money. The young woman was so hardworking that she begot many children, got chickens and goats and a barnful of yams and other crops. Her husband got her initiated into Ozo and Ekwe titles. She was called *Nwanyi Ekwe, Lolo Oriaku.* Another woman went to school and studied studiously and graduated as a doctor of medicine. She became in charge of a hospital. After all her educational qualifications, she came home to take the Ekwe title in order to support her culture.

Chapter 2.2

In the mode of life, we say, "*Ibughi onye oku iburu onye oru.* In ancient Igbo land, men were brought up as farmers or as craftsmen or as both for we say, *onye na nke ya, onye na nke ya, onye ghara nke ya ogbenye ama ya.* For you to become, you have to pay attention to what will make a man. Parents will check the following occupations: farming trade, blacksmith's trade, goldsmith's trade, building, cloth weaving, harvesting of ripe palm fruits in the bush, carpentry, tailoring and painting. King JaJa of Opobo, an Igbo ex-slave, was trained to be a palm produce trader by his master. He put all whims and caprices into action when trading in palm produce. His master and all the villagers made him a chief and on his master's death, he became head of the village. When he paid all the debts owed by his master (a regent of the king), he became King JaJa of Opobo. When he was instructed, he obeyed willingly. He became a celebrity. Another man was brought up as a blacksmith. He established a workshop and had five apprentices. His business produced all the farm implements for the village farmers. He made iron pots and plates. He became rich and had many children, some of whom became doctors and some, lawyers. He took the Ozo title and his Ozo title name was *Akubuenwata* (wealth has made a man great). There was one *Udozor Mgbeoji,* a tailor, who did a lot of improvisation in his trade. He did not have enough thread for sewing cloth together. Accordingly, he would take up some short pieces of thread and join them together to form a long stretch of thread and then he would start sewing with this newly formed thread. But it would not be long before the new thread got broken and he would go on and re-join the pieces again and start sewing again. This attitude gave him this name-calling epithet: *Udozor Mgbeoji, erir,i eriri, nkwobiri, nkwobiri, nzochi ,nzochi; Udozor Mgbeoji, eriri- eriri, nkwobiri -nkwobiri, nzochi, nzochi.* Another personality is a woman who was very industrious in peddling food. She would sell *akara* (fried bean balls) and akamu (corn porridge) and moimoi (boiled bean bread) in the morning, and in the afternoon and evening, she would sell *ukwa* (cooked African breadfruit) to people. Her household was always busy with boys and girls preparing foodstuffs to be cooked by her. She was called mama *Agidi,* Onye fufu food dealer. This name made her well known and rich. She could boast of having got many children through school and well educated. She was a prosperous and noble lady. These are products of home training.

Chapter 3.1

As has been said already, Igbo counselling, teaching, and upbringing are spread out in activities, rituals and festivities such that when you are dancing, you are also, at the same time, worshipping God because the tune of the music you are dancing to is framed with praises to God and to high dignitaries; you are also paying some homage and respect to elders and ancestors. At the same time, the learning process is taking place. This mood keeps you psychologically sound that you are doing what everyone else regards as the proper behaviour. This brings us to a story of a wild beast called *Nwaikpirikiti,* (the impossible). Once, a man raised a vegetable garden full of *anara* (African eggplant) and *Nwaikpikiti* liked to eat *anara* very much. One day, *Nwaikpirikiti* and its young ones invaded the garden and left it desolate, shorn of its vegetable inhabitants. Thus, the gardener conjectured he would not catch this formidable animal by himself outright but he must render it helpless. He made a big soup of *anara* and *ogbono* (peach family), both vegetables which contain slimy, sticky mucilage and he spread this mucous stuff all over the garden and went to sleep.

In the night, the beast came, but unknowingly, it was overwhelmed by the slippery stuff on the ground. Then, the beast began to cry:

kpurunumee nkwaranuma,
kpurunumee nkwaranuma
onya gi magburum nkwaranuma,
kpurunumee nkwaranuma.

The gardener, feeling something had happened, sneaked to the backyard to see if his plan had worked. Surely, the giant beast was lying on its back helpless. When the day broke, he called all his people to come and assist him in getting hold of the animal. The Igbo wise saying goes, *ocho ihe ukwu nyara ama damirida, ocho ihe puo aba; onwugidi gidi nwuiga aka na ogwu; otancham ncham tabiri ire ya.* He, who says it is impossible to catch him and he will always prevail, does not know that a slight clever thought catches a lion. So, while the hurly-burly is raging, always use your fertile mind to figure out ways and means to tackle a never-ending obstacle.

Chapter 3.2

Igbos were part and parcel of Ancient Egypt in their glorious royalty, military, spiritual, mercantile, and agrarian expressions, such that, in Igbo land, every town has its own administration of three hierarchies - *Ndeze, Ndenzo, and Ohali Amala* - which confer to administer the welfare of all citizens. A typical Igbo man is so imbued with the principles of social equality and justice and fair pay for fair work that he always believes that his fame depends on the strength of his honest struggle. He does not care if he has to start from the bottom rung of the ladder of honour and glory provided there is a fair pay for fair work, for the scriptures say,

"Stay in the same house, taking what food and drink they have
to offer, for the labourer deserves his wages."
—Luke 10:7.
The Jerusalem Bible & Popular Edition

Darton Longman & Todd 1974, (p. 87).

Land is shared according to families, age groups, and merit of honour in serving the community. The question of land is very important in that every family must provide food for its members and therefore, must farm the land to do so. All Nigerian languages especially the Igbo language are linked together to the Ancient Egyptian language. Here are some examples:

Ancient Egypt rekh re = skilled mouth, wise in speech
Igbo: ire nko = skilled tongue, wise in speech

Ancient Egypt: rehreh = to burn out
Igbo: orele = it is burnt out

Ancient Egypt: res = tongue
Igbo: ire = tongue

Ancient Egypt: tut = to collect
Igbo tuta = to collect what is lost.

Ancient Egypt uta = to thrust out the arm in hostility
Igbo ita uta = to blame
uta = arrow that shoots out.

Ancient Egypt: uga = to chew and swallow
Igbo: uga = that part of the mouth used in chewing

We have freedom of speech but not freedom for slander and false witness.

Chapter 4.1

It cannot be stressed enough about the importance of good home training on children until we see a product of it. *Eziokwu si kwute ya; Anu abuba na afu onweya oku* (that which is self-evident needs no proof. "All the same, wisdom is proved righteous by its works"

(Mathew 11:19). Children are always counselled with respect to the efficacy of good behaviour, good works, and good life. When a girl is being tended for marriage by a boy, parents always lay out before them the need for honest dealings, diligence, good appearance, clean words and consciousness of what is and what is not, the thought of things in future events and the lifestyle that married life entails. They are told not to be licentious as there is time for a sex life. They are told to aim high but work steadily and systematically to reach the goal. You should not be Jack of all trades and master of none but you should do one thing at a time nimbly until the last piece of the task is gone.

Chapter 4.2

For a short period of colonialism, African culture and personality were devastatingly robbed of their past glory. Our ancestors had been successful in all ways of life until the advent of European mercantile civilization because, the Europeans said they came to trade with us. The African continent, the first land mass to appear, was the centre of the ancient land mass known as "*Gondwanaland*" (Planet Earth by Jonathan Weiner p. 45) some 500,000,000 years ago and had the privilege of having all wealth of nature within and without it. Abundant minerals (mineral complex) and abundant animal and plant life make Africa unique and temptingly attractive to outsiders. Enough is not said, nor is the correct history given until an adequate reference of everything has been made to Ancient Egypt. In Ancient Egypt, cities were first named after the god that controls their destinies. So do we today name our cities after our gods (example: Ala Mgbidi). Rivers have their goddesses (*Obana Ezenwanyi, Mgbidi)*. Ancestor worship was observed in Ancestor Egypt. Likewise, it is observed today by all Africans. So, do Christians ask for intercession of all the saints?

In Ancient Egypt, it was observed that the three stars of Sirius and Orion rose at the same time with the sun in the year 3300 BC at the beginning of summer (June) (Egyptian Mysteries by Lucie Lamy p. 74). This incidence continued to be used by the Egyptians as a sign for the start of farming every year. These three stars are actually made from seven stars - three of Sirius and four of Orion. When they merged as husband and wife, only three stars appeared, the fourth being hidden. In Igbo land, these three stars are called *Okoronato of Orion*, the appearance of which is an indication that it is time to start farming every year as narrated by my mother. This is what is said by an astronomer, Carl Sagan, in his book, Cosmos (pp. 196-7) about Orion's stars: "The constellation of Orion, the hunter, is outlined by four bright stars and bisected by a diagonal line of three stars, which represent the belt of the hunter. "My people, at the sighting of these three stars (*Okoronato*), offer farm sacrifice (*aja oru) to Ahijoku*, the farm god and start the cutting of bush to mark the beginning of farm season."

Today, the world has become a global village. New innovations have brought us together in this village and our former cultures have given way to new ones. We are learning how to live together in peace even though many things are equalizing out yet, some of us cling to the selfish arrogance of a "holier than thou" attitude. They are talking about democracy but when they draw up the governing constitution, they put up their own practices and taste of life, ignoring those of others. We, therefore, are faced with the struggle between real life and theoretical life as defined by calculated rules and laws other than the natural laws. We are beginning to know we are polluting our environment, our foods and our characters by our technological and social practices. Mad cow disease, avian flu, swine flu (influenza), Ebola virus, the covid-19 pandemic, global warming, and European use of wars to dominate the planet are a few of all ills generated by the wrong use of technology. Let us first, like the scriptures have said, cultivate the earth to raise adequate foods to feed ourselves and then lower the glut for riches by reducing our high salaries and high prices of commodities. We just work for moderate living for all and stop wars. *The Ancestral Legacy of Family Counselling* is based on natural wisdom in which our parents are edified and continuously educating their children based on their natural intuition, not knowledge acquired from an academic field. This is wisdom embodied in them by nature. From their natural counselling, their children acquire the ancestral wisdom which enhances their cognitive reasoning. The educated parents play music, read story books, use toys, TV, Internet work, different kinds of apps and symbolism to edify their own children but our illiterate parents use ***totems and folklore*** to groom us. As you are now exiting from reading this book, I would love you to remember two things read throughout the passages; these are the "Time keeping animals and the "Birds of omens" which our ancestors cherished in their time and taught us. To refresh your memory; here are the lists of them:

The signs of Omens
1. Obu (Cuckoo the bird of "fortune and misfortune)
2. Udele (Vulture is a diviner of sorrowful omens).
3. Rainbow (something significant to happen)

The Signs of Time Keeping
1. Cock-Cow Igboland timekeeper

2. Okwu (Bush fowl) Igboland timekeeper
3. Shadow
4. Sun and moon
5. Egyptian start Sirius
6. Sun clock, Sundial shadow Clock, Sun clock and water clock; all are Egyptian timekeepers
7. Baboons Egyptian timekeeper animal
8. Stars of Sirius and Orion (reminder of farming season-Egyptian)

Thanks for reading and may the wisdom of our parents remain with you amen.

Chinedum Joachim Konye Nwadike, Hfsn. (Rose Ann).
London United Kingdom
Febuary 8, 2022

BIBLIOGRAPHY

- Ackerman, Diane. (2004). Alchemy of Mind. New York: Simon & Schuster, 11.
- Albert, Einstein. Htts://www.goodreads.com
- Asiedu, J. J. (1999). Processing Tropical Crops London UK: Macmillan Education Ltd, 189-194.
- Barack Obama. (2008). Change We Can Believe In. Random House, Inc., New York: Three Rivers Press.
- Bateman, Graham. (1985). All The World's Animals: Birds, Owls, Parrots, and Waders.
  Torstar Books. Inc, 63,64,86, 96, 114, 125, 144.
- Bateman, Graham. (1985). All The World's Animals: Songbirds. New York Torstar Books Inc. 40, 52, 72, 79, 146.
- Boorstin, Daniel J. (1983). The Discovers: A History of Man's Search to Know His World and Himself. New York: Random House,4-78.
- Budge, Wallis E. A. (1978). An Egyptian Hieroglyphic Dictionary Vols I, II. New York: Dover. Publications Inc.
- Budge, Wallis E.A.9(1989). The Mummy- A History of Extraordinary Practices of ancient Egypt.
  New York: Bell Publishing Company, 298-301, 361-363.
- Bunch, Bryan and Jenny Tesar. (2000). The Penguin Desk Encyclopedia of Science and Mathematics. New York: Penguin Books, Inc.
- Carnegie, Dale. (1985). How To Stop Worrying and Start Living. New York: Pocket Books, 113-127.
- Cavalli- Sforza, L. L, A. (1996). Pizza and P. Merozzi. The History

and Geography of Human Genes. New York: Princeton University Press, 69.

- Dike, Onwuka K. (2000). Trade and Politics in the Niger Delta, 1830-1885. Westport,
  Connecticut: Greenwood Press Publishers. 181.182-201, 203-222.
- Diop, Anta Cheikh. (1974). The African Origin of Civilization: Myth or Reality. Chicago, Illinois. Lawrence Hill Books. 76-84.
- Eleanor Farjeon. (1881). Celebration Hymnal for Everyone, 1490.
- Emeka George Ekwuru. (1995). Igbo Cosmology and The Ontogeny and Hermeneutics of Igbo Sculpture Studies in African Ethnoaesthetics, 123, no.3.2.5.
- Finch, Charles S. III, M.D. (1999). Echoes of the Old Darkland. Decature, Georgia: Kheen.
- Grove, Noel. (1997). Atlas of World History. Washington DC: National Geographic Society,2am.
- Jackson, John G. (2001). Introduction to African Civilizations. New York: Citadel Press, 196-223.
- Jay, James M. (1978). Modern Food Microbiology, 2nd Ed New York: D. Van Nostrand Company, 260-284.
- Litvinoff, Sarah. (2004). The Confidence Plan. Printed and bound by Ashford Colour Press Ltd. UK,
- Lamy, Lucie. (1989). Egyptian Mysteries. New York: Thames and Hudson Inc, 6-9, 74-78.
- Mazrui, Ali A. (1986). The Africans- A Triple Heritage. Boston, Massachusetts: Little Brown and Company,63, 239.
- Njoku, Fr. Greg Udo. (2001). Counselling Is A Community or Village Enterprise. Miami, Florida: Ubuntu Enterprises, 35. 36.
- Njoku, Fr. Greg Udo. (2001) Counselling Is A Community or Village Enterprises. Miami, Florida: Ubuntu Enterprises, 8-9, 73-74.
- New World Translation of Holy Scriptures. (1984). New York: Watch Tower Bible And Tract Society of Pennsylvania.
- Obrien, James A. (1986). Management Information Systems. Chicago, Illinois in Richard

- D. Irwin. (1986). A Times Mirror Higher Education Group Inc, 513-518, 9-23, 281-295.
- Oakes, Lorna and Lucia Gahlin. (2002). Ancient Egypt - An Illustrated Reference to Myths, Religions, Pyramids and Temples of Land of the Pharaohs. New York: Hermes House, Anness Publishing Inc. 2002, 330-331.
- Restak, Richard M. (1984). Receptors. New York in Bantam Books. (1994); 12-31.
- Rodham Clinton, Hillary. It Takes a Village. New York: Simon & Schuster Inc. Rockefeller Center. 1996.
- Sagan, Carl. Cosmos. (1983). New York: Random House, 196-197.
- Sharma, Robin. (2003). Family Wisdom From The Monk Who Sold His Ferrari
- Nurturing The Leader Within Your Child: Published by Jaico Publishing House First Jaico Impression.
- Smith, Hudson. (1996). The Religions of Man. New York: Harper and Row Publishers.
- Strudwick, Helen. (2008). The Encyclopedia of Ancient Egypt. London. UK: Amber Books Ltd, 166-167, 446-451.
- Ali A. Mazrui. (1986). The African Cheikh Anta Diop, Origin of Civilization, 124-155.
  Africans pp. 41-79.
- The Divine Office the Liturgy of the Hours According to Rome Rite IV Ordinary Time Weeks, 18-34 p. 630.
- The Divine Office the Liturgy of the Hours According to Rome Rite II Lent and Eastertide Easter Octave: Wednesday (p. 389).
- Thomas, Clayton L. (1998). Taber's Cyclopedic Medical Dictionary. Philadelphia, Pennsylvania. F.A. Davis Company, 2076-2077.
- Vertosick, Frank T. Jr. (2002). Genius Within – Discovering the Intelligence of Every Living Thing. New York: Harcourt Inc, 21.
- Weinert, Susan J. (1984). North American Wildlife. Pleasantville, New York: Reader's Digest, 42-71, 74-195.
- Wheeler, Mary Bray, Alice C. (1984). Ewing and John A. Fribley.

Webster's New Reference
- Library-An Encyclopedia of Dictionaries. New York: Thomas Nelson Publishers.
- William Shakespeare, Webster's Encyclopedia of Dictionaries by John Gage Allee, Ph.D.; 835.
- https://en.wikpetha.org/wiki/mememorandumofunderstanding